P9-DDD-439

SUIHO RESERVOIR

Chongjin

Hiesanjin

Nanam

Ch'osan

CHOSIN
RESERVOIR

Kapsan

Yudam-ni

FUNSEN
RESERVOIR

Songjin

Uisan

Hagaru-ri

Pukch'ong

Tanch'on

Iwon

Anju

CHONGCHON

Tokch'on

Koto-ri

Hamhung

Sinanju

KAEDONG R.

Sunch'on

Yangdok

Hungnam

P'YONGYANG

NAN R.

Wonsan

SEA
OF JAPAN

Sariwon

YESONG R.

Kosong

Yonan

Ichon

IMJIN R.

Kumhwa

Inje

Yangyang

Kaesong

Panmunjom

Ch'unch'on

38º

Kimpo

SEOUL

Hoengsong

Samch'ok

Inch'on

HAN R.

Wonju

Suwon

Osan

Yongju

Ulchin

Ch'onan

Ch'ongju

Ch'ungju

Yech'on

Yongdok

KUM R.

Sangju

Andong

Taejon

Kasan

Kunsan

Chonju

Taegu

P'ohang-dong

NAKTONG R.

Kwangju

NAM R.

Chinju

Masan

Pusan

Sunch'on

120 MILES TO
JAPAN

Yosu

T'ongyong

KOREA STRAIT

TSUSHIMA

THE KOREAN WAR

Uncertain Victory

Books by Donald Knox

Death March
Delta Force (with Charlie A. Beckwith)
The Korean War—Pusan to Chosin: *An Oral History*
The Korean War—Uncertain Victory

Donald Knox

With additional text by

Alfred Coppel

THE
KOREAN
WAR

Uncertain Victory

The concluding
volume of
AN ORAL HISTORY

HARCOURT BRACE JOVANOVICH, PUBLISHERS

San Diego   New York   London

HBJ

Extracts from The Black Watch Diary,
Lt. J. G. Moncrief's report on the
Second Battle of the HOOK, 26 November 1952,
are Crown copyright material reproduced
by permission of the Controller of
Her Majesty's Stationery Office.

Library of Congress Cataloging-in-Publication Data
Knox, Donald, 1936–1986.
The Korean War.
Vol. 2 additional text by Alfred Coppel.
Maps on lining papers.
Includes bibliographical references and index.
Contents: [1] Pusan to Chosin — [2] Uncertain victory.
1. Korean War, 1950–1953.   I. Coppel, Alfred.
II. Title.
DS918.K53   1985   951.9'043   85-8567
ISBN 0-15-147288-2 (v. 1)
ISBN 0-15-147289-0 (v. 2)

Designed by Janet Taggart based on a design by Joy Chu
Printed in the United States of America
First edition
A B C D E

TO MOTHE

Contents

Publisher's Note

In 1985, after three years of intense work that included interviews with hundreds of Korean War combat veterans, historical research, and concentrated writing, Donald Knox completed *The Korean War: Pusan to Chosin*. That first volume of this oral history covered the opening six months of the savage conflict, from June 24, 1950, to December 31, 1950.

He then outlined the second volume and drafted eight chapters. But on April 19, 1986, at age 50, he died without warning of a heart attack. Because the work is so important in itself, as well as it was to Donald Knox, the publisher requested Alfred Coppel to conclude it. He has done so with eight additional chapters and a valedictory. The result is *The Korean War: Uncertain Victory*, which carries this deeply moving, personalized history through July 1953 to its tragic, haunting conclusion.

On behalf of the authors and the publisher, it is meet to express appreciation to all those individuals at government agencies whose generous assistance proved immensely valuable. Thanks are due to Kathleen Rucker for her unstinting help in editing and reviewing. Finally, and above all, to those veterans who shared their experiences in these pages and whose history this is, the fullest measure of gratitude is sincerely given.

WINTER

1 January-29 January 1951

Capt. NORMAN ALLEN *
I Company/5th Cavalry

New Year's Eve
35 miles NE of Seoul

Mother darling,

The ROKs [Republic of Korea troops] have a thin screen in front of us along the 38th [Parallel], but it has gaps in it and the enemy can give them trouble. We're kind of stuck out on a limb here.

We all rather expect to have the Chinese attempt to give us a New Year's present so we are on a 50% officers alert [one off, one on]. It's my trick awake and I am dressed and sitting next to the radio in the command post which is in a dirty little farmhouse.

There is a little celebration of sorts going on—the booming is nothing new on New Year's, except this year it's not pots and pans making the racket, but artillery.

[Into the wilderness Korea had become, the New Year of 1951 arrived like a raging lion. Just seven months before, in June 1950, those other

---

* A Californian, Allen was a professional soldier who had been awarded two Purple Hearts in the Second World War, when he campaigned in the Pacific. In Korea, he had earned three more. He was twenty-seven years old and the father of a daughter.

beasts of war, hatred, chaos, and pestilence, had been let loose when Communist-ruled North Korea invaded its neighbor, South Korea, and the United States rushed air and naval units to help her democratic ally. On the day the war began, 25 June, the United Nations had issued a resolution demanding that the Communists stop fighting and withdraw to the 38th Parallel, the border between the countries. When the North Koreans ignored the demand and captured Seoul, the South Korean capital, President Harry Truman ordered U.S. ground troops to Korea, and the UN asked its member nations to aid South Korea.

July had seen outnumbered and outgunned American and South Korean troops reeling from the hammering they were absorbing; August saw the allies blunting the North Korean offensive at the Pusan Perimeter and the first American victories; September, the Inch'on landings behind enemy lines, the crumbling of the Communists' offensive, and the Allies' breakout from the Perimeter; October, the UN's forces crossing the 38th Parallel and seizing the enemy's capital, P'yongyang; November, the entry of Communist China into the war and wicked fighting near the Yalu River; December, bitter winter weather, massive Chinese attacks on all fronts, and the UN's long withdrawal back to South Korea.

As 1950 drew to a close, the Allies had dug in below the 38th Parallel and were waiting for the Chinese to come again. North of the Parallel the enemy continued to build up its forces and was making plans to continue its drive on Seoul.

The United Nations Command (UNC) was led by General of the Army Douglas MacArthur. From his headquarters in Tokyo, he received orders from President Harry Truman and the Joint Chiefs of Staff acting as executive agents for the UN's Security Council. The general's command comprised the U.S. Eighth Army with attached units from fifteen member states of the United Nations,* the Army of the Republic of South Korea, the Far East Air Forces, and the Far East Naval Forces. In Korea, all ground forces were directly responsible to Lt. Gen. Matthew B. Ridgway, who had replaced the late Gen.

---

*There were contingents from Great Britain, Australia, Canada, New Zealand, South Africa, France, Greece, the Netherlands, the Philippines, Thailand, Belgium, Turkey, and Luxembourg, as well as medical units from Sweden and India. Units from Ethiopia and Colombia would arrive later.

*Walton H. Walker as commander of Eighth Army.** These forces, nearly 365,000 men, included the ROK Army, which was under his control but not part of Eighth Army. Across the border in North Korea, the enemy was estimated to number nearly half a million men, with twice that number believed to be in reserve north of the Yalu River in Manchuria.*

On the last day of the old year of 1950, after more than six months of savage fighting and unthinkable destruction, the opposing armies faced each other along the same boundary line that had, from the end of the Second World War, so uncomfortably separated the two Koreas. Artillery fire, mostly outgoing, continued throughout the day; then, after sunset, it intensified, especially the incoming. American units were put on 50 percent alert. The night was very dark and very cold.

1950 had been a bad year; 1951 would be worse.]

S/Sgt. W. B. WOODRUFF, JR. † ‡
L Company/35th Infantry
Around midnight the CCF [Chinese Communist forces] struck an ROK division to our right [the 1st]. The sound of firing, including artillery, was audible for hours, and the sky was filled with arching tracers. The New Year thus came in accompanied by a tremendous fireworks display.

Cpl. LACY BARNETT
Medical Company/3d Battalion/19th Infantry
The Chinese attacked and soon broke through the South Korean unit [the 2d ROK Division] on our left flank. Suddenly, we realized the

---

*Walker had been killed in a vehicle accident on 23 December 1950, and Ridgway had assumed command on the twenty-sixth.
†Near the end of the Second World War, "Woody" Woodruff had seen some combat in Burma. After the war he returned to school and received a law degree from the University of Texas. In September 1950, Woodruff, who had stayed in the Active Reserve, was recalled to duty and shipped to Korea. He joined Love Company on 8 December during Eighth Army's long retreat from North Korea.
‡The rank given is that held by the man at the time of the experience he relates, and unless otherwise specified, the unit denotes his company and regiment.

enemy, who had swept away everything, was about one mile in front of the aid station and between it and our line companies, which were now north of the Chinese. Each vehicle that tried to reach these rifle companies was destroyed or turned back. Many of these vehicles were loaded with ammunition, and that New Year's Eve we saw some of the most spectacular fireworks any of us had seen.

Even though our battalion was suffering casualties, none of them could be brought to us through the Chinese roadblocks. And if the enemy had continued its advance in our direction, our battalion headquarters, aid station, and artillery would have been overrun. Why the Chinese didn't was strange and puzzling, considering their superiority in manpower. We were situated in a valley with only one mountain pass leading out toward the south. A small Chinese force could easily have put a cork in the bottle and trapped us.

A few of us who had been in Korea six months strongly believed we had no alternative but to get out of the valley where we were. We prevailed upon the battalion surgeon to make the move. He and the assistant battalion surgeon, a newly arrived officer, agreed to try. The battalion CP [command post] was about 1,000 yards away. Between midnight and 3:00 A.M. the surgeon made numerous trips to this CP. Each time he returned, he looked more confused and dejected. Finally, he admitted to us that even though he was convinced the aid station should be moved, he hesitated to ask headquarters for permission to make this move. He was afraid the battalion authorities would think the movement was for personal reasons. He had been "burned" by his former unit, which had resulted in his receiving a bad efficiency report, and he didn't want or need any further black marks on his record.

We remained in our location throughout the night, and although the battle was raging nearby, we received not one casualty for treatment. Shortly after daylight a battalion officer discovered the aid station was still in the valley. He immediately ordered the surgeon to get out of the valley and through the pass. We moved quickly and without incident, and were soon in a new location where later in the day we would begin to receive the wounded that poured in.

[At daybreak on New Year's Day, after a night of solid artillery preparation, nearly 500,000 enemy troops launched a major offensive south *of the 38th Parallel. Attacking all along the snow-covered front, the Chinese directed their major efforts toward the capture of Seoul and the port of Inch'on, the corridors to which were defended largely by ROK units. Deep penetrations were made almost at once and a wedge driven between the ROK 1st and 6th Divisions. When only scattered reports reached Eighth Army headquarters during the night, General Ridgway hurried forward to see for himself what he could.]*

Lt. Gen. MATTHEW B. RIDGWAY
Commanding General, Eighth Army

I drove out north of Seoul and into a dismaying spectacle. ROK soldiers by truckloads were streaming south, without order, without arms, without leaders, in full retreat. Some came on foot or in commandeered vehicles of every sort. They had just one aim—to get as far away from the Chinese as possible. They had thrown their rifles and pistols away and had abandoned all artillery, mortars, machine guns, every crew-served weapon. *

[When the Eighth Army commander returned to his command post, the news he received was even more ominous. Increasing Communist pressure in the west made a breakthrough likely, which Ridgway knew the enemy could swiftly and skillfully exploit. The general—only six days after taking command—decided to be prudent and ordered his forces to withdraw to a bridgehead position north of Seoul.]

<u>1 January 1950</u>
The battalion withdrew from the Imjin River Line without ever receiving an attack due to the deep [enemy] penetrations east of us.

    EXECUTIVE OFFICER'S JOURNAL, 3D BATTALION/35TH INFANTRY

---

* Gen. Matthew Ridgway, *The Korean War* (Garden City, N.Y.: Doubleday, 1967), 93, 94. Hereafter, Ridgway.

S/Sgt. W. B. WOODRUFF, JR.
L Company/35th Infantry

A mess truck drove up to our position burdened with the traditional army holiday meal of turkey and all the trimmings. A chow line promptly formed. Maybe ten men had been served, and three or four were seated on the ground taking the first bites; the rest of us were in the line, mess kits at the ready. Suddenly, a truck column approached at high speed, led by an officer in a jeep. The latter hit the ground shouting orders to close the chow line and mount the trucks on the double. Marmite cans were slammed shut and thrown back on the chow truck, men already served stopped eating and dumped out the turkey and dressing, and everyone put away his mess gear. I believe we were loaded within two minutes of the trucks' arrival, and were moving shortly afterward.

Thus began what I characterized in my own mind as the "runaway." Trucks would haul us an hour or so, then drop us off to return for some other unit, then pick us up again for another ride. This schedule was adhered to with no regard to whether it was daytime or darkness. Packed aboard the open trucks like sardines, we were often certain we had frostbite. When we were ordered to dismount, our first efforts went to fire building, for which the main fuel was rice straw. I regret to say, however, that it was customary to feed the fire with anything flammable which could be scrounged up, including considerable amounts of household furnishings, as well as doors, ceilings, flooring, and so forth.

Before dawn on January 2 we dismounted for the second or third time, but this time were directed to dig in; here an effort would be made to hold. In the darkness the breakfast chow line was set up, and was very welcome as we had not eaten since breakfast the preceding day. Quickly, the word was passed back up the chow line: the menu was turkey and dressing! It had been on the road with us some twelve hours, and was quite frozen. The gravy was of special interest; it was a sort of gravy sherbet. We spent the day in reconnaissance, digging positions, and developing signals and other coordinating measures for the defense.

2 January 1950

The morale of the command has had a noticeable decrease during the withdrawal. The men, far from having a defeatist attitude, would welcome an order to attack.

EXECUTIVE OFFICER'S JOURNAL, 3D BATTALION/35TH INFANTRY

Sgt. ARTHUR MACEDO
Headquarters/38th Infantry

Things were again looking pretty bleak. When I went on my rounds to check the perimeter security posts, I was quite scared. I trudged through knee-deep snow and tried to bury my head in my neck to avoid the biting wind. No one knew how close the Chinese were, or whether one had you right then in his sights.

Sgt. F/C WARREN AVERY
G Company/21st Infantry

Late in the afternoon [2 January] Lieutenant Gillman volunteered the 2d Platoon to go out in front of Hill 1157 in the Uijongbu area, where we were expecting a Chinese attack.* He was a real gung-ho second lieutenant who was going to make first lieutenant even if it killed us. The lieutenant was constantly volunteering us for patrols, or to advance on the point each time the company was in the attack. Our mission after New Year's was to go out and report when the Chinese arrived. In other words, we were going to be a listening post. A squad was put in each valley leading to a small hill, and my unit was on the left of the platoon headquarters. We were connected to each other by sound-power telephones.

As best as I can recall, it was around midnight when the Chinese began moving into our area. There was snow on the ground, so we were hiding in a small wash. We notified the platoon headquarters about the Chinese but received no orders to pull out. We stayed where we were. Cold and dark. About the time it began to lighten in

---

* All hill numbers in Korea refer to height in meters above sea level.

the east, we heard shots near where the platoon headquarters was set up. We whistled through the sound-power. A Chinaman answered and told us the rest of our unit had been captured and that we, too, should lay down our weapons and return to the headquarters area. I forget what our platoon sergeant told the Chinaman to do with himself, but we took off and moved southward toward Hill 1157.

As dawn broke, the F-80s [Shooting Stars] came over.* I thought at first they would strafe us by mistake, but they wiggled their wings and stayed with us for as long as they could. A couple of hours later, a flight of Hellcats [F6Fs] came over and kept the Chinese off us. Around dusk we finally got back to our lines on top of 1157. Everyone wanted to know why we hadn't pulled out of our listening post earlier than we had. The best answer we could give was that no one had ordered us to move back.

S/Sgt. W. B. WOODRUFF, JR.
L Company/35th Infantry

An hour or so after darkness fell, it was back to the trucks. That night [2 January] we drove through Seoul. In fact, we had a considerable tour of the city, for we got lost. This required movement back to the north, which took quite some time, then back south on a different route through Seoul and across the Han River.† We eventually dismounted at Kimpo Airbase.‡ The Air Force was already gone. Around us were piles of supplies, including ordnance, which had been set afire; in the flames sundry ordnance exploded regularly, sending pieces of metal whirring through the air. We took shelter in a large hangar and got some needed rest.

---

* Although new to Korea, the F-80 was the U.S. Air Force's oldest operational jet fighter.
† A broad river bordering Seoul on the south.
‡ Korea's largest airfield was ten miles west of the capital.

Lt. Gen. MATTHEW B. RIDGWAY
Commanding General, Eighth Army

In general the Eighth Army had fallen back in good order and with almost all its equipment. But our situation now was dangerous indeed. At our backs we had the Han, an unfordable river, choked with huge cakes of floating ice which might tear loose the pontoons of our only two bridges. Jammed into a tight bridgehead on the north bank of the Han, we had more than a hundred thousand UN and ROK troops with all their heavy equipment, including British Centurion tanks and U.S. 8-inch howitzers. And pressing upon us was the imminent possibility that panic-stricken refugees by the thousands might overwhelm our bridge guards and hopelessly clog our bridges—while enemy artillery, if resolutely pushed forward at night, might soon have the crossings within range.

In discussion with our two U.S. corps commanders [Maj. Gen. Frank W. Milburn commanded I Corps, and Maj. Gen. John B. Coulter, IX Corps], with the ROK Army chief of staff, and with the chief of MAG [U.S. Military Advisory Group to the Republic of Korea], it became clear that a combination of enemy frontal attack and deep envelopment around our wide-open east flank, where the ROK had fled in panic, could soon place the entire army in jeopardy. I had not yet found sufficient basis for confidence in the ability of the troops to hold their positions, even if they were ordered to. Consequently, I asked our ambassador [John J. Muccio], on January 3, to notify President [Syngman] Rhee that Seoul would be once more evacuated and that withdrawal from our forward positions would begin at once.

I also informed the ambassador and what part of the ROK government still remained in Seoul that from 3 P.M. [3 January] on, the bridges and main approach and exit roads would be closed to all but military traffic. All official government vehicles would have to clear before that hour, and there would be no civilian traffic permitted from then on.

Just how these hundreds of thousands of frightened refugees would react when told to get off the only bridge that led to safety, no one could predict. My specific orders to [Brigadier] General [Charles D.] Palmer [who was placed in charge of the bridge crossings], therefore, were to instruct his MPs that if civilians refused to stay clear of the highway, the MPs were to fire over the heads of the refugees; and if this failed to stay the tide, the MPs were, as a last resort, to use their weapons directly against the offenders. *

Cpl. LEONARD KORGIE †
Headquarters Company/2d Battalion/21st Infantry
We arrived in the outskirts of the capital late one day. What a mess! Civilians—clothed, half clothed, some barefooted; millions of them, all trying to get south with whatever they could carry or drag with them. It tore at my heart. I couldn't imagine how the poor devils could do it.

Our convoy had a terrible time trying to move through these masses of civilians. How these people managed the will to live through those conditions, I'll never know. A scene that has haunted me all these years, and whose sounds I still hear, was when we attempted to cross the bridge spanning the Han River. ‡ Our reports claimed the Chinese were entering Seoul from the north, and here we were a few miles south trying to get over a bridge. MPs tried everything in their power to clear the bridge of civilians so the military convoys could get through. There was the smell of urgency in the air. The convoys were being threatened with capture or destruction. Part of our convoy finally crawled onto the bridge and began to move along it. Frenzied, hysterical refugees broke through the cordons and flooded onto the bridge. They were alongside our vehicles, in front and behind them. There was no reasoning with them. The trucks stopped. An officer on the roadway in front of us made a decision. Then, and now, I don't know what alternative he had. "Bring 'em through! Move! Move! Get going!" God! The trucks began rolling. The civilians couldn't get

---

* Ridgway, pp. 94–96.
† Leonard Korgie was born in a small Nebraska farm town. In high school he lettered in baseball and basketball. He then attended a Catholic seminary in Cleveland before dropping out in 1948 and enlisting in the regular army. Korgie had been fighting in Korea since just after the fall of Taejon in July 1950 when, as a replacement, he had joined L Company, 34th Infantry.
‡ All permanent bridges across the Han had long before been destroyed. Two military pontoon bridges, a redecked railway bridge, plus five floating footbridges remained to carry the exodus from Seoul. The deeply frozen Han could also be crossed in places on foot.

out of the way, pressed tightly as they were on the roadway. I still hear the smashing of bodies.

Sgt. ARTHUR MACEDO
Headquarters/38th Infantry
There were lines of escaping refugees along both sides of the road. Mothers tugged at little children, who were more interested in the smoke and what else was happening behind them than in keeping up. Old men with long gray beards, bent over by the weight of the heavily packed A-frames on their backs, shuffled along next to the trucks. Everyone pushed or shoved and tried to get ahead of the person in front of him. Ugly black trees burnt free of limbs stuck out in the snow. I thought, We humans can escape, but trees, too, are living things and are destroyed and can do nothing about it.

The day was gloomy and cloudy, and behind I could hear the booming of either artillery or great explosions; it was difficult to tell one from the other.

[By 4 January, Seoul was again in flames. The bridges were blown at 2:00 P.M. By evening the capital had changed hands for the third time in a little more than six months. Eighth Army, delaying only momentarily below the Han, moved south. Once the supplies were removed from Suwon, it, too, was abandoned, as was Osan, where six months before, almost to the day, the first U.S. unit to enter the Korean War, Task Force Smith, had met an enemy column and had been forced to withdraw.]

Sgt. ARTHUR MACEDO
Headquarters/38th Infantry
My convoy stopped at Miryang, the very place I remember arriving in when I came to Korea in August. To think I had marched deep into North Korea only now to return to where I had started. It made me sick. Six months before, this hamlet south of Taegu had been a major staging area for the Naktong River battles. In January it appeared it would again become a place of nightmares.

S/Sgt. W. B. WOODRUFF, JR.
L Company/35th Infantry

By my reckoning we had yielded up to the enemy some eighty miles during the runaway, 100 miles altogether since I joined the company on December 8. I had seen no enemy, fired no round, and the company had sustained no casualty. I felt disgusted, ashamed, and frustrated. Talk that Eighth Army was about to evacuate Korea was common; there was lots of speculation as to the port from which we would depart. My morale was at bottom.

[The Chinese did not aggressively follow up their advantage in the west, and the two Eighth Army Corps,* south of Seoul, were able to pull back to the vicinity of P'yongt'aek and Ansong (known as Line D) on 7 January. During the withdrawal, contact with the enemy fell off dramatically.

The 1st Cavalry Division reached its new assembly area and set up defensive positions near Ch'ungju, sixty miles southeast of Seoul.]

Capt. NORMAN ALLEN
I Company/5th Cavalry

After we crossed the Han, the [3d] battalion moved to the rear and took positions on the Mun'gyong Pass [about twenty miles south of Ch'ungju and eighty miles southeast of Seoul]. From one end to the other, the pass was thirteen miles long and carried Eighth Army's MSR [Main Supply Route] over the mountains. Here, K, Company was assigned the south end; L Company, the top of the pass; and I Company, the north end.

---

* I Corps, farthest west, consisted of the U.S. 25th Infantry Division, the ROK 1st Division, the Turkish Brigade, and the 29th British Brigade; IX Corps, on their right (east), comprised the U.S. 1st Cavalry and 24th Divisions, the ROK 6th Division, the 27th British Commonwealth Brigade, and a battalion each from Greece and the Philippines.

Pfc. JAMES CARDINAL
I Company/5th Cavalry

7–8 January
South Korea

Dear Folks,

Our company is set up on a hill overlooking a mountain pass
. . . through which what looks like the entire Eighth Army is
moving south. We've been here two days already and thousands
of vehicles and tens of thousands of troops have gone by. We
expect to be here another two days before we too will head south.
It looks like the beginning of the end. The Chinese are kicking
hell out of us; there are just too many of them in Korea for us
to fight. If the big wheels in Washington decide to continue
fighting it will be the biggest mistake they ever made. I don't
think we can hold the Chinks.

Keep those packages coming just in case we don't get evacuated. If we do, I can always eat them in Japan.

Cpl. VICTOR FOX *
I Company/5th Cavalry

As it had been in North Korea, up on the Mun'gyong Plateau it was
numbingly cold, with temperatures at one time as low as −22° F. In
1951 there was no such thing as "windchill factor"; men dug in on
the pass thought it was very windy. Many days, heavy snowstorms
blew through the pass and over the plateau, bringing most activity to
a halt. It didn't stop the mail, though.

When we were first in the Pusan Perimeter near the Naktong
River in late August 1950, Sergeant Blackie Furlan talked me into
writing Doris Day in Hollywood, to tell her she had been made Queen
of the 3d Squad, 3d Platoon, Item Company, 5th Cavalry Regiment.
At Mun'gyong Pass, five months later, damned if I didn't receive a
large envelope postmarked Hollywood, California. It contained eight

---

* Fox, born in Sault Ste. Marie, Ontario, had decided he wanted to see more of the world and
enlisted in the U.S. Army. In 1951 he was eighteen years old.

large black-and-white glossies of the actress—all autographed! A covering letter from her secretary thanked our 3d Squad for the honor. Some of the autographed photos were given to men who didn't know why she had sent them, since only Sergeants Hughes and Furlan and Corporals Haltom and Fox were left from the original squad that had "voted."

[While the west remained unnaturally quiet during the first two weeks of January, the central and eastern fronts saw heavy, chaotic fighting. Maj. Gen. Edward M. Almond's famous X Corps,* assigned to Eighth Army in late December,† was ordered forward on 2 January and assumed control of three ROK divisions (the 2d, 5th, and 8th) on the central front between the U.S. IX Corps on its left (west) and the ROK III Corps on its right. During this period, the enemy shifted units eastward and concentrated on driving a hole between Almond's command and the ROKs. In the rugged mountains east of Hoengsong, the South Koreans collapsed, and X Corps was forced to fall back toward the vital road and rail junction of Wonju. Some of the worst weather in a winter that became infamous for its cold and snow compounded the problem by limiting the number of close-support sorties that could be flown by Far East Air Force. Four enemy divisions attacked the U.S. 2d Division at Wonju on the eighth. After a series of grim battles fought in knee-deep snow, the Indianheads were forced to give ground when the ROK line on their right disintegrated.‡ § By the tenth, large numbers of enemy troops were pouring through the gap east of Wonju, and North Korean guerrillas were threatening to cut the MSR. Ridgway called for Maj. Gen. Oliver P. Smith's 1st Marine Division,‖ now completely recovered from its heroic thirteen-day

---

* Almond's X Corps now comprised the U.S. 2d and 7th divisions; the 1st Marine Division had been detached and put in Army reserve. The Corps had conducted the Inch'on landings in September and fought in the mountains around the Chosin Reservoir and northeastern Korea in November and December.

† Up to that time X Corps had been an independent command.

‡ Second Division was so named for the division's patch, which shows an Indian wearing a warbonnet.

§ On 13 January, the 2d Division's commander, Maj. Gen. Robert B. McClure, was replaced by Maj. Gen. Clark L. Ruffner, Almond's chief of staff.

‖ The division consisted of the 1st, 5th, and 7th Marine Regiments. The 11th Marines was the division's artillery regiment.

*battle in the Chosin Reservoir area, and ordered it to stop further
enemy penetration southward and to protect the supply routes to the
ROK units from being cut by North Korean guerrilla units.]*

Pfc. JOHN BISHOP
*I/7 **

We were told we were going to hunt and destroy North Koreans
who'd been left behind and were now acting as bandits by raiding the
homes of citizens. Well, before we went out, my friend Zena and I
stole a case of sick-bay alcohol—didn't know when we'd get another
drink. Worse luck, the first sergeant saw us do it. I'd served with him
in Camp Lejeune, and I knew he hated my guts because he rode my
ass all the time. Well, anyway, he sent word with a corporal that he
wanted to see me. I said to Zena, "Well, I've had it this time." I
went with the corporal to the headquarters tent, where the first sergeant was waiting for me. He thanked the corporal and told me to
come with him. "Bishop, I want to show you something." We walked
behind some tents, and when there was no one else around he told
me he'd seen me take a case from the aid tent. "Now, you best make
it easy on yourself and Zena. First, what was in the case?" I was
nervous. "Six half-gallon cans of sick-bay alcohol, First Sar'nt." He
said, "Have you any idea what a mistake it is to sled government
property during wartime? If I bring you up on charges, you'll get a
general court-martial." Boy, this was going to be bad. "Now, I'll tell
you what I'll do, Bishop. I'd hate to see you go to the brig, so I'm
going to let you make a choice. You either go see the cap'n or take
my punishment." Not much of a choice there. "I'll take yours, First
Sar'nt." "Okay," he said, "right after chow you make sure five of 'em
cans are in my tent; make sure no one seez ya. And you and Zena
make sure you never mention how easy I let ya off or you'll be a
sorry-ass Marine—you know what I mean, don't ya?" I told him I

---

*To help distinguish Marine units from Army units, the former will be shortened. Marine
companies will be designated by a letter only, battalions by a number. Numbers following the
slash indicate regiments; thus, I/7 is I Company, 7th Marine Regiment, and 2/5 is 2d Battalion,
5th Marine Regiment.

understood. To this day I thank my lucky stars that the sonovabitch was a big drunk. Next day we went out looking for guerrillas.

[The 1st Marine Division moved northward from Masan, where it had been recuperating and receiving replacements, and closed on Pohang on 16 January. Two days later the Marines went guerrilla hunting.]

Pfc. DAVE KOEGEL
B/7

As a warm-up to the main event with the Chinese, we made two patrols, one of two weeks and one of ten days, from a base camp at Pohang. We trooped over the hills for contact with guerrillas who had been organized after they'd been cut off following the breakout from the Pusan Perimeter in September 1950.

The fear and tension of combat seem a whole different thing from the gloomy clouds that hang over various other experiences of war. Chief among these clouds was the successive agony of lugging yourself and equipment up interminable hills. Most of these instruments of torture had numbers in meters, and a typical hill would be named 740 or 860. Sometimes we'd meet enemy resistance on them; and even when we didn't, we'd still have the gut-straining pull of *climbing* them. As you bent over under the deadweight of your pack and equipment—in my case, a thirty-four-pound "light" machine gun—you'd occasionally raise your head to gauge the distance remaining to the top. But the top was never the top; it was always just the first ridge in a succession of ridges. All reaching the "top" would do is give you a false hope that you had reached the objective. About halfway up, we'd usually pass Korean burial mounds. In our misery we'd speculate how tough it must be to lug a body up a hill, as the Koreans did.

When we'd finally reach a peak designated our objective and begin to lay out positions, the platoon sergeant would be around picking men to scramble down the hill and return with cases of C rations and ammunition. Needless to say, the prospect of another trip the same day lay like deadweight on our already leaden spirits.

Our new company commander, Captain [James J.] Bott, who

had joined us at Masan as a replacement,* had to unlearn a few of the principles that OCS and Advanced Infantry Leadership courses had inbred in him. On the first night out on the Pohang patrol, we found ourselves at the end of a long march on frozen rice paddies. Like the well-trained officer he was, he took stock of his terrain and then gave the order that no man was to get into his sack until the company was securely dug in.

The frozen, granite-like hills we usually occupied could resist the most well-directed and ferocious chops of an entrenching tool. But usually, after backbreaking work, we were able to scoop out a defensible foxhole. These frozen rice paddies were another story. Digging in them was like trying to make a hole in concrete with a spoon. Between the clanging of entrenching tools and the cursing of the bitter, exhausted men there was an Anvil Chorus that went on until the singers collapsed into the inch-deep "holes" they'd been able to batter and scratch out. If Captain Bott was testing the old Marine dictum about morale, "The men are not really happy until they're bitching," he must have thought that night he had molded the company into a love fest.

Several weeks later the company found itself some miles from the secondary camp where our sleeping bags and food remained. It was a chilly February day. A unit of North Koreans, which we had engaged in a firefight earlier in the day, had taken off in full flight, and the word came down that Baker Company was to hold its position overnight. The thought of a night on a hill without food or the warmth of a down sleeping bag began to look like a painful reality.

Captain Bott sensed the needless misery we faced and, by radio, roused battalion HQ and chewed a little rear-echelon rear end. Most of what he said I've forgotten, but I do vividly recall the words "We're coming in!" They were spoken not as a simple statement but as a determined command. The radio did not reply. At once the jubilant shouts from the men, "We're going in!" marked a swift change in our morale.

---

*On the way down from the Chosin Reservoir, Baker 7 had lost five company commanders, three of whom went down on the same day, 8 December.

Pfc. JACK WRIGHT *
G/5

They said the area we moved into was the home of an estimated regiment of North Korean regulars that had been cut off when we made the Inch'on landing and the army broke out of the Perimeter. These troops had turned guerrilla and had been raising hell all up and down the countryside, and it was going to be our job to go in and get them. That's when we learned we were going to be fighting a different kind of war. Always before it was taking ground or losing ground; now it was just kill the enemy, and ground had nothing to do with it.

We mounted into trucks and headed for the area where the guerrillas were supposedly operating. The day was bitter cold and overcast. We reached a place where I saw real steep hills on our left and the road turning right before it cut between two mountains. From one of these mountains we began to receive mortar fire. We all jumped out of our trucks and hit the ditch. Our platoon sergeant ordered us forward, and in a skirmish line we started across a frozen rice paddy.

When we reached the base of a hill we began to assault the enemy's position. We all noticed this one colored guy in our outfit, a BAR man we called A.C., beginning to fall farther and farther behind. Well, you can imagine what we thought of that. On top we found our mortars had taken care of the North Koreans. There was blood everywhere and rice scattered all over. About then A.C. came up and joined us. We didn't say anything, but you can imagine what we were thinking. A.C. was the first Negro we had had in our outfit.

We climbed off the hill and entered a nearby village. Our motor transport came in back of us. In the village we found four North Korean soldiers who all had dysentery in a bad way. The corpsman trying to treat the guys was gagging and sputtering. He poured enough paragoric into them to float a battleship. The Communists were surprised at the treatment, as they had expected we would kill them.

---

* Private Wright, who was nicknamed "Archie" after the comic-strip character, had arrived in Korea in early August as a member of the 1st Provisional Marine Brigade. He had fought in the Pusan Perimeter, landed at Wolmi-do as part of the Inch'on landings, and hobbled out of the Chosin Reservoir. Aside from some frozen feet in December, Wright had never been wounded.

That night the company set up on one of the hills above the village. Being the extra man that night, the way the squad was set up, I went down and stayed in a nice warm hut which had been turned into a headquarters. It was pretty late at night, and I had just begun to doze off when an enemy tracer went through one window and out the other. An officer jumped up hollering, "Who struck that match?" Well, we weren't answering, as we were too busy getting our gear together and making a run for it. Then I heard burp guns firing outside. I saddled up, got out the door, and began climbing the hill. Suddenly, I heard one of our BARs cut loose. Some NKs were trying to come down a ridge that lay to our rear. This BAR stopped them cold. I figured it had to be A.C., and I was right. The guy was all over this hill that night. Every time some place got hot, that's where we would hear A.C.'s BAR. I rejoined the rest of the outfit, and during the night we had a pretty good firefight going. Some tanks on the road below began shelling, and we moved forward. We assaulted the enemy position and they took off into the bushes. About this time A.C. came up. One of the guys turned to him and asked, "Hey, what the hell's the scoop? Yesterday, you acted like a yeller nigger—I'm not gonna mix no words—yesterday, we couldn't get you up a hill to save ourself. Tonight, you're all over the place. Now what's brung on the big change?" A.C. was a pretty big guy. He just looked and grinned. "Hell, white boy, can't you tell the difference? In daytime I stand out like one sore thumb. At night, I got it made." After that there were no problems. It was standard procedure: when we went into the assault in the daytime, A.C. dropped back. When we set up at night, A.C. went out front. Nobody said a thing. That's just the way it worked out.

[Enemy troops sliding through the gap in the east central front in mid-January had also infiltrated behind IX Corps and into the area held by the 1st Cavalry Division.]

2d Lt. ADRIAN BRIAN [*]
I Company/5th Cavalry

One time we were trying to destroy a guerrilla stronghold which was causing trouble on our supply route. We went in and flushed out a bunch. After quite a bit of fighting, we captured about fifty men, whom we collected in a field; all of them wore civilian clothing and looked all to the world like farmers. One of the ROKs in the battalion S-2 section [intelligence] was a huge, tough-looking guy. He joined our group guarding the POWs. We chatted a few minutes and discussed whether any of these captives could, in fact, be civilians coerced into serving the enemy. The big ROK then walked over and stood directly in front of the kneeling prisoners. They all had their eyes glued on him. Suddenly, he snapped to attention and barked a command in Korean. All of the prisoners, except one old man, jumped to their feet as if they had one pair of legs and stood at attention. He shouted a few more commands, and each time the group faced left, faced right, and did a couple of about-faces. Then, one by one, you could see the "I've been a sucker" light come on in their eyes. No longer would they be able to play the poor dumb farmer role. We kept the old man behind while we marched the rest to a POW collection point.

Pfc. JAMES CARDINAL
I Company/5th Cavalry

14, 17 January
South Korea

  Dear Folks,
  We are still in central South Korea guarding a mountain pass against guerrillas. It's colder than the North Pole and we are getting miserable chow.
  I don't think I can impress you with how lousy our chow is

---

[*] A West Point graduate, class of 1949, Brian had served in Korea since July 1950, when the 1st Cavalry arrived in-country. Related on his mother's side to the abolitionist Harriet Beecher Stowe, he was known to the men as "Beech."

or how little we get. That's why I'm counting on your packages so much. In your next package send some boxes of raisins and sweet cocoa, a can of boneless ham, sausages, pumpernickel bread, fruit cake, salt and pepper, salad dressing, fudge, Hershey almonds and pre cooked rice. You can make two packages out of all this.

[Month after month of relentless fighting, marching, and dying began to take its toll on men who'd been in Korea since the summer of 1950. The roar of battle had rolled across the land for eight months, and the casualties stretched out endlessly. The soldiers could not know how much longer the fighting would last, but by midwinter, 1951, they felt it had been with them forever and might go on forever. It was a time of doubt and disillusionment. Life on the lines never got better, only worse. With the men living as they were, in the open, in a hole in the ground, broiling in the summer, freezing in winter, all the while being shot at or bombarded, the first month could have been called an ordeal; the second month, cruel; the third, an outrage; the fourth, torture. By January 1951, there were thousands of GIs in their fifth, sixth, and even seventh month of living under these conditions. They were weary, less certain of things.

Combat was always bad, but some times were worse than other times. Some days the chances of being killed or maimed were greater than on other days; it often depended on luck—where you were, where the enemy was. Some units just happened to miss contact with the enemy; others, it seemed, encountered the enemy wherever they were. The 5th Cavalry's Item Company, for example. They had had to cross three enemy-held rivers—the Imjin in September, the Taedong in October, the Ch'ongch'on in November. The men of the company had arrived in Korea in late August, and by mid-September were grappling with the North Koreans on an insignificant piece of hell called Hill 174. When their company commander, Norman Allen, wrote the following letter, he was spending his 149th consecutive day of living either in a hospital ward (he'd been wounded three times) or in a hole in the ground. Captain Allen was tired.]

Capt. NORMAN ALLEN
I Company/5th Cavalry

24 January
near Sangju

Dearest Mother,

Trying to convince us that we aren't just so much sacrificial cattle will be difficult to do. Let no one question our fighting heart, for there is no doubt if we go down it will not be without a nasty fight first. But if anyone is attempting to be idealistic, well—don't try our reason. It is nothing more than survival, sheer, base, common survival. This place holds no value now, military, political or idealistic. The only thing of value it holds for the men here is a 6 x 6 x 6 plot of burial ground and what future is that to look forward to?

Heard where a "friend" of mine who works in Pusan is on a rest and recuperation to Japan. Frontline companies get two men a week, and the battalion one officer. Then to hear some son-of-a-bitch stationed in Pusan—where he is so safe he doesn't even carry a gun, has hot showers every day, sleeps in a steam heated room between sheets, and has sufficient white women, liquor and cigarettes—gets to go to Japan. My God! No justice! I'm beginning to hate those rear-echelon bastards as much, or more, than the Chinese. No wonder combat soldiers begin to carry chips on their shoulders. Mail is the only reason we aren't convinced we're members of a forgotten legion.

Heard on our radio someone singing "Old Man River." Oh, was that really nice.

[But if the fabric that held Eighth Army together, as represented by the weary veterans of Taejon and the Pusan Perimeter, of the Ch'ongch'on and "the Gauntlet," began to show signs of wear, there were always the fresh, young replacements pouring into Korea to strengthen it.]

Lt. Gen. MATTHEW B. RIDGWAY
Commanding General, Eighth Army

Before going on the offensive, we had work to do, weaknesses to shore up, mistakes to learn from, faulty procedures to correct, and a sense of pride to restore. GHQ in Tokyo, the entire military establishment at home, and the Japan Logistical Command were all working at forced draft now to meet our needs. Gradually our armor and artillery were strengthened, and our ranks began to fill up with well-trained replacements.*

Pfc. BEN JUDD †
F Company/23d Infantry

I was green when I arrived in Pusan from Japan as a replacement. *Green.* I met my friend Reed, and we were shoved onto a slow-moving train heading north; rumbling, slow (almost walking speed), stopping sometimes for an hour—always heading north with precious replacements. We was warned there were guerrillas in the area. Personally, I really had my doubts about this news—how little I knowed. We arrived all right. Then Reed and I were carried a ways on trucks. When we got down from them is when we met the famous men of the 2d Infantry division and their officers. It was some meeting.

We two replacements, Reed and Judd, were taken to a platoon which was having a type of meeting. We were told to stand over on the side and just listen. We did. We stood, our mouths hanging open awhile. One look at these fellers and Reed and I knowed they meant business. It was easy enough to see they'd come through some rough times. The lieutenant [platoon leader] was telling them how proud he was of how they'd come through, and at the end of his talk notified them he had received a whiskey ration of two bottles, of which

---

* Ridgway, 97.

† Judd was born on a hillside farm in the rural South in 1932. As a mountain boy he learned how to shoot. For each round he used, he was expected to come home with a squirrel or rabbit. On his eighteenth birthday, he enlisted in the Army, where he was trained as a mechanic.

one would be shared among the men. There was one drink to each man. They'd all watch each other careful and make sure each man took one drink. When the bottle passed down the line, Reed looked at me. "What'll we do?" "Well," I answered, "pass it by, naturally. Thank 'em kindly and pass it along." It hadn't been a long time since we'd had a drink of whiskey. So we passed it on without drinking, and they respected that. I knowed how they'd have felt if we'd tipped their bottle. And who could've blamed them? I doubt if we'd ever have had a friend. It wasn't gonna be easy, anyway. Who needed added trouble?

Someone then handed Reed and me over to sort of a small feller with a loud, rusty voice called Sergeant Ennimore [a squad leader in the 2d Platoon]. He would prove to be a fine one. Rest assured, there was no slack in that boy, none whatever. He was from the North, one of the big cities—New York or Chicago, I forget which.

Ennimore tried to orient us to the situation and called over a seemingly slow-moving guy—called him Bowen. Bowen was slow talking and didn't have a lot to say. He was supposed to look after our safekeeping. Bowen didn't like this, not one bit. He called Sergeant Ennimore aside and made no bones about how he felt, being a nursemaid. I mean, he was nice enough, but it wasn't anything that would be hid; he just didn't like greenhorns coming in under his wing. Ennimore had other things to do, and he assured Bowen that Bowen would cooperate, which he promptly did. But it was a matter of time before Bowen got around to doing much talking.

When Bowen got to talking to Reed and me, he spent a lot of time talking about some place called Kunu-ri.* He let us know what a terrible place it had been. I wanted to know what a North Korean or Chinese looked like. Bowen finally got to talking more and more. He said to me one day to answer the question I had asked over and over, "You'll know 'em when you see 'em." Now that's not much of an answer for a greenhorn, but I soon found it was the true answer.

---

* Although the 2d Division's 23d Infantry Regiment had escaped the worst of the Chinese trap set at Kunu-ri on 30 November, the division's other regiments, the 9th and 38th, had been nearly annihilated.

Cpl. DONALD CHASE *
B Company/19th Infantry

I can't remember my first impressions of my fellow squad members,
but I do know that along with many young fellers there were a large
number of men my age or older who'd been called back into active
service from their reserve units. These men had already served their
time in World War II (I had been in Europe with the 89th Infantry
division), and I doubt any of them had ever thought they'd be called
back, let alone fight another war. I was still single and had volunteered, but I thought what a tragedy it was for the men who were
married and had families. There was one feller, Sergeant Stark, who
had a machine-gun squad, who'd been in Korea awhile. He told me
this war was nothing like the one we'd fought against the Nazis. The
Koreans all looked alike, there was no way to tell friend from foe,
and the enemy seemed to be everywhere. He was one of the men
called back from a reserve unit and often talked about his family. Sad
to say, later on, he was killed.

S/Sgt. RICHARD TURNER
C Company/23d Infantry

When I reported to Charlie Company, I climbed out of the truck
and asked for the CO. I found I was talking to him; he looked like
anyone else, certainly not like an officer. Told him I had some replacements and machine guns for him. "That's great," he said, "we've
been expecting you. Already given you assignments." I looked around
and asked, "How far are we from the front lines?" He began to laugh.
"I know this doesn't look like anything, but you'll get used to it. This
is what the front looks like." I had a vision of the front lines being, I
don't know, maybe a big white tape stretched across the earth, with
us on one side and the bad guys on the other. Here, instead, was a

---

* Don Chase went into the Army in 1944 and served as a rifleman with Patton's Third Army.
When the war ended he reenlisted and spent time in Alaska. Chase was discharged in 1948
and went back to work as a carpenter; on weekends and holidays he drove stock cars on race-
tracks in Rhode Island and in Massachusetts. Shortly after the Korean War broke out he reenlisted, asking to be sent to the Far East. Although timid by nature, he says he found being
part of adventurous doings gave him a certain recognition he enjoyed.

bunch of guys lollygagging around, eating, sleeping, writing. I didn't see anyone charging up a hill with a bayonet. I couldn't believe I was actually at the front.

Two days later some F-80s flew over and strafed the area to our front. I also heard nearby some small-arms fire. Gee, I thought, this really is the front.

Cpl. VICTOR FOX
I Company/5th Cavalry

Naturally, we pumped the replacements for stateside news. The only information we got about home was through the mails or the *Stars and Stripes* newspaper—if it wasn't too badly soiled or shredded by the time you got to read it. Among other things, we all wanted to know what the current hit records were. The new men looked at us like, "Where have you guys been?" but it did not take long for them to realize we were not pulling their legs. They told us everyone had eventually gotten sick and tired of "Goodnight, Irene," and it had been replaced by another big hit called "Mockin' Bird Hill."

[In mid-January the combat situation along the eastern and central fronts improved, and enemy pressure gradually lessened.* But nowhere was this improved situation more noticeable than in the west, where it appeared the Chinese had actually withdrawn northward, leaving only thin screening forces in contact with the UN lines.† It seemed that only the Marines in the South were making substantial contact with the enemy, and this with North Korean guerrillas. Accordingly, General Ridgway concluded it was time to go back on the offensive. The attacks in his new scheme would fully exploit the UN's superiority in artillery, armor, and air power.

Operation Thunderbolt, the first of these methodical advances, jumped off on 25 January with the objective of seizing the area south

---

*The UN later estimated that the Chinese and North Korean divisions participating in the offensive had lost 38,000 men during the first twenty-six days of January.
†Launched on 15 January, Operation Wolfhound, a reconnaissance in force, met only light enemy opposition while advancing through Osan to Suwon.

of the Han River.* Territory gained, however, was secondary to the primary objective: regaining solid contact with the enemy, then destroying him—a tactic that quickly became known to the foxhole GI as "the meat grinder." During the operation, the UN's advance was anything but reckless, with Ridgway insisting on thorough artillery preparation and close lateral contact between units.]

Pfc. ROBERT HARPER
Headquarters/3d Battalion/19th Infantry

Some days we would advance two or three miles; some days we wouldn't advance at all. There were days we would go five, ten miles, then be held up for a day or more. We were told there were probably a million Chinese waiting for us in the mountains of North Korea. We began to capture quite a few prisoners, many of whom were wounded. These Chinese were treated by our medics, then moved farther south to a POW compound. Our artillery and airplanes were doing a tremendous amount of damage to the enemy. There were times when we overran Chinese first-aid stations so quickly that the medics did not have time to take their surgical equipment with them. We would find a tremendous amount of blood and bandages lying around. We knew then we were hurting them pretty bad.

S/Sgt. W. B. WOODRUFF, JR.
L Company/35th Infantry

Each day meant a foot march. Sometimes it was on flat ground, which meant an easy march, arrival on schedule at the objective, the comfort of accompanying tank support, evening chow on time, and ample time for digging in at night. Other times the route lay along winding mountain trails, where ambush was more likely and the tanks could not follow. Two miles on the battalion S-3's map might translate into many hours of slow climbing on the ground, and it might be midnight before the objective was reached. In these cases a piti-

---

*The operation was conducted by Eighth Army's I Corps (on the left) and IX Corps (on the right), each of which contributed to it one U.S. division and one ROK regiment.

fully shallow foxhole would be chipped out of the frozen and rocky earth. On reaching the objective, the CO must locate his sector, boundaries, and defensive line, and apportion these among his platoons; then each platoon sector must be apportioned among its squads and occupied by them. Finally, the squad leader must position and designate each of his two-man foxholes, typically ten to twenty yards apart. At night, in rough country, this process of reconnaissance and assignment of sectors could take an hour or more before the troops could actually begin digging. Then flanking units must be hunted out, contact established—sometimes not possible—and any gaps in the line filled by outposts or connecting patrols. These required coordination to insure against being fired on by friendly troops. Also, positions had to be specially selected for supporting weapons.

Sometime during this process chow would arrive—usually. One man from each foxhole would go to eat, while the other continued digging. Sometimes the bearers would bring along a supply of overcoats, which would be issued—until they ran out—one per two-man foxhole. The remaining time until daylight next morning would be computed and divided into four watches, each usually from two to three hours long. One man would take the first and third watch; the other, the second and fourth. The man off duty got the overcoat, if there was one. While one stood guard, the other would hunker down in the bottom of the foxhole, wrap himself in any covering available, and try to get some rest until called for his watch or roused by enemy activity—the latter occurring during this period about once in each two nights, on an average.

The temperature at night must have dropped to around zero. Commonly, one was too exhausted to stay awake and too cold to stay asleep. As the night passed, one roamed back and forth across the line between being asleep and awake. Each state in its own way was acutely uncomfortable.

It was noted regretfully that infantry combat rarely occurs on low or flat ground; it is always in rough country. Frequently, an enemy patrol would approach within maybe 300 yards, usually around eleven at night, and fire a few short bursts with a burp gun or other automatic weapon. It was supposed that this was an effort to draw return fire, so that the location of our line—and especially of our supporting weapons—could be ascertained with a view to engaging at close

range an hour or two later. Our standing orders were that fire was
not to be returned unless a suitable enemy target existed. Maybe this
strategy worked; we did not experience enemy infiltration of our main
defensive line. My belief is that the CCF conducted these nightly
patrols for less ambitious purposes. They harassed us, creating fear
and preventing rest. They may well have been designed, also, to
maintain aggressiveness and offensive spirit among their own troops.
I had already learned how difficult it is to maintain morale and aggressiveness during a lengthy retreat.

Our first significant enemy contact came shortly after the 35th
was committed, possibly about January 22 or 23. Digging in one
night we observed a lone farmhouse out to our front, at a distance of
400 or 500 yards. The CO decided to outpost it with a squad, I
believe from the 2d Platoon. The men went out after dark to avoid
observation, and a commo crew went along and laid phone wire back
to the company. Sometime in the night the phone went dead, though
no sound was heard. Next morning the squad did not return and
could not be raised. It had disappeared. I recall some insistence by
the parent platoon on commencing a search-and-rescue effort, but
the CO flatly refused. It was near time to begin our assigned mission
for the day; the rescue effort might have got a whole platoon into an
ambush, from which the company would have been ill positioned to
extract it. The CO, however, put his refusal on the ground that it
was the outpost's own fault; they must have gone to sleep on the job,
or we would have heard sounds of combat. He would not in those
circumstances jeopardize others in a probably fruitless rescue effort.
The decision was hard to accept at the time, but I judge it to have
been correct. I had long emphasized to 3d Squad that in no event
was any member to be abandoned to the enemy; either we would all
come out or none of us. I thought this necessary to maintain esprit
and unit cohesion, and to encourage the offensive spirit. However,
my instruction was based on the assumption, at least implicitly, that
the member in trouble got there by doing his duty rather than by
negligent failure of duty. The missing outpost was, in fact, captured;
some of their names we saw in the press years later among the POWs
exchanged. This experience was troubling; it did nothing to enhance
unit pride or individual confidence.

The next significant action worked out much better. It would occur a few days later at a place we christened "Hand Grenade Hill."

[*Like an enormous, deadly snowplow, Thunderbolt proceeded cautiously, methodically along a solid front, valley by valley, ridge by ridge, phase line by phase line. Ridgway's advance was new to Korea and totally different from the road-bound, motorized columns pushing toward the Yalu three months before, which had proved to be so vulnerable to enemy attacks. The UN was serving notice that it had regained the initiative and intended to keep it. Sweeping broad expanses of its front clear, Thunderbolt—with more* thunder *than* bolt—*ground forward, at first meeting little resistance.*]

Cpl. DONALD CHASE
B Company/19th Infantry

One morning we were given extra bandoliers of ammunition and extra hand grenades and C rations, and we began to move toward the enemy. Our objective was a ridge that led to a higher ridge that led to a higher ridge, and so on. We left the road and walked on dikes running along frozen rice paddies. Tanks back on the road we'd just left began firing over our heads, blasting the ridge we'd been ordered to take. The day was cold and gloomy. Bullets cracked overhead. "Please, Lord," I murmured, "don't let me be blinded or paralyzed." Other types of injuries, I felt I could cope with. When the enemy bugged out we took the ridge. This pattern went on for days—ridge after ridge. It seemed, no matter how high the ridge we were on, the next ridge was higher. Many times the ground was too hard to dig in, so we'd build walls with loose rocks. There were casualties, but it seemed the enemy was only fighting delaying actions.

Capt. LUTHER WEAVER *
A Company/35th Infantry

The company attacked a village on a rail line just south of Suwon [January 25]. My platoon was slightly to the rear and left of the two

---

* Captain Weaver had been promoted on 20 January.

forward platoons, and taking long-range rifle fire from the village across the tracks. Apparently, someone had called back for ammunition. To our amazement, a jeep and ammo trailer came barreling up a dirt track that ran along our flank. We knew he would not get far before the Chinese picked him off. He actually got about 200 yards past us before the Chinese opened up on him. The jeep came to a screeching halt and the driver dove out of the vehicle and landed in a ditch. We watched him crawl back to cover, then up the trail to safety.

From where I was, the jeep did not appear to be shot up or out of action. I instructed the squad farthest on the left to cover me while I tried to retrieve the jeep and ammo trailer. I worked my way forward under cover until I reached the vehicle. The engine was running, and apart from the windshield being shattered and one flat tire, it appeared to be okay.

I dashed for the jeep and immediately backed it down the trail about twenty yards until I had enough room to swing around and head it back in the right direction. I received no enemy fire until I started backing off the trail; then a round hit an empty 5-gallon jerry can strapped to the rear of the jeep. The sound was so loud I thought the trailer had exploded. I bailed out on the ground and heard a few more shots crack overhead. When the firing stopped I decided to give it another try. The engine was still running, and I had it headed in the right direction. I jumped in and floored it; flat tire and all, it banged down the trail. When I got it behind some cover, I turned it over to the shaken driver. The men in the platoon made some jokes about Chinese marksmanship. As this was the second jeep I had rescued in as many months [the first from a roadblock in North Korea near the Ch'ongch'on River in late November], I became known in the company as the vehicle rescue officer.

We continued our attack on the village next morning, and to our surprise discovered that the Chinese had moved out during the night.

[On 26 January the 35th Infantry's 1st Battalion occupied blocking positions and patrolled into enemy territory. Its 2d Battalion cleared the western portion of the old walled city of Suwon while the 3d Battalion, including L Company, began screening the area east of the city.]

S/Sgt. W. B. WOODRUFF, JR.
L Company/35th Infantry

Our route led over a range of hills and down into a valley. Meandering down the valley was a narrow roadway—really, a wide trail—which passed through several small villages. We checked these out and found all deserted, which was unusual and a warning. Toward noon, as we proceeded down the road, a couple of shots rang out. These seemed to come from a hill to our front, the bullets making the usual ugly sound as they passed overhead.

Lieutenant Fry [the platoon leader] immediately moved 1st Platoon off the road and up on high ground to our direct left, on the double. From the forward edge of our hill, we could observe the enemy position on top of the next hill, which was at the same approximate elevation and about 500 yards to our front.

Lieutenant Fry, Sergeant Goggins, and I took turns studying the CCF position through the lieutenant's field glasses while we awaited arrival of the company commander, with whom we were in radio contact. We observed a dozen or so Chinese soldiers move forward from the reverse slope to their foxholes on the forward slope of their hill. It was standard CCF tactics to dig in on both slopes, occupying the reverse slope positions initially, to avoid incoming artillery. Often, they would also fall back to these positions in final stage of the defense to prepare for counterattack. I noted two things about them. First, none that I saw had firearms; second, judging from both the number of positions and the number of observed personnel, I estimated them to be in platoon strength, possibly twenty-five to forty men, whereas we had an entire company. I also knew the Chinese soldiers often did not have rifles or other individual weapons. They did use snipers, some of them all too accurate; and there usually was at least one submachine gun—we habitually called them "burp guns"—per squad. Most or all of the rest of the squad, however, might have nothing but hand grenades. These were of the potato-masher type, with wooden handles to aid in throwing, and were "offensive" grenades, relying mainly on concussion for effect rather than fragmentation, as was the case with our "defensive"-type grenade. This made them less dangerous, at least in daylight; if you hugged the ground, one of their grenades detonating six feet away was unlikely to do you harm. American soldiers have for centuries equated *infantry* with *riflemen*, but in other armies this is not necessarily so. The typical Chinese peasant draftee at that time lacked comprehension of the basic principles of mechanics and physics involved in marksmanship. However, in an army trained mainly for the night assault, this was not as much a disadvantage as it might at first appear. At night, or in other conditions of poor visibility, a rifle can leave you feeling pretty helpless. Also, where our people normally carried three or four grenades per man, the Chinese carried twenty or more.

We fired a few rounds to try the range and see what we could stir up, with no effect. By this time the CO was looking the situation over, and engaged in a brief discussion with Lieutenant Fry. I continued study with the binoculars. The enemy hill had a rather flat top, with foxholes dug along the forward edge of the flat area. Just in front of these positions, the hill fell away almost straight down for a distance, then sloped gradually out toward us. The face of the hill was heavily eroded, cut with many ravines and ditches. One large ravine looked like it would provide cover for an attacking squad all the way from the base of the enemy hill up to within a few yards of the flat summit. While advancing down the slope of our hill and crossing the narrow valley between the two hills, we could be placed under fire but at or beyond maximum effective range for ordinary riflemen. I pointed out this possible avenue of approach to the two officers, whose discussion had indicated some concern for the delays involved if we should be forced to undertake a flanking maneuver.

The idea was promptly approved, a base of fire on our hill provided for, and Sergeant Goggins ordered to commence the assault with 3d Squad. He led us down our hill and across the valley on the double; I was not aware of any incoming fire during the transit. However, we were widely dispersed on beginning the climb up the enemy-occupied hill, and the ravine turned out to be a tangled and zig-zag mass of ravines. I kept taking whichever fork seemed to head most directly toward the top. Others following, when they could not see me, would make their own choice as to which branch to follow. On arriving at the head of the ravine I found Bacon still with me. The others, I felt certain, were near and headed for the same objective, but on account of the roughness of the ground, Bacon and I had lost all visual contact with the rest of the squad.

Just at this time the first grenade exploded, off to our left. We forgot the rest of the squad, giving our entire attention to the enemy positions directly above us. Grenades then began exploding around us regularly, and this kept up for a considerable time. Directly above me there appeared briefly the head and face of a Chinese soldier wearing their version of our pile cap, ear flaps flapping; I judged the distance to be thirty yards. He was apparently in a short trench, as his head would appear at one position, then at another a few feet away. He would peer out just long enough to aim and toss a grenade, then disappear; he would then reappear at the other end of the trench, throw another grenade, and repeat the exercise. I could not get a good shot at him until I caught on to the regularity of his movement. Then I began lying in wait for him; that is, aiming at his alternate position, where I would just have time to fire as his head was exposed. This went on for some time—at least six or eight rounds, which also meant six or eight of his grenades—while we both seemed to have a charmed life. I was beside myself, trying to figure out how I could miss that many times at that range, when suddenly it dawned on me: my rifle sight was set on "battlesight," 300 yards. I was shooting a yard over his head. There was no time for adjusting sights; I used Kentucky elevation and aimed my next round a yard low. This was rewarded by the sight of his cap flying off, and no more grenades came from that sector. Meantime Bacon, lying alongside me and observing my lack of accomplishment with the rifle, undertook to throw one of his grenades uphill into the enemy position. He tried this a couple of times, but the range was a little too much for his arm, and there appeared some chance his grenades might roll back down upon us.

About this time I was struck in the left temple by a minute fragment from a grenade that went off only about four feet to my front; this smarted enough to emphasize that we were engaged in serious, even deadly, business. The enemy were now keeping their heads down so that we had no target, but they continued the grenade barrage. Still there was no sign of our comrades. It seemed a bit foolhardy for Bacon and me to contemplate a two-man charge on the top of the hill, and if we stayed where we were it was only a matter of time until an incoming grenade would be too close to dodge, especially if we were bracketed; that is, if two grenades were to hit

simultaneously, one on either side. I told Bacon we ought to draw
back enough to get out of grenade range while we gave the situation
further study; he concurred. We had scooted backward and downward on our bellies about fifteen yards, when we heard voices behind
us. There came the rest of the platoon in skirmish line, using marching fire. Lieutenant Fry grinned and said something about coming to
the rescue; they had watched our initial progress and subsequent dis-
comfiture through the binoculars. By this time we were masking any
supporting fire, so they came on the double.

The enemy position was then promptly overrun. We took a couple of prisoners, and off on the right flank captured a light machine
gun. It was our luck that in coming out of the ravine Bacon and I
were just far enough to the flank that the machine gun could not
bring fire on us. In fact, it seemed to me the enemy position was
poorly selected—a mistake the Chinese rarely made. From this hill
they had good observation and fields of fire upon the valley roadway,
but were ill disposed to defend against an attack from the direction
we came. Perhaps it was also good luck that Lieutenant Fry, when
we first received fire, moved us off to our left, instead of to the right;
or perhaps this was the result of good tactical sense on his part.

The enemy had not really made much of an effort to hold this
position, and did not succeed in delaying our advance more than a
couple of hours. I never understood why they had left such a small
and poorly armed force, which was bound to be sacrificed for little
or no gain. I never saw this mistake repeated. Possibly, they had
intended to reinforce the position but had had insufficient time; possibly, they had more people in the area who were constrained to
depart early by the speed and vigor of our reaction. In any event, 1st
Platoon had for the first time met the enemy in a stand-up contest to
determine who owned a piece of real estate, and our title had prevailed.

As we reorganized on the objective, preparatory to continuing
the day's march, I do not recall that we gave any thought to these
questions of strategy and tactics, much less to any deeper philosoph-
ical meaning that might be attached to the day's events. This would
only come later. There was a feeling of relief that the platoon had
come through without loss. The sight of enemy casualties scattered
about the position brought no rejoicing, but rather a vague uneasi-

ness in the pit of the stomach. We marched away feeling more than usually drained, both physically and emotionally.

[Following the firefight for "Hand Grenade Hill," Love Company and its parent battalion, the 3d, continued to play their assigned roles in Operation Thunderbolt and resumed the advance north and northwest of Suwon. Life for these units had taken on a routine. Along with the marching and fighting there was housekeeping and bureaucracy. A peculiar symbiosis was forged, as it is in all fighting armies: riflemen and machine gunners, clerks and cooks, platoon leaders and battalion staff officers—dancing partners, but not always moving to the same music.]

27 January

Ever since the attack began we have a great deal of foot trouble. Primarily care of feet is related to leadership. In a static situation the problem is simple. In a rapidly moving situation excellency of leadership by squad, platoon and company commanders alone will insure proper care of feet. Unit commanders must be made to realize that daily inspections, change of socks, must continue in spite of the tactical situation.

EXECUTIVE OFFICER'S JOURNAL, 3D BATTALION/35TH INFANTRY

28 January

One reason for our vehicles getting in such rough shape is the fact that service company is too far to the rear to do the jobs they are charged with doing. Our own first echelon driver-maintenance has improved considerably.

EXECUTIVE OFFICER'S JOURNAL, 3D BATTALION/35TH INFANTRY

S/Sgt. W. B. WOODRUFF, JR.
L Company/35th Infantry
Lieutenant Fry was a youngish man—I judged him to be in his first year out of college—but a fine officer. He had common sense, sound judgment, and a high and conscientious devotion to duty. He was my platoon leader in 1st Platoon, Company L, 35th Infantry Regiment, from the time I joined the unit on 8 December 1950 until late

January 1951. With some of the old-timers, like Platoon Sergeant Goggins, he would engage in small talk; the two had a very close relationship and ran a good platoon. But with me, as one of his squad leaders, he was always all business. That was the way we had both been trained. There was mutual respect and loyalty, but no cameraderie. I never learned his first name, nor where he was from, nor where he had gone to school.

Early, I noticed he never wore his insignia of rank. Once Goggins told me in a more or less confidential tone that Fry was still a second lieutenant. I had a distinct impression that he just felt it unwise to advertise his youth and inexperience among frontline combat troops by wearing the gold bar. To me, it was his business and made no difference either way.

Sometime about mid-January, Lieutenant Fry received his promotion orders to first lieutenant. On went the shiny silver bar. Congratulations were sincerely offered by all hands. Lieutenant Fry struggled to maintain a dignified and gracious acceptance of these good wishes, but couldn't suppress a wide, happy, and very boyish smile.

One night [29 January]—it was just after we passed Suwon—I slipped on a frozen dike at the edge of a rice paddy and sprained an ankle. I limped to the aid station and got it bandaged. Next morning I could hardly walk. Goggins sent me to the company CP to see if there was a chance for a ride that day, but no vehicles were moving with the company. Lieutenant Schilling, the company executive officer, pointed out the road along which the company would be moving and told me to follow it as best I could, so that sooner or later I would catch up. I found there were two others in the "sick, lame, and lazy" category, and as soon as the company cleared we fell in behind it. The company was soon out of sight ahead of us.

29 January
0830 Bn moved forward in the attack.
                              UNIT JOURNAL, 3D BATTALION/35TH INFANTRY

30 January
0950 Received call from G-1 (Captain Apgar) regarding Rest and Relaxation. Personnel will leave Taejon on 5 February 51.

Enlisted men will report to 25th Replacement Company 3 February 1200 hours. They will fly to Atami Field.
1000 Call from G-1 regarding Lt. Hoskell's trial. Lt. Garresam, Pvt. Stegner, Capt. Watson (Company L) to report to Judge Advocate at 25th Replacement company as soon as possible.

S-1 JOURNAL, 3D BATTALION/35TH INFANTRY

S/Sgt. W. B. WOODRUFF, JR.
L Company/35th Infantry

In an hour or so my ankle warmed up and felt much better. With each step my limp was less pronounced. I took my leave of the other two and began stepping out. I left them far behind, and by noon caught up to the company, which was taking a C-ration break in a village. The company had been in battalion reserve the past twenty-four hours or so, and there had been no enemy contact. However, when we moved out after lunch, L Company was advance guard for the battalion. First Platoon was designated lead element of the company. In turn, 3d Squad—mine—was designated point squad. We moved out of the village across a large valley covered with rice paddies. There was considerable snow, but the noonday sun had brought a slight melting; I noted a very small trickle of water running through the snow in the bottom of the ditches on either side of the road. Ahead loomed high hills at the north end of the valley.

We had been moving about an hour without incident, clearing the few houses and small villages as we went, when a shot rang out, apparently from high ground to our left front, the bullet striking the road amid 3d Squad. We took cover in the right-hand ditch and tried to locate the enemy position. Immediately, I was conscious of Lieutenant Fry running forward up the ditch; crouching, he ran past me and stopped about ten yards ahead of me, alongside the lead men in the squad. A newsreel cameraman had been with our company the last several days, off and on. He also ran forward and halted as he came alongside me. I heard Fry ask if anyone had located the source of the incoming fire. I believe the thought running through all our minds was that we had come upon another enemy rear guard or defensive outpost. These generally resulted in slowing our advance for a time, but had never presented a serious problem. As soon as we got supporting fire deployed and got down to serious business in the attack, the enemy, his delaying mission accomplished, would begin withdrawing.

I saw Lieutenant Fry rise up on his knees, exposing himself from about the waist up, studying through his binoculars the suspected enemy position to our left front. A second shot rang out. Lieutenant Fry fell back into the ditch, saying distinctly, "Gee, I'm hit." I went to him and found the bullet had entered his left chest. It was plain he was breathing his last.

Another squad member came up; I have no memory of who it was. We decided to bandage his wound. I think we both knew it was a hopeless gesture, but it seemed the least we could do. We started working as fast as we could, crouched in the snow and mud of the ditch. We loosened his clothing and, noting where the bullet had exited his lower back, realized we would need two bandages. We began racing against time. I was dimly aware of a thought that if we could just get the bandages on before he expired, by a miracle he might live. We got the bandages on. The miracle did not occur.

I looked up, feeling doubly defeated, suddenly conscious of a whirring sound to my left. There knelt the cameraman five yards away, still filming, camera pointing directly at us. I was shocked. To me it was a gross invasion of privacy. I could not imagine any circumstances in civilian life in which a cameraman would be permitted to film the act of one's dying. Death on the battlefield in the service of our country was even more sacred. This stranger had intruded on the scene and on our grief in an acutely insensitive way. I fixed a long stare on his face, which I imagine was a compound of sorrow, indignation, and abhorrence, turning gradually to pure hate. He stopped filming and looked the other way.

An ambulance crept forward up the road. Medics placed Lieutenant Fry's body on a stretcher, then into the ambulance. Goggins came up to personally supervise this. He made no effort to control the flow of tears which, on his weathered face, seemed totally incongruous.

This brought a number of men out on the road, but there was no more firing. It was my first, but not last, such experience. I never knew the Chinese to fire on a rescue party seeking to recover the dead or wounded. This may have indicated a mature and civilized approach to war, or merely a sort of professional courtesy; it was something else to ponder.

Then our company commander strode up. Brusquely, he ordered Goggins to take charge of the platoon and immediately counterattack the hill mass to our left front. I stared in disbelief. The size of the designated objective was more appropriate to a battalion than a platoon attack. Its base was half a mile away across an open rice paddy. Moreover, the enemy had us under observation and zeroed in, while we did not know his position nor strength. Furthermore, the captain had said nothing about air, artillery, or even mortar support. I calculated 1st Platoon was about to go the way of its leader.

Nevertheless, we formed up in the left-hand ditch and on Goggins's shouted orders commenced movement to the left front in a forty-man skirmish line. Immediately, the Chinese opened up with rifles and automatic weapons. By the time we were able to take cover in a drainage ditch about 100 yards out, two men had bullet holes in their clothing, and one of these had his hood penetrated and briefly set afire by a tracer bullet. Miraculously, no one was hurt, but a machine gun was raking the forward edge of the drainage ditch. After a few minutes the attack was canceled, and the mission turned over to friendly troops advancing along the high ground to our left. They were in position to take the enemy position in flank.

29 January

1330 Call from Mr. Harrison on report of compliance of memo "Why Are We Here?"* Informed him that message was read to frontline troops two days before.

S-1 JOURNAL, 3D BATTALION/35TH INFANTRY

---

* To improve morale in his army, Ridgway had written a memo he called "Why Are We Here? What Are We Fighting For?" which, on 21 January, he directed be read to every individual assigned or attached to Eighth Army. His answer to the first question was simple—because as soldiers they were ordered to be there. The general gave the answer to the second question this way: "In the final analysis, the issue now joined right here in Korea is whether Communism or individual shall prevail; whether the flight of fear-driven people we have witnessed here shall be checked, or shall at some future time, however distant, engulf our own loved ones in all its misery and despair."

S/Sgt. W . B . WOODRUFF, JR.
L Company/35th Infantry
Two hours later the company was in its position for the night, on a
low hill. Chow had been brought forward to a village just behind the
hill. During this respite, while I was waiting for the end of the chow
line, the newsreel cameraman sidled up to me. He mumbled something about how we all have our job to do, and his actions ought not
to be taken personally. I looked him in the eye and gave him another
long, cold stare, then turned and walked away. I never saw him again;
if I had, it would have been too soon.

29 January
1700 Set up Command Post approx 5 miles N of Suwon. Result
      of days action: 1 off-4 EM KIA [killed in action] (Lt. Fry
      KIA); 1 off-9 EM WIA [wounded in action]. 28 En pris-
      oners taken 44 enemy killed.

                          UNIT JOURNAL, 3D BATTALION/35TH INFANTRY

S/Sgt. W . B . WOODRUFF, JR.
L Company/35th Infantry
That night about eleven, right on schedule, an enemy patrol somewhere to our front saluted us with a couple of short bursts. As usual
we held our fire but went on 100 percent alert. It had been a long
day, filled with unusually disruptive and disturbing events. But, with
the familiar enemy patrol action, our life seemed to have returned to
its normal routine.

29 January
2315 Received 45 replacements, also returnees from 25th Re-
      placement Co. Took replacements to Hq Co., given sup-
      per and bedded for the night. Summary of day: usual
      administrative duties.

                            S-1 JOURNAL, 3D BATTALION/35TH INFANTRY

CHIPYONG-NI

29 January-1 March 1951

The day Lieutenant Fry was killed, farther east a patrol from Captain Norman Allen's Item Company was ambushed by a strong enemy force. On the twenty-seventh, the 5th Cavalry had moved out of reserve and attacked through the 8th Cav, which had stalled in front of phase line A. By the twenty-ninth, the regiment had advanced generally to the area of phase line B. That morning I Company sent one of its platoons out on patrol.

Pfc. JERRY EMER *
I Company/5th Cavalry

The deuce-and-a-half driver's name was Wayne. Also in the front seat were the patrol's leader, Lieutenant [Walter] Cadman, and a sergeant from Texas named Hardie. The rest of the platoon was riding in the back of the truck. Nothing unusual, the road we drove along paralleled a valley lined with hills. When the first bullets cracked overhead and one went through the windshield, narrowly missing Lieutenant Cadman's head, Wayne slammed—and I mean *slammed*—on the brakes. The sixteen or so of us riding in the back ended up

---

* One of thirteen children, Emer grew up in Wisconsin. As soon as he graduated from high school he was drafted into the Army, but the Japanese surrendered before he saw action. He left the service in 1946, but in less than a year had reupped.

on the floor in a tangle of arms and legs. As soon as we untied ourselves, we scrambled out the back and piled into a deep ditch running along the road. The fire was coming from a high hill to our left, and when we weren't pinned down, we fired in that direction. The ensuing firefight turned into a rather aimless affair. Someone murmured almost prayfully, "Christ, I hope those bastards don't have mortars." Except for the four or five brand-new replacements who were too scared and confused, the rest of us knew what the prayer meant. I'm sure each of us thought to himself, Amen! Amen! I know I did. As it turned out, this prayer was answered.

Eventually, Lieutenant Cadman decided someone would have to return to the village where the rest of the company was bivouacked and tell Captain Allen of our predicament. The lieutenant *asked* the driver if he wanted to go. When he said no, he asked everyone else. No one wanted to leave the ditch and get back to the truck, which then needed to be turned around and run through the gauntlet of enemy fire. There was no cover on that road. The lieutenant could have ordered Wayne to do it, but he wasn't that kind of an officer. What he did next won him the Silver Star. He dashed back to the truck and carefully cranked it around till it pointed in the right direction. Leaving the engine idling he ran back to the ditch. The truck was hit several times by gunfire, but Lieutenant Cadman returned without a scratch on him. He told Wayne and me to get going and to bring back Captain Allen. Wayne and I made the truck okay and got back to the company in one piece.

Capt. NORMAN ALLEN
I Company/5th Cavalry

29 January
Between Chonju and Sangju

Mother dear,
Today wasn't near as quiet as it had been around here for the past three weeks. One of my patrols got into a tough fight and was pinned down by 100 of the enemy armed with machine guns and rifles. The patrol had fought toward the base of a hill the enemy was on, when it learned a group of about thirty-five

of the enemy was coming around to hit it in the rear. The patrol had been in a truck, and when the men dismounted and took up the fire, the truck got away. I alerted a platoon and took off after notifying the colonel [Edgar Treacy, 3d Battalion's CO]. Went two and a half miles and stopped when I thought I was about 700 yards from where my patrol was pinned down. I had just raised my hand to halt the rest of the column and opened my mouth to order dismount, when an enemy MG [machine gun] opened up on me. The men didn't need my order. With that first burst of fire they piled out so fast it looked as if a giant hand had turned the vehicles on end and tumbled them out. First thing I knew, I was behind a stone wall ten yards from my jeep. I couldn't at first determine where the fire was coming from, but set up a base of fire and maneuvered into a frozen river bottom. Then I moved up on to some high ground that looked across a small valley and opened up with everything I had. Our riding up so boldly had thwarted the enemy's efforts to outflank the patrol. I kept up a heavy base of fire and yelled to the patrol across the valley to secure their wounded and come out under our cross fire.

I sent twelve litter bearers up the draw to meet them, and we were able to get everyone back. The patrol's lieutenant, a sergeant and two men were in pretty bad shape; two others were slightly wounded. Sure am sorry to lose Walt [Lieutenant Cadman]; he was a fine-looking officer with a fine career ahead of him.

[Through the last days of January, the Eighth Army meat grinder slowly rolled on. Chinese prisoners stated that all that lay in front of the advance was two divisions, a clear sign that the enemy's mission was nothing more than to screen and delay Eighth Army.]

Sgt. GLENN HUBENETTE
F Company/7th Infantry *

We moved off one ridge and the next day moved to another. This mountain formed a natural defensive position for the Chinese, and they didn't want to give it up. After two days we finally climbed to the top but were still fired on by snipers and well-dug-in machine guns. Every time we left our holes we were shot at. The terrain was quite rugged, and the enemy was dug in on a high, rugged outcropping of rock and pines. On the morning of the third day our platoon sergeant, Ted Turkos, a veteran of World War II who'd fought on Okinawa, was hit in the head. I ran over to him and, after pulling him behind some rocks, yelled for the medics. I could see the back left side of his head was gone. Our medic, Mac, put two large field dressings over the hole and told me it was doubtful Ted would live. We knelt there waiting for him to die, but he didn't. That morning Ted and I had had an argument about where to have my squad dig in. He'd finally said to me, "Put your men where I tell you and stop arguing! I'm your sergeant and I know what I'm doing." What could I say to that? I felt he was right, but I still called him a Greek SOB. We were tired and grumpy. Ted turned and gave me a dirty look that said, "Just do it!" A half hour later, I was kneeling by his side expecting him to die. When he hadn't and another half hour had passed, I said, "We'd better get him down the mountain." I cut two small pine trees to make a litter, and someone went and got a shelter half. Our new platoon leader told me I'd take over the platoon when I returned. Then three volunteers and I began to carry Ted off the mountain.

We had to work hard because the sun was melting the frost, and the trail was slippery. When blood and saliva blocked Ted's breathing we'd stop and clear the passages. When we reached the road, there was no litter jeep to be found. Thirty minutes or so later, a jeep pulled up. I was really pissed, but the guy driving said they'd just been notified by radio. I apologized. Ted seemed to know what was

---

* The U.S. 3d Division, comprising the 7th, 15th, and 65th Infantry Regiments, had joined Thunderbolt on 27 January and was attached to I Corps.

going on. After he was loaded he raised his head slightly as if he was about to say, "So long," but the jeep roared off.*

When I returned to the top of the hill, the fight was still going on. The lieutenant told me another sergeant had taken over the platoon. I never got the promotion.

[By Wednesday, 31 January, it was apparent to United Nations Command that south of the Han, in front of both I Corps and IX Corps, the Chinese were finally climbing back into the ring. No longer content to jab and move, the Communists would begin counterpunching. Below Seoul, they would try to stop Thunderbolt.]

Sgt. F/C WARREN AVERY
G Company/21st Infantry
We were near the Han River when the 3d Platoon was ordered to go out with some attached tanks and patrol the area to our front. We moved our obstructions from the road so they could pass through. We felt we were pretty safe, as the battalion had recently patrolled about thirty miles in front of the MLR [main line of resistance] and not found any Chinese. When the 3d Platoon and the tanks got about 500 yards down the road all hell broke loose. They were hit by a good-sized enemy unit and pinned down by machine-gun and mortar fire. One of the tanks giving covering fire from a small hill threw a track and had to be blown up. My platoon was ordered out to help get our men back. We didn't take the machine guns, just grabbed our rifles and carbines and ran toward the firefight. When we got into the area, we kept running. I jumped over an enemy foxhole; the Chinese soldier looked up at me and I down at him. I didn't have the guts to blow him away with my carbine, but I did throw a grenade after I got beyond him. At least I didn't have to look at him when he died.

I saw the Chinese had their mortars set up behind a small village about 1,000 yards to the north. Each time one of the tubes fired, it

---

* Sergeant Turkos was taken to the Swedish Red Cross Hospital in Pusan, where he was fitted for a steel plate. He died later in San Francisco.

blew some of the thatch or straw off the roofs. I gave this news to our platoon leader, who told the tanks. It wasn't long before the village just wasn't there anymore. After that, the battle kind of faded away, and we returned to our roadblock position. That night reinforcements came up and helped us man our perimeter.

Sgt. THOMAS RANDELL
Heavy Mortar Company/7th Cavalry
George Company, to which I was attached as an FO [forward observer], was to move out at 4:00 A.M., cross a series of rice paddies, and take a hill held by the Chinese, who were estimated to be there in company strength. Ours was to be a sneak attack; no shots were to be fired, only bayonets were to be used. If we could get to the top of the hill undetected, it was believed the objective would be ours for the taking.

We crossed the rice paddies in the dark without incident, and the company began to quietly ease up the steep slope. Everything was going according to the plan. Then, as we were sneaking past an enemy sentry, someone, forgetting the order to use his bayonet, shot the Chinese. Within seconds the hill came alive, and we were raked with machine-gun fire. With the element of surprise lost, our only chance of surviving was to get back across the rice paddies in the dark. If we waited, the sun would rise, and in its light, caught in the open, we'd be cut to pieces.

We hugged the ground while the murderous enemy fire literally cut down the small trees around us. On my left, a bullet smashed into the face of a GI, entering one cheek, cutting off the tongue, and exiting the other cheek. He bled badly but still tried to talk. A guy on my right took a slug in the stomach; he lay gasping in the snow.

I got an arm around each and tried to help them down off the hill. We slipped on the hard, crusted snow and at first slid, then fell, tumbling end over end.

At the bottom the company crouched and waited for orders. The enemy fire slowed, then stopped. A voice from above called out in perfect English, "Hey, George Company, we have two of your wounded. We'll hold our fire while you come and get them." A platoon officer new to Korea muttered, "Nobody can trust them lying

Chinamen." But a Sergeant Berryman, a West Virginian and an old-timer with George Company, picked four men and was soon on his way up the hill to retrieve his wounded buddies. Keeping their word, the Chinese held their fire, and in a short time Berryman's small group returned with the wounded men.

It was growing lighter in the east by the minute, and we were all anxious to get across those rice paddies while it was still gray. The company commander cautioned us not to run, but to withdraw slowly and in an orderly manner.

I carried the boy with the stomach wound for the first 100 yards or so. He'd become so weak he could no longer stand, let alone walk. Thinking he was dying, he repeated the Lord's Prayer so often that I lost count. I told him he'd be okay, that the medics would take care of him. But I have no way of knowing whether he made it or not.

When we reached our lines, the wounded were quickly evacuated to the rear. The following day, after a mortar and artillery barrage, we took the hill and found the Chinese had already withdrawn.

[In IX Corps, the 19th Infantry was the spearhead of the 24th Division's piece of Operation Thunderbolt.* Toward the end of the first week of February, it began to run into vigorous enemy resistance.]

1st Lt. WILLIAM CALDWELL III
L Company/19th Infantry

We were the lead element in a reconnaissance in force that made contact with the enemy to our north. A month earlier, when my company returned south of the 38th Parallel, I had approximately seventy men left. I began at once to receive replacements and one day received as many replacements as I had men in the company. In civilian life these men had been laborers and bakers, mechanics and candlestick makers; they weren't infantrymen. But I will confess these soldiers *were* dedicated. They were determined, mature, and willing to learn, and by Operation Thunderbolt I felt they had become a very effective fighting force.

---

*Twenty-fourth Division had been in Korea since early July, having been the first U.S. unit sent from Japan to try and stop the North Korean invasion.

In early February, out in front of the regiment, we ran across a very determined enemy and found we were nearly cut off. We suffered heavy casualties before extricating ourselves and withdrawing.

[The 19th Infantry was forced to give ground, and fell back behind a screen hastily established on the first defendable terrain by the 1st and 3d Battalions of the 21st Infantry Regiment. The Chinese force, later estimated to be a division, closely pursued the withdrawing Americans. That night the weather was cold, and there was snow on the north face of the ridgeline where the Americans expectantly lay in wait. The enemy collided with the GIs just after dark on 5 February.]

1st Lt. CARL BERNARD
L Company/21st Infantry

Soon after dark, we received word of probing attacks in the area of the 1st Battalion. Next, our 3d Battalion, on Hill 296, was probed by forward scout elements moving up the ridgeline. The Chinese then began to assault the hill in force and came at us in three waves. The first, men armed with grenades, crawled to the company's forward position and in a coordinated effort threw all they had. Once the last grenade exploded, the second wave—a line of men armed with burp guns—sprinted through L Company, firing as they went. The main assault followed in a classic fire-and-movement maneuver and forced the company's platoons off the hill. The company had just received its monthly payroll, and left on top of the hill was this payroll and a box of money.

At first light, the platoon on the left attempted to return to its original position on the hill, but was beaten back by close-in machine-gun fire. At the same time the right platoon and a platoon that had been attached to it from King Company were also turned back. Several men leading this counterattack were killed before they'd gone more than ten yards.

Shortly after 11:00 A.M. [6 February], Love Company made a coordinated attack to regain the hill. With the artillery battalion commander [of the 52d FA Battalion] personally calling in fire, barrage after barrage was placed directly in front of the men and aided them in their attack. Another battery fired on top of the hill and kept the enemy pinned down. (It was at this time—because the artillery was tearing up the down bags we'd been forced to leave behind, and the feathers were flying everywhere—that Hill 296 became known to us as "Sleeping Bag Hill.") The men in the assault crawled forward until nearly into their own fire, then requested an "add five-zero" to the concentration. They repeated this procedure until they were able to get into a final assault position. A grenade attack helped take a particularly nasty machine-gun nest, and seven serviceable Bren guns were captured. The last Chinese soldier in this position was an extremely brave man who, in spite of his hopeless situation, fought to his death.

Each of the four artillery tubes, which kept the crest of the hill under continuous fire, then fired white phosphorus, which indicated they were lifting their "fire for effect" barrages. With the explosion of the last "willy-peter," we launched an attack which carried the top of the hill. The artillery fire was then adjusted on the enemy who, in their white parkas, were withdrawing in the valley below. The platoon on the right was reorganized in its original position, and by 3:00 P.M. the lines were restored to the positions Love Company had held on the fifth.

That night, around 10:30 P.M., the depleted company was again hit by heavy, probing attacks, but these were not followed up on as they had been twenty-four hours earlier. It is probable the Chinese were fixing in place our forward elements while they withdrew northward.

Enemy dead, which we counted next day, added up to 169. Our own casualties were forty-one, of whom sixteen were killed. Those killed included three men who had been with the company from the time we arrived in Korea in early July 1950.

[The Chinese vigorously contested Thunderbolt's methodical advance for more than a week; then, on 9 February, they suddenly disappeared. In the west, patrols all across I Corps's front raced forward through a heavy snowstorm and, without firing a shot, reached the Han River. The next day, Inch'on and Kimpo Airfield were again in the hands of the UN. By nightfall units of the 25th Division had arrived south of Seoul and were looking across the Han at the battered capital.]

S/Sgt. W. B. WOODRUFF, JR.
L Company/35th Infantry

Yongdungp'o was a large city,* though considerably the worse for wear. I had been here twice before, and would be here three times more later on. On this day we followed a rail line for a time, then climbed out over the embankment and threaded our way through what looked like a warehouse or industrial district. Around noon we came upon the Han River. At this point there was a dike, or levee, along the south bank of the Han to keep the river in bounds, and the high ground lay on the Seoul, or northward, side. The levee was some twenty or more feet high, and wide enough at the top to accommodate a two-lane paved highway.

Atop the levee the platoon halted. Lopez [1st Platoon sergeant] was sent out over the river ice with Baker's [2d] squad to check out a small island in midriver to our front. A little later I went with Skirvin's [3d] squad to check out a large two-story building down on our left flank. From the blackboards and other contents, we judged it had previously housed a high school or small college. It was the most prominent building we could see, all other structures in the area being small mud brick shacks with thatched roofs. Both patrols were uneventful. We dug in atop the levee, along the north side, overlooking the river. As the sectors were finally assigned, the large school building was just outside and to the left of our platoon and company sector. Our platoon CP was set up in a shack below and south of the levee, and an additional shack was taken over by each squad as a "warm-up shack" for the off-duty shift. The company CP and mess area were located about 300 yards to the rear. In setting off to chow you were initially protected by the levee from enemy fire originating from the high ground north of the river, but you were exposed the last 200 yards or so. From time to time the CCF let it be known they were still in place on the north bank, so the orders were that the shift going to chow would go singly, keeping a good interval between men. Inevitably, when nothing happens for a day or two, Americans get careless. Sure enough, a shift from 2d Squad one day took this route,

---

* Yongdungp'o was an industrial suburb southwest of Seoul, and at the time of the Inch'on landings the scene of some tough fighting between the North Koreans and the 1st Marines.

swinging their mess kits and walking along together, talking. In came a single mortar round—one of the Russian 120-mm heavy mortars—and Baker was suddenly short half a squad.

Capt. LUTHER WEAVER
L Company/35th Infantry
On February 13 I was notified that I had been selected to take over as company commander of L company and was to report to the 3d Battalion's CO, Lieutenant Colonel James H. Lee, as soon as possible. As is always the case in frontline units in combat, a move from one unit to another is a simple matter of telling the old unit's first sergeant so he can make an entry in the morning report, and possibly notifying the supply sergeant so he can drop your weapon, compass, watch, binoculars, or anything else you might have been issued. No baggage, footlockers, or reams of published orders are necessary. Everything necessary, you're wearing or carrying on your back.

I reported to Colonel Lee, a tall Texan, who in his winter parka looked like a grizzly. He briefed me on what I would find at L Company and told me I would be their fourth company commander within a matter of some five or six weeks. I could see from what he told me, I'd have my work cut out for me.

I arrived at L Company's CP about 4:00 P.M. and met the acting company commander and the 1st sergeant, John Mills. My primary concern before dark was to take a good look at the company's defense line on the levee along the Han.

The river, which was to our front, was frozen over with a good foot or more of ice. I made a hasty tour of inspection and found many things I wanted to correct, like installing trip flares, but due to the time of day, I decided to wait until the next day before implementing them. The few men I had a chance to talk with briefly struck me as being rather shaky and unsure of themselves.

S/Sgt. W. B. WOODRUFF, JR.
L Company/35th Infantry
The same day our new company CO, Captain Weaver, arrived, there also appeared in our platoon CP shack a full keg of beer. It was

immediately and abundantly clear that this wholly unexpected item
was the sole property of Joe Alford. I never asked him where it came
from, and he never told me.* I may have been just a little surprised,
but I knew that if anybody could find a keg of beer in the middle of
the Sahara Desert, it would be Sergeant Al. My recollection is that I
never had a taste of it. It is possible Alford may have offered me a
drink. It is equally possible he may have told me, Lopez, and Paul
"Scosh" ("Scosh" meaning "little") Myers that it was our duty to
remain alert and sober at all times. Or, the beer may have been
acquired for medicinal purposes. Anyway, that night Al was medi-
cating at a steady rate. Somewhere about his sixth or eighth beer,
there came a sudden burst of small-arms fire back to the rear. Alford
allowed it may have come from a mortar unit set up several hundred
yards behind us. He undertook to get them on our field phone. The
sergeant of the unit, a long-time acquaintance of Alford, promptly
answered, but in a whisper. What he whispered was, in substance,
that "they" were "all around my CP," and "for God's sake please
don't make my phone ring again"; also, to please not talk so loud, as
"they" might hear. In Alford's then-medicated condition, this situation struck him as being fraught with humorous possibilities. He immediately, and as loud as he could talk, demanded to know who the
hell "they" were. He further demanded that the sergeant "Speak up,
man, I can't hear you." He then pretended to be unable to hear, and
announced that he guessed he was going to have to ring again as no
one had answered. After he had prolonged this torture a while, Alford put down the phone and lay back. Over his countenance spread
a look of total contentment, which to Alford was the equivalent of
anyone else's belly laugh.

About an hour passed, and all was quiet. The incident back at
the mortar unit had been forgotten. About midnight the calm was
suddenly shattered by a long burst from a burp gun and a series of
grenade explosions. This racket came from atop the levee and no
more than fifty yards away. I ran out of the dimly lighted hut into a
night that was pitch dark, and eased up to the top of the levee. I
whispered to the man in the first foxhole I came to; he whispered

---

* There was a brewery in Yongdungp'o.

back that the firing was to his left, and that was all he knew. About that time I heard Fisher yell, "Grenade!" It was not incoming; it was an American grenade and exploded out on the low ground in front of the levee. Then it dawned on me: In basic training you are taught to yell "Grenade" upon throwing one, as a warning to others in the vicinity. It is like a golfer yelling "Fore," or a powderman yelling "Fire in the hole." Fisher, in the midst of the action and understandably excited, had reverted to his basic training—and warned the enemy he was heaving a grenade. Simultaneously with the explosion, our people fired a volley of rifle shots, also down into the low ground immediately forward of the levee. Somebody yelled that one of the enemy had been hit and was lying down on the pavement, and to watch out for him, as he might still be alive. As it happened we had no BAR in this immediate sector, and rifle fire is not effective against a moving target on a dark night. The one enemy on the pavement was the only casualty we inflicted; but he turned out to be a North Korean squad leader, who still had his burp gun. He was probably leader of the patrol.

Capt. LUTHER WEAVER
L Company/35th Infantry
Right at the point of loosening my bootlaces with the intent of getting some shut-eye, I had heard firing from the direction of the dike. Within seconds, the 3d Platoon had called to report they were under attack. I immediately called for my runner to get a 536 radio* and follow me. I also told a private manning a field phone back to battalion to tell them Love was having another probing attack. Within seconds I was in contact with the 3d Platoon and told them I was on the way. A few minutes later I was approaching the dike.

---

* The SCR-536 was a short-range, frontline, platoon-to-company radio set, amplitude modulated, weighing about ten pounds. Its range was about one mile.

S/Sgt. W. B. WOODRUFF, JR.
L Company/35th Infantry

At this time no more than fifteen minutes had passed since our first contact, and we were still edgy. I became aware of a noise down the paved road to our right. I could not identify it, except that it appeared to be coming closer. The night was still absolutely pitch dark. I had not been back to the platoon CP, and had not seen Alford or Lopez—they were out along the line somewhere, but we had not encountered each other—so I was unaware of any contact we might have had with the company CP. My rifle was bearing on the strange noise coming down the road, when I suddenly recognized it as radio transmission. Next, I could make out, waving against the night sky, the outline of a long antenna. Then I could make out two men; it was our new CO, Captain Weaver, and his runner. He had come down to check on us and our situation.

This was a first. Until then I had no idea what company commanders did at night, and had never thought about it. All I knew was that I had never before seen one out strolling along the front line in darkness, much less in practically the middle of a firefight and accompanied only by a radio operator. Pondering it the next day, I concluded it was a rather foolish act on Captain Weaver's part; he stood equal chances of running into an enemy patrol or being shot by mistake by some of his own people. That night I just stood there with my mouth open. Clearly, this Georgian had different notions about running a company from anything I had experienced before. He told us what was known at his level of the enemy activity just concluded, and got a report on 1st Platoon's participation, which appeared to satisfy him. I believe he indicated that night that next day we would change our dispositions some.

We did. He had us move our foxhole line down to the base of the levee, on the forward, north side, explaining that this would allow us to put grazing fire out to, and partly across, the river. Plunging fire, from the top of the levee, offered less chance of being effective against an enemy attack of any size. All my military life I had heard of "plunging" versus "grazing" fire, but up to that time it had all been theoretical to me. This practical example made me an instant expert—my education had advanced another notch. The captain also personally relocated the light machine guns for mutual support, and had us put out trip flares and booby traps. Of course, once we were thus set up for them on the levee, the enemy never again made contact with us.

Pfc. JAMES CARDINAL
Headquarters Company/3d Battalion/5th Cavalry

13 February
South Korea

Dear William,

We are now near the Han River getting prepared for a big attack. They say we are going to assault Seoul real soon. I just hope that my luck continues to be as good as it's been in the past. I've been here five months and have hopes of being rotated home sometime this summer. They say there are a lot of replacements coming over soon which makes me very happy. I'll only be too glad to give somebody else the honor of fighting for the UN for a while.

Today's my 22nd birthday. It seems very strange. This is only my second birthday away from home. My 18th I spent in Italy but that was a lot different from today. Then I had the world by the tail. Now I just hope to stay alive until my next birthday. It's as simple as that.

I am now in HDQ Company attached to the I & R [Intelligence and Reconnaissance] Squad. Its job is to run patrols into enemy territory. It's pretty interesting. Only trouble is that every so often it gets wiped out. Gives you something to think about.

[*Although some UN units were on the Han, the Chinese still retained a considerable amount of ground below the river. Although he defended it tenaciously, it would only be a matter of time before the enemy lost this foothold entirely. Unfortunately, at the time, he didn't know this. What he did know, however, was that I Corps must be prevented form sending reinforcements eastward, where the Communists' main effort would next be directed.*]

Sgt. GLENN HUBENETTE
F Company/7th Infantry

The guys in the squad laughed it off, but I knew that on February 13 I was going to get killed or wounded. We were outside an old walled city [Sansong-ni] and had taken over from the 1st Battalion. I detailed a man to guard our baggage, and the rest of the squad moved east until we stood at the base of a big horseshoe ridge. It was a long way up, and a man named Coffee and I sang "The Tennessee Waltz" while we climbed. As we approached the top we stopped singing. Someone behind us on the hill suddenly yelled and it sounded to me like "Help!" My BAR man, Tanner, stood behind me. Then Lieutenant Chris [Frank Christianson] shouted, "Get down!" We did, and all hell broke loose! Tanner and I had dropped into a shallow ditch. Uphill of us a machine gun opened up. I lay facedown while that Chink tried to get me. Slugs slammed into the hard dirt. This was the first time I knew—really knew—what gut fear was. I'd been scared many times before, but this time it was different. Pure, unadulterated fear ran up and down my spine. I whispered to Tanner, "You okay?" "Yeah," he answered. "How do we get out of this mess?" I said, "Listen for when the gun fires off in the other direction. Then turn around. Go slow, though." The lieutenant called up to me to see if we were okay, then told us to come back down to where he was. Lord, I don't know how Tanner and I did it, but we slid around until we faced downhill. We waited for the Chink to fire in another direction. I thought, My ass must be sticking up in the air. That Chink is gonna nail me not on the right, not on the left, but right in the middle. The machine gun fired again. For many miles I'd been carrying a rifle grenade and the launcher, and thought maybe now would be the time to use it. I'd never fired one before and had only seen movies on how to launch it. Hell, before Korea I'd been an engineer who had served in a warehouse.

The machine gun opened up on a target off to our left. I yelled, "Now!" Tanner and I got up and sprinted to where the lieutenant waited.

For the rest of the day we stayed where we were, shooting and taking cover, pumping clip after clip into the Chinese positions. Our mortars tried to silence the Chinks, but failed. Then the Air Force sent some planes to strafe. We ducked—so did the enemy.

We lost men this day. A young soldier named Cox was hit and died before our eyes. The week before, he'd been notified his wife had just had a baby. This happened in the company often enough to cause us to wonder if it wasn't bad luck to be notified you were a father. Seemed like everyone who was, was soon dead.

The Chinks tried to outflank us but were turned back. That one machine-gun emplacement still held us up. As the afternoon wore on, we found ourselves packed together tight on the slope of that ridge. Word reached us that Sergeant Molesky had been hit trying to bring replacements up the hill. Word also had it none of the replacements made it either—they'd been ambushed.

Late in the afternoon we held a conference. Captain Ladd decided we were going to charge the Chinese. "Fix bayonets" rang out. Damn, if I couldn't get my bayonet out of its scabbard! I sat there in frustration. It was then that a shell exploded behind me. The blast killed Lieutenant Chris, Sergeant Coffee, and Corporal Meyers. It blew me down the hill. I found out it had also wounded Tanner and Bill Giard, and put a hole in Lieutenant Miller from H Company.

I was the last wounded man taken off that cursed hill. On the way down we were ambushed. The medics dropped my stretcher and hid behind some rocks. When the Chinese were finally driven off, they came back and carried me to the road.

Later in the evening, Tanner and I and Lieutenant Miller were in the same ambulance. It was a wild ride.

I banged on the window and the driver stopped quick and ran back to us. "What's the matter?" "For Christ's sake, take it slower, there's guys hurt back—" "Can't help it, we're being shot at." "We'll hang on—let's go!"

In a MASH [Mobile Army Surgical Hospital] outfit, Tanner and I watched while the doctors removed big, jagged pieces of metal and fatigue jacket cloth from the hole in Lieutenant Miller's side. What a bloody mess. Next, we were sent to a hospital set up in a schoolhouse that was handling a lot of men. One young lad sitting next to me in the hallway was hysterical. He'd shot himself through the foot. When I'd been treated, a doctor/major began working on the young GI. Told the kid if he had his way, he'd let him bleed to death, and that the guy didn't belong in the same army with men who'd been legitimately wounded. The major might as well have saved his breath;

the GI didn't hear a word he'd said. Who knew what the kid had gone through before he shot his foot? When the GI and I were alone in the hallway, I told him, "Take it easy, kid."

Later, I learned F Company lost twenty-six men on the slopes of that big horseshoe-shaped ridge.

[Tuesday, 13 February was a bad day for more than Sergeant Hubenette and those twenty-six men in Fox Company. Farther east, in the area of General Almond's X Corps,* a battle was shaping up that day that would be as savage as any the war had seen.

The major players in this drama, the men of Col. Paul L. Freeman, Jr.'s 23d Regiment Combat Team, had gone on stage innocently enough ten days before. The setting was unimpressive—a cluster of the usual mud, stick, and straw dwellings in a valley ringed by a maze of high, snow-covered hills. In the center of the village, two roads crossed. The huts and the farmers living in them were not important; the roads were.]

S/Sgt. RICHARD TURNER
C Company/23d Infantry
Along with the French [battalion], my company marched into Chipyong-ni on the railroad tracks [3 February].† They were airstriking and blasting the area to our front. There was some resistance, but not much.

[Colonel Freeman realized he did not have an adequate force to hold the hills above the valley and chose instead to establish his perimeter in a tight circle on the low hills immediately around the village. Companies A, C, and L dug in along the northern boundary; I and K

---

* This command consisted of the U.S. 2d and 7th Regiments and three ROK divisions (the 2d, 5th, and 8th).
† The 23d Regimental Combat Team that took over Chipyong-ni comprised the 23d Infantry Regiment (three rifle battalions); 37th Field Artillery Battalion; French Infantry Battalion; B Battery, 82d AAA [antiaircraft artillery] Battalion; B Battery, 503d Field Artillery Battalion; B Company, 2d Engineer Battalion; 2d Clearing Platoon, Clearing Company, 2d Medical Battalion; 1st Infantry Ranger Company—in all, about 5,600 men.

held the eastern lines; E and G, the southern; and the French, the west. Freeman placed his artillery in the center of the rectangular perimeter, which roughly measured 4,000 yards east and west by 2,000 north and south.]

Pfc. JOHN KAMPERSCHROER
L Company/23d Infantry

In Chipyong-ni our company CO [Capt. Chester Jackson] had us dig our foxholes deep. He must have known something was up, because for the first time in the war we placed logs on top of them, then sandbags, then dirt. We felt very comfortable in them, and warmer.

We came into Chipyong-ni after the battle of Twin Tunnels,* which had reduced our platoon strength by 25 percent. After receiving replacements we had one of the regiment's strongest companies, 98 or 100 men [instead of the normal 211].

[The weather in the valley was deplorable. Temperatures, near zero in the day, plummeted at night. Storms covered the 23d's perimeter in a foot or more of snow. Patrols were sent out daily, but in general the regiment spent a quiet time in their covered bunkers. Most of the men remember they were bored.]

Pfc. WEBSTER MANUEL
Headquarters Company/23d Infantry

I was in the commo [communications] section, and at Chipyong-ni assigned as a switchboard operator, which I hated like hell because I had reenlisted and volunteered for Korea to see some action. I particularly disliked it whenever the regimental XO [executive officer], Lieutenant Colonel Metzer, would ring the switchboard and greet the operator, "Hello, girls!"—this would chap my ass no end.

Captain Walker's [regimental communications officer] favorite saying to the men in his section was "Fuck up here and you'll be in

---

*The battle of Twin Tunnels took place 30 January–2 February 1951. The area was named for two railroad tunnels located three miles southeast of Chipyong-ni.

Charlie Company." Poor old Charlie Company had been wiped out two or three times in Korea, and we all knew being assigned to Charlie was like being sentenced to death.

We had a regular switchboard with about twenty drops [plug-ins], plus two more boards including an infantry company board [five drops]. Needless to say, everyone who was someone had a telephone, and they were everywhere, including the officers' shit house—a luxury in those days.

It's a known fact throughout the world that we "girls" on the switchboard stay on a little longer than is necessary after a line connection. Not eavesdropping, mind you—never.

The day the battle of Chipyong-ni began, I was assigned the 4:00 P.M. – 12:00 midnight shift on the switchboard.

[The 23d Infantry's heroic ordeal that would soon begin had been set in motion on 5 February, the date Ridgway ordered X Corps and the ROK III Corps to begin an offensive similar in execution and objectives to that made in the west by Thunderbolt. In advancing, the ROKs did not keep up with X Corps, and Almond discovered his right flank was open. The enemy increased the pressure north of Hoengsong and shunted reinforcements eastward. On the night of 11–12 February, a combined force of Chinese and North Koreans broke through three ROK Divisions and poured into the gap, creating a deep salient which threatened Eighth Army's rear. Ridgway ordered a withdrawal to Wonju. The 23d RCT stayed at Chipyong-ni and formed a peninsula in X Corps's broken lines. Soon it would become an island.]

S/Sgt. RICHARD TURNER
C Company/23d Infantry
One day some cargo planes flew over and dropped supplies inside the perimeter. To us new men this seemed strange. Why not use the road? we wondered. A veteran commented, "They don't generally do that unless you're surrounded."

[On the afternoon of the thirteenth, the 23d's Recon Company discovered one of the Chinese columns advancing toward Wonju had turned westward and was arriving in the hills above Chipyong-ni.]

Pfc. JOHN KAMPERSCHROER
L Company/23d Infantry

We ran a patrol out, which crossed some frozen rice paddies to the hills on the other side of the valley. The advance men began receiving fire from two directions. The fire then spread along the front and began falling on our platoon. I was in my usual position as a medic, following my platoon leader, Lieutenant Richard Palmer. Tracer bullets floated down the hill and zipped between Palmer and me. Palmer thought I'd bought the farm, and I feared the worst for him. One of the replacements behind me was hit in the bladder.

Pfc. WEBSTER MANUEL
Headquarters Company/23d Infantry

For me, the shit began hitting the fan about 4:30 P.M. Elements of the 2d Recon Company came under enemy fire while they were guarding the southern route. There was a lot of yelling on the phone, and I could hear firing. Incoming calls then began to pick up.

[Earlier in the afternoon, faced with encirclement, General Almond flew into Chipyong-ni by helicopter and discussed with Colonel Freeman the advisability of a withdrawal. Almond then returned to his command post and spoke with General Ridgway. The Eighth Army Commander, a veteran of D Day and the Battle of the Bulge, adamantly refused permission to abandon Chipyong-ni.]

Pfc. WEBSTER MANUEL
Headquarters Company/23d Infantry

Late in the afternoon the 2d Division CO [Maj. Gen Clark L. Ruffner] and Colonel Freeman were talking; I don't remember who called whom. Colonel Freeman wanted to vacate Chipyong-ni in the worst way, but the division CO kept saying the Old Man wanted us [the 23d] to stay put. I believe the "Old Man" General Ruffner was referring to was General Almond. Colonel Freeman said, "Well, if we get out of this alive I'm going over to headquarters to kick some ass."

My relief from 12:00 – 8:00 A.M. never showed up—no big deal, except Captain Walker chewed me out for not getting relieved.

By now I knew we were all in deep shit. The switchboard was lit up like a Christmas tree.

[Around 10:00 P.M. long columns of torches could be seen in the hills above the valley. Three Chinese divisions had arrived at the battle-field. The curtain was about to go up, and the deadly drama would soon begin.]

S/Sgt. RICHARD TURNER
C Company/23d Infantry

We got hit first about ten in the evening. Everything happened so fast. A machine gun way off to our front, up in the dogleg, began firing at our position. Right away my machine gun opened up. My squad and I were so green. I didn't have enough savvy to know all the Chinese were doing was pinpointing our automatic weapons. Someone shoots at us, shoot back—wrong! We then took a halfhearted banzai attack. They came at us and we opened fire. I crawled between foxholes checking on my people. I got up once and was crouched over to run somewhere, when my 57-mm recoilless rifle fired; the backblast blew my helmet off and knocked me over. I thought I'd been mortared. I collected myself and crawled to one of the holes. I called to a foxhole on my right to see if everyone there was okay. I didn't receive an answer. My God, I thought, they're all dead. I jumped out of my hole and ran to see what had happened. The 57-mm opened up and again blew me down the hill. I then stayed in my hole until daybreak.

[For three days the Chinese threw themselves at the Chipyong-ni road junction, and for three days the men of the 23d RCT threw them back. The fighting was savage and formless. The days belonged to the Far East Air Force and the American and French infantrymen; the nights to the Chinese. It was firepower against human-wave attacks. Who won would depend on who could endure the pounding longer.]

Pfc. BEN JUDD
F Company/23d Infantry

One of the new replacements, some other soldier, and I seemed to have a habit of simultaneously firing at the same enemy target. One morning we did this, fired directly into a Chinese soldier who was running in front of the rising sun. He simply jumped four feet in the air, kicked, and burst into flames.

That hillbilly music they played on that hill there at Chipyong-ni didn't get me homesick—I'd just gotten there—but it did rub me the wrong way. It got me sort of angry, don't know why. It was probably the surrender talk that went along with it.

S/Sgt. RICHARD TURNER
C Company/23d Infantry

The next night they hit us again, but this time they opened up with mortars. Big mortars. I was with two other men in a hole which had been enlarged; they were happy about this—it cut down their watch time at night. The mortars landed around us, and the enemy came at us in droves. A platoon sergeant nearby directed our mortar fire, and he was responsible for killing a lot of Chinese. We killed a lot of folks, too. I don't know how many because in those days we didn't go out and conduct body counts. We had strung barbed wire to our front. In the morning there were a lot of dead on the rocks, a lot in the fields, and a lot on the wire.

Pfc. JOHN KAMPERSCHROER
L Company/23d Infantry

The weather was on our side. Had we not had air support, we'd all have ended up in POW camps. The fighter pilots were super. The C-57s flew over and dropped food, ammo, and gas in brightly colored chutes. When one of the chutes wouldn't open, the boxes would hit the frozen rice paddies and bounce.

Our aid area was near the village. The 3d Battalion was on some high ground, and casualties were not as high as in the other two battalions, or in the French battalion. Since we could not get the wounded we had out, we kept them in tents. Enemy artillery and mortar fire kept the helicopters busy in more ways than one. The landing areas hummed with activity. I drove a litter jeep. This meant I noticed who at regimental collecting was flown out and who wasn't. Those with the best chances of surviving got out first. One man with a particularly bad head wound lay so I could see him for several days. Even if he had gotten out, it is doubtful whether he would have made it.

S/Sgt. RICHARD TURNER
C Company/23d Infantry

Once I watched the French make a bayonet charge.* They dug two series of holes, one row behind the other. When things got touchy, they'd get out of the forward holes and drop back to the second line of holes. Once the Chinese attacked and got into the front holes, the French knew where they were and would finish them off. Ingenious, those French.

Pfc. JOHN KAMPERSCHROER
L Company/23d Infantry

Once I was sent with my jeep to an area down the road, where I picked up a wounded man. Several men helped load him, and I took off for the aid tent. When I arrived I had a call to go back and pick up another guy from the same area. I went back. This time the guy was dead, and I recognized him as being one of the men who had helped load the wounded man earlier. The doctor was very upset that I had used the litter jeep as a hearse.

One of the most disturbing things I saw was a fellow brought in who had lost both legs to a mortar round which dropped into his foxhole. He and his buddy were lying head to toe to each other. Of course, the round had killed his buddy. I remember the poor soul asking over and over how his buddy was. No had the heart to tell him.

---

* The all-volunteer French battalion had arrived in Pusan in November. Its commander, Lt. Col. Ralph Monclar, a Foreign Legion veteran, had given up his general's stars to take the battalion to Korea. Later the battalion fought in Indochina and in Algeria, where it was known as the Battalion of Korea.

Pfc. BEN JUDD
F Company/23d Infantry

It was there in the valley of Chipyong-ni that I met Alabama, the wild one. He was simply the best machine gunner in all of the 23d Infantry. I say this not because he was a friend of mind, but because of his skill, dedication, and deadly accuracy—those were the qualities that made this man the best. Alabama wore a size-ten shoe, stood six feet tall, and weighed around 210 pounds. He had as much courage as his size could carry. This size also enabled him to manhandle his .30-caliber air-cooled machine gun. Even while carrying this weapon, he moved with the speed of an untamed horse. His gun chattered continuously into the mountains and into the Chinese soldiers who attacked us at Chipyong-ni, ceasing only long enough for him to reload or change barrels. When the heat from the barrel threatened to jam his gun, Alabama would call out, "Judd, I'm gonna reload," or "Judd, I'm gonna have to change barrels." It was at these times that the burden shifted to a few rifles. All too often I heard those terrible words, "Runnin' low, Judd. Can you handle it?" "Take care of what you must," I'd say, "and get it finished." Firm assurance from someone who had his own doubts. Had I enough ammunition? Would I shoot fast enough? Straight enough? Would my fingers move with speed and ease in the below-zero cold while I reloaded a clip? Had I uncovered in the few moments between enemy attacks the clips in my bandoliers which would save precious seconds? There could be no loss of movement, no slack in doing my job.

[While the 23d RCT fiercely defended its perimeter, the 5th Cavalry Regiment (then in IX Corps reserve) was ordered to set out the evening of the fourteenth for Chipyong-ni. Colonel Marcel Crombez, the 5th Cav's commander, immediately formed a task force of tanks and infantry to travel the fifteen miles. The column, driving on the road from Yonju, had advanced about half the distance when it was forced to halt around midnight in front of a blown bridge.

    The next morning the regiment's 1st and 2d Battalions attempted to gain control of a dominating ridgeline held by the Chinese. The enemy held, and Crombez realized he would not be able to slug his way into Chipyong-ni. He organized, instead, a quick strike force of *twenty-three tanks [M26s and M4A3 Shermans].* To protect them from fanatical infantry attacks, he ordered the 3d Battalion's Love Company to ride on top of the tanks. About 3:00 in the afternoon, the rifle company mounted up. Lieutenant Colonel Edgar Treacy, the 3d Battalion's CO, decided to accompany the riflemen on the tanks as an afterthought.]*

Sgt. CARROLL EVERIST
L Company/5th Cavalry
Before the company climbed aboard the tanks, most of us wrote letters home. This was also the first time I ate assault rations; they sure beat C rations.

On the tanks we had no means to communicate with the tankers who were buttoned up inside. I've read that each tank had one man on the outside machine gun—maybe, but not ours.

Just before the first halt, we fired from the tanks at the Chinese who were all along the road in the hills above us. My carbine would not fire automatic, so I was forced to use it single shot.

[Tanks Force Crombez traveled two miles and was south of Koksu-ri when the Chinese hit it first. The tanks and infantrymen stopped and engaged the enemy. Colonel Crombez realized success depended on the ability of the tanks to keep moving, and ordered them to continue the advance. Thirty or more riflemen who had dismounted to take cover were left behind. The tanks managed to get about 1,000 yards north of Koksu-ri before the Chinese stopped them again.]

Sgt. CARROLL EVERIST
L Company/5th Cavalry
We were then hit hard again from both sides of the road, and I felt a heavy bang in my knee. The tanks were forced to stop, and because we had no cover, the men riding them jumped off. I managed to

---

*The tanks were drawn from D Company, 6th Tank Battalion, and A Company, 70th Tank Battalion.

climb off but could not get off the road. Colonel Treacy, who was in a gulley, shouted for me to join him and the men with him. When I limped over, I saw he'd been hit in the mouth. He appeared to be more worried about the rest of us than he was for himself. The colonel gave me his aid pouch to use, as he could not use anything in it where he'd been hit. There was blood all over his face.

[Colonel Crombez again ordered the tanks north, and again the riflemen of L Company, deployed by the side of the road, were caught by surprise and left behind.*]

Sgt. CARROLL EVERIST
L Company/5th Cavalry
The tanks then began to move again, and we were left behind. The Chinese were then all over us. I was instructed to drop my weapon in the snow, and as there was absolutely no chance to fight our way out, I obeyed the order. There were seven of us in the group around Colonel Treacy. A sergeant kept begging for the Chinese to release him—later I heard they murdered him farther down the road. The Chinese began to try to get us to move off with them. Due to my wound I was unable to walk, so Colonel Treacy lifted me on his back and carried me. He never complained and carried me what I believe to be several miles before we stopped in a clearing that had a building without sides. The Chinese decided to move faster, and they prevented Colonel Treacy from carrying me again as this would slow them down. I last saw him and his small group on the night of February 15. Before the Chinese left, they took my watch and everything personal I had; they did, however, return a little prayer book sent to me from my home church in Mason City, Iowa. The Chinese marched the little group away and I was left alone. After a little while, a Chinese soldier came back to me and tried to get me to walk. It was no good— I couldn't. I knew I would now be shot. The soldier aimed his rifle at me, and the feeling that I had is impossible to describe. I froze

---

*Of the 160 riflemen and 4 engineers who had originally been on the tanks, only 70 remained when the task force advanced after the second halt.

and could not move. I was not very brave. I went into shock, and I believe the enemy soldier thought I'd gone crazy, because he left without shooting me.

[Several hours before Sergeant Everist was left behind by his captors, Task Force Crombez, after fighting a continuing running battle with the enemy, entered the 23d RCT's perimeter and lifted the siege of Chipyong-ni.* The Chinese began to abandon the hills above the valley and were caught in the open by U.S. artillery. Task Force Crombez spent the night in the perimeter. A few flares sputtered over the village and circling hills; but for the first time in three nights, the Communists did not attack, and the valley lay quiet.]

Pfc. BEN JUDD
F Company/23d Infantry

The night was dark, and our communications lines got cut. Somebody had to go look see. The lines had to be repaired. Well, this I could do easy enough. Them pitch-black hillsides weren't no stranger to me and didn't bother me a bit. They worried the rest of the platoon, but then they didn't have an idea what was out there. All I could think about was, If those lines weren't repaired I'd have to carry a big, heavy radio that'd slow me down to a drag. I volunteered to go. I barreled out around one o'clock in the morning, heading across a little valley and then up a long, sloping hillside fairly well covered with timber. I followed the wire to the top. I eased around those woods, quiet as an old country boy carrying a pint of still liquor. I crept out to the edge of the timber, and in the moonlight found a large field. I could hardly believe my eyes. There in the field, lying every which way, were hundreds—no, thousands—of Chinese. Thousands of thousands. Dead. Maybe sleeping. I returned quick with the news. "Hey, Sarge, there's thousands and thousands of dead men lying out there in the field. They might not be dead, they might be asleep." "Well," he said, "the captain will want to hear of this."

---

* Of the seventy men who had remained on the tank decks after the second halt, only twenty-three reached 23d RCT's perimeter—thirteen of whom were wounded.

Later we found it was dead men I'd stumbled onto on that hilltop around them mountains of Chipyong-ni.

[Toward dawn on 16 February, the battlefield became shrouded in a swirling snowstorm. That afternoon, escorted by tanks, nineteen ambulances and twenty-eight trucks carrying food and supplies drove northward from the Yoju and, without seeing anything of the enemy, pulled into Chipyong-ni.

The battle had been costly to both sides, but to the Chinese it had been a catastrophe. Nearly 5,000 of their dead lay on the hills or in the valley and were covered by several inches of freshly fallen snow. For the first time in Korea, the Chinese had lost a battle. At Chipyong-ni, Eighth Army had gotten it right. On the morning of the seventeenth, the 5th Cavalry moved north to relieve the 23d RCT in position.]

Cpl. VICTOR FOX
I Company/5th Cavalry

In fighting its way through to the 35th's perimeter, Task Force Crombez left behind on that road a human carnage right out of hell. All along the flanks of the steep, winding road, I saw the bodies of hundreds of Chinese piled in grisly heaps. Everywhere I looked were these mounds of frozen Chinese bodies lying every which way in their mustard-colored quilted uniforms. Artillery and tank fire must have blasted the Chinese at point-blank range. I never saw such carnage, not even on Hill 174.* Even today it is almost unbelievable when I think of the horror that lay along that winding, fifteen-mile corridor to Chipyong-ni.

Capt. NORMAN ALLEN
I Company/5th Cavalry

From our new positions at Chipyong-ni, we looked down on the results of the Chinese attacks against the 23d Infantry, and they were,

---

* Item Company had taken and held Hill 174 for six days in September 1950.

to say the least, awesome. There were many, many enemy dead—
far too many to count. The 23d had done its job very well indeed.

Sgt. ED HENDRICKS
F Company/5th Cavalry

Worse thing I ever saw in my life—twenty, thirty trucks lined up
carrying American dead out of Chipyong-ni. Columns of deuce-and-
a-halfs, one behind the other. The corpses couldn't be flattened out,
because they'd frozen the way the men were when they'd been killed.
Blankets couldn't cover the arms and legs sticking in every direction.
Bodies on top of bodies, fitted together like jigsaw puzzles. The whole
valley around Chipyong-ni was full of dead people. In every war it's
the same—bad. But to see this number of people wiped out in a
place like Korea . . . Iwo Jima, Okinawa—that was global war, when
we were fighting for our own survival. Korea? Hell, we were there
fighting for somebody *else*'s survival.

Pfc. BEN JUDD
F Company/25th Infantry

When the mountains of enemy were torn down and were no more,
Alabama reported one of his machine gun barrels was burned up. He
was told he would be charged for it and pay taken from his check. I
think this took some of the sharp edge off Alabama's skills. I do not
know if he actually had to pay or not, as I was to see very little of
him after Chipyong-ni.

Pfc. WEBSTER MANUEL
Headquarters Company/23d Infantry

What happened at Chipyong-ni is history. Colonel Freeman became
a hero, and the 23d Regiment got a visit from General MacArthur
and a presidential unit citation. As for ole W.M.—me—I got transferred to a rifle platoon, not to Charlie Company, but to King. Shortly
afterward my platoon leader got killed, and I was made acting platoon
leader and my grade elevated to corporal.

[After he was left behind by Task Force Crombez and the Chinese, Carroll Everist remembers very little of the three days he wandered in the bleak hills around Chipyong-ni.]

Sgt. CARROLL EVERIST
L Company/5th Cavalry

I do remember seeing Chinese riding horses. I ate snow and icicles. I made a tourniquet from my belt and a stick, and I was able to stop the blood flowing from my leg. At night I would loosen it a little.

On February 18 I looked over the valley and saw an American patrol [from I Company, 5th Cavalry Regiment]. I yelled and yelled until I was hoarse. A sergeant came over to me. When he cut off my boot, it was packed with frozen blood. The men gave me their C rations. The franks and beans tasted like Thanksgiving dinner. I was carried to the road, where I learned that several Americans had been found dead along the way, but none of the bodies belonged to Colonel Treacy.

I lay on a stretcher and waited for an ambulance. Colonel Crombez came by, and I told him I believed Colonel Treacy was the best officer the Cav had. He didn't seem to be interested in what I had to say.

Capt. NORMAN ALLEN
I Company/5th Cavalry

18 February
Near Chipyong-ni

Mother darling:

The night of the 15th and 16th were black days for Swing Blue [3d Battalion/5th Cavalry]. Our mission was to take a tank/infantry task force and bust through several heavy Chinese roadblocks to relieve the pressure on the surrounded 23d Infantry. "L" Company rode the tanks in. The task force broke through heavy resistance and got into the besieged regiment. "L" Company had 160 men—twenty-six missing, the rest dead and wounded. Among the missing is our beloved battalion commander, Colonel Treacy. We are all *sick*, heart broken and lost. We have pieced information together and it is almost conclusive that he is a prisoner. We shall carry on and fight but our hearts aren't in it, not for a few days anyway. Bob Greer [I Company's executive officer] was transferred to another battalion so I have lost both my right arm and my heart.

I am okay and the company is on a cold, snowy, windy hill.

19 February

This afternoon the regiment moved northward about three miles. My battalion [3d] is in reserve and my company is providing security to the regimental installations and artillery batteries. The other two battalions are holding at Chipyong-ni. Because of the shellacking we took on the task force the regiment will give us a few days to get organized.

It is very hard getting used to the fact that Colonel Treacy isn't with us. God, it's almost impossible to believe. Captain [Ralph] Curfman, Lieutenant [Joseph] Llynes and I went through the colonel's effects and all three of us were in tears. He was so wonderful and one of the ablest and finest officers I ever knew. We found out that when the task force went in, Colonel Treacy refused to get into the tank he was riding on and when the column was attacked the tank swung its turret to go into action and knocked the colonel off. He had been hit in the mouth by a bullet splash but not seriously. He had then climbed on Sergeant Smith's tank and continued on. Lieutenant Chastain and two other men climbed on with him. They went on a little ways until the tank took a direct mortar hit. The commander in the following tank saw the colonel fly through the air, hit the ground, then move a little. A little later we received reports from three wounded men, one of whom [Sergeant Everist] the colonel had carried for a short time before a Chinese guard told the colonel to put him down because they were being forced to move fast. This wounded man was later picked up so it's almost conclusive that Colonel Treacy is a prisoner. He is mentally and physically capable and resourceful and if anyone can make it out, he will. *

[Besides Chipyong-ni, Wonju had also held. UN artillery and hundreds of close-support sorties flown by FEAF had broken the back of the enemy counteroffensive, and by the eighteenth, North Korean and Chinese units were streaming northward. The assurance ebbing out of the Communists seemed to flow into Eighth Army. On the nineteenth, X Corps, with the ROKs on their right, were approximately where they'd been before the withdrawal. X Corps ordered combat patrols sent forward to find where the enemy had gone.]

2d Lt. ADRIAN BRIAN
Intelligence and Reconnaissance Platoon/5th Cavalry†

Around noon, the jeep I was riding in ran over a mine. Actually, it ran over two mines simultaneously—one went off in the left rear; the other, the right front. I flew way up in the air and soared over the hood and down. I grabbed my helmet with both hands and tried to remember to tumble just like in gym class. CRACK! Instead, I landed flat on my back. The next thirty seconds went by in slow motion. I felt pain in my back, and I was unable to catch my breath. I attempted to lift myself by my suspenders the way I remembered the trainers at West Point tried to help football players get their breath back after a crunching tackle. The tanks in front of me began firing their machine guns at the ridgeline on both sides of the hollow we were in. I tried to do about four things at once; catch my breath, see

---

* In 1953, after all POWs had been repatriated, then-Major Allen met at Fort Benning, Georgia, an Air Force colonel who had been a prisoner in P'yongyang with Edgar Treacy. The colonel stated that Treacy had died on 15 May 1951, and had been buried on a high hill north of the capital in an area Major Allen recognized as being close to the school building in which Item Company had been billeted in October 1950. Lieutenant Colonel Treacy's death is officially listed as having occurred on the last day of May 1951.

† Lieutenant Brian had recently left E Company and had been given command of the regiment's I & R platoon. He would be that platoon's seventh leader in five months. Brian lasted five weeks, and at the time had had the longest tenure of the seven. Interestingly, one of the earlier leaders of the platoon had been Joseph Toomey, a classmate of Brian's at West Point (class of 1949) who, with Brian, had also served in the 5th Cavalry's Item Company. Toomey had been wounded and captured by the Chinese in November 1950 and died subsequently.

what the tanks were firing at, reach some kind of cover, and stop moaning. I believe the jeep I'd been in had been hit by a flat-trajectory gun of some sort, and I expected it to open fire again. About then my foot started to hurt. I finally caught my breath and stopped moaning. One of the other jeeps drove up. I had the men look after our Korean interpreter, who had a back injury. My driver and radio operator were dazed but not hurt, and they continued on with the patrol. I was back at the battalion aid station in five minutes and, though I didn't know it then, on my way home.*

[General Ridgway was determined to capitalize on his command's new aggressive spirit and to give the enemy neither rest nor opportunity to reorganize.]

Capt. NORMAN ALLEN
I Company/5th Cavalry

20 February
Near Chipyong-ni

Mother dear,
Today we moved forward four miles and have entered the 23d Infantry Regiment's perimeter for the night. Tomorrow we will move off into the attack; should be pretty hairy. But as long as our mission is to kill Chinamen, we might as well get started. Always have a little shaky feeling in the pit of my stomach when the order is issued. Never will get over that, I guess.

Today was a beautiful day. I hope the AF [Air Force] gave the Chinese much hell. Winter is still here; quite brisk, the hills are very high and I am out of shape from my hospital days.

---

*Brian spent eighteen months in Letterman General Hospital in San Francisco waiting for his damaged foot to heal. Ironically, command of the regiment's I & R was next given to another officer from I Company; this time, 1st Lt. Robert Geer.

21 February
0630

Shoving off in the attack with the hour. Going to be a little rough, but lots of artillery support. I am the lead element of the offensive designed to pinch off 35,000 Chinks. Feel good about it—more we kill the sooner it will be over. Wish me luck, darling.

[On 21 February, Ridgway launched an offensive in the sectors held by IX Corps (west central) and X Corps (central mountain), which had as its objective the destruction of all enemy units east of the Han's upper reaches. Operation Killer, as it was sanguinely called, completed the cycle from concept to plan to execution in just three days. The 1st Marine Division, relieved of its guerrilla-hunting duties around Pohang, was attached to Maj. Gen. Bryant E. Moore's IX Corps.* The operation called for the Marines to advance through the Wonju basin in a northeasterly direction and seize control of the high ground below Hoengsong.†]

Pfc. PAUL MARTIN
Reconnaissance Company/1st Marine Division
Our officers gave us a briefing on the overall situation and then a gung-ho pep talk. The whole world, we were told, was watching the Marines because we were going back on center stage. Here was our chance to show how we had recovered from the Chosin Reservoir, and that we were better than ever. We veterans of Inch'on and Chosin would set an example of courage for the replacements. These words helped smooth out whatever fears we had about going back onto the line.

The first day [of Operation Killer, 21 February] we were carried

---

* Moore had assumed command on 31 January. At the time of Operation Killer the UN's order of battle, west to east, was Milburn's I Corps (U.S. 3d and 25th Divisions, British 29th Brigade, Turkish Brigade, and ROK 1st Division); Moore's IX Corps (U.S. 1st Cavalry, 1st Marine and 24th Divisions, ROK 6th Division, 27th Commonwealth Brigade, a Philippine battalion, and a Greek battalion); Almond's X Corps (U.S. 2d and 7th Divisions, ROK 2d, 5th, and 8th Divisions); ROK III Corps (7th and 9th Divisions); and ROK I Corps (Capital Division).
† In X Corps's zone, Killer was to have the U.S. 7th Division move northward from Yongwol to P'yonch'ang.

across a wide river [the Som] by tanks, and the rifle companies behind began to push forward.

We found ourselves on foot and in no-man's-land. The ground was beginning to thaw, and muddy hillsides made walking difficult. The huts we trudged past were deserted, and there was no sign of the enemy. While climbing on a mud-slicked hill, the officer who had given the gung-ho speech slipped in the goo and slid backwards on his butt. I asked him, "Is the whole world still watching us?" The laughter made us all feel a little better.

When we got near the top of a tall hill, one of the replacements said he couldn't wait to see beyond the ridge line. He hadn't learned that there was nothing in Korea to see but another ridgeline. We followed the ridge for a while, and in one place we could look behind us. Back in the distance I saw artillery and tanks blasting a hill that was being assaulted by a line outfit. Everyone felt good about pushing forward again, but I worried we might be too far forward and in danger of being cut off.

At dusk we came in sight of a river [Som] that branched in two directions. We dug in and established an outpost near one of the branches. Our orders were to avoid contact with the enemy, if possible.

About two hours after sunset, I saw movement toward the river; the Chinese were pulling sections of a bridge into the river, and once it was assembled, a column of troops began crossing. Then, later, animals carrying equipment walked across the bridge. Before dawn, Recon Company quietly withdrew from the area and took up new positions farther down the river, where they waited—not for the enemy troops but their animals. We figured one cargo-carrying mule was worth ten enemy soldiers. After a short wait, the enemy troop column passed our ambush. A few minutes later about fifty donkeys and mules came into sight. It was like being on the rifle range, and each Marine selected a target. Once the first donkey crossed the clearing, everyone opened fire. The animals just dropped where they were. We got laughing, it was so easy. Someone fired a tracer and a mule disintegrated in a ball of flame. A guy near me shouted, "Light up a Camel!"

Once we finished the job, we withdrew; enemy troops would be on our tail quickly. Each platoon took turns covering the leapfrogging maneuver, and we returned that day to our command post area. We were all on a high.

Pfc. JACK WRIGHT
G/5

The company got together and they told us what was going to happen. Next, the platoon assembled in its area, and our platoon leader told us what each of our assignments would be. Then the squad leader got us together and went over all of it again. It was supposed to be quite a sight. We were going up this valley and jumping off in the assault with two regiments abreast [the 1st and 5th Marines] and another coming up in reserve [the 7th]. Our company and platoon would be out front.

In the morning we jumped off and moved along the valley and nothing really happened. The next morning [23 February], before we got started, the word came forward, "Wright to the rear with your gear." Well, I was dumbfounded; I didn't know what the heck was coming off. When I reported to the platoon CP, I was told I was to stay in the rear and guard the packs we were leaving behind; then, when the vehicles came up, I was to load the gear and to stay with them. What I didn't know was they had started rotating men home; in fact, one group had already rotated out. No one told me I was going to be in the next group—I was the only man in my platoon left from the original brigade. The superstition was, when you got toward the end of your tour, you always got hit. Well, soon as the word came out that I was to be rotated home, my company commander [1st Lt. Charles D. Mize], who was also a brigade man and my platoon leader, pulled me back. Eventually, I learned what the deal was, and I thought it was pretty good.

I joined the platoon later with the gear. The next day we made contact with the Chinese [24 February]. "Saddle up, we're going in." My lieutenant—we'd lost so many platoon leaders I couldn't keep track of their names—walked over to me. "Wright, you're staying here with the gear." Okay. I scrounged me up a pair of binoculars, and I watched the guys assault a hill. All of a sudden, a Marine from another platoon shouts he's seen a column of Chinese moving toward our left front. There were seven of us left behind, so we hurried over and got in front of the Chinks and waited. I lay thinking, Hey, this is gonna be great; one last firefight before I go home. Then a Corsair flew over and made a pass. It dropped a bomb, and the Chinese took off running.

Later, the platoon came back off the hill. We settled in for another night. Then I got the word: "Wright, pack your gear, you're goin' home." I spent the night on the hill, but I couldn't sleep. In the morning I was told to report to the company CP. I was pretty excited. I sat down with one of my buddies, Jack Davenport. He said, "You lucky sonovabitch. Get the hell out of here, Archie. Don't even wanna talk to ya!" I laughed. Before I went to meet the truck, I left behind everything I could think of, including a package of goodies I'd just received from home. I left that to the squad. Then I walked down the road and away from the front.

[The day Private Wright left George Company, General Ridgway called a halt to the advance until ammunition and supplies could be brought forward. Orders were issued on the 25 February to begin the second phase of Operation Killer on 1 March. The evening before, the first phase had officially ended with all preliminary objectives seized. From the ridgeline south of Hoengsong, the Marines could look across a swampy river plain to their next objectives, the six hills north of the ruined town.

The day Operation Killer commenced, and the Marines were meeting no resistance above Wonju, the 1st Cavalry Division,* near Chipyong-ni, had also jumped off [21 February], but unlike the Marines, the Cav advance was held up not by enemy resistance, but by the combined difficulties of thawing snow, sleet, slush, and flooding rivers.]

Cpl. VICTOR FOX
I Company/5th Cavalry
The company was now in the lowlands and surrounded by numerous tributary streams which flowed into the Han. Heavy rain and the

---

* The 1st Cavalry Division was commanded now by Maj. Gen. Charles D. Palmer.

melting of the heavy snow cover caused a quick rise in the water level, and riverbanks everywhere overflowed.

At one curve in a broad stream, now a swirling rage of rushing white water, combat engineers from the 8th Cav somehow rigged guideline ropes for us to use when we crossed. By using them we managed to pull ourselves through the torrent and reach the other side and some nearby high ground. The company and other units close by became stranded on the tops of hills which the flooding had made into islands.

Pfc. JERRY EMER
I Company/5th Cavalry
It was terribly miserable. We began to get a lot of cold rain and sleet, and the hills became slippery and soggy. We started taking weather casualties, guys with terrible coughs, maybe some with pneumonia and pleurisy. Several nights we spent without sleeping bags and lay in our shallow holes, shivering and shaking.

Sgt. JAMES HUBER
I Company/5th Cavalry *
Before the company moved onto a new hill, the men were ordered to leave their mountain sleeping bags at the foot of this objective. It was two days of cold drizzle and mist before the men saw their bags again.

When these fellers came off the hill they were so damned cold and stiff they walked like a bunch of stiff-jointed zombies or mechanical robots. Of all my experiences in Korea, I think this one was the most touching. I never heard one word of complaint from anyone in the company that morning. I knew how they had to be hurting so damned bad from the cold and wet. It's not easy to make me cry, but I think if I ever wanted to cry it was then. Hell, I just wanted to put my arms around each one of those guys.

---

* Huber was I Company's supply sergeant.

Capt. NORMAN ALLEN
I Company/5th Cavalry

24 February
Above Chipyong-ni

Mom darling,

It's been pretty rough here the last few days. Shoved off out of Chipyong-ni on the morning of the 21st, fighting toward my objective which was Hill 227. Got a toe hold on the ridge with two platoons but had to give it up at nightfall 'cause my flanks were open. Second Battalion [on the left] and 1st Battalion [on the right] were unable to get up on line. In our battalion zone I company was on the right and K on the left. "K" really caught hell. Their CO was killed the first day and they had twenty wounded. The second day the new CO was hit and K had fifteen killed, forty-four wounded. They didn't play it easy and sock their objective with artillery the way I do. On an equivalent piece of ground, similarly defended, I lost one killed, six wounded. But the man I lost was a favorite of mine and a hell of a nice kid. In the seven and a half months he had been with me I had promoted him from Pfc. to Sgt. F/C. Nice looking boy, about twenty-three; I am just sick about it.

The weather is terrible; cold wind and driving rain. I was soaked to the skin for two days and nights and just froze. Despite the weather the lads fought hard. Took our hill again yesterday and last night held on to it. Today pushed on to another. I pounded the Chinese hard with artillery and then rooted them out with bayonets and grenades. We killed sixty-four yesterday—but the bastards are really dying hard.

I've finally dried out, partially at least. Dried this paper before a small fire in my foxhole tonight. Writing this by candle. To show you how heavy yesterday's fight was, my company fired 16,000 rounds of machine gun and 21,000 M1 rifle rounds, and this is not counting artillery, mortar and recoilless rifle rounds. I'm okay but getting weary of climbing to the top of these damn hills. I'm afraid it will be a long war.

Pfc. JAMES CARDINAL
Headquarters Company/3d Battalion/5th Cavalry

24 February

Dear Folks,

It's a cold, gray day and the wind chills me to the bone. Off in the distance air and artillery are pounding the Chinese. Navy Corsairs are strafing and rocketing them, too. Believe me, I don't know how those SOBs can take it. It looks like we'll run out of shells before the Chinese run out of troops for us to kill. And the cold hurts them much more than us. A few days ago I found three of them frozen dead on a hill. Two miles away in a field and on the side of a hill [near Chipyong-ni] there are 600 dead ones, all killed by planes and artillery. And still they fight.

Pfc. JERRY EMER
I Company/5th Cavalry

The days we spent as part of Operation Killer were like a bad dream. We advanced slowly, ridge by ridge. Patrol, assault, patrol again, assault again—and again, and again. The weather was miserable, and we were often soaked to the skin by cold drizzle or sleet. During this period Hagob Hananian was hit. He was my best buddy—after Jim Cardinal, who'd transferred to the battalion headquarters company. Hananian was from Haverhill, Massachusetts, and as his name indicates, an Armenian. Stocky, powerfully built, everyone in the company called him "Beast."

Maybe a week after Chipyong-ni, the company on the assault was pinned down in a shallow depression, and I was lying next to Hananian when a machine-gun slug slammed into his gut. "Doc!" I bellowed. Our corpsman, Bernard McKenna, hustled over in a low crouch. Hagob was gritting his teeth in pain. Doc gave him a morphine shot, then calmly and deftly cleaned and dressed the wound. I saw the bullet had entered a bit to the right of Hagob's cartridge belt, gone through an ammo clip, and exited a little above his right kidney. Then Hananian decided he could walk down to the litter jeeps on his own—and, by God, he did! We hadn't nicknamed him Beast for nothing.

This day would get worse. Shortly after Hananian started his trek down the hill to the road, Corporal Moan got hit real bad. I believe he had come into the company as one of our December replacements. He'd been a veteran of the CBI [China-Burma-India] Theater in the Second World War and afterwards gone into the inactive reserve. A big man with reddish-blond hair and a ruddy complexion, he looked to me like a Viking chieftain. The kids in the outfit called him "Pops."

On this day, on this cold, Godforsaken hill, in the shallow hollow, I'd been having trouble with my SCR-300.* Finally, to my surprise, I got in contact with Item 6, which was Captain Allen. More surprising, a tank, one of four down the valley on our left, joined in our conversation. When he heard the problem we were having, he moved his tank along the valley floor and clanked up behind us. My radio transmission with him now was "Loud and clear, five by five." Sergeant Hardie, on my right, was jubilant. Acting as an FO [forward observer] he called in fire on the Chinese bunker that was slowing us down. The tank's first round of HE [high explosive] burst a little to the right. Hardie hollered, "Left, tell him a bit more left." "Just a bit more left." Then I heard the tanker's voice, soft but excited, "Got visual sighting." "They've spotted it," I yelled to Hardie. A few seconds went by. I tried to get lower in the hollow. WHOOOSH BLAM! Bingo, right into the mouth of the bunker—a hole in one. Hardie and the others shouted with joy. I yelled into the radio and told the tanker how happy he'd just made the 2d Platoon of Item Company. Faintly, I heard the babble of voices in the tank—everyone was happy.

A few days after the Beast and Pops were hit, it became my turn. The 2d Platoon was taking a break, about ten of us lying or sitting in a ragged line. I was lying on my stomach. A Russian-made machine gun opened up. A slug from the first burst got me in the back of the left leg, a few inches below the knee. It felt like I'd been belted with a ballpeen hammer. I jumped up. "Medic! Medic!" Everyone else scrambled for cover. Limping badly, I staggered toward a squad that

---

*The SCR-300 radio was a short-range, frontline, company-to-battalion packset. It was frequency modulated, had forty channels, and weighed almost forty pounds.

had the medic. While I made my way toward them I heard our BAR and M1s returning the fire. Undaunted, this Joe Chink gunner stayed right on my butt. I got into some high brush and felt another sharp blow, this one in the back of my thigh. I slipped and slid down into the hollow where the other squad was hunkered down. I was blowing like a horse—really winded. A medic subbing for Doc cut away my pant leg. Sergeant Lee was there, the guy who'd helped me pull Cardinal out of the quicksand during the Imjin River crossing four months before. The pain was excruciating. Sergeant Lee plunged a Syrette of morphine into my thigh. He said, "Christ, he caught one up here too." The pain by this time was unbearable. I sobbed and prayed, "Jesus, Mary, Joseph!" then I recited the Hail Mary. I begged Lee to give me one more Syrette and he did.

Someone other than me had the SCR-300 this day, and I heard him report back, "WIA on Item Two patrol—WIA." I was warm and floating on a sea of morphine. Battalion reported on the radio, "We roger you, Item Two. Litter jeep on way." It happened that my friend Jim Cardinal was at battalion just then and asked the operator there to find out who in his old platoon had been hit. When he heard it was me, he rode up with the jeep and met me while I was being carried down the hill.

Perhaps a half hour later, Captain Allen came into the aid tent where I was being worked on. He was full of his usual piss and vinegar. He asked how I was doing, the usual stuff. Then as he left, he turned and thundered, "Take good care of this man, he's one of the Old Guard!" I thought, "Gosh, what an exit line." *

Capt. NORMAN ALLEN
I Company/5th Cavalry
On February 28 there was a general attack that should have brought adjacent companies and the British [27th Commonwealth Brigade] abreast of us. The new battalion commander [Maj. Charles J. Parziale] told me I Company would not have to advance because we were

---

* A few days later Emer was flown to a hospital in Japan, where his leg was operated on. He returned to duty and I Company in late May.

already sitting ahead of the line. I still anticipated something, so I got a patrol out to Hill 235, 2,000 yards ahead of my position. Sure enough, at 3:00 P.M. the order came down to move forward to Hill 235. My patrol had been sitting there all day engaged in a small firefight. I pushed out quickly. [Lieutenant] Curfman—who again had K Company—and I decided to consolidate on this hill. Our right flank was having quite a fight, and it looked as if we wouldn't capture the objective before dark. Curf and I put our platoons into position. I situated my MGs [machine guns], and had my men dig in. One half of both companies went down the hill to a shelter spot where hot chow was awaiting them.

Cpl. VICTOR FOX
I Company/5th Cavalry
Against resistance, we climbed to positions on a ridgeline snarled with dense undergrowth, its slopes covered with trees. Third Platoon finished digging two-man holes and setting up fields of fire in front of, and below, the company CP.

I then committed a grievous mental error and walked along the skyline. Below me Captain Allen shouted, "Get that man off the skyline!" At that moment, from the thickly wooded area below our front, I clearly heard the coughing sounds enemy mortars made. I also heard the banging report of an SP [self-propelled] gun. Everyone in the 3d Squad dove over one another for holes and cover. The shells dropped right into our positions. There had been no registration; they just began dropping on top us.

Capt. NORMAN ALLEN
I Company/5th Cavalry
CRASH! CRASH! CRASH! The first rounds burst into the trees and scattered fragments all over the place. I ran toward my foxhole. I looked over my shoulder and saw a ball of fire beside me. I soared through the air and I knew when I landed I'd be in one piece. I flew through my own tent and landed in a hole. Curf, returning from chow, was forty yards away when he saw me flying. He sent my 1st sergeant up to get me, since he wanted to remember me the way I'd

been. [Lieutenant Curfman would also be wounded in this mortar barrage.] When I came to, I looked for my top sergeant or my executive officer to turn the company over to.

Cpl. VICTOR FOX
I Company/5th Cavalry

When it was over, everyone looked around and saw some South Koreans and a GI medic carrying a badly wounded Captain Allen past us. One of the Koreans, the one called Harry, had the captain's helmet and, I believe, a pack. Everyone was really upset.

Capt. NORMAN ALLEN
I Company/5th Cavalry

Next thing I knew I was being carried down the hill. Found one of my trusted sergeants [M/Sgt. Edward Reuter] and turned command of the company over to him until an officer [Lt. Joseph Hynes] could be sent up.

There followed some periods of unconsciousness, then a litter jeep, an ambulance, the battalion aid station, and division clearing. All this was followed by a bone-breaking twenty-eight-mile ambulance ride over a muddy road. One lad riding in the ambulance— there were five of us—had a bad belly wound and screamed at every bump, and there were three million, six hundred thousand, nine hundred and forty-two bumps. Shortly after we arrived at the MASH, the boy died.

I was flown to Pusan, transferred to a hospital train, then placed in an ambulance for a short drive and lifted on an electrical elevator. When I was unloaded I found I had finally arrived at my destination—the Navy hospital ship USS *Consolation*.

The day Allen arrived on the Consolation *was his twenty-eighth birthday. In surgery, forty-two mortar fragments were removed from his legs, back, and groin. He never again saw the men in Item Company, 5th Cavalry Regiment, the unit he had led for two years.*

The last day of February, the Communist front south of the Han collapsed and General MacArthur confidentially reported to Washing-

ton that he was ". . . entirely satisfied with the situation at the front, where the enemy has suffered a tactical reverse of measurable proportions." * On 1 March the UN's forces were thirty miles south of the line they had defended New Year's Eve and were stretched solidly across Korea from Kimpo Airfield in the west, to above Kangnung in the east—no gaps, salients, or soft spots anywhere. The sun was growing warmer, and birds, oblivious to the surrounding desolation, began to sing. Unmistakably, spring was in the air.

*Commander in chief, Far East Command to Department of the Army, 1 March 1951.

HAN RIVER

2 March-15 March 1951

Cpl. JAMES CARDINAL
Headquarters Company/3d Battalion/5th Cavalry

March 2, 1951

Dear William:

The stories you've been reading about terrific Chinese casualties are true. In this area alone [IX Corps], artillery and planes killed several thousand in the space of a few weeks. I've seen the bodies myself so I know it's true. Killing them in droves, however, doesn't seem to be enough. They still come on and on and on, like waves pounding on a beach. If this keeps up, either the last units in the Chinese armies are going to be destroyed in Korea, or else, much less likely, they will break through and drive us to the sea. Of course, there's a third possibility (the obvious and sensible one)—the Chinese top brass, growing tired of watching their troops slaughtered, will accept some sort of cease-fire.

[With the Communists obviously stumbling, Ridgway was determined to continue his unrelenting march back to the 38th Parallel with a new offensive—Operation Ripper. All Corps would advance through successive phase lines and seize a line designated phaseline Idaho, just below the border between the two Koreas. In the west central and central zones, IX and X Corps were to attack northward, creating an enormous salient that would force the enemy out of Seoul by envel-

oping it from the east. Ripper would commence when the U.S. 25th Division crossed the Han River near its confluence with the Puk-han,* † approximately twenty miles east of the capital.]

Although the 35th RCT was engaged with the enemy through-out practically the entire month of March, the most significant single operation during the period was the assault crossing of the Han River. . . .

The initial instructions were received by the Combat Team Commanders on 3 March. During the morning the command-ing officer [Col. Gerald C. Kelleher], S-4 [logistics section chief] and assistant S-3 [operations and training section] were called to the [25th] division command post for a briefing. At this briefing the broad outline of an impending operation was sketched. The division was to make an assault crossing of the Han River in its assigned zone and attack to the north.

COMMAND REPORT, 35TH INFANTRY REGIMENT

Capt. LUTHER WEAVER
L Company/35th Infantry ‡
The 35th RCT moved into a forward assembly area on the south bank of the Han River [4 March] approximately six miles southeast of Seoul.

S/Sgt. W. B. WOODRUFF, JR.
L Company/35th Infantry
There came a day [4 March] when Love Company was ordered back into the line [one week earlier, it had gone into division reserve]. We rode in a truck column most of the day, in a downpour of rain. I

---

*The 25th Division comprised the 14th, 27th, and 35th Infantry Regiments.
†From the mountains of eastern Korea, the Pukhan flows south to the Hwach'on reservoir, then southwest before entering the Han.
‡L Company, along with I, K, and M Companies, made up the regiment's 3d Battalion. Companies A, B, C, D made up the 1st Battalion; E, F, G, H, the 2d Battalion. Companies D, H, and M were heavy weapons companies; the others, rifle companies.

recall that in crossing one long valley with flooded rice paddies stretching out to either side, the "road" was just a sea of mud and water. The heavy trucks were grinding along, slipping and sliding, their dual tires continuously squeezing the mud off the roadway and down into the borrow ditches to either side. But not to worry, men! For standing almost shoulder to shoulder in both ditches, as far as the eye could see, knee-deep in mud and water, were men in the faded blue uniforms of the Korean Service Corps, each armed with a long-handled shovel. As the mud slipped into the ditch, they picked it up and shoveled it back onto the roadway. It looked to be a nip-and-tuck contest, whether the road would hold. I placed my bet on the Koreans; I knew what labor they were capable of, and figured they could outlast the spring rainshowers.

Capt. LUTHER WEAVER
L Company/35th Infantry
Our 3d Battalion bivouac area was about 3,000 yards south of the Han River but forward of the 1st and 2d Battalions. From this I assumed the 3d would be the assault battalion. The Turkish Brigade was dug in and holding the line to our front. My L Company occupied a small, deserted village [Isong-ni] and waited for whatever mission it was assigned.

> During the early evening of 4 March an officer courier arrived at the regimental command post with Operations Order Number 27, 25th Infantry Division, which assigned the Combat Team mission. The essence of the mission was to assault the line of the Han River and seize the zone bounded on the west by the Pukhan River (inclusive) and on the north and east by the division boundary.
> Next in consideration [after available forces] was the terrain. A catalog of its salient features might list first the two rivers— the Han and its northern branch, the Pukhan. At the confluence of the rivers lies a hilly island about 1600 meters long by 500 meters wide. The Han varies from approximately 150 to 300 meters in width in the regimental zone, but is divided into

channels, 120 and 160 feet wide, by a small flat island about a thousand meters upstream from the confluence. Hydrographic surveys indicated that at the time of the crossing the current would be moderate but that the river would at no point be fordable by men or vehicles. There is high ground on both sides of the river throughout the zone. In the right and central portions, the hills fall abruptly into the water, while on the left, they recede leaving strips of low, flat ground from 200 to 1500 meters wide on either shore. North of the Han the ground rises in a series of ridges and hills, some as high as 600 meters. A single track, standard gauge railroad following generally the north bank of the Han passes through six tunnels in the regimental zone.

The fact that the covered route to the river terminates several thousand yards from the crossing site, coupled with unobstructed observation of the near shore from the high ground on the enemy side of the river, meant that troops and vehicles would be exposed to whatever fire the enemy could bring to bear for well over four thousand meters before arrival at the crossing point. Some means, either natural of artificial, would have to be employed to limit enemy observation in this critical area.

Consideration of these factors was a continuing process through the night of 4 March and the morning of 5 March. Meantime preparations for the assault went forward. In the early morning hours [5 March] General [George B.] Barth [Division Artillery Commander] and Colonel [John H.] Michaelis [Assistant Division Commander] and members of the division general and special staffs met at the regimental command post for a conference with staff representatives from all regiments in the division. Details of various phases of the operation were discussed with special attention paid to the coordination of traffic on the main supply route [MSR] on "D" Day, which was now scheduled for 7 March. Not only did the narrow four mile stretch of the road which constituted the final link of the main supply route have to handle supply and evacuation for three regiments, but at an early hour on "D" Day a bridge train of over ninety very heavy vehicles would have to advance over it to the crossing sites. The bridge train would have absolute priority after "H" Hour. Other matters pertaining to use of the road were arranged among the staff representatives of the three regiments before the conference adjourned.

Commencing at 0900 hours on 5 March each company of the Third Battalion received two hours of training in assault boat technique. Methods in launching, loading and handling were explained and demonstrated and drill conducted by the engineer personnel made available for the purpose.

COMMAND REPORT, 35TH INFANTRY REGIMENT

S/Sgt. W. B. WOODRUFF, JR.
L Company/35th Infantry
What was new and different was briefings from engineer personnel, including a chance to look at, feel, and lift their assault boats. These would be off-loaded in darkness, as near as possible to the river-bank—meaning 200 to 300 yards. From that point the infantry would hand-carry and drag them to the water's edge at the appointed hour. Each boat would carry about a squad of infantry, depending on the actual strength of the squad and what heavy or extra equipment was to go with it. The engineers would provide a crew of two men, one stationed at the bow, with rope, and the other astern, to steer. In each boat were paddles with which the riflemen would, as silently as possible, provide the propulsion. For many uses these boats were equipped with outboard motors, but for this particular mission it was thought better that we not try to wake up the entire Chinese army. We cheerfully accepted the rowing alternative.

At 1500 on the fifth, the battalion commanders and operations officers with the commanders of the Heavy Mortar Company, and attached units, assembled at the Combat Team Command Post to receive Operation Order Number 14 assigning unit missions for the attacks. Given the Combat Team mission, the force and the terrain factors noted earlier, the basic decision involved the selection of objectives for the assault waves. An arc roughly 2,500 meters from the crossing site seemed desirable for several reasons. It afforded reasonably attainable objectives for two battalions; it lay in the first high ground north of the Han; it secured the crossing site from small arms fire; and placed the nucleus of the road net in friendly bounds. The Third Battalion, crossing in boats, could move northeast approximately a thousand yards with both flanks resting on the convergent river. While this advance was in progress, the First Battalion could cross on the footbridge to be constructed by the Engineers and, as the right flank of the Third Battalion (advancing north) swung away from the Han, attack east in the gap thus created. Following the assault echelons, the Second Battalion, in Combat Team Reserve, could cross and take up positions in the bridgehead. This, then, was the plan as transmitted to the assembled commanders on the afternoon of 5 March.

COMMAND REPORT, 35TH INFANTRY REGIMENT

Capt. LUTHER WEAVER
L Company/35th Infantry

The two assault companies would be King and Love—Item would be the reserve company. The assault crossing would jump off at 0615 hours on March 7, with Love Company on the right and King on the left. Love Company's objective would be the high ground consisting of Hill 72 and Hill 106, plus a small village at the base of the hills. Some 1,000 yards of flat river-bottom terrain would have to be crossed to reach either Hill 72 or the village.

Upon returning to the company with the normal maps of our sector showing checkpoints, phase lines, and boundary lines, I prepared a briefing for all platoon leaders, the XO, and 1st sergeant. This briefing was more or less an alert as to the general situation and what to expect, but not the final attack order, which I would give to them on the sixth. Based on what we could see from the map, our objective obviously would be the key to the successful crossing of the 35th RCT. The men knew King Company's objective was more or less open terrain and therefore could not be defended very strongly by the enemy. On the other hand, one of our objectives, Hill 106, could be strongly defended, and probably was.

S/Sgt. W. B. WOODRUFF, JR.
L Company/35th Infantry
News of the assault crossing came as a bit of a shock, but probably shouldn't have. Our unit had arrived at the Han, in Yongdungp'o, month earlier. Sooner or later, it should have been obvious somebody was going to have to figure a way to get troops across. We— meaning the 35th and its sister regiment, the 27th—had been elected to make the initial crossing. I thought back to Mark Twain's story about the miscreant who, having been tarred and feathered, and in the process of being ridden out of town on a rail, mused to himself that if it were not for the honor of the thing he would just as soon be somewhere else.

> On 6 March battalion staff and company commanders made their reconnaissances. The First Battalion moved into an assembly area closer to the river in order to be the more readily available for prompt movement to the crossing site on "D" Day. Throughout 6 March telephone lines and couriers between division and regiments, regiment and battalions, and among the regiments, carried a heavy load of messages effecting last minute coordination of details and minor changes in plans. Observation posts reported minor enemy activity across the river from time to time. A weather forecast predicted that "D" Day would be cloudy with visibility possibly limited by snow or rain.
>
> COMMAND REPORT, 35TH INFANTRY

Capt. LUTHER WEAVER
L Company/35th Infantry
Love Company was a beehive of activity. Everyone was making sure his weapon was oiled and ready, and that he had a sufficient supply of ammunition. Platoon leaders began to break their men down into boatloads. My WW2 experience had taught me that once our boats reached the opposite bank, the men had to keep moving. To freeze under fire on the opposite bank would be suicide.

On the afternoon of the sixth, I was jeeped back to one of the forward artillery liaison airstrips. I was then flown in an L-4 spotter plane up and over the river where I could observe my next day's objectives. This being my first and only recon by air over an objective, I must say it was a most valuable experience. Although the flight was not conducted without our receiving some calling cards in the form of small-arms fire from the enemy on Hill 106, I was able to get a good view of the terrain, from the north side of the Han all the way to the rear side of Hill 106. Most important was the view I got of the enemy defense positions and how he was arranged on the two hills. The sighting of newly dug positions also indicated the enemy was reinforcing his positions daily for an expected attack by our forces.

After some fifteen minutes of flying and dodging enemy ground fire, I signaled to the pilot to head for the friendly shore. By then I not only had a complete picture of the terrain, but I had discovered where I believed the enemy's strongest defense to be. I also became aware that my pilot was a skilled veteran observer as he very calmly maneuvered his plane in evasive actions that confused the enemy guns on the ground. I am afraid that the loud cracking of bullets coming in around our cockpit was more disturbing to me as I sat fastened in the plane than my many experiences on the ground under similar circumstances. When we landed we checked out the plane, as I was convinced not all the small-arms fire had gone wild. My thinking was confirmed when I discovered four or five new holes in the plane's wings and tail section. The pilot, whose name I should have remembered but didn't, rather nonchalantly said, "It happens all the time." To him it was just another flying mission.

By the time I reached our battalion headquarters, I was ready to brief Colonel Lee [battalion CO] on what I estimated enemy strength to be and how I planned to carry out the attack. Once I had briefed him and gained his approval, I was ready to issue our attack plan.

Since we still had several hours of daylight left, I called for my platoon leaders with all their NCOs to assemble between two buildings near the company CP.

S/Sgt. W . B . WOODRUFF, JR .
L Company/35th Infantry
During the day of March 6, we were dimly aware through the increasing tension that commanders at higher levels were completing reconnaissance flights, planning sessions, and meeting at which

directives were issued and details coordinated. Alford went up to the company CP late in the afternoon to get the picture on Love Company in general, and 1st Platoon in particular. Our preparations completed, we waited. It was the longest wait of a long day.

Capt. LUTHER WEAVER
L Company/35th Infantry

With what maps we had, and by sketching on the ground, I covered every facet of how the company would proceed to its objectives. In general, our attack from the river would move swiftly in spread column straight northeast up a slight depression—which would give us some cover. This, along with the darkness of the hour, would help us bypass the 1,000 yards or so of flat ground between the river and our first objectives, Hill 72 and the village. Calculating from the crossing time of 0615 hours, I felt that, unless something unforeseen happened, we could be on the flank of our objective and ready to assault Hill 72 by daylight.

First Platoon, led by Master Sergeant Joe Alford, had as its objective Hill 72, which screened from the northwest the approach to the village and Hill 106. Joe Alford, a tried and true combat veteran, was a soldier all the way; his sense of perception in knowing how to outsmart the enemy and his fearless leadership qualities made him a superb leader. His talents were at their best during a firefight.

Next in line would be the company command group—myself, my runner with an SCR-536 radio, and two company communications men with the SCR-300 radio.

The 3d Platoon would follow next, together with the 57-mm Recoilless Rifle Section.* The platoon would be slightly echeloned to the right wherever the terrain permitted. Third Platoon's leader was 1st Lieutenant Fleming, a very fine officer with excellent leadership capabilities. He had a good sense of humor and was well respected by his NCOs and men. Lieutenant Fleming's orders were to

---

* Firing conventional shells in a flat trajectory, the recoilless rifle had a range far in excess of the bazooka. It was breech loaded and could be fired from the shoulder. In Korea this infantry-carried artillery was eventually replaced by heavier RRs (75-mm and 105-mm).

attack on the right flank of 1st Platoon, and secure the approach to the village. He would then wait for my orders to attack the village.

Second Platoon would follow 3d Platoon as reserve and be prepared to move to the rear of 1st Platoon after that platoon made its turn and launched its attack on Hill 72. Second Platoon would also be responsible for making visual contact with King Company on our left flank. The 2d Platoon leader was 1st Lieutenant Garretson. He had recently arrived and was rather aggressive but not reckless—a trait I admired.

Lieutenant Freeman and his Weapons Platoon with its 60-mm Mortar Section would follow 2d Platoon and bring with them the litter bearers. Freeman would clear the crossing site and advise me when Love Company cleared the river. Lieutenant Freeman had been with the company for several months and was a very capable officer, well liked by his men. He was very quiet, but could do a fine job when called upon. He and I had an understanding: if my luck ran out at some point during an operation, he was to take charge of the company without hesitation.

My executive officer, 1st Lieutenant Joe Schilling, and 1st Sergeant John Mills were to remain behind after the company left for the river crossing. They would take charge of the company vehicles, drivers, mail clerk, and all equipment we left behind, such as bedrolls and overcoats. They would also maintain communications with battalion rear. Additionally, if the operation went as planned, and the engineers could get a pontoon bridge in, we would expect them to send a hot meal the evening of the assault.

After these final instructions were given, I dismissed everyone to return to his platoon area.

S/Sgt. W . B . WOODRUFF, JR.
L Company/35th Infantry
It was already after dark when Alford returned, and we gathered around in some mixture of relief, eagerness, and foreboding. While we waited a little longer for all the squad leaders to arrive, Alford stayed busy studying his notes and the map, saying not a word, giving us not a clue. It was for Alford to know and to plan; it was for us to listen close when he was ready to speak, and to carry out his orders. Joe

Alford was at that moment the essence of "old Army," the absolute autocrat, doing the job he was getting paid for, all business and totally confident. We would not have wanted it any other way, and were glad we had him.

Then he laid it out. First, the time schedule. The purpose was to land on the north bank just before first light. Computing backward in time, it meant we would get up at 2 A.M. and breakfast at 3 A.M. By 5 A.M. we would have moved the mile or two through the Turkish lines and up to the boats. There, we would wait for the twenty-minute artillery preparation. When it concluded, we would move the boats to the water, get aboard, and paddle across. In our company zone there was a village some few hundred yards north of the river, and in the northerly part of the village was a long, low ridge, or hill—Hill 72—which was our initial company objective. Beyond that lay a higher hill—Hill 106—our final objective for the day. Essentially, our job was to hold along the line of the latter hill a day or so while bridges were erected and supplies and equipment brought across to make the bridgehead secure.

The ground directly between the enemy-held village and the river was flat and open. However, along our left boundary, a small creek flowed southward down to the river. Along this creek we would make our main advance, taking advantage of the broken ground and brush for cover and concealment, until we came abreast of the village; then we would turn right to take it in flank. This creek was the approximate boundary between Love and King Companies, King being next to the Pukhan and we on their right. To our right would be the 1st Battalion.

My recollection is that the company, once across, would move initially in a column of platoons, 1st Platoon leading. Then Alford got into the details of who and what would ride in which boat, and it was at this point that I received a severe jolt: A 57-mm recoilless rifle and its crew had been attached to 1st Platoon for this operation, but there would be no room for this detachment in the first lift; it would have to wait for the boats to return and cross in the second echelon. I was detailed to take charge of this element—about four men under their own section sergeant, plus the 57-mm and ammo— with the mission of ensuring it moved as rapidly as possible to catch up with and rejoin the company. Being separated from the platoon in an action of this importance was bad enough; being assigned as nursemaid to a recoilless rifle and crew—given the usual rivalry between the riflemen and heavy-weapons people—was worse. I felt demoted, and grievously disappointed. I do not remember the rest of Alford's instructions. The excuse I made for myself was that since I had nothing of any significance to do, there was no point in my trying to recall all the details of the platoon's operation; I would not be there, anyway. I regret I was of very little help to my platoon leader during the rest of the evening's preparations. I was nearly overwhelmed by a temptation to argue with Joe Alford about my assignment, but at least I had sense enough not to do it. Of course, I eventually resolved to do my best with my piddling part of the operation.

The squad leaders rushed off to clue in their people. (At this time, these were, in order by squads, Wright, Baker, Skirvin, and Pelfrey.) Alford and Lopez sacked out but did not turn off the light; they continued studying notes and maps, occasionally discussing some point. I drifted outside the tent. A few men had gathered around a small fire, where one of them was playing a harmonica. The musician was Corporal Smallbone, from upstate New York. I barely knew him before that night, and do not recall any circumstances surrounding his recently having joined 1st Platoon. He had the largest and most elaborately decorated harmonica I'd ever seen, and he played it beautifully. During an occasional rest from playing, he told us some of his ancestors had brought it over from the old country, Germany. We kept urging him on, until he had played every song he could remember. Most of the others wandered off to bed, until only Smallbone and I were left. We talked, he played; we talked some more, he played some more. I think we both hated to end the evening. When we broke up I am sure he was exhausted. I felt I had made a new friend, and one I valued greatly.

At 1930 on 6 March, a tactical Command Post was opened in the village of Kwirin-ni about three thousand meters south of the crossing site. Then at around 2200 hours the telephone lines began to fall silent and the day-long surge of urgent messages was replaced by a quiet succession of negative hourly reports from the battalions.

COMMAND REPORT, 35TH INFANTRY REGIMENT

0315 Breakfast served for troops in preparation for movement.

S/2-3 JOURNAL, 3D BATTALION/35TH INFANTRY

Capt. LUTHER WEAVER
L Company/35th Infantry

Sergeant F/C Joe Wlos [L Company's mess sergeant] was right on time with breakfast, as usual; and his warm pancakes from marmite cans were readily consumed with lukewarm coffee. Each man was given one day's assault ration to carry in case the evening meal did not reach him. In mingling and talking with a number of the men while we were having breakfast, I sensed a feeling of confidence that they were ready. They all seemed to know exactly what we were going to do and how we planned to do it. Some were telling me, "If so-and-so doesn't get a move on when we reach that north bank of river, he will get a kick in the ass with a wet boot." I also overheard, "The captain said we had to move to stay alive, and by God, when that rubber duckie [boat] scrapes dirt on the other side, we are going to be *moving.*"

S/Sgt. W. B. WOODRUFF, JR.
L Company/35th Infantry

Around 3 A.M. next morning I dutifully linked up with my recoilless rifle crew. I'm afraid I treated them with a good deal less than soldierly comradeship. I set a brisk pace throughout, ignoring entirely their heavy load of gun and ammo. The 57-mm weighed about fifty pounds, and was very awkward to carry. It was still winter, with considerable snow on the ground, but the men would all be sweat-soaked before we caught up with the company. They would have been justified in shooting me.

As we approached the river's south bank in complete darkness, I almost stepped on a Turkish soldier dug in alongside the trail. Dimly, I could discern that he was sprawled out in a shallow hole, all alone, awake and alert but looking quite relaxed, and only vaguely curious about what we were up to.

While the Infantry Companies were moving forward in the dark along a trail at the base of the high ground, tanks of the 89th Tank Battalion using a parallel trail close to the river towed assault boats to the crossing site. Depositing the boats at the designated points, the tanks took up positions nearby from which they could support the assault by fire, and were at the same time prepared to take the first opportunity to cross and continue their support as the assault waves moved inland. This was accomplished prior to 0530.

At 0555 hours four battalions of 105-mm howitzers, a battalion of 155-mm howitzers and a regiment of British 25-pounder guns opened a twenty-minute preparation barrage on previously designated targets in the Division Zone.

COMMAND REPORT, 35TH INFANTRY REGIMENT

S/Sgt. W. B. WOODRUFF, JR.
L Company/35th Infantry
Then the artillery preparation began. It was, and remains, indescribable. At Fort Sill years before, in basic training, I had seen firepower demonstrations involving multibattalion concentrations; but nothing prepared me for this. The earth shook, and a deafening roar went on and on. Across the entire visible expanse of these mountains shells burst in absolute profusion, each burst first flaring orange, then turning to black smoke against the whiteness of the snow. I watched, nearly hypnotized.

Capt. LUTHER WEAVER
L Company/35th Infantry
Some of the men joked about Joe Chink being fed lots of hot metal for an early breakfast. As artillery continued, I moved the company down to the bank of the river, where boats were being positioned by tanks.

As 0615 hours arrived, the 1st Platoon was to push off from the south bank. As suddenly as the artillery preparation commenced, it ceased.

0615 Bn moved out in the attack, crossing the Han River.
S/2-3 JOURNAL, 3D BATTALION/35TH INFANTRY

Capt. LUTHER WEAVER
L Company/35th Infantry
As we pushed off, straining for a view of the other side of the river
through the darkness filled with smoke and haze, the most audible
sounds on the river were the swishing of boat paddles and the grunts
and groans of men determined to reach the other side before the
enemy started reacting.* We knew we were in range of his mortars,
but were not sure of his artillery capability.

S/Sgt. W. B. WOODRUFF, JR.
L Company/35th Infantry
Once the boats vanished into the darkness, I moved my little group
down to the water's edge, straining for the first glimpse of a returning
boat. This was also the crucial stage of the operation. What if the
enemy lay in wait on the opposite bank? At what instant might 1st
Platoon come under a hail of gunfire, exposed in those puny boats,
wearing sixty pounds of equipment, in the center of a river where the
water was ten to fifteen feet deep and icy cold? When I calculated
they had had time to complete the crossing, and the night was still
silent, there was vast relief. Then came into view the first of the
returning boats.

I grabbed the first one with no effort to identify it as the correct
one, got my gun crew aboard, and moved out smartly. It now came
to me that first light was not far off, and I did not want it to catch us
in midstream. The thing to do at such a time is to keep everything
and everybody moving. In quite short order the boat scraped bottom
on the north bank. The engineer at the bow leaped out with his rope,
pulling the boat up as far as he could. We clambered ashore. I looked
about and made out the shapes of a small group of men not far away.

---

* Each assault company was allocated eighteen wooden boats. This broke down roughly to
about twelve men per boat.

I went over and asked if they were Love Company. No, they were King Company. In the darkness, the current had carried us downstream, out of Love Company's zone.

> The initial wave moved rapidly across the river and inland on the far shore. Then at 0635 the assault companies had moved up the gentle rise from the river banks coming under heavy enemy small arms fire 300 yards inland, less than one half hour had elapsed since the embarkation. The small arms fire seemed to be coming from a nose of the first higher ground on the battalion's right flank. At 0635 the battalion commander [Lt. Col. James Lee] requested artillery fire on the nose, which was promptly delivered.
>
> COMMAND REPORT, 35TH INFANTRY REGIMENT

Capt. LUTHER WEAVER
L Company/35th Infantry
Captain McGraw continued to pound Hill 106 and the village area [on the battalion's right] with 81-mm mortar fire. As we continued to move to the point where 1st Platoon was to make a right turn and attack Hill 72, we began to receive long-range MG fire from our right flank, directed across the open, flat ground toward the river crossing site. I had suspected the enemy would have that flat terrain covered with fire from positions near the village and also the foothills of Hill 383. A frontal attack across the flat ground to seize the village would have been suicidal. I called the 2d Platoon to see if they had cleared the river, and received an affirmative. I warned them to be careful on approach from the river, as daylight was breaking and an enemy MG was firing across the rear of 3d Platoon. I called battalion and reported Love Company had cleared the river and was now in position to attack Hill 72. There was very light resistance so far. A few rounds of rifle fire had come from our objective, but due to poor light, no one had been hit yet. I informed Lieutenant Garretson [2d Platoon] that 1st and 3d Platoons were ready to attack, and as we moved in for the attack, for him to continue forward and establish visual contact with King Company and to get in position to attack later when I needed him. Alford [1st Platoon] said he was ready to

attack the back side of Hill 72 and the railroad embankment, adding, "Captain, I believe we're gonna surprise them by hitting their flank." I told him to start moving in and, if needed, 3d Platoon would be ready with a base of fire. The 1st Platoon launched their attack on Hill 72, utilizing some protection from various brush-covered fingers and irregular terrain that tapered off from Hill 72 and Hill 106. By now the enemy appeared to be recovering from the artillery plastering he had endured an hour before. Enemy small-arms fire was picking up, but mostly from enemy riflemen, as their MG emplacements apparently were dug in to cover a frontal attack. As 1st Platoon gained a foothold on Hill 72, I told Lieutenant Fleming [3d Platoon] to attack to the right flank of 1st Platoon and to get in position to assault the village as soon as we cleared Hill 72 and the railroad embankment. I then ordered the 2d Platoon, which was now in about the same position as the 1st Platoon had been in when they had launched their attack, to swing right and attack and clear several fingers that tapered out from Hill 106. I told Garretson to hold up as soon as he reached the railroad. We were now getting quite a lot of enemy mortar fire. I called Lieutenant Freeman, who was following the 2d Platoon with our 60-mm mortar section, to get his mortars in action and to take under fire whatever they could locate as targets on Hill 106.

I had now moved up with 1st Platoon, which was on phase line Baker, the railroad. I gave battalion a progress report and was informed the 1st Battalion was now crossing the river prior to launching their attack on my right flank. Also, the 89th Tank Battalion would soon be getting some tanks across, and I was to use them wherever I could. I informed Blue Six [Colonel Lee] that we now held the rear of Hill 72 and the approach to the village. Because I knew the enemy had MGs covering the flat, open ground between the village and the river, I told him I preferred to hold up on attacking the village until after the 1st Battalion crossed and the tanks reached us. We continued to receive enemy mortar fire from Hill 106. Third Platoon, which was in position to attack the village, was not receiving any fire from the village; but to attack now would place it between the enemy's machine guns and the 1st Battalion and the tanks crossing the river. Colonel Lee concurred and said to do whatever I thought was best.

In the meantime the litter squad, which was carrying a couple of wounded men back to the river, was caught on the flat ground by enemy MG fire and had two corpsmen down. After getting this information, I instructed all platoons not to send any wounded back until I was sure the area had been cleared. It was now about 9:00 A.M.

Lieutenant Kelly, my FO [from the 64th FA Battalion] had now joined me by the railroad. While we were being held up, enemy mortar fire from Hill 106 continued to harass us. I instructed Kelly to get some fire on the crest of that hill. Shortly afterward we heard a barrage [of 105-mm howitzers] go over our heads like a swarm of angry bees and crash into Hill 106. A few more salvos, and the enemy mortar fire ceased.

From time to time enemy snipers picked men off. One was a young kid with the 1st Platoon who was about ten yards from me and my runner. I can't recall now the young soldier's name—he had only been with the company a few weeks. Before the sniper shot at him, several men had told him to keep his head down. But he just could not seem to resist the temptation of standing up to see where our artillery fire was landing. He raised up one time too many; the sniper was waiting and shot him right dead through the forehead.

S/Sgt. W. B. WOODRUFF, JR.
L Company/35th Infantry

My gun crew huffed and sweated, traded places on the recoilless rifle, and begged for a break. Those I gave them were few and short, and not graciously extended. At length we climbed yet another of the endless ridges, until there before us lay the west end of Hill 72, and, extending along it in an apparently relaxed state, a company of men, some of whom I immediately recognized. We were home. The time was 9:30 A.M. It had been almost two and a half hours since we stepped ashore on the north bank of the river. We must have crossed almost the entire width of King Company's zone.

As soon as we came in under the ridgeline, my gun crew fell out, exhausted. I started making the rounds, shaking hands, greeting people as though I hadn't seen them in a decade, and inquiring for news of their obviously successful attack. There was one item of bad news—Smallbone's death. He'd been picked off by a sniper.

I found Baker and Lopez sharing a rather small foxhole—probably dug by the somewhat smaller Chinese—on the forward [north] slope of the ridge. They told me Alford had gone to the company CP to report and get any further instructions. Through trees and brush ahead, I could make out the railway station. Baker told me that, seeing movement inside it, they had had the happy thought of getting Fisher to put a 3.5-inch rocket launcher round in it,* which he had proceeded to do, right through a window. This had so unnerved three Chinese occupants that they would not come out; Baker's squad had to go in and run them out. Baker and Lopez were especially happy about the morning's work, and were laughing and telling jokes. I sat down to join them. I thought they felt rather sorry for me, as I had missed all the action; but being gentlemen they did not allude to it. I described my morning to them briefly, trying with no real success to put as heroic a cast on it as possible.

At just that instant, Lopez jumped as though startled, and grabbed his right arm. All remained quiet. He rolled up his sleeve: there was a neat, round hole in his forearm, about midway between his wrist and elbow. We remained alert for a moment, but when there was no further sign of enemy activity, Baker started helping Lopez with a bandage. Suddenly laughing aloud, Baker said, "Lopez, you lucky son of a gun, that is a Pusan wound." Lopez joined in the laughter, then reached back for his pack. Going through it quickly, he handed out to those gathered round what, just a minute ago, had been his most prized possessions—several pairs of dry socks, along with a pack or two of cigarettes, and the like. He said he would not be needing them where he was going, and that while he rested between clean sheets back at the hospital, he would think of us. This completed, Lopez waved good-bye and set off in high good humor to hunt out the aid station.

No sooner had Lopez gone than another man was struck: The

---

*The 3.5-inch bazooka had replaced the obsolete 2.36. It weighed fifteen pounds and fired an 8.5-pound shaped charge which was capable of penetrating armor plate.

sniper was back at work, and an ordeal began that would last about two hours. They were among the longest hours I ever endured. Once every few minutes a sniper's bullet fell on the ridge. It seemed to me that about one bullet out of three found a human target. We never heard the sound of the rifle firing, nor could we find the sniper's location. He must have been on high ground a considerable distance to our front—maybe half a mile or more. The ridge on which we lay afforded no protection; the enemy sniper was high enough to aim at any point on the ground we occupied. One place was as safe or as dangerous as another. There was nothing we could do except sit and wait—and gradually develop a nearly overpowering urge to advance, even without orders, on our next objective. Nothing, we thought, could be worse than sitting here providing target practice for the sniper. A radio operator out of company headquarters sitting six or eight feet away from me suddenly lay over on his side, blood running from a hole in his temple. Another bullet kicked up snow from the ground between my feet. The aid men worked with superhuman effort: no sooner would they get one man to the aid station than there was another—and of course they were as exposed as everyone else. Our platoon aid man, Doc Moore, who had been with us since December, was never the same afterward. I never saw him smile again; he had a pinched look that never left him. He was transferred a few days later, and we never saw him again. Nor did Lopez return to the unit. I estimate we took twelve or fifteen casualties during the two-hour period—all except Lopez either killed or seriously wounded.

We had a little reorganizing to do. I moved up into Lopez's place, but do not remember the circumstances. I can imagine Alford said in his Hoosier twang, "Ah, Woody, you will have to take over for Lopez," but I really do not remember. He may have just taken it for granted without any formal announcement. Pelfrey moved up to my old job, Lorenz taking over 4th Squad.

In the regimental OP [observation post] the commanding officer [Colonel Kelleher] continued his watch over the crossing. At 1100 hours the 1st and 3d Battalions would move out toward their final objectives. Anticipating the completion of a fifteen ton raft capable of ferrying vehicles, Colonel Kelleher assigned priorities for its use. The 3d Battalion was given first priority and a tank platoon forded the river to close behind the battalion.*

COMMAND REPORT, 35TH INFANTRY REGIMENT

Capt. LUTHER WEAVER
L Company/35th Infantry

Blue Six called and told me I would have four medium tanks that were on their way, and that I was to make contact with the tank platoon leader and use them wherever I thought best. In contacting the platoon leader on the radio, I was informed he had one tank that could not be used due to some problem with the tank gun's traversing and elevating mechanism. I asked him if the tank was mobile. "Oh, yes," was the reply. "Nothing wrong except the big gun." I said, "Okay, send two tanks to the northeast side of Hill 72 and Hill 106. Bring the others—including the one with the bad gun—up to the rear of Hill 72. We will use the one with the inoperative gun to carry wounded back to the river. I want the other one to stay on low ground and protect the flank of my platoon, which is ready to clear the village. Tell your tank commanders to be on the lookout for enemy MGs firing across open ground between the village and the river. Love Company is deployed along the railroad track. When your tanks come up to the northeast side of 72 and 106, they will be looking right into Hill 106. Have them start firing on anything that appears to be bunkers or emplacements." "We are on the way," he replied, "and will be in position within a few minutes."

I told the platoons what we were doing, and also to have their wounded escorted under cover to the base of Hill 72, where they would be picked up by a tank and evacuated. Shortly afterward, the tanks were in position and firing on targets they picked out to our front. I then sent Fleming's 3d Platoon in to clear the village. There had been very little resistance coming from houses in the village.

While the two tanks on my left had a field day knocking out bunkers and we waited to attack Hill 106, I moved down to the 3d Platoon, which was searching houses.

---

* At 9:15 A.M. Colonel Kelleher had directed the commander of the attached 89th Tank Battalion/25th Division to assign one platoon of tanks to each battalion.

The squads were moving from house to house, and Fleming and I joined them. Together we moved toward one of the houses. I told my radio operator to take a break but to let me know if battalion called. Fleming and I began to check this one house. We kicked open the door and jumped in—nothing. I checked one room, then another. I edged into the hallway, my carbine ready. Suddenly, out of the corner of my eye I caught sight of someone moving. I wheeled and fired a full blast. A mirror shattered and in the remaining shards I could still see parts of myself looking very foolish. Fleming, who saw it all, was darn near rolling on the floor. A very good practical joker, he never did let me live it down.

Time		Serial	
In	*Out*	*No.*	*Incidents, Messages, Etc.*
1050		11	Phone: L Co. knocked out SP Gun . . . They are still receiving S/A fire fr Hill 106 and mortar fire fr 27 RCT Area. . . . Ready to move out at 100 hrs for obj.
1126		12	Phone: K and L Co's jumped off at 1100 hrs. . . . L Co working towards 106.

S-3 UNIT JOURNAL, 3D BATTALION/35TH INFANTRY

Capt. LUTHER WEAVER
L Company/35th Infantry
Like a bolt of lightning, an artillery salvo from our rear came over our heads and exploded right into my 3d Platoon. I immediately radioed battalion to tell them we had been hit by our own artillery, and that we needed litters and jeeps immediately. Lieutenant Kelly, the FO, was immediately in contact with the 64th FA Battalion. Fortunately, we received no more friendly fire, but it certainly held up, temporarily, a well-coordinated attack we were making up the hill. Two men from 3d Platoon were killed, and four seriously

wounded. Being fired on by your own forces has a much more de-
moralizing effect on a unit than enemy fire. I later tried to find out
what artillery unit fired on us, and who called for the fire, but, as
things go in the thick of battle, I could get no positive answers. In
war when someone makes a mistake, he doesn't come forward and
apologize.

The wounded were moved off the hill and 3d Platoon's shock at
being shelled by its own artillery quickly disappeared. We continued
the attack.

Time		Serial	
In	Out	No.	Incidents, Messages, Etc.
1200		13	Phone: Co. K . . . shooting en as Co. L runs them off of Hill 106—Co. L moving up 106. Has 3 KIA and 13 WIA so far.
1205		14	Phone: L Co. is 200 yds fr Obj Hill 106.

S-3 UNIT JOURNAL, 3D BATTALION/35TH INFANTRY

Capt. LUTHER WEAVER
L Company/35th Infantry
Sergeants Alford and Woodruff called me to say they were in position
to make the final assault. I could tell from their voices they were
pleased. I gave Alford the go-ahead. Lieutenant Garretson with the
2d Platoon [on the left flank] had reached the big finger that pro-
truded north, and with the tanks, was having a field day firing on
enemy troops trying to leave the hill. Third Platoon was just then
reaching the crest on the right of 1st Platoon. Except for a few enemy
routed out by 1st Platoon, Chinese resistance was minor.

On my left I watched the 1st Platoon move to the top. Shortly
afterward, 3d Platoon reached the crest. I then reported to battalion
that we were on our final objective. Very little mopping up was nec-

essary, as the enemy left behind nothing but his dead. According to my diary, the time was now 1230 hours.

A couple of hours later, we were dug in on the most suitable and commanding high ground and were ready to defend our newly won territory.

Later, my radio operator, whom I had left at the spot where the company CP would be located, sent someone forward to tell me the battalion S-3 wanted to speak with me. Contact was made, and the assistant S-3, a young West Point officer, told me that according to their map Love Company should move forward about 200 yards, to map coordinate so and so. I explained the situation and told him he had better check his map again as his coordinates would put us on ground we would not be able to defend. Furthermore, we were established and I preferred remaining put. We broke contact. Shortly afterward, the S-3, a major, called. He appeared rather steamed up. "I want you to move 200 yards forward to coordinate such and such." When I explained the situation to him—getting hot under the collar myself—he told me that his orders were from the regimental S-3. I informed him then that before I would accept the responsibility for the lives of Love Company in an indefensible position, I would have to talk to Blue Six. Shortly afterward, Lieutenant Colonel Lee called. "What's your problem?" "I don't have a problem," I replied, "but Blue Three [regimental S-3] does. Either he can't read a map, or his map is not like mine." I explained the situation to him, and what the terrain 200 yards to my front was. His reply: "Okay, Captain, remain where you are. You know more about the terrain from your position than the map readers back here do. Are you tied in with King?" I replied, "Affirmative." Colonel Lee said, "Real proud of Love's operation today, damn good job. Engineers have made a bridge across and you should have a hot meal arriving pretty soon. Any questions?" "Not at this time." "Okay, Roger and out."*

Prior to dark the word came through that Lieutenant Schilling and Sergeant Wlos had come through with hot chow. They were in the village at the base of the hill. Overcoats for use that night had

---

*On 7 March, L Company/35th Infantry sustained five KIA (including the two by friendly fire) and eleven WIA. Enemy losses in front of L Company were forty-five dead and an estimated seventy-five to a hundred wounded; fifteen POWs were taken.

also been brought up, plus batteries for the radios and ammunition. Platoons were told to start sending their men back to eat in shifts. About dark, as I was on the way down the hill, following a pretty well worn trail—the first shift had already eaten—I encountered a group of men returning to their position. They were loaded with bundles of overcoats for their respective squads. I am sure all of them were tired, but they did not want to show it. At the time, I knew all their names; and as we passed along the trail, I told them what a good job they had done. When I arrived at the chow jeep Lieutenant Schilling met me with a big smile, as always, and brought me up to date on what had been going on back across the river that day, the status of some of our wounded, and so forth. Whenever I left Joe behind, I knew he'd be good at keeping up with the overall situation. With Schilling back there I always knew if anyone would get hot meals, Love Company would. Of course, he already knew of my using the disabled tank to move the wounded back, and the company being hit by our own artillery. Having heard the men talking before I arrived, he knew of more individual acts of courage and bravery than I did. When he started to laugh and said, "What's this I hear about the captain about to shoot himself in a mirror?" I knew Lieutenant Fleming had already been down to eat.

8 March
At 0800 hours the 1st and 3d Battalions moved out in the attack, as ordered, from the positions secured on the previous day and, encountering relatively minor opposition, quickly secured their assigned objectives.

COMMAND DIARY, 35TH INFANTRY REGIMENT

S/Sgt. W. B. WOODRUFF, JR.
L Company/35th Infantry
On the following day [9 March] a platoon-size patrol was ordered out to the front. This patrol was made up of some elements from the 4th Platoon—a 60-mm mortar and crew, as I recall—and some from the 1st Platoon, which provided Skirvin's 3d Squad and possibly another squad. Lieutenant Freeman, then 4th Platoon leader, was patrol leader, and I the senior sergeant. Freeman told me to take the

rear of the column and keep it closed up, while he stationed himself at the head—all of which was SOP (standard operating procedure). However, in this instance, it left me with the heavy weapons, about which I knew little and cared less; and it put Freeman with rifle squads—with which he had not the intimate acquaintance I had. He put Skirvin's 3d Squad on the point.

John Skirvin was from Iowa and was the kind of hardworking, capable, and conscientious soldier I routinely came to expect from that state. He was wholly dependable, and the kind of man who in his midforties tried to reenlist for the Vietnam War. Yet, in my appraisal, he was not a great soldier, for he was also quite religious and—possibly for that reason—lacking in the killer instinct. Further, he could hardly bring himself to send any man out on a mission of any danger; he was more apt to go himself. This sometimes would put him in a position where he could not well supervise his squad. On this particular day all these factors came into play at once.

We had been marching slowly and cautiously for maybe an hour and a half, when I heard from the head of the column four or five shots. The mortar crew immediately set the base plate and prepared for a fire mission; I left the mortar sergeant in charge and went forward on the double. At the head of the column I found 3d Squad, less Skirvin, lying prone along the crest of a hill, all hands keeping a sharp lookout to the north. There had been no more firing, and I could see no movement. The men reported Skirvin had been out in front—acting as his own first scout, naturally—and that he had been hit by a sniper. (That this was incorrect I did not learn for many years. Since the experience on Hill 72 the morning before, we all had "snipers" on the brain.) At the time I never thought to question what they reported, and concluded the sniper must be on the next mountain, 600 or 800 yards to the front. They pointed out where Skirvin lay, fifty or sixty yards down the forward slope of the hill in front of us. I said that we must get Skirvin out. I think every mouth in the squad opened, but the first one to get out the words "I'll go with you" was Corporal Billy Hatfield.

Hatfield was from Missouri, and another recent transferee into Love Company, arriving about the same time as Smallbone. I don't believe he stayed very long; this was almost the only occasion I was closely associated with him. He told me he had come from an MP unit. I asked for no details, and he didn't volunteer any, but there came into my mind fleetingly an ancient and time-honored custom of the army in wartime: When a man got into disciplinary problems in a unit of another branch, he was quickly transferred to the infantry. Whether this was so in Hatfield's case, I have no idea; but he was in any event a fine combat soldier.

I ran down the hill and hit the dirt alongside Skirvin, and was immediately followed by Hatfield. Skirvin appeared unconscious from a head wound. We saw no trace of any other wound. The next question was how to get him back. Directly up the hill was steep, and Skirvin was a big man; I figured he outweighed me by twenty or thirty pounds. Also, in moving directly up and over the crest of the hill, the three of us would make an excellent target for the supposed sniper. What we decided was to move him to our left around the side of the hill and along the same contour, until we reached a better place to get him up to the top. This task consumed well over half an hour and was hard work. We pulled, pushed, dragged, and half-carried Skirvin to keep him moving but not sliding downward, as he had a tendency to do. He struggled against us, muttering in the monotone I had by now associated with head wounds that he was tired, he hurt, and he wanted to be left alone and to rest. I thought him semiconscious and out of his head, and figured that this was for the best to prevent his feeling the pain. At last we reached a gentler slope, somewhat out of the direct line of observation of the "sniper." Hatfield and I fashioned a stretcher of our two rifles and field jackets and got him over the top. About this time Doc Moore arrived with a litter, and took over.

Lieutenant Freeman had by now received orders by radio to withdraw the patrol when ready, its mission—to make enemy contact if possible—having been accomplished. I confirmed to Bressard that he was to take over 3d Squad, and we returned to the company area.

(I had sporadic correspondence with Skirvin following the war, and was aware he used crutches for years, and then a cane for many more years. I assumed this was caused by paralysis resulting from his head wound. It was thirty years before I got a full account from him. There had never been a sniper. What happened was that out in front of his squad, as he passed the crest of the hill, he came face to face with a Chinese soldier, probably one assigned to lookout duty but who had been caught napping. The enemy soldier jumped and ran, and Skirvin got off one round with his M1, which missed. The Chinese then whirled and gave him a short burst with his burp gun. Skirvin was hit not only in the head, but also in both legs. I think at least one leg had been broken. The pain, and probably great additional damage done to this fracture by our half hour or more of dragging him around the hill, makes me wince today just thinking of it.)

Several days later [14 March], 1st Platoon was sent out north maybe three miles on outpost. We moved past the hill where Skirvin had been hit, and finally set up our outpost, with the platoon CP in a lone farmhouse. This also turned out to be a mistake of sorts—that is, sending Alford out on an independent mission outside the company area. For Sergeant Al immediately got inebriated, or more accurately, roaring drunk. I never saw the liquor, nor him drink it, and I am mystified to this day as to where it came from. But of the end result there was no doubt. Toward late afternoon he got out of the shack and began visiting the various foxholes and weapons positions. His suggestions and instructions, of course, made no sense. When he reached Fisher, the latter lost patience and announced in the patronizing voice commonly used toward a drunk that he was going to put Al to bed. Al challenged him to do any such thing, and the two struggled briefly. Fisher, who was quite big and strong—not to mention younger and sober—promptly had Alford's shoulders pinned to the ground. Al suggested that if Fisher was ready to concede who was boss of 1st Platoon, he would release him. Fisher did. Al went back to the platoon CP and pondered this for a while; then, about dark, he really went on a tear. Picking up the field phone in the presence of several of us, he pretended to engage in a lengthy conversation with the company CP. The phone switch, which had to be pressed to talk, was never pressed. The purported conversation related to a major attack by a horde of Chinese who were in the process of annihilating the entire company. Al started shouting orders for us to go on full alert, for me to check the line and keep everyone on their toes, and to get the machine gun on full load instead of half load. Finally tiring of this game, he lay down and fell into a sound sleep— to the relief of all. Next morning he was hung over, in an ill humor, and would hardly speak to anyone.

Toward noon we were ordered to return to the company area; Love Company was being relieved and would go into reserve. We entrucked and went back across the Han, this time crossing on a new bridge, courtesy of the engineers, within 100 yards of the point we had crossed in assault boats a few days before.

Love Company returned south of the Han River on 15 March and, with its regiment, went into I Corps's reserve. On this same day, Seoul fell to the UN.

NORTHWARD

7 March–21 April 1951

The same day the 25th Division crossed the Han, the other units in Operation Ripper also began moving forward. While I Corps made a feint and held the Chinese in place in the west, IX and X Corps, which carried the brunt of the offensive, jumped off toward their objectives in central Korea.

In the rugged mountains east of the UN's Han River bridgehead, it dawned clear and cold on Wednesday, 7 March; but by afternoon clouds had rolled in, and snow began to fall. The IX Corps advanced in the direction of its primary objectives,* the road centers of Hongch'on and Ch'unch'on, and on the first day recorded substantial gains. Then, for more than a week, the Corps ground northward, encountering light resistance from an enemy that was satisfied to delay but not stop the attack.†

---

* The IX Corps was commanded now by Maj. Gen. William H. Hoge, replacing General Moore, who had died of exposure and a heart attack after a helicopter in which he was riding crashed into the Han River. Major General Oliver P. Smith, USMC, had temporarily succeeded Moore and had taken charge of the Corps until 5 March, when Hoge assumed command. General Hoge was best remembered for his bold seizure of the Remagen Bridge in the Second World War.

† In March it was estimated that 227,119 Americans (110,871 of whom were in Eighth Army, the rest in the Air Force and Navy) now served in Korea. This element, when added to the 21,184 men serving in UN member states' ground forces and the 249,815 officers and men in the ROK Army, gave the Allies a combat strength of 493,503. Communist forces in Korea were estimated to be sixteen Chinese armies (each about the size of a U.S. corps) and five North Korean armies—a total of about 504,000 troops. These did not include rear-area service

Sgt. THOMAS RANDELL
Heavy Mortar Company/7th Cavalry

Sometimes, when a Chinese unit on a hill withdrew, it would leave behind two or three men manning a well-dug-in machine gun, whose job was to slow us down. Often these men fought to the death.

One cold, snowy morning Easy Company, to which I had been assigned as an FO [forward observer], was ordered to knock out one of these fortified machine-gun nests. Before the men moved out, I met an old acquaintance named Blackburn, whom I had known from our garrison duty days in Tokyo.* He had come to Korea with the division in August, and was one of the few that still remained from the old company. We talked for a while, and he told me about his friends, now all dead or wounded. I asked about a mutual chum and learned he had been hit in the spine and sent home paralyzed.

I moved onto the hill with Blackburn. At one point he and I lay next to each other and peered over the brow of the hill. A rifle grenade fired by a Chinese landed between us on the hard, frozen ground. The grenade had not been armed before being fired, and did not detonate. This was one close call too many for poor Blackburn, who took one look at the unexploded grenade lying next to us and completely cracked up. The man had reached his breaking point, then gone on beyond it.

I never saw Blackburn again, although later I talked to his company commander. He assured me Blackburn had not received a reprimand, and until that moment on that frozen hill, had been a fine and dependable soldier. The burden had become just too heavy to bear—regrettable but unavoidable.

After Blackburn had been led down off the hill, our interpreter tried to talk the Chinese machine gunners out of their pill box. They were having none of it. Pinning them down with rifle and machine-gun fire, three infantrymen crawled close enough to lob grenades into the enemy fortification. The Chinese threw them back, and they exploded in the newly fallen snow. An officer yelled to the GIs to

---

elements or the strength of eight Chinese armies reported, but not confirmed, to be in Korea. Huge reserves waited north of the Yalu in Manchuria to make up losses.

* Before the outbreak of the Korean War, the 1st Cavalry Division had been one of the divisions in the army of occupation in Japan.

release the spoons on the grenades earlier before throwing them. This procedure was followed, and the grenades exploded inside the pill box, killing the three Chinese die-hards.

In a similar incident the following day, our interpreter was successful in talking two Chinese into surrendering. The enemy soldiers walked toward us with their hands raised. One of them suddenly bolted in the opposite direction and was immediately cut down. The other Chinese soldier began to sob. The interpreter asked why he was crying. The man replied that we had just killed his brother.

Sgt. F/C WARREN AVERY
G Company/21st Infantry
Funny, one of our objectives was Hill 1157, the same hill 2d Platoon had been captured on in early January [January 2]. We had a hell of a fight trying to get the Chinese off of it. The objective was taken in company assaults which lasted all day. That night a battalion perimeter was put in on top, and our defense was in depth, foxholes one right behind the other. No one was going to break into our positions. All day Korean mule trains brought up ammunitions, so we had plenty. The Chinese came up at night, blowing their whistles and bugles. By now we were used to this and laughed at it. We mowed them down—wore out a lot of machine-gun barrels. That night we really did a job on the Chinese.

Cpl. DONALD CHASE
B Company/19th Infantry
As usual we were up in the mountains trying to take the highest ground.* In some places the snow had melted, revealing partially decomposed bodies still in their foxholes on hills that had obviously been fought over sometime in 1950. Some of the prisoners we captured had horribly swollen and blackened hands and feet.

On March 11 we were pinned down in midmorning by enemy fire no one could see. I volunteered to climb out on a projecting

---

*The 19th Infantry, a regiment of the 24th Division, was in the IX Corps's west central zone.

ledge to see if I could find its location. Putting my rifle down, I inched out onto a ledge and across a small valley. Off to one side, I saw the enemy machine gun. I didn't think he had spotted me and half turned to reach for my rifle. I was wrong. He turned the gun and got off several rounds, one of which went clear through my thigh. It felt as if I'd been clubbed, and it scared the hell out of me. I flopped off the ledge and fell heavily back behind some cover.

The problem now was to get me down to the aid station, which was somewhere far below. Each company had Korean civilians with them who took the place of mules. The loads these men—we called them Chiggy Bears—were capable of carrying on A-frames strapped to their backs were unbelievable. I was put on a litter carried by four of these human mules, and with a GI guide we started down the mountain.

It was a strange feeling to be wounded. I knew I hadn't been crippled, so I didn't mind too much. I also realized I would now be put into that special group of fighting men who carry scars that show they were "there." Strange as it seems, being wounded makes you just a little bit different.

Once the shock wore off, my leg and hip began to hurt, then throb terribly. Hours went by, and I felt we were lost. Would I be captured? What chance would I have with a wound to survive a prison camp? When we finally reached the aid station it was very dark and had been so for several hours. I'm sure I was crying.*

[*By Sunday, 11 March, elements of Hoge's IX Corps had reached the first phase line—Albany. The 1st Marine Division, forced to slow down earlier and wait for an Army unit on its right flank to catch up, resumed its advance.*]

Pfc. PAUL MARTIN
Reconnaissance Company/1st Marine Division
We received new orders to patrol deeper into the hills south of Hongch'on. In front of our platoon was a wide valley of rice paddies,

---

*Chase was sent to the Swedish Red Cross Hospital in Pusan, where he was operated on. He returned to B Company in mid-April.

with a ridgeline rising behind. Orders were received to cross this valley at dusk. I studied the ground for the rest of the day and memorized the number of rice paddies I'd have to cross before getting to the other side.

When the sun set, the platoon set out. We signaled each other by tapping our rifle butts—two taps meant stop; three, advance. I began counting paddies: four forward, three left, then five forward and I was at the base of the ridge. Crossing in the open at night is extremely nerveracking; one amber cluster overhead would reveal our vulnerability. This night it remained dark, and the platoon reached the other side without incident.

We lay at the bottom of a hill and listened for a half hour before we began to climb. Slowly, the platoon crawled up the hill, stopping often and listening for sounds of the enemy. We eventually reached the crest and before sunrise set up an observation post [OP].

When the sun brightened the sky, I saw across a narrow valley some Chinese leaving a native hut. I then noticed many more moving toward the dark shadows created by the nearby hills. Next, I saw a column of enemy troops walking away from us through the hills. We called to our company to join us, and a few men at a time, they crossed the rice paddy valley and climbed the hill our OP was on. We learned the rifle companies were trying to cut off the Chinese before they could withdraw.

At sunset we returned to the rice paddies of the night before and guided Marine rifle units across them. They climbed the hill and dug in there for the night.

I was assigned to a listening post about 300 yards beyond the defensive perimeter and given orders not to fire except in self-defense. A short time later I noticed movement on a nearby trail. A column of Chinese passed several feet in front of me. The first ten men carried burp guns over their shoulders; after that, only one in three had any weapon. An hour later, another group of around fifty Chinese followed the first column; then another column, farther away, passed. If this continued we would be trapped behind enemy lines, and when the sun rose we'd be helpless, if spotted. At times like this you feel very powerless and close enough to death to touch its corners. Suddenly, our line outfit—above, in their perimeter—opened fire. The

Chinese began yelling and running around. We had evidently taken them by surprise. I could see muzzle flashes on the nearby hills to the rear and knew the first column I'd seen had also been bush-whacked. Bullets skimmed the trees overhead, and it was impossible to know whether it was unfriendly or friendly fire—it didn't seem to make any difference. The noise allowed us to call on a walkie-talkie. We were told to stay put and not give away our positions by firing. A few mortar rounds began to fall around us. We could see small groups of the enemy moving back toward the hills to our front.

When the firing stopped before dawn, we were ordered to return to our own lines. I remember thinking I was on borrowed time.

As the sky grew lighter, the rifle companies began to attack the hills the Chinese had retreated to and, before noon, secured their objectives. My platoon received orders to return to the CP. We arrived in time to learn the division's main objective, Hongch'on, had been taken [15 March].*

[Two days later, while the still-well-dug-in Chinese were being cleared from the hills north of Hongch'on, the UN's commander in chief paid a whirlwind visit to the Marine division.]

Maj. Gen. OLIVER P. SMITH
Commanding General, 1st Marine Division
We got the word from General MacArthur that he was coming over by plane to Wonju [17 March] and wanted to be met there by jeep, and that he wanted to make a tour of the Marine division without getting out of the jeep.† So I took my driver and we met the plane. General Ridgway rode in the jeep with General MacArthur and myself. We started out on the road and I said, "Now, General, we are scattered"—I don't know how many miles we were scattered, maybe sixty miles or so up the road—"and you said you had three hours

---

*On 15 March also, L Company/35th Infantry recrossed the Han and went into division reserve, and Seoul fell to the UN.
† General MacArthur made eight quick visits to the war zone between January and March 1951.

that you could spend here. We can't make the rounds in three hours."
He said, "I've got the time." I said, "All right—if you've got the
time."

So we went and picked up the reserve regiment of the division
[5th Marines], which was the first unit we ran into—[Col. Richard
W.] Hayward was in command of it at the time—and General
MacArthur didn't get out of the jeep; he talked to Hayward. We went
up by my CP, and he didn't get out of the jeep; he shook hands with
some of the staff officers. Then I said, "The 7th Marines are up the
road by the Hongch'on River; that's quite a distance." He said, "I've
got the time." So we took off for the river. I was hoping [Col. Homer
L.] Litzenberg hadn't crossed the darn thing yet, because it was a
deep and fast-flowing river that we would have to ford. But we got to
the south bank of the Hongch'on and Litzenberg had gone on, so we
forded it in the jeep. We actually floated at times, and on the other
side we got out of the jeep. We got it going again and found Litzenberg and talked to him. Then General MacArthur said, "I want to
see an assault battalion." My gosh! We kept going up the road and
found [Maj.] Webb Sawyer and his battalion [1/7];* all the Marines
crowded around. Nobody told these Marines it was General Mac-
Arthur who was coming up the road, but all of them had cameras.
My God, there were a lot of cameras!

After we talked to Sawyer, we drove back to Wonju. I don't
know how many miles it was, but if you've ever ridden for four or
five hours in a roughriding jeep, you've got to go to the head. Well,
no one suggested stopping before we got to Wonju. The general
marched majestically off to his plane and all the rest of us just disappeared. General Ridgway came up to me and asked, "Smith, why
in hell didn't you suggest we stop to take a leak?" "Well," I said,
"you were the senior, and I think it was up to you to suggest that!"
Maybe the old man had a rubber bag or something.†

---

*The day before, the battalion had had to attack bunker after bunker with grenades before the
Chinese were driven off Hill 399.
†General O. P. Smith interview, Oral History Collection, Marine Corps Historical Center,
Washington, D.C. Hereafter, Smith interview, MCHC.

*[By Tuesday, 20 March, Ripper had reached its second phase line—
Buffalo. The Communists had chosen again to withdraw and, as the
U.S. 24th Division had done in that terrible month of July 1950,
trade space for time. The enemy in March, as it had been eight months
before, was made up of North Korean units that would be used to bob
and weave until the Chinese reorganized, regrouped, and mounted
another offensive. The front was now covered in perpetual haze as the
Communists burned green wood in order to hide their movements from
UN aerial observation.*

*The same day, Ripper moved on toward its third objective, phase
line Cairo.]*

S/Sgt. W. B. WOODRUFF, JR.
L Company/35th Infantry

By this time it was known that Alford was first in line for rotation, as
soon as rotation was ordered in effect. We were still short of officers,
and it appeared that when he left I would have to try to fill his boots
as acting platoon leader. I worked even harder, trying to learn everything I possibly could from him. I remembered how green I had been
as a replacement back on December 8, and how very combat-wise
Goggins and Lieutenant Fry had then appeared to me. Within three
months—long ones to be sure, but still just three months—I had
been given Joe Goggins's old job, and it appeared that within another
month I would have Fry's. The jump to acting platoon leader was a
quantum one by comparison with those preceding; I would come
into the map, field glasses, and radio. I would also come into the
daily presence of the Old Man; and in carrying out his orders there
would be no one immediately present that I could turn to except
myself. The looming responsibility looked awesome.

One day [20 March] we climbed a hill [648] that was the grand-
daddy of them all. We were relieving a regiment of the 24th Division. We spent most of a day climbing, arriving atop the hill just at
dark, and near exhausted. We had orders to attack north from this
hill the next morning. In the distance we could see the Hwach'on
Reservoir. We knew that beyond it lay the 38th Parallel, and beyond
that, North Korea.

However, the immediate problem was to put in a line for the night, and we could find no trace of the unit supposedly on our flank. Bob Baker's squad drew the task of locating our left-flank neighbor, and it was long after dark when he returned to report he had found them. There was over a mile gap between our respective lines.

This news made me jumpy, or rather, more jumpy. Besides, I was concerned the exhausting climb had created more than the usual danger of men going to sleep while on guard. About 3 A.M. I was out checking the line for probably the third time, when I noticed a light in the pup tent that had been set up for the CO in the company CP area. The fastenings on the shelter halves were worn out, so that the ends did not fasten securely, exposing a light from inside. I went over, intending to give warning of the light problem, for Captain Weaver had set up practically in the line of foxholes.

When I got close enough to see the crack in the tent, I saw Weaver lying on his stomach and holding a flashlight. On the ground before him, under the light, lay his map, which he was studying intently—at 3 A.M. I then knew why he was awake at such an hour. He was planning the next morning's attack, and would seek all night, if necessary, for a route affording the best cover and concealment, and the best chance for a quick seizure of the objective with the least loss to Love Company. I left as quietly as I had come, and forgot about the problem of the escaping light. The captain was engaged in business of such importance that he did not need to be disturbed, certainly not for a matter as trivial as in infraction of light discipline.

Early next morning [21 March] battalion contacted us by radio and canceled our attack mission, directing that we return to base.

Captain Weaver, ignoring the winding trail we had come up the day before, led us directly off the hill and straight down. Still footsore from yesterday's all-day climb, I took note that in only twenty-five minutes we were back down on the valley floor.

2nd Lt. EDMUND KREKORIAN *
C Battery/3d AAA AW Battalion (SP)/3d Division †

I had just taken command of the 2d Platoon of self-propelled anti-aircraft guns when, one night, the field telephone rang in the command post [24 March]. I picked up the phone and flipped the butterfly switch. "Fireplug X-Ray Two." "This is Fireplug Six" [1st Lt. Tony Zelenko, the battery commander]. I said, "Yes, sir." "Get this down," he ordered. I dug out pencil and paper. "Battalion has assigned your platoon to the infantry [3d Battalion, 15th Infantry] for a close-support mission tomorrow morning. Their objective is Hill Fox Nan Mike. Artillery will fire on the objective from 0600 until 0630. Then your platoon will fire until 0640. After the infantry jumps off, help them any way you can. Are you getting this?"

"Yes, sir."

"You're to meet a liaison officer from the Third Battalion at 0530. He'll be at the road junction about five hundred yards up the main supply road from your CP. Any questions?"

I couldn't think of any.

He asked, "How are you fixed for fuel and ammunition?"

"Okay—we're up on both."

His voice then became very reassuring. "Ed, I know this will be your first mission with us. The Old Man and I will be pulling for you. And Ed, some of the infantry is still skeptical over using ack-ack to support them. Tomorrow you'll get a chance to see them on us. Do a good job, boy."

After he had rung off the switchboard, I cranked the phone a couple of times and waited.

"Fireplug Two," responded the switchboard operator.

"Call all the sections," I told him. "Have the section chiefs and

---

* Born in Boston, Krekorian graduated from high school in 1943, and at age seventeen enlisted in the Marine Corps. He spent eighteen months in the Pacific, and when the war ended was honorably discharged. He enrolled in Emory University but in 1948, bored with academia, enlisted in the Army and was made a 2d lieutenant. In the summer of 1950 Krekorian married; six weeks later the Army shipped him to Korea.

† Battery C of the 3d AAA Battalion had arrived in Korea with the 65th Regimental Combat Team in late September 1950. During the war it fired missions for both the 15th and 65th Infantry Regiments.

squad leaders here at the CP in one hour—at 2200. Do you know where the platoon sergeant is?"

"Yes, sir. He's over at Section Seven, fixing a gun."

"Have him come, too."

"Yes, sir."

"That's all. Break it down."

I settled down to wait for the men. Some of them had to come from areas several miles out, so it would be at least an hour.

I threw a few precious pieces of firewood in the stove and dug out a jar of instant coffee from my gear, along with some little paper sacks of sugar and an old coffee pot I had picked up. There was enough water in the 5-gallon can to almost fill the pot. It made a hissing sound on the hot stove.

In the flickering candlelight I began writing in my notebook the items to be discussed. I remember the battery commander's instructions: Sell ack-ack to the infantry.

Ack-ack is antiaircraft artillery. My platoon was made up of four M19s and four M16s. The M19 was a full-tracked light tank with twin 40-mm cannons capable of firing hundreds of high-explosive shells with phenomenal accuracy. The M16 was a half-tracked armored truck. Its armament was four .50-cal machine guns fixed to a single electrically powered mount. One man firing all four guns could put out thousands of rounds a minute.

These weapons were intended for use against aircraft, but in Korea, many of our antiaircraft units were used against ground targets.

My squad leaders began to arrive at the CP. In the few days I had been in the platoon I had found these men to be smart and capable. They knew their men and equipment well. I liked them.

"There's hot water on the stove," I invited, "and here's some coffee and sugar."

"What, no cream?" someone said.

While the coffee pot made the rounds, the platoon sergeant helped me spread my map on the ground. The men crowded around, alternately stirring and sipping their coffee.

I made a small circle on the map with a blue grease pencil. "Here is our position," I said. "Tomorrow at 0515 we'll assemble here at the CP, move out to the MSR, then up to this road junction, where the Third Battalion liaison officer will meet us."

We moved to a different section of the map as I continued: "This is where the Third Battalion is at present. Tomorrow, after an artillery preparation from 0600 to 0630, we will fire for ten minutes. Here is the objective." I drew a red circle around a hill labeled 644.

The mission was then explained in detail, after which the remaining items in my notebook were taken up. Were there any questions?

A squad leader asked, "Can we carry spare gas cans on our tracks?"

"No—the gooks have started putting incendiaries in anything that looks as if it might have gasoline in it."

"Suppose we run out of gas?"

"There'll be a six-by-six truck at the battery CP, loaded with gas. If we get pushed for fuel, we can radio for it."

Someone else asked about ammunition.

"Carry as much as you can. We can get more, using the same routine as for gasoline."

"How about carbine ammunition and hand grenades?"

I thought a minute; several tanks had been overrun by Communists in the early days of the war. "Bring plenty," I told them.

I was ready to dismiss the men, when I remembered the last item on my list.

"Wait a minute before you go," I said. "Tomorrow we won't have a forward controller with us, which means there won't be any air support. The tanks will be in another area, so we won't have tank support. In other words, tomorrow the ack-ack will do all the softening up. We've got the firepower the infantry needs. Let's sell 'em on that idea."

The men left the CP quietly.

I blew out the candles, took off my boots, and wormed my way into the cold sleeping bag. I reached for the field phone and asked the operator to give me a call at 0330.

The ground seemed mighty hard as I tried to burrow a ditch for my hip. I was too excited to sleep. I was worried and scared, too. A wrong order, a misinterpreted order, or an error in judgment could

result in many casualties—in my platoon or in the infantry. It was
frustrating to lie there and try to anticipate every unexpected development. I found myself up against a mental brick wall of anxiety,
anticipation, excitement, and fatigue. I prayed, asking God to be with
us the next day; then I drifted off.

The ringing field phone snapped me awake.

"Sir, you asked me to call you at 0330." It was the switchboard
operator.

I mumbled, "Thanks—would you call the squad for a readiness
report?"

"The platoon sergeant did that about half hour ago. All squads
are ready except number seven. It's got generator trouble. The sergeant's gone out to look at it."

"Thank you." I replaced the phone, fumbling around in the
dark for its box. I lit a couple of candles, pulled on my combat boots,
and thanked Heaven for a good platoon sergeant.

The stove was out. The water left on it the night before was now
ice. However, the water in the canteen I had slept with was still
water. It was enough for a combat-type shave. I became aware of the
steady patter of rain on the CP roof. "Hell!" I muttered, and nicked
myself again.

The growing roar of engines told me the platoon was arriving. I
finished dressing. Since I slept with my clothes on, this was a simple
procedure. The finishing touch was my holster, into which I slipped
the pistol from the sleeping bag—my other nighttime companion.
Into another went 100 rounds of pistol ammunition—the heavy weight
was reassuring. I picked up a couple of candy bars, slapped on my
helmet, and stepped out into the rain.

Five vehicles were already lined up at the CP. "Who's missing?"
I asked the platoon sergeant.

"Section Two Four is stuck in a creek bed; Section Two Seven
got lost in the dark. I sent Two Five after both of them."

The radio in a nearby M19 crackled: "Fireplug X-Ray Two, this
is Fireplug Jig, over."

I walked to the vehicle. The man inside handed me a mike.
"This is X-Ray Two. Go ahead, Jig."

"King and Nan are with me. We're on our way in."

"Roger, out." I handed the mike back.

The rain was falling with a vengeance. The men looked soaked and they *were* soaked; yet their spirits were up and their joking did much for my own morale. At last the missing tracks pulled into line. I climbed aboard the lead M19 and spoke into the mike: "This is X-Ray Two—report in order."

Back came the voices with rapid precision: "How—Item—Jig—King—Love—Mike—Nan—Oboe."

"This is X-Ray Two—move out."

The platoon rumbled over wet grass and mud, then turned onto the main supply road. My orders were to proceed up the MSR some 500 yards to meet the liaison officer from the infantry. I hoped we wouldn't miss him, as this road went clear to the Yalu. I thought of the infantry boys we would be supporting and said a little prayer for them.

A hand touched my shoulder; the squad leader pointed fifty yards ahead, where a jeep was parked just off the road. The platoon ground to a halt. A major got out of the jeep and came over to me. "Are you the ack-ack commander?"

"Yes, sir."

"The colonel would like to see you a few minutes. You can leave your tracks here and ride in my jeep."

"Okay," I said. Then to the squad leader, "Call the platoon sergeant, tell him where I've gone, and to keep the platoon here until I get back."

I hopped in the back of the major's jeep, and we tore off down a small trail, past some demolished huts, to a wrecked schoolhouse which now served as a battalion command post. As we entered a large classroom, I noted blankets over all the windows and maps and charts over all the walls. The raspy hum of Coleman lanterns blended with the several conversations. A scholarly-looking officer came over to us. He looked from the major to me.

The major introduced us. "This is the ack-ack commander, Colonel."

"Oh, yes, how are you, Lieutenant?"

We shook hands, then walked to some maps on the wall. He pointed and said, "The Communists have an estimated two battalions on and around our objective. They mean to hold it. We mean to take it. There are machine guns up there, and we've had reports of antitank guns; but so far no tanks or self-propelled guns have been spotted."

This was vital information. Ack-ack is very vulnerable to tanks.

The colonel talked briefly for a few more minutes. He asked if I had any questions.

I replied, "No, sir."

We shook hands again. "Thanks very much for coming. Good luck," he said. I saluted and walked out.

Back with my men, I ordered the platoon off the MSR and down a muddy mess that had been a road. We crossed several swollen streams without mishap. I strained to find some landmark I could identify. When we tried to climb some slippery hills, the half-tracks began to slide sideways down the hill. It must have been a combination of driver skill and God's help that kept them from tipping over and crushing the crews. The more powerful and stable M19s went to the rescue and towed their buddies up the hill. At last we were deployed in firing position, facing what I thought was the objective.

The platoon sergeant reported all units ready to fire. "Great," I told him. "Send two men and a walkie-talkie to the infantry. Have them call in any targets they want engaged."

With my binoculars I tried to poke a hole in the rain and fog. It was awful. I could not make out the objective, which meant the platoon couldn't fire. We could hear the slamming-door bang of the artillery behind us and the swoosh of the shells passing over. We could hear the crunch as the shells exploded on the objective, but we could not see the bursts. Then the artillery stopped. All was quiet, except for the rain and a machine gun far off.

Infantry began moving through our positions, down the far side of the hill, disappearing into the fog. A message arrived from the two men we had sent to the infantry. The objective was taken. The Chinese had abandoned it when the artillery began.

I was disgusted. I had done a fine job selling ack-ack to the infantry—we hadn't fired a single round! "Let's head back to the MSR," I told the platoon sergeant. Soon the platoon was slipping and sliding its way back down the muddy hills that had been so much effort to climb. I decided to call the battery commander to give the platoon report.

"Fireplug Six, this is Fireplug X-Ray Two, over."

"This is Fireplug Six, over," came the answer.

"Mission is over; no rounds fired. We're on our way to the MSR."

"Too bad, Ed. Maybe next time."

"Roger," I said. "Over and out."

An hour later we pulled onto the MSR. Much to everyone's surprise, the battery commander was there in his jeep waiting for us.

"What's up?" I asked him.

He spread out a map on the hood of the jeep. The rain soaked it good. "Right after I got your message, I got a call from the Old Man. There's an infantry company over here"—he outlined an area with his finger—"that's run into a hornet's nest. They're pinned down by much machine-gun fire. We can't get any planes because of the weather. A tank went down to help but got hit. Do you want to have a go at it?"

"I'm for it," I said eagerly. "How about you, Sergeant?"

"What are we waiting for?"

The platoon followed the battery commander's jeep. We headed north and soon passed through a village. The Korean huts were in ruins, and the ruins were burning. Farther on, we noted, white phosphorous was setting some woods on fire. We stopped by a small side road. The battery commander got out of his jeep and walked back to us.

"Ed, down this road about two thousand yards you'll pass a village with a shrine on the left. Five hundred yards beyond the village, the road passes between two long, narrow hills. The road then drops down to another village. A friendly tank is knocked out in the village. The gooks are in the hills on beyond. Our troops are between the village and the gooks. I've got to leave you here and get over to the First Platoon."

"I'm worried about our gas—it should be getting low."

"Okay," he said, "I'll radio the battery CP and order the gas truck to meet you in the first village."

I waved good-bye as he drove back down the MSR.

The eight tracks made quite a noise moving down the road toward the first village. The rain had slowed to a fine mist. As we passed through the village, the sun began making efforts to break through. This was a good omen. The sounds of combat began to reach us over the noise of the engines, and I spotted the two hills between which the road ran. They looked like good positions for ack-ack. I called the trailing six tracks: "Jig, King, Love, Mike, Nan, Oboe, move into position on the right."

The lead M19 and M16 continued down the road, past the two hills, to descend into the village. We moved through the town to the far corner. The hit tank was there, sitting quietly beside a partly collapsed hut. We parked behind it. Only a lone tank corporal was to be seen.

"What's going on?" I asked him.

"There's an antitank gun up there—it got my tank but hasn't fired since. I think I can show you about where it is." He took my binoculars, braced them on the edge of his tank, focused, then took his head away so that I could peer through. All I saw was rocks, dirt, and more rocks. Then I did see something shiny, like a brass shell case, or something. Looking around with the binoculars I saw many Communists, some of them moving boldly over the crest of the hill. We would soon put a stop to that.

Suddenly, machine-gun bullets stitched the ground by our feet. The corporal and I jumped behind his tank. "Lieutenant, you'd better get the hell out of here," he said. Something sounding like a hornet whizzed by my ear. I ran to the M19. "Go, man, go!" I told the driver.

Again, the machine gun stitched the ground, a long burst this time. Closer, too. The M19 engine roared as we raced for the protection of the two hills we had passed. We hadn't quite reached them when the first AT [antitank] shell hit the ground some thirty yards away. By the time the second round hit we were behind the hills, safe. We pulled into firing position.

With my binoculars I found the spot the tank corporal had shown me. Figures were moving toward the crest of the hill. I squeezed the mike button: "Fireplug units, stand by to fire fifteen seconds on my indicated round, then shift fire to sectors assigned." I knew the platoon sergeant had given each track an area to cover. To my own gunner I ordered, "Sight on that double peak at ten o'clock."

"I'm on it," he responded.

"Come down that draw to the left. When you reach the end, go right five mills and fire one round."

I watched the twin snouts of the cannons move down, stop, then move over and stop again. Wham! The tracer streaked for the hills and burst in a puff of black smoke. It was too far to the right. "Go left two mills, fire," I ordered.

The twin snouts moved slightly—again a single tracer sped off. The black smoke appeared again, in line with the target but a few yards behind. "Add one mill, fire ten rounds." I squeezed the mike button: "Fire on next round."

Again a single burst of black smoke appeared on the hill ahead. Our position erupted with noise as eight 40-mm cannons and sixteen 50-cal. machine guns poured their fire into an area about twenty yards by twenty yards. I watched as the tracers then swung to pre-designated sectors of fire. Dozens of figures began running back toward the ridge. We poured it on for everything we were worth. Periodically, our machine guns swept the ridge clean, then eased down, spraying the area to within 100 yards of our infantry. The bullets made little twinkles of light as they hit rock. Black smoke from the rapid-firing forties began to cloud over the hill as the tracers leaped for cracks, crevices, caves, emplacements—anywhere that a man could hide. The commies must have thought they were caught in a cloud-burst of lead. At last I ordered, "Fireplug units—cease fire, repeat, cease fire."

The noise diminished, then stopped. A voice behind me said, "Mighty fine shooting, Lieutenant."

I turned to see an infantry captain and his radioman standing by my M19. Together we watched the black smoke over the hill turn gray and disappear. We watched his men move cautiously past still forms. The radioman spoke briefly into his mike, then handed the mike and headset to the captain. He listened for a moment. His face grew serious. I was worried. What was the matter? Had my platoon hit some of his men by accident? The captain's face changed to a huge grin. "We've got the hill," he told us happily. "We didn't lose a single man."

The battery commander must have been sitting on his radio waiting for my call. "Why in hell haven't you sent me any progress reports?" he snapped as soon as I called him. "Do you think this is your private war?"

"The infantry have the hill," I informed him. "How about our gas and ammo?"

"I know the infantry took the hill—I had to get my information from the Old Man." His voice suddenly sounded pleased. "It looks good, Ed. I hear you made it real easy for the footsloggers. The gas and ammo trucks are at the village you passed on your way in. I thought you all might like some hot chow, so I sent the chow truck along."

I ordered the platoon to form on the road. We headed toward the little Korean village, eager for the hot chow waiting there for us.*

[The enemy continued to withdraw and in many places broke off contact. Ripper averaged gains of thirty-five miles a day, and toward the end of a wet and muddy March, the operation came to a close. Eighth Army stood poised on line Idaho, just below the 38th Parallel.]

Cpl. JAMES CARDINAL
Headquarters Company/3d Battalion/5th Cavalry

March 27, 1951

Dear Folks,

We are now in Corps reserve about twenty miles south of the 38th Parallel in central Korea. Before being relieved we had advanced to within eight miles of the 38th Parallel and into the city of Ch'unch'on. I certainly hope we don't cross the Parallel again. If we do cross the line there will be more fighting, more casualties and less chance of rotation home.

Pfc. DAVE KOEGEL
B/7

Rumor was, we were not going to stop at the 38th Parallel—a situation that gave painful promise of our continued presence in Korea. The weather turned quite pleasant and was in contrast to the cold

---

*Edmund A. Krekorian, "A Lesson In Fire Power," V.F.W. *Magazine* (January 1959), 14–15, 34–37. The operations report for this mission (25 March 1951) states 462 rounds of 40-mm and 1,400 rounds of 50-caliber were fired. Fifteen enemy were killed and forty captured. There were no U.S. casualties.

rain and mud we had endured in late March. Our heavy down sleeping bags were replaced by lighter bags, made of a single layer of wool with a water-repellent cover.

[Rumor turned to fact when Ridgway followed Ripper with Operation Rugged, another limited phase-line advance toward a new objective— phase line Kansas. This new line would command high ground north of the 38th Parallel and include in the center the large water barrier of the Hwach'on Reservoir. The 115 running miles of phase line Kansas—from Munsan-ni on the Imjin River, to Yangyang on the Sea of Japan—would also create a base of operations designed to threaten the Chinese build-up in the Iron Triangle, a heavily fortified valley bounded by Ch'orwon, Kumhwa, and P'yonggang.

The UN's fifth offensive in two months got underway on 5 April.*]

S/Sgt. W. B. WOODRUFF, JR.
L Company/35th Infantry
Sometime in early April 1951 we reached and crossed the 38th Parallel. The chief clue that we had crossed was that the map quality deteriorated. The U.S. forces had updated, corrected, and modernized the old Japanese maps covering South Korea, and reprinted them in color and with much data shown in English. The only available maps of North Korea, however, were in black and white with most information not reprinted in English. In the most mountainous areas, where we now were, the contour lines were so numerous as to create an almost meaningless maze.

Pfc. DAVE KOEGEL
B/7
Keeping up morale seemed to be a major project of the rumor mills, which were grinding out continually hopeful views of what lay ahead. Before Thanksgiving and the Chosin Reservoir it had been "Out of

---

* Elements of the ROK I Corps had crossed the Parallel on 27 March and captured the North Korean town of Yangyang four days later.

Korea by Christmas." When we had dragged ourselves out of the mountains and were in the Bean Patch, the absolutely straight scoop was "Marines would never again be used outside of Naval gunfire." The division's assignment in February to the west central zone [IX Corps] killed that rumor as dead as "Home by Christmas." The next one was "We will not again cross the 38th Parallel." On April Fools' Day the news turned grim, and that rumor too sank from sight.*

In the spring of 1951, with no hope of the war ending and some of the veterans of the brigade's action in the Pusan Perimeter rotating home, we began to speculate on when our own turns would come. We sat around and counted the guys ahead of us on the priority list.

S/Sgt. W. B. WOODRUFF, JR.
L Company/35th Infantry

Sometime about mid-April [the sixth] there came our last day for this tour in the line. That night we were to link up with the 24th Infantry and be relieved by them, the 35th reverting to division reserve the following day. There is something about the last day in the line that makes it different from the ones preceding. We were getting pretty well exhausted. But it was more a mental problem; nobody liked the idea of getting through twenty or twenty-five days and then becoming a casualty on the last day. On this morning we were to begin with an attack on the next hill, then continue the advance across an extremely rough and brush-covered area. The map indicated it would be one ridge after another, all day going either straight up or straight down, ridgelines zig-zagging in all directions. To this extent the map proved entirely accurate.

Breakfast chow was late that morning, delaying our jump-off. My sense of foreboding increased; I would have much preferred to climb that first hill at first light. The arrival of a section of tanks to support us did not help my feelings. On account of the ground, they would be able to accompany us only a few hundred yards; in other words, to the base of the first ridge. There they would assist us in

---

*The 7th Marines, attached to the 1st Cavalry Division, advanced northward in early April and crossed the 38th Parallel on 4 April.

taking the hill, but after that we would be on our own. Also, adjusting artillery or mortar fire in this rough country could be extremely difficult, and if brought in, they were apt to be ineffective. I looked for a bad day.

The first ridge was of a soft sandy soil, and hard climbing. Just as we neared the top, one of the supporting tanks opened up with its machine gun, tracer bullets striking the ground no more than ten yards above us. I frantically waved them to cease fire. At that time I had never served in tanks and had no real feel for their capabilities. I did not fully realize that the turret-mounted machine gun was equipped with telescopic sights and capable of extremely accurate fire; in fact for all I knew, they were firing the bow gun, which was much less accurate. I later learned they had sighted a Chinese on top of the hill. By thus keeping his head down and distracting his attention, the tank may have saved us a lot of trouble. For immediately afterward, Baker reached the top, being the first man to do so. There, he found himself face to face with a Chinese soldier. I heard him yell "Hey!" at the top of his voice. When he yelled, the Chinese had thrown down his rifle and run like a rabbit; he got clean away. By the time I got to Baker to get these details, Bob was laughing at himself. He had been so taken by surprise that he forgot, for an instant, the rifle he was carrying.

The Chinaman's presence raised a big question as to what the enemy's plans were. Was the lookout's mission to call out a defending force, or merely to let them know it was time to withdraw? We continued over the successive ridges, moving slowly and cautiously. At one point, while taking a break on top of a ridge from which we had a good view of a portion of the front, we heard one of our KATUSAs [Korean Augmentation to the U.S. Army] yell, and saw him point northward. Out there at a distance of maybe 800 yards we saw a detachment of Chinese moving across our front. In the same instant, out of the corner of my eye, I saw our Korean throw down his rifle. I looked around to see what would cause this unusual behavior. In a state of excitement he was pulling out of his pouch a hand grenade, which he immediately drew back and threw with a mighty effort in the direction of the enemy force. He got pretty good range, but of course fell about 750 yards short. We did not take time out to laugh at the Korean until later (he was quite embarrassed); we

put some long-range rifle fire on the enemy and had the limited
consolation of seeing them take up the double time until they disappeared from view behind another ridgeline.

About this time we entered an area of burned-out forest. Everywhere the brush and stunted trees were still smoldering and smoking;
some were still aflame. We assumed this had been caused by our
artillery, but were afterward told the CCF had set the fire to assist in
covering their withdrawal. It would have worked better if there had
been real timber to burn. As it was, our visibility was considerably
reduced, the smoke was irritating, and it was even harder to locate
any known point on the map. I gave up, but Alford kept worrying
about it, hardly taking his eyes off that map the entire day. He had
his rifle slung and was holding the map in both hands as we walked,
looking constantly from it to the surrounding hills and ridges. The
smoke was thick as a light fog, giving the scene an eerie quality. The
heat was also noticeable.

We saw nothing more of the enemy. About sundown we emerged
from the burning brush onto a road. Up the road no more than a
hundred yards was the village that was our last objective for the day.
How he did it I could never figure, but Sergeant Alford had brought
us through once more, direct to our assigned objective after a long
day's march through the burning forest and rough country. I had
been totally lost for hours. Our only casualty was one of the new
draftees who had stumbled and stabbed himself in the eye on his
neighbor's bayonet. The wound was not serious.

Next morning [7 April] the 24th Regiment was hustling about,
taking over our zone. Soon we entrucked and were en route to our
reserve position.

Cpl. DON THOMAS *
K Company/23d Infantry
I arrived at the K Company command post on April 7. Some things
never change, for we still had the same old water problem—not fro-

---

* A Californian from Merced, Thomas had joined the Army in 1947, when he was fifteen years
old. Discharged two years later, he reenlisted shortly after the Korean War began. Thomas was

zen, just scarce on the tops of mountains. But the smells were different: The fields were fertilized with human waste. I was with the company CP for about two days before catching up with the rifle platoons. We replacements arrived with a load of supplies at the base of the tallest mountain I had ever seen in Korea [in X Corps's central zone]. A group of South Koreans were there to lug the supplies up the mountain to the platoons. However, it was obvious at once that there were more supplies than Koreans to carry them. The excess was distributed amongst us returning GIs. I began to climb, carrying thirteen bandoliers of rifle ammunition, four grenades, a box of .30-caliber machine-gun ammo, and a can of four 60-mm mortar rounds— plus my own rifle, poncho, and blanket. I was out of condition after my months in hospital and weighed about 200 pounds.

The pack train started out at about nine in the morning. Not long afterward I unloaded the mortar rounds on someone. A couple of hours later I managed to get rid of the machine-gun ammo. All that day we climbed, and around seven, when we weren't yet at the top, stopped and camped on the trail. Twelve hours later we began climbing again and reached the rifle platoons just before noon chow.

At the summit the trail led to the 1st Platoon area. Most of the guys were out of their holes taking it easy. I began to look around to see if any of the guys I used to know were still here. Sure enough, there he was—Pete "the Short Man" Naranjo from Holbrook, Arizona. In November he had been in the 3d Squad while I had been in the 1st. Pete and George [Chamberlain, the platoon sergeant] used to kid about who was tallest. Both were just over five feet. Pete asked me to join his squad. He was the squad leader now. We got an okay from Jack Brown, the new platoon sergeant. I learned Brown was a veteran of the Second World War, in which he'd been a master sergeant. He had lost his stripes in the States for fighting and drinking, and had been reduced in rank to a Pfc. When the war broke out he had asked for service in Korea in order to get his stripes back—which he did on the average of a stripe a month. [In June, Brown would again make master sergeant.]

---

shipped to Korea in November and met his rifle company in the Ch'ongch'on River Valley two days before the Chinese launched their massive winter offensive against Eighth Army. He had been wounded near Hoengsong on the last day of 1950.

Pete told me Masters had been killed the week before by our own artillery. I paired up with Pete, and we dug and shared the same foxholes for a while in the area. This was a good break for me, as the hike up the mountain had really done me in. The squad leader and whoever paired up with him did not have to participate in the nightly 50 percent alert [one man awake, one man asleep]. Therefore, I was able to get much needed rest until I worked myself back into shape. It didn't take long, not with C rations and daily hill climbing.

We didn't have to wear many clothes now—just a set of fatigues, regular boots, and the steel helmet. We carried a blanket rolled up and tied to the back of our pack harness. A poncho was again hung over the rear of the cartridge belt, and we still carried the canteen, shovel, bayonet, and first-aid packet on the belt, and ten clips of rifle ammunition in our pockets. The rolled-up blanket was tied with short sections of communications wire. Later we would use "liberated" nylon parachute cord.

This period is described in the Division history book as the "April Preliminary." The company and rest of the 2d Division ranged over mountain peaks and ridges in a screening and patrolling mission which was intended to find out the enemy's intention, strength, and location. We sometimes would take over positions the enemy had held moments before. At dark we'd set up a perimeter defense on a commanding ridge or peak, and dig in for the night. It rained a lot. We would spread our ponchos over the holes, with three sticks to support the front. This allowed us a slot to look through, down the slope. We also rigged a long stick above the hole and tied the center of the poncho to it so the rainwater would run off. Then we'd add straw to the bottom of the hole, and presto—instant home. We moved every day and dug in every night. Usually no fires were allowed, so we ate cold C rations.

Sgt. GLENN HUBENETTE
F Company/7th Regiment
I returned to the company around April 8 after goldbricking for six days in the big repo depot [replacement depot] north of Seoul. My wound was still draining, and I had diarrhea again and felt I needed

a few more days' rest. I was traveling with Joe Kudelka, who was wounded at Huksu-ri and only now returning to the company.* The first sergeant had finally caught us through a morning chow head-count, and that afternoon he saw to it that Joe and I were on the truck bound for the 7th Regiment.

Although on my return I was given a squad in the 1st Platoon, I did not forget my buddies in the 2d Platoon, and brought them two fifths of Four Roses. One morning we were moving up to the front [phase line Kansas], when we were told to take a ten-minute break. I broke out the two fifths. Soon 2d Platoon was feeling no pain. We sang some raunchy barracks ballads, like "The First Sergeant's Whore." The "Top" [first sergeant] yelled back to us, "Knock off that goddamn singing!"

Pfc. DAVE KOEGEL
B/7
The action in the early weeks of April took the form of brief encounters when the enemy would resist our hilltop assaults on their bunkers. Heavy artillery barrages and close air support from Corsairs and P-51s firing rockets and dropping bombs made our work easier. We'd battle rearguard units while the main body of enemy troops withdrew northward.

Pfc. PAUL MARTIN
Reconnaissance Company/1st Marine Division
My patrol crossed the Pukhan River in rubber boats and advanced into the hills [8 April] to see if we could link up with the ROK 6th Division [on the Marine division's left]. We passed many undefended ridgelines and, when we had not made contact with the ROKs that night, set up a defensive perimeter.

Around sunrise I spotted some Chinese on a ridge to our north, watching us. We quietly withdrew. Reaching the banks of the Pukhan

---

*Huksu-ri was a road junction in North Korea approximately twenty miles west of Majon-dong, which the Chinese had attacked in early December.

at midday we discovered the river had evidently been hit by a tidal
wave and was now much, much wider and flowing too swiftly for us
to cross it in our rubber boats.* We walked about six miles downstream to use the pontoon bridge the engineers had built, but found
it had broken loose. The patrol spent the rest of the day north of the
river, and that night was picked up by some DUKWs [amphibious
trucks].

I went out on several more patrols in succeeding days, but they
were all conducted without incident.

[During the third week of April, UN forces crept forward; Hwach'on
Dam was captured on the sixteenth; and on the east coast, Taep'o-ri
fell. The I and IX Corps felt their way toward phase line Utah and
encountered negligible resistance. Elsewhere along the front, the Communists broke off contact with X Corps and the ROKs. By 19 April,
I and IX Corps were on Utah and preparing to enlarge the bulge by
advancing to phase line Wyoming.

It was during this period of cautious advance toward phase lines
Kansas then Utah that many of Eighth Army's frontline units had a
chance to pull back and go into either division or corps reserve. For a
few days at least, GIs and leathernecks got a chance to stand and
stretch and not worry about being picked off by a sniper's bullet; to
eat hot chow three times a day; to shower with hot water; to change
clothes; to defecate in a real toilet; to sleep on level ground in something with walls and a roof—and to grow restless. Men found in their
own ways that the adrenalin high of combat was a hard habit to kick.]

Cpl. JAMES CARDINAL
Headquarters Company/3d Battalion/5th Cavalry

Dear Folks,
We are camped about twenty miles NE of Seoul and have been
in reserve since March 25th, Easter. I figure they're holding us

---

*The enemy opened several penstocks, and spillway gates of the Hwach'on Reservoir, sending
floodwaters through the Pukhan Valley on 9 April.

back for the big Communist offensive expected when the rainy season begins in May. Anyways, the war seems very far away. It's just like garrison duty back here. We have reveille and retreat, inspections—have to wash and shave every day and keep my clothing clean and shoes polished. Of course all this nonsense will go out the window just as soon, as we return to the front lines; meanwhile, it's a pain in the neck.

Sgt. F/C WARREN AVERY
G Company/21st Infantry

At one point we captured a large enemy force. Our trucks ran back and forth stacked full of Chinese soldiers. Along with the troops, we captured all kinds of equipment. Anyone who wanted one could get his very own Mongolian pony. Some of the boys from Texas and out West were hot to ride them; they used to have rodeos down in a dry creek bed. Everyone was having a ball until one boy was thrown and broke a leg. The battalion commander ordered us to give the ponies to a neighboring ROK unit. We figured, since the Koreans didn't want to fight, they could use the animals to resupply us. Next thing we found out was that the ROKs had had a big feast and eaten all the ponies.

[On 10 April the Marine division received orders to stop where it was. The leathernecks spent the next ten days patrolling and strengthening their position.]

Pfc. DOUG MICHAUD
Headquarters & Service Company/1/5

With time on our hands, we "requisitioned" a rooster from a nearby village. The six guys in the tent decided to fatten him up before eating him. We didn't dare let him outside the tent for fear he'd be stolen by some other Marines—you have to understand, there was a big difference between our requisitioning and others' stealing. We made a leash out of the laces from our boondockers [boots], and with it tied the rooster to the ridgepole in the center of the tent. The rooster had the run of the tent on his leash, and he flopped around all over our racks. Once he was fat enough, we'd have ourselves a feast. First morning, before sunrise, the bird began crowing. Everyone threw at him whatever was handy—"Shut up y'sumbitch!" Second morning was a repeat of the first, with boondockers flying through the air. The third morning the rooster awoke before dawn and did his thing again. I heard "You sonovabitch!"—"*Squawk!*" One of the guys had reached out and wrung its neck. We ate the bird that night.

Pfc. DAVE KOEGEL
B/7

Spring was all around, President Truman had just fired MacArthur, and we had little to do but think up ways to torment the new replacements, who probably found sitting around the front lines pretty exciting. One such fuzzy-cheeked private became the all-too-willing fish in a story that grew to incredible proportions.

We were camped for a few days on a ridgeline, hearing and seeing nothing of our Chinese enemies. Someone suggested to this young replacement that as the newest man, he'd have to draw outpost duty. Pointing to a nearby hill, the veteran said, "That's crawling with Chinks. They'll probe us tonight—probably send a company." The kid's duty was to patrol the base of our ridge alone and warn the rest of us when he spotted the Chinese. He bit the bait. Sure, he'd do it alone—even when he was told few men had ever returned from such a mission. "Okay," he said. The kid was *game*. Unable or unwilling to stop the prank, we led the recruit to the platoon leader, who immediately picked up the drift of things and added a few more suicidal details of his own. When the kid continued to accept the mission, the sergeant, a more principled man than we, suddenly exclaimed, "Good grief, I can't stand this anymore!" He then explained to the replacement how he had become the platoon's entertainment for the afternoon, and that the kid's time to show his grit would surely come but not manning a lonely outpost in the face of certain death. In truth, we were all relieved, as we had not anticipated the guts the kid had shown. Putting someone's strength on trial was a good deal less satisfying than testing his weaknesses. We spent the rest of the day playing poker and making up stories about our sexual prowess.

S/Sgt. W. B. WOODRUFF, JR.
L Company/35th Infantry
During this reserve period new men came in, in considerable numbers. It thereafter became common to have the platoons 50 percent overstrength—at least, while in reserve. After a tour in the line we would be as shorthanded as ever, but then be given another big bunch of the draftees. They were good enough men, but young, confused, bewildered, and with no conception of infantry combat. If they lasted long enough, they learned, just as we had. Too many of them did not last long enough. Our nonbattle losses were probably the heaviest; too many were physically or mentally not up to it. I remember one man, seemingly older than most, maybe in his late twenties, who said he had been a professional boxer. He convinced us—he was the "punchiest" individual I ever hope to see. At night he would lose his head, and anybody who got within twenty yards was apt to be shot, bayoneted, or grenaded. Made it tough on sergeants accustomed to checking the foxhole line two or three times every night. You had to know his location, call out to him, and be fully identified before daring to approach. Others showed up with back backs, bad knees, bad elbows, et cetera. I gained a poor opinion of the screening process that made riflemen out of these guys. Sometimes it appeared the infantry got more than its share of the culls. But there were many exceptions. As rotation got underway, some of these new men quickly began rising in our esteem and in the responsibilities assigned them.

The day came when Joe Alford bid us good-bye—characteristically, this did not take much time, nor many words—and departed on rotation. He was gone only two or three days, because there was a mixup in orders somewhere. When he returned, nobody was happier to see him than me. I had things in a real mess. What I had done was try to do too much, supervise too much, get too involved in petty details. It is a common error on the part of a new leader or commander, at all levels; and I have since seen many others make the same mistake. I did not discuss this with Alford, but his return gave me a chance to sit back and see what I had done wrong. It is also likely he detected the problem; he may well have helped me understand what I was doing wrong, without ever alluding to it directly. As I say, he was a complex man.

Within a couple of days, Alford left again and this time did not return. Now I went about my job differently and had no more trouble. By this I mean I gave mission-type orders, and let the squad leaders figure out the details of accomplishment. Not only were they capable, but this method allowed them to fully develop their own capacities.

Pfc. DAVE KOEGEL
B/7
On April 21 we moved unopposed onto the forward slope of a hill well advanced from our last fortified position. The enemy seemed nowhere in the area, and the encampment took on a casual air. That the enemy seemed equally unwary of our presence was attested to by a lone Chinese soldier who sauntered out in front of us as if nothing was wrong. He was armed with a machine pistol and may have been a courier or scout. He never completed his solitary mission, as he was cut down almost at once.

Sgt. GLENN HUBENETTE
F Company/7th Infantry
We were dug in along a big irrigation canal up on the Hant'an River.*
Each night we had sent forward one squad to act as a listening post, and on April 21, a Saturday, it was my squad's turn. Not one of us knew it would be the last peaceful night we'd have for some time.

Cpl. DONALD CHASE
B Company/19th Infantry
I rejoined my company on April 21. My wound had healed fairly well in the Swedish hospital. To get it closed the doctors had had to cut out a large piece of tissue, which somewhat weakened the leg. I was nevertheless anxious to get back to the company. It had been about six weeks since I'd been hit in the thigh, and if I didn't return

---

*The Hant'an flows into the Imjin River near the head of the Uijongbu Corridor.

soon, I was afraid I'd be sent to a different outfit—something every-one tried to avoid. Sometimes, though, it happened. So even though I wasn't 100 percent recovered, with the shortage of frontline man-power it was not difficult to show that I could be returned to active duty.

When I got back to the company it struck me right away how many new faces there were. When I asked about certain fellers, the answer was "dead" or "stateside wound." Very few men did I recog-nize as having been with the company when I'd been hit. There was little time to reflect on the meaning of this or much of anything else, for the next day the Chinese launched their major spring offensive.

[*During the first five months of the Korean War, General MacArthur had not opposed Washington's handling of the fighting. However, once the Chinese entered the war in November, he began to disagree—mildly at first, then more vehemently—with the directives under which he operated in Korea. The general wanted to bomb the enemy's bases in Manchuria and use other all-out methods to bring the conflict to an end. President Harry Truman feared such measures might lead to global war. He also found MacArthur's megaphone diplomacy to be objectionable and a direct challenge to his authority as the nation's commander in chief. The war of words between Tokyo and Washing-ton escalated in early 1951. Truman finally decided he could no longer accept the general's open disagreement on national policy and on 11 April ordered the chairman of the Joint Chiefs of Staff to send MacArthur a message directing him immediately to turn over his com-mands to Lt. Gen. Matthew B. Ridgway. Lieutenant General James A. Van Fleet was sent from Washington to replace Ridgway as com-mander of Eighth Army and attached forces. General MacArthur and his family left Japan for the United States on 16 April.*

A confident Van Fleet, a firm believer in the principles of offen-sive warfare, was prepared to keep Eighth Army moving northward, but was warned by Ridgway of an expected Chinese offensive. That the Chinese would attack was a foregone conclusion—the only ques-tions remaining were where and when.]

ATTACK

---

22 April–25 June 1951

The UN Command had been waiting for weeks. Along the front lines the Americans, ROKs, Thais, British, Filipinos, and Belgians had also waited. The night of 22 April, the waiting stopped. By the light of a full moon, the enemy hurled four army groups, nearly 350,000 men, against the seventy miles of the UN's lines defended by the U.S. I and IX Corps.* Suddenly, all the hills between Munsan-ni and the Hwach'on Reservoir were on fire; and in the brilliant flashes of thousands upon thousands of explosions, the Chinese could be seen moving forward.

In the west, the full thunder of the Chinese assault crashed down around the British 29th Independent Brigade, which had the unfortunate luck of holding the hills above the Imjin River near the tiny village of Choksong. Through the brigade's sector ran the twisting road that from time immemorial had been the main route of invasion from the north, and the one the Chinese had decided would carry their victorious armies southward in April 1951, through Uijongbu and into Seoul.

---

* General Van Fleet's frontline strength numbered about 230,000 men, with another 190,000 infantrymen in reserve. Eighteen fighter-bomber groups were also available.

Twenty-ninth Brigade had positioned astride this road two of Britain's oldest and most illustrious combat units. The 1st Battalion, Royal Northumberland Fusiliers, formed in 1674, was dug in on the right; the 1st Battalion, The Gloucestershire Regiment, raised in 1694, was on the left. These battalions were supported by the 45th Field Regiment, Royal Artillery. Behind, in reserve, were the Royal Ulster Rifles and the tanks of the 8th King's Royal Irish Hussars. East of the brigade was the U.S. 3d Division; west, the ROK 1st Division. The sector the British held was doubly important to General Van Fleet because near the positions of the Northumberland Fusiliers, the UN's front lines curved sharply northward before bending back at Yonch'on toward the east. If the enemy could slice through the hills held by the 29th Brigade, he could twist in behind Van Fleet's divisions and cut them off.

The Communists' main effort in the west, therefore, fell on the British. A series of vicious battles was fought under the light of that full moon on the night of 22–23 April as each hill near the road, separately and together, was attacked again and again and again by waves of Chinese troops. The memoir of a young English captain, and the laconic extracts from the British brigade's radio log, typed by a clerk while the battle raged near enough to hear clearly the gunfire, tell much of the story of the first crucial sixteen hours of the Chinese spring offensive.

Time	From	Event
22 April		
2220	170 Mortar Bty	C Coy of Belgians [attached to 29 Ind. Bde.] being attacked
	1 GLOSTERS	Ambush patrol engaged
2340	170 Mortar Bty	They and 45 Fd Regt RA engaging . . . enemy movement in village

Time	From	Event
23 April		
0055	1 GLOSTERS	Report they are firing salvos . . . in front of A Coy
0057	1 GLOSTERS	Report that patrol from 1 NF are in contact with enemy who have infiltrated between 1 GLOSTERS and 1 NF
0120	45 Fd Regt RA	OP with Belgian report enemy patrol got round behind them. . . .
0121	45 Fd Regt RA	Enemy got to junction of the 2 rivers [Han and Imjin] near bridges
0145	1 NF	Report lot of firing in area of ULSTER river crossing
0205	45 Fd Regt RA	Tracers visible in this area coming from direction of W Coy, 1 NF
0215	1 RUR	Report carrier dvr returned, says the patrol ambushed over second river. . . .
0220	1 GLOSTERS	D Coy being attacked. Attack being held by our MOR DF [mortar defensive fire]

Capt. ANTHONY FARRAR-HOCKLEY
1st Battalion/The Gloucestershire Regiment

The attackers enter: hundreds of Chinese soldiers clad in cotton khaki suits; plain, cheap, cotton caps; rubber-soled canvas shoes upon their feet; their shoulders, chests, and backs criss-crossed with cotton bandoliers of ammunition; upon their hips, grenades—rough stick grenades. . . . Brown eyes, dark eyes beneath the long peaks of their caps peer forward to the back of whatsoever "comrade" they are meant to follow. Those in the forefront of the battle wear steel helmets that are reminiscent of the Japanese. Their weapons—rifles, carbines, "burp" guns, and Tommy guns that we supplied Chiang Kai-shek—are ready in their hands. Behind, on mule or pony limbers, are drawn their guns and ammunition. Between the two lines, on sweating backs, or slung between two men upon stout bamboo poles, their mortars and machine guns travel forward. No Oxford carriers, no jeeps and trailers, no gun prime-movers here; but if they lack these aids to war, they do not lack what we do most: men. The hundreds grow to thousands on the riverbanks as, padding through the night, they close with us: eight hundred Glosters stand astride the road to Seoul—the road the Chinese mean to clear at any cost.*

Time	From	Event
0230	Belgians	SITREP [situation report] Enemy has attacked the bridge and climbed on to slope of hill occupied by C Coy and have put automatic weapons on it.
0250	1 GLOSTERS	Attack continues on A and B Coys. No ground given.

*Captain Anthony Farrar-Hockley, *The Edge of the Sword* (London: Frederick Muller Ltd., 1953), 23. Hereafter, Farrar-Hockley.

Capt. ANTHONY FARRAR-HOCKLEY
1st Battalion/The Gloucestershire Regiment
The Vickers guns cut across the cliffs and slopes by which the Chinese forces climb to the attack. Long bursts of fire—ten, twenty, thirty, forty rounds—are fired and fired again: the water in the cooling jackets warms, the ground is littered with spent cases. The mortars and the gunners drop their high explosive in amongst the crowded ranks that press on to the hill slopes from the river crossings.

The weight of defensive fire is so great that the enemy has realized he must concentrate his strength in one main thrust up to each hilltop. As the night wanes, fresh hundreds are committed to this task, and the tired defenders, much depleted, face yet one more assault.*

Time	From	Event
0335	Col FOSTER [CO NF]	Coys holding but hard pushed. X Coy pulled out—some have got back.
	1 GLOSTERS	A and D Coys still under attack, but holding firm.
0405	1 NF	Right platoon Z Coy heavily engaged. Enemy possibly trying to by-pass to east.
	1 GLOSTERS	Enemy still attacking A, B and C Coys.
0425	1 NF	. . . except for X Coy posn is firm.
0430	1 GLOSTERS	A and B Coys still under attack. Some abatement in D Coy.

* Farrar-Hockley, 26.

131	0435	45 Fd Regt RA	X Coy NF now behind guns.
132	0445	Belgians	C Coy being attacked all around—grenade fighting.
133	0510	Belgians	B Coy attacked from north and west—attack repulsed.
134	0600	45 Fd Regt RA	OP with C Coy Belgian reports they are still being attacked.
135	0610	1 NF	Right hand pl of Z Coy pushed back.
136	0612	45 Fd Regt RA	200 enemy being engaged.
137	0615	1 GLOSTERS	Heavy attack still being made on C Coy.
138	0645	1 GLOSTERS	Still being pressed by enemy in considerable strength. Air support essential.
139	0647	Belgians	Left hand end of C Coy being overrun. 1Pl has been lost and remainder of Coy pinned down on their posn. Enemy infiltrating between C and A Coys. Posn becoming dangerous.
140	0650	45 Fd Regt RA	Co 1 GLOSTERS [Lt. Col. J.P. Carne] reports that posn in front of A and D Coys serious. Did not give much hope of lasting much longer against the 1000 enemy reported in the area. Could the people on the right [NF] do anything to help.

Time	From	Event
0651	45 Fd Regt RA	Report D Coy 1 GLOSTERS very hard pressed.
0730	1 GLOSTERS	Very hard pressed. Told by Comd to withdraw if necessary—Regt strength against them.
0735	Belgians	Need assistance if possible. C Coy overrun. Comd says tanks will be sent as soon as road through NF open but can't estimate time.
0735	Comd	To CG 3 Div explained situation

Capt. ANTHONY FARRAR-HOCKLEY
1st Battalion/The Gloucestershire Regiment
There were no planes that day; there were targets and more else-where. The guns and mortars fired . . . but the Rifles and Fusi-liers—to say nothing of the brave Belgians—needed support, too. There were so many of them. At about half past eight it became apparent that the positions of A and D Companies had become un-tenable; little by little they were being swamped by a tide of men. The time had come when the advantage of holding the ground for-ward would be outweighed by the loss of much or all of two rifle-company groups. The order to withdraw was given over the wireless.*

Time	From	Event
0845	MEMO	Prepare move HQ to rear. . . .
0900	1 NF	Bringing Y back, trying to re-cover right of Z Coy.

* Farrar-Hockley, 30–31.

0910	1 RUR	Engaging enemy.
1020	1 RUR	Report large number of enemy on N and W slopes of Hill 587.
1115	Belgians	Ammunition supplies being brought up. . . . Told probable order to move to Line KANSAS tonight.
1145	1 GLOSTERS	Enemy on Hills 148 and 182 [their flanks].
1215	1 NF	Will try to counter-attack soon.
1240	Belgians	C Coy under attack.
1300	1 NF	Counter-attack NOT successful —many enemy on right.
1320	1 NF	Large number of enemy.
1330	45 Fd Regt RA	Unknown number of enemy moving.
1400	1 GLOSTERS	Position secure. Action diminished. Own casualties about 45— enemy casualties hundreds.

[Sixteen hours before, in front of IX Corps, the Communist lightning bolt had fallen heavily on the ROK 6th Division, which defended the line between the U.S. 2d Division on its left and the 1st Marine Division on its right. The ROKs were blown away, and the enemy poured into the gap. With dismaying accuracy the Chinese had again found the weakest spot in the UN's lines and had pounded it until it broke. The Marines reacted swiftly to the potential disaster.]

2d Lt. JOSEPH REISLER
C/1
By midnight we were all on trucks and rolling on the roads north.
Mile after mile, all the roads were covered with remnants of the
ROKs who had fled. Thousands of them were straggling along the
road in confusion.*

Pfc. PAUL MARTIN
Reconnaissance Company/1st Marine Division
Many of the replacements in the company boiled over: "I come six
thousand miles from home to protect those cowards?"

When we arrived at our destination we were divided into patrols
and sent off to various key terrain positions. The drivers were ordered
to round up ROK stragglers wherever they could be found.

[*In the early hours of the twenty-third, the Chinese collided with the
Marines, and heavy fighting erupted around Maj. Web Sawyer's 1st
Battalion, 7th Marines.*]

Pfc. DAVE KOEGEL
B/7
The Chinese came at our position in waves, and were supported by
heavy machine-gun fire. Much of the action was hand-to-hand. That
Baker Company withstood these swarming attacks of rank upon rank
of enemy infantryman had to do with the skill and guts of the artillery
FO attached to the company. By the time the first rounds of our
artillery ploughed into the area at the foot of the hill, the Chinese
had passed it and were higher on the slopes. The FO, marking the
first rounds, walked succeeding volleys up the hill until they crashed
into the front ranks of the attackers just yards below Baker's positions.

---

*Lieutenant Reisler letter, as quoted in Lynn Montross; Maj. Hubard A. Kuokka, USMC; and
Maj. Norman W. Hicks, USMC, *The East-Central Front*, Vol. 4 of *U.S. Marine Operations
In Korea, 1950–1953* (Washington, D.C.: Historical Branch, G-3, Headquarters, U.S. Marine
Corps, 1962), 105. Hereafter, Reisler.

23 April

0610 It is reported that there are wide gaps on both flanks and
      elements of 1st Marine Division . . . are under attack.
      ROKs retreating and situation obscure. It does not look
      good.

           OPERATIONS LOG, 27TH BRITISH COMMONWEALTH BRIGADE

*[The first graying flush of dawn on Monday, 23 April revealed the
enemy in motion across the whole of Korea.]*

Pfc. PAUL MARTIN
Reconnaissance Company/1st Marine Division

My patrol walked up a long valley, then did some steep climbing
[Hill 902]. All this walking and climbing made me feel too tired to
think about being killed or wounded. We placed an outpost that
overlooked many lower hills and a wide valley, behind which were
more ridges and more hills. To the right the Chinese had set a large
fire, and great clouds of white smoke rose in the sky.

Pfc. LYLE CONAWAY
F/1

The Chinese tied up bundles of straw, lit them, and ran them through
the dry grass at the base of the hill we were dug in on. They also tied
burning straw to a donkey and chased it into the grass. At first it
didn't register with us what they were doing, then the fires really got
going and we knew. The Chinese came up right behind the flames
and smoke. It reminded me of a cowboys and Indians fight. Like
most of the daylight attacks they tried, this one failed.

     When the Chinks got around our flanks, we had to withdraw to
a high ridge in our rear. During this move we ran into an enemy
machine gun down the road about 1,000 yards that lobbed its shells
at us mortar-fashion. It wasn't very accurate fire, but it sure was harassing. Whenever the gunner ran out of a belt, a couple of his crew
would leap out of a nearby ditch and help him reload. A few of the
men, including me, were sent forward with our BARs and told to get
rid of this pest. He ignored us and also a couple of 60-mm mortars

that were fired in his direction. All of a sudden, from behind me, came two Corsairs [F4Us] no more than 100 feet off the deck. Their machine-gun bullets kicked up a wall of dirt and rock all around this guy. Everyone of us cheered those pilots. When the dust cleared, the Chink was still there firing away.

1st Lt. GEORGE JAMES, JR.
21st AAA Battalion (SP)/25th Division *

I picked the day the Chinese hit us to make a trip over to the 3d Division area, on our left, to try and see my brother-in-law, Ed Krekorian. In reserve, I'd grown bored [James had arrived in Korea ten days before] and picked April 23 for the visit. When I arrived on the 3d Division's MSR, I found a hell of a lot of disorganized traffic all frantically streaming south, directed by some brigadier general who was standing in the middle of the road. He cussed and stomped and tried to achieve order from near chaos. I discovered then that the Chinese were trying to rearrange some real estate. By the merest chance I connected up with Ed. I piled into his jeep while mine followed behind, and we had a nice visit, all the while heading south in the traffic jam.

Perhaps an hour went by before I said good-bye. I figured I ought to head back to my own unit, as my division probably wouldn't think too highly of my visit. Waving good-bye to Ed, my driver, Master Sergeant Russ Whiteside, and I headed north toward the connecting trail and the Chinese. What a mess—traffic thick as fleas on a dog's back, and if it wouldn't move it was burning on the roadside. I remember the forwardmost installation I saw was the 3d Division's QM (quartermaster) dump, now a raging inferno. We kept going and eventually found traffic getting light. In fact, Russ and I saw very few people until we reached the road junction where we had to turn right on a narrow trail to get back "home." At that point there was a standard build-it-yourself wooden military bridge and some engineer peo-

---

* Lieutenant James's platoon was attached to C Company/35th Infantry, which, at the time of the Chinese offensive, was in regimental reserve near Chip'o-ri.

ple with weapons waving frantically for Russ and me to stop. It appeared they were in the process of blowing the bridge, as the thing was wired up with primer cord and pretty yellow blocks of TNT. I explained to the engineer sergeant who tried to appear to be in charge that I had to get over his bridge before he blew it. He got sort of a "ya gotta be kidding me" look on his face and shrugged his shoulders. "Okay, Lootenant, I guess ya know what you're doin'," and he waved us through. We drove over and were about 100 yards down the road when, BALLOOOEY! No more bridge.

On we went. It was indeed a lonely country road, peaceful and quiet. We didn't see a soul for miles. Then, KRRRUNCH, KRRUNCH—two 105-mm HE rounds landed nearby. Several more followed in rapid succession. BLAM! BLAM! The jeep was now going full bore through dust and smoke. I had no idea that the bugle-playing Chinese were out in front of us hiding like possums in a swamp. Then it grew quiet again. Another mile more and we ran into folks dressed in green. Fortunately, they were GIs from Charlie Company, 35th Infantry. I learned later that the shells that had missed us were our own—the battalion FO registering his fire for the night.

That night we got probed, and the following day all hell broke loose in our sector. I remember thinking, Wonder if I'll make it.

[From one end of Korea to the other, from the Yellow Sea to the Sea of Japan, there was fighting on 24 April. The U.S. 24th and 25th Divisions, the first American units to enter the war ten months before, now seasoned and confident, gave ground grudgingly. Van Fleet ordered the British Commonwealth Brigade and the 5th Cavalry Regiment to get ready to plug the hole left by the disintegration of the ROK 6th Division. In the meantime the Marine division would fall back, all the while guarding itself against Chinese attacks from the west as well as the north.]

Pfc. PAUL MARTIN
Reconnaissance Company/1st Marine Division
American fighter planes flew all around the valley and over the nearby hills. The lieutenant crawled over and gestured with his head. "The

Chinks have broken through in that direction. There's nothing between them and our regiments but our platoon. That's why we're
here." I looked at him in disbelief. "We're to stop the whole Chinese
army?" "Who else, if not us?" he said. "There isn't anyone else." He
was new to the company, and I admired his courage. Another replacement asked me questions which showed his fear. I answered,
"Whistling shells fall far away—longer the whistle, the farther away
they are. Don't worry about bullets and shells. Think of walking on
the sidewalk and of all the cars that pass close but don't hit you." I
found giving advice helped smother fear, but the truth was, I was
more scared than any of the kids. I knew what could *really* happen
to me.

When we hadn't seen any signs of the enemy for an hour or so,
I told the lieutenant that my experience at the Chosin Reservoir was
that we wouldn't see the enemy until our planes left the area. About
thirty minutes later, the planes flew off. Shortly afterward one of the
guys spotted a few Chinks leading horses and mules across the far
end of the valley. These were followed by infantrymen. Our lieutenant told us other OPs had also begun to spot movement. The planes
returned, and when they did, the Chinese hid in the lengthening
shadows.

A little time later, several of our line companies, along with
heavy machine guns and mortars, began arriving. What a relief! I
knew then our lieutenant had been kidding about holding the Chinese
alone. We were then ordered down to the road. I thought it was all
over for us. I was wrong.

The company was issued two days' supply of field rations and
ordered to set up observation posts along the western flank of the long
valley we had overlooked from the high hill. The sun dropped lower
in the sky, and the shadows grew longer. Many of us grumbled about
being shifted around like this. There's nothing faster than a pencil
stroke across a map to indicate movement. Those planners should
have to walk from one end of their drawn arrows to the other, as we
did. We climbed the far side of the valley in the dark and, as the
moon began to rise, took a break. The world was very quiet.

Someone hissed, "Listen!" I heard voices in the distance shouting what sounded to me like "Marine." As I tried to figure this out,

green amber clusters suddenly lit the sky over the hill we'd been on that morning. All hell broke loose in that direction, with small-arms fire and artillery rocking the hill and surrounding ridges.

[It was 8:00 P.M. on the twenty-fourth when the Chinese, pouring through the gap left by the ROKs, finally turned east and barreled into the Marines who were dug in on a hill mass called Horseshoe Ridge.]

2d Lt. JOSEPH REISLER
C/1

They came on in wave after wave, hundreds of them. They were singing, humming, and chanting, "Awake, Marine. . . ." In the first rush they knocked out both our machine guns and wounded about ten men, putting a big hole in our fire—and those grenades, hundreds of grenades. There was nothing to do but withdraw to a better position, which I did. We pulled back about fifty yards and set up a new line. All this was in the pitch-black night with Chinese cymbals crashing, horns blowing, and their god-awful yells.*

Pfc. FLOYD BAXTER
Weapons Company/1

The hair on my neck stood up. Trying for some humor, I told my foxhole buddy, "They sure can use some music lessons."

All of a sudden it got quiet. You could hear the guys bracing themselves, you know, getting ready. I thought, Who's gonna live and who's gonna die?

It finally happened. They hit us from the rear while at the same time they hit Charlie from the front. Several times the Chinks got into our positions, but each time we beat them back. The guys from the security platoon did a fantastic job holding the enemy out of the 81s' [mortars] gun pits.

*Reisler, 113.

We began to get low on ammo. All us carriers started down to the truck. At one machine-gun position the gunner held his fire, and one at a time, we inched past his position. The line of trees where the Chinese were was about fifty yards below the truck—we could see their muzzle flashes. We managed to get enough ammo to keep the 81s firing. Made two trips.

Once we began to withdraw, we received a lot of small-arms fire. The Chinese set up a machine gun to cover a draw we had to cross. One at a time, running zigzag, we managed to get across. Johnnie Savona caught a bullet in the kidney; it went right through. When J. J. Baresh helped put him on a stretcher, he was shot in the arm and chest. Two 'copters [from VMO-6] tried to land, but it was impossible. One was shot down, the other escaped. We loaded the wounded on jeeps, trucks—on anything with wheels.

We made our way through the thicket where the Chinese had been during the night. A kid named Bagley, right behind me, yelled. I thought he'd been hit. But it was only his sleeping bag which was knocked off his pack. I laughed at his expression and relief when he realized he hadn't been hurt. A little later a guy named Crow was wounded and put on a truck. In a few minutes a sniper put one through his heart. We lost several of the wounded this way.

We were out of food and water, and almost out of ammo. We couldn't get water from the streams we crossed, because of the bodies lying in the water. My tongue felt twice its size.

Snipers stayed with us the whole way. I saw bits of dust jump up at almost every step I took.

When we finally arrived at our perimeter, a lot of guys were amazed to see us. They had received reports that One One [1st Battalion, 1st Marines] had been surrounded and wiped out. I told the guys who asked me about the report to check with the other men; I didn't know anything about it.

[Frontline units disengaged and, on General Ridgway's orders, withdrew to phase line Kansas.

The Communist offensive now shifted westward, and it became apparent that its main target was Seoul. The I Corps, in front of the capital, began receiving the full might of the Chinese onslaught as 337,000 enemy troops lashed Van Fleet's divisions. Enormous pressure was exerted on the left flank, and the ROKs, west of the British brigade, disappeared. The Chinese drove into the hole and turned to attack the Glosters, who now alone held the key to Van Fleet's orderly withdrawal. If the Glosters could be destroyed and the rest of the British brigade driven off, the Chinese would be able to roll along Eighth Army's flank, devouring the UN's divisions one by one.

With the ROKs gone, the British brigade suddenly found Chinese crawling all over its flanks. The brigade's radio log recorded the growing catastrophe.]

24 April

Time	From	Event
0341	RUR	Coys under attack.
0530	GLOSTERS	Road is open to enemy who is using it.
0615	GLOSTERS	Think 1 enemy regiment passed GLOSTERS.
0630	NF	Enemy battalion sighted . . . enemy crossed river. . . . Air strikes required immediately.

[During the morning, with the Belgians, Fusiliers, and Rifles barely holding their own, the Glosters, riding the center of the Chinese whirlwind, fought their way to a hill overlooking the mud huts of Solmaeri. There, on Gloster Hill, time after time the enemy threw himself at the British riflemen—and again and again they defied him.]

Time	From	Event
0900	GLOSTERS	Told to fight way out if necessary—decision left to CO [Carne] but commander [Brodie] concurs.

Time	From	Event
1130	GLOSTERS	. . . Enemy all around and unable to move without drawing machine gun fire. Difficult now to see enemy but can see them to SOUTH.
1645	GLOSTERS	Need batteries and ammunition URGENTLY—also want food and water.

[To the right of the British was the U.S. 3d Division. During the daylight hours of the twenty-fourth, the Americans had managed to hold their own, but during the night the Communists hit the division hard.]

Pfc. JAMES CART
H Company/7th Infantry *

At the time my outfit got overrun by the Chinks in the middle of the night, I was in the mortar platoon as the third gunner. I was the jerk assigned to carry the base plate. It weighed sixty pounds; after carrying it five miles, it weighed 600. On this particular night the 81-mm mortars were a few hundred yards behind the rifle companies. We could hear all the gunfire to our front, but nobody called in the mortars. One of the men from a line company ran into our perimeter. He told us the Chinks had overrun his position and that they were heading in our direction. My platoon sergeant told me to pick up the mortar base plate and head back for the hills to our rear. It would only be a matter of minutes before the Chinks had us surrounded. Along with the base plate I lugged my M1 rifle, three bandoliers of rifle ammo, my web belt, canteen, mess gear, and helmet. Before I got started, the sergeant gave me a thermite grenade and told me to put it in the engine of one of our jeeps. We didn't even have

---

*The 7th Infantry, along with the 15th Infantry and 65th Infantry, made up the 3d Division.

the time to get our vehicles out. I used the grenade, then ran as best I could into the night and headed for the hills I knew were behind our lines.

Somewhere along the way I met up with a BAR man from Fox Company. He too was loaded down with gear, which included six grenades and his 16-pound automatic weapon. A little later we ran into a medic, and throughout the rest of the night the three of us climbed hills. In the morning we walked another four miles or so, until we saw a group of GIs at the foot of the hill we were on. We walked down and joined them. The first gunner from my platoon was there. First thing he said to me was, "What'n the hell you doin' carryin' that base plate for?" "Hell," I said, "sarge told me to. Why ya askin'?" "Damn, we don't have no mortars—left 'em behind. Left everything behind." If I'd have known that, that danged base plate would have got sailed.

[*By 25 April, Van Fleet's gate carrying the withdrawal had swung wide, and the units riding it were safely behind a new line. It was time then to extricate the hinge, and the British brigade was ordered to fall back. For the Northumberland Fusiliers and Royal Ulster Rifles, it would be a tortuous fighting withdrawal.*]

25 April
1215 All companies were in the assembly area at Main HQ, orders were issued to company COs. The plant was to march out along the road and the RV [rendezvous] and go into a blocking position.
WAR DIARY, 1ST BATTALION/ROYAL ULSTER RIFLES

Rifleman LEONARD JONES
1st Battalion/Royal Ulster Rifles
We held the line as long as possible—for three nights and two full days. On the third day the Rifles and the Northumberland Fusiliers were ordered to make a fighting withdrawal. By then the Chinese were all around us, so it was get out the best way we could.

Our artillery opened up when we came down in groups from the hills above Happy Valley. A lot of the lads got hit from short rounds. We were very tired and dirty. There had been no time for things such as a wash.

At the bottom of the hill, we gathered into groups of twelve or less. By then the Inky Pinks were on the hills above us, on each side of the valley and in front of us. It was as if the Imjin River battle we'd fought in early January was starting again from the beginning.

Rifleman HENRY O'KANE
C Company/1st Battalion/Royal Ulster Rifles
We were to make for our old positions down the road, where we were told transport awaited us. There, B Company held a blocking position, near the slopes of Kamak-San [Hill 675]. We in C Company had spent our first night high on the hill when we returned to the 38th Parallel on March 31.

We knew the distance was about four miles, a mere stroll, but the effects of the last three days had taken their toll. Lack of sleep, a shortage of food and water, and the constant strain of battle had wearied us. As we were about to move out, some shells fell amongst a neighboring platoon, causing casualties. We learned that the 25-pounders were under fire from Chinese snipers, and that 29th Brigade HQ was also under attack. It was going to be a long four miles.

1225 First company crossed to road

WAR DIARY, 1ST BATTALION/ROYAL ULSTER RIFLES

Rifleman HENRY O'KANE
C Company/1st Battalion/Royal Ulster Rifles
When we at last started down the road it was fairly quiet, except for the 3-inch mortars that were letting off the last of their bombs. The men of my unit [9th Platoon] seemed fairly subdued; there was none of the usual banter or joking that went on. Remarks such as "We're going down the road again" and "We've done it all before" were heard along the column. The terrible days of the third and fourth of January at Happy Valley were still vivid in our minds—the withdrawal had cost the RURs over 200 casualties. That action had taken place in darkness, and C Company itself had borne a heavy toll. Now

we were going down the same road, this time in broad daylight, the hills on either side and in front full of Chinese. We had no option but to follow orders: "Go straight down the road. Lead on, C Company!" It wasn't long before the sound of firing increased all around us. But most of it seemed to be coming from up ahead, in the direction we were heading.

> 0300 As battalion got onto the road moderate to heavy LMG [light machine gun] fire began to fall. The battalion deployed in open order and the advance continued. Within ten minutes it was impossible to move except in short rushes, which were hard to control.
>
> WAR DIARY, 1ST BATTALION/ROYAL ULSTER RIFLES

Rifleman HENRY O'KANE
C Company/1st Battalion/Royal Ulster Rifles
Suddenly, we began taking fire from the hills to the west. There wasn't anything to do but stop at intervals, return fire, then keep on going. We were without cover at this point. The fire became strong. A section of 3-inch mortars joined in. Suddenly, I was hit in the leg. After crawling to a paddy, I ditched my gear, except for my rifle, and managed to keep on going. We began to take further casualties as we dodged from cover to cover, bund or brush, though there was very little of either. Later on, we seemed to put heads down and kept on going. The fire was intense, but we tried not to notice it. A group of Royal Engineers acting as infantry were hunched under the lee of a Centurion [Mark III] tank that had shed a track; they shouted to us to get down, but we kept on going. We passed two more tanks that were knocked out and on fire. Farther down the road an RUR Oxford carrier lay with its dead crew spilling out. The name on the side read *Ballymacab.*

Later—much later—we eventually reached our old positions, still held by what was left of B Company. Centurions [of C Squadron] of the 8th Hussars were waiting to carry as many as they could on the final run to Uijongbu. The rest of the battalion turned left into the surrounding hills. Before we moved out on the tanks, I saw

men, their ammunition having been expended, climbing at a fast
pace.

Rifleman HENRY O'KANE
C Company/1st Battalion/Royal Ulster Rifles
It was a wild, swaying ride. It didn't last long, but I shall never forget
it—the dust, the rattle of the tracks, the screams of wounded men as
we were repeatedly hit. Suddenly, we were surrounded by the Chinese.
They came along the road with Molotov cocktails and pole-charges;
the tanks killed many of them. Later—how much later, I don't know—
I came to a ditch, or stream, by the side of the road. A few yards
farther on, a tank was slewed across a paddy, its track off and its
petrol tank burning. I was covered in blood, my nose and ears bleeding from concussion. I had lost my rifle—it was the only thing at
this particular moment that worried me.

As I lay half submerged in the small stream by the side of the
road, I soon realized I was not alone. Along the banks small groups
of men were lying; most were wounded, some were dead. We were
soon engulfed by the intense fire of machine guns and mortars. Much
of it was directed at the nearby burning tank and at some of the lads
who were heading for the hills and freedom. By now the Chinese
were darting across the road and the paddy fields in hot pursuit of
the rest of the battalion. They passed us by without a glance. After a
time men started to move about, trying to help one another. Someone removed my bloody camouflage smock, splashed water over me,
put a bandage around my head, and gave me a drink of rum. The
feeling of preservation then returned.

As I awaited my fate, a great silence seemed to settle over me.
The noise of battle was dying. No more tanks rattled past with their
Besas firing. The machine-gun fire and mortars that had been going
for so long had almost stopped. Three Chinese soldiers suddenly appeared and handed us safe-conduct passes. One, who spoke a little
English and appeared to be of fairly high rank, said "Good fight,"
then disarmed my group. We marched with our hands on our heads
down the road and across to our old positions. Wounded who were
unable to walk were left behind. They were never seen again.

1830 Remnants of RNF and 1RUR were ordered to hold the Tokchong area for 1½ hours until relieved by a bn, 15 Regt [US 3d Division]. By then everyone had been fed but there were few Brens [machine guns], no wrls [wireless] or tele comms
ephones] and no picks or shovels. At this time the men began to arrive in ones and twos and in one case approx 30. Cpl. Keenan [1 Section] brought in a further 7 and reported that the enemy were digging in large numbers 4,000 yards due north singing and blowing bugles.

2330 Bn relieved without incident and began to march down the Uijongbu road.

WAR DIARY, 1ST BATTALION/ROYAL ULSTER RIFLES

[The order to withdraw, receiving the morning of the twenty-fifth, came too late for the Glosters.]

Capt. ANTHONY FARRAR-HOCKLEY
1st Battalion/The Gloucestershire Regiment

We read so often in histories . . . that one or another company of such-and-such a battalion was "cut up," "cut to pieces," "destroyed." What does this mean exactly? How is this done to a hundred-odd men, organized and armed to fight a semi-independent battle, with all the means to hand of calling down artillery fire to support them?

In Korea, in the battle of the Imjin River, it was done like this.

The whole company front is engaged by fire—fire from heavy machine guns well concealed in hollows or behind crests which take our artillery from other, more vital tasks if they are to be engaged. There is fire from mortars and from light machine guns at a closer range. Meanwhile, the enemy assault groups feel their way forward to the very edge of our defences; and, finding the line of our resistance, creep round our flanks to meet each other in the rear. To the defenders, these circumstances do not constitute disaster. Holding their fire for sure targets; exploiting their advantage of positions carefully sited for just such attacks as these, they are undaunted. Again and again, they see the shells from their artillery burst amongst the crowded ranks of the enemy. Their own small arms pile up another dreadful score of casualties. Each enemy assault is beaten off without great difficulty. For hours, this repetition of attack and repulse continues, the night wanes, the dawn begins to break. Little by little, a terrible fact becomes apparent to the men of the defence. This is not a battle in which courage or tactical and technical superiority will be the means to victory: it is a battle of attrition. Irrespective of the number of casualties they inflict, there is an unending flow of replacements for each man. Moreover, in spite of their tremendous losses, the numerical strength of the enemy is not merely constant but increasing.[*]

Time	From	Event
0605	Comdr [Brodie]	GLOSTERS given permission to break out.
0610	GLOSTERS	Very hard pressed, asking for air support . . . on any enemy sighted.
0620	GLOSTERS	Surrounded impossible to withdraw.
0755	GLOSTERS	Only another 30 minutes of battery left.

Capt. ANTHONY FARRAR-HOCKLEY
1st Battalion/The Gloucestershire Regiment
Back on the ridge, I saw that Jumbo was waiting with the main body just above Support Company Headquarters, where a section of the machine guns was established to cover Hill 235. "A" Company moved off, and I rejoined Battalion Headquarters; for A Company were now so weak that one officer could command them without difficulty. I

[*] Farrar-Hockley, 42–43.

reached the Colonel [Carne] just as he finished talking on the Rear-Link wireless, and I saw that his face was grave.

"Let Sam know," he said, "that I have just been told by the brigadier that the guns are unable to support us—the gun lines are under attack themselves. Our orders are quite simple: every man to make his own way back."

[When it was clear that the Glosters would not be able to break out of the trap, the brigade commander, Brigadier Brodie, in what must have been a very emotional moment, picked up a pen, and across the radio log which had recorded the long ordeal, he wrote, "Only the Glosters could have done it."

Eventually, thirty-nine survivors of Gloster Hill managed to reach the UN's lines. It had cost 29th Independent Brigade more than 1,000 casualties, but for sixty crucial hours the British had stemmed the tide of the Chinese advance. It was a glorious achievement at a terrible cost.

Elsewhere, the twenty-fifth was a day of enormous activity as Eighth Army attempted to give the decimation of the Glosters its full meaning and justification by containing the Communists north of Seoul.]

Sgt. F/C W. B. WOODRUFF, JR. [*]
L Company/35th Infantry

By noon [25 April] we were rolling by truck up the main road. Our convoy soon slowed, and we encountered a column of men from the 27th [Wolfhound] Regiment marching south. We'd been friendly rivals since early in World War II, and whenever we met them along the roadways, it was our custom to greet them with a derisive chorus of wolfhowls and whistles. This time it was different. The men of the 27th looked tired but not whipped; we respected them. The conversation this time between the men of the two regiments was friendly and sympathetic. One of our men called out, "How was it?" Back came the reply: "Rough."

---

[*] Woodruff had been promoted and became 1st Platoon sergeant and acting platoon leader in mid-April.

Cpl. JOHN VENEZIA
724 Ordnance (M) Company/24th Division

A guy named Oliver Wilson and I were told to wait and assist some infantrymen who were withdrawing [25 April]. When they got to our truck convoy, we loaded their wounded into the ambulances and trucks, then we were told to drive along the road and pick up any South Korean ammo bearers we ran across. It was obvious the enemy was pushing hard in this area—the wounded riding behind us told a grim story. I was therefore very relieved to be ordered to the rear. I was a reservist called back to active duty, and my job was repairing everything, from trucks to mess kits. In no way was I used to seeing infantrymen in action. The combat troops around us this day were from the 5th RCT, the Triple Nickel [555th Field Artillery Battalion], and the 6th Tank outfit. There were probably no more than fifteen of us guys from the 724th Ordnance driving trucks.

We picked up about a dozen ammo bearers before turning south to get out of reach of the Chinese. I was pretty certain we were one of the last large groups to start south.

Suddenly, we came under heavy fire. My assistant driver, Oliver Wilson, pointed to both sides of the road, and when I looked, all I saw were Chinese on the ridges above and in the ditches along the road. We had driven right into an ambush. What a nightmare! Wilson and I learned right then, real quick, how to fight. We could not move forward because the first few trucks, towing artillery, had been hit hard and their drivers killed. Dead Americans, mixed with some Chinese, lined the road. Concussion grenades exploded around me. The truck stalled and wouldn't start. Machine-gun fire tore into the back. Wilson and I dragged the wounded out. The trap was really tight.

A lieutenant I'd never seen before asked for volunteers to assault a ridge where heavy fire was being directed at us. A sergeant claimed it would be suicide to try. The lieutenant agreed but said, "We gotta stall the Chinks, gotta get the wounded and others out." I gulped and volunteered, "I'll go, but not alone." The lieutenant said, "We'll help 'ya—give 'ya covering fire." I must confess that a few minutes earlier I was about to run off with the others who were making for the hills, but when I saw all those dead guys in the truck and then the wounded firing at the Chinese, I became very pissed off. If they could do something, so could I. So Wilson, me, and eight or nine others charged up the hill. The lieutenant kept his promise, and with others by the side of the road gave covering fire. We ran and ran. When I reached the summit I heard bugles and whistles, and all hell broke loose again—machine-gun fire, rifle fire, concussion grenades. Some of the guys bled from their mouths and ears. I was blown off my feet; mud and gravel hit me in the face. I saw an arm throw a potato-masher-type grenade at me. I tried to toss it back. It exploded before I got to it. The explosion stunned me. I shot the Chinese who threw it. Bullets kicked dirt around where I lay. The Chinks were in ditches everywhere and coming at us. We killed several more. Some of our guys, to get out of this mess, ran down the hill—one or two made it. Then it happened—my carbine jammed. I couldn't fire it. While I was trying to kick it clear, the guys around me kept up their fire; but no one saw a Chink with a burp gun looking directly at me—couldn't have been more than twenty-five feet away. He looked completely surprised, like he didn't know who I was. Maybe he mistook me for one of his own; I was wearing a fatigue hat and a pile vest, and this might have confused him. I said to myself, Here goes. I grabbed the carbine by the barrel and lunged forward. To my great relief one of our guys with a BAR shot him before I reached him.

Next thing, we all got the hell off that hill and ran back down to the road. The lieutenant was gone, and everyone else was running along a secondary road; besides, it was getting darker and no one could see real well.*

Capt. LUTHER WEAVER
L Company/35th Infantry

Our position was rather precarious.† In the afternoon [25 April], even after deploying all four rifle companies, I had two open flanks—the worst being the one on the right. There just were no other units to

---

*Venezia and Wilson safely reached their own lines that night.
†On 25 April, L Company's 3d Battalion was on a hill overlooking the Hant'an River, southeast of Ch'orwon. The 35th Infantry's other two battalions were in a blocking position behind the 24th Infantry. To the west was the Turkish Brigade and the U.S. 3d Division; to the east, the U.S. 24th Division.

tie into. The company's mission was to hold in the event of a Chinese breakthrough and permit all the units forward to clear through us before we withdrew. I had the company curl around in a horseshoe, and put my CP in the middle, just below the crest of the ridge. From there I could plainly see to my rear the battalion CP tent at the base of the ridge. On the north bank of the Hant'an—at this time no more than a stream—there was a rail line that ran into a tunnel on our right. In the early afternoon a rifle squad with a unit of halftracks mounting quad .50s had checked out the tunnel and found it empty.

There was the muffled sound of artillery fire in the distance. As the afternoon wore on, the sound got closer. Reports from battalion mentioned certain units being hard-hit, others told about Chinese breakthroughs.

Sgt. F/C W. B. WOODRUFF, JR.
L Company/35th Infantry

My platoon runner was Scosh Myers. Back in January it had been discovered he was still only seventeen years of age—too young, according to regulations, to be in combat. He was sent back, but soon returned to the unit; before they could get him out of the country he had turned 18. He weighed maybe seventy pounds dripping wet; it was alleged he never had to dig a foxhole because he could crawl under a helmet for protection. A field jacket made a perfect blanket for him. He worked all the time, never admitted to being tired, never complained, and was always in good humor. The State of Pennsylvania ought to erect a statue in his honor. With Scosh Myers in charge, our communications never failed—except this one time.

Just as darkness fell, the radio suddenly emitted a raucous series of noisy squawks. A very Chinese singsong voice repeated the same phrase, over and over, and at maximum volume, "Wu-da-ruh-fu, Wu-da-ruh-fu. . . ." Myers looked at me in astonished alarm, more shook than I had ever seen him, and said, "Sergeant Woodruff, they're calling your name." My heart skipped a beat; I pictured four million Chinese, all out to get me personally. I recovered with a nervous laugh and told Myers to try to raise company on the field phone; it was obvious our radio frequency had been found and would no longer permit secure transmission even if the jamming stopped. (It didn't, and we eventually turned the radio off.) Myers said he knew the phone was all right, he had just checked it a few minutes ago. But this time the line was very dead. I hoped this meant the wire had somehow been cut accidentally; the alternative was that enemy patrols were already swarming our area.

Capt. LUTHER WEAVER
L Company/35th Infantry
About dusk, Lieutenant Fleming's 3d Platoon reported seeing troops in the distance, going south. I knew the Turks were in that direction, but because of the bad light and distance, we could not tell with any certainty who exactly these men were. They continued to move past us until we could no longer see them in the darkness. About then I felt Love Company was in the eye of a storm. Around 8:00 P.M., Colonel Lee over at battalion called to say the situation to our front was worsening, and that the 3d Division on our right had been hit hard. A few minutes later, rifle fire from the direction of 3d Platoon broke the stillness. The phone rang. Fleming told me there were people—he was sure they were Chinese—in the brush to his right. Then battalion called. I informed them that I believed the enemy was bypassing us and going toward them up the ridge to our rear. Third Platoon opened up again, and this time the firing was heavier. I could also now hear firing from the direction of the battalion CP. Within moments Colonel Lee was on the phone telling me he was moving out. I asked, "Do you have any instructions for me?" He answered, "Get out the best way you can." I gave the platoon leaders the situation, "Be ready to move back on the trail toward where battalion was. We're probably gonna have to fight our way out, but we're going out as a company! Keep your squads intact. We're going out together." Second Platoon on the summit was to move back first and be the point during the withdrawal. Third Platoon was to keep pressure on the enemy on the ridge until I told them to come in. First Platoon was to hold on the left as long as they could, or until 1st Battalion had cleared our positions. I sent Lieutenant Schilling, my exec, back down the trail with a few company headquarters personnel and instructed him to have 2d Platoon move along the trail

about 100 yards, then to spread out and wait. Men on the right were to keep fire on the right; those on the left, to keep fire on the left.

Once 2d Platoon began firing on the high ground, I brought 3d Platoon back. Because of the hill's contour and where I was, I could not now reach Woodruff's 1st Platoon over the 536 radio. I told Schilling the column would move as soon as I went forward and returned with the 1st Platoon.

On the trail a stray bullet slammed into an empty 55-gallon drum and both my runner, Private Haitz, and I ducked.

Moments later, I ran into several men I recognized from our 1st Battalion, not the least of whom was my old friend Sidney Berry, who was that battalion's S-3. Of course, we did not have time to chat about our old times with A Company, but as we hurried off in opposite directions he called after me, "Good luck, Weaver. I'm sure glad it's you and Love behind me now. There's sure a lot of Chinks following us." I found Woodruff, who by then was growing concerned that we'd forgotten his platoon.

Sgt. F/C W. B. WOODRUFF, JR.
L Company/35th Infantry

My confidence was well placed, for after a time Captain Weaver personally appeared out of the darkness. He told me the company had orders to withdraw down the wagon trail, and that 1st Platoon was to move out immediately. In his voice I thought I detected reproach because we were not already moving. This caused me to say that I had presumed someone would inform us we were to move, since our radio and telephone were both out. He smiled and told me he knew our communications were broken, but insisted we hustle.

Capt. LUTHER WEAVER
L Company/35th Infantry

I ran back to where Schilling and the rest of the company were waiting for me. I radioed 2d Platoon to start moving. Our walking fire kept the enemy on the ridges above the trail guessing, and relieved the tension of the men. We passed a vehicle or two, and a couple of abandoned half-tracks that could not negotiate the trail's hairpin curves.

We moved back at a good walk. When we received fire we returned it, but did not stop to do so.

About dawn, the terrain opened up, and the company arrived at a small village which had been the regiment's CP. Most of the houses were still burning, as were a number of vehicles and ambulances which had obviously been ambushed. A few hundred yards beyond the fire and dense smoke, we came upon some troops and tanks firing on a small ridge to our left [east]. I ran into Colonel [Gerald C.] Kelleher [the regiment's CO], who was standing by the road observing the firefight. I told him that as far as I knew, mine was the last company to leave, and asked if he knew where Colonel Lee was. He thought Lee was forward but, due to the situation, was not certain of this. The sun had risen now, and it was light enough to see where we were. Through all the smoke and haze I noticed a lot of movement along a small ridgeline which dropped into an area of rice paddies. Although we were receiving no fire from that direction, I knew we had ourselves a good opportunity. The company was spread all along the road, sitting or lying down, waiting for things to move ahead up front. I was with 3d Platoon and about midway in the company column. I told Fleming to get his men up and begin firing on the ridge. By now the enemy was moving across the rice paddies. I called Woodruff's 1st Platoon up. Second Platoon was too far forward to help, but a couple of its squads in the rear got the word, anyway. With two platoons in position, we opened mass fire on the ridge and rice paddy area. Volley after volley slammed into the Chinese. When the smoke cleared we saw no one standing in that direction, but we heard a lot of moaning and groaning.

Shortly afterward, I got a call from battalion, which I thought we'd lost communication with. They wanted to know where I was, and had I heard a lot of firing in the direction of the burning village? "Yes," I said, "there was a lot of firing. I think we surprised a bunch of Chinks." Colonel Lee told me then that things looked clear up the road.

A few miles along the way, the company mounted some tanks that took us back to an area where we set up another blocking position.

I learned the next day that when a task force of tanks and infantry returned to the burning village to recover American bodies from the ambushed ambulance convoy and some equipment which had been left behind, they discovered about fifty dead Chinese that L Company had killed on that small ridgeline and in the rice paddies.

[Throughout all of Thursday, 26 April, the Chinese kept their shoulders to the wheel and cut the Seoul-Kansong highway. In both the west and central sectors, the enemy pressed the withdrawing columns of tired, sweaty, and hungry GIs. Deep Chinese penetrations had made it impossible to hold phase line Kansas, and further withdrawals were ordered. Eighth Army units everywhere tried to disengage and fall back.]

Cpl. DONALD CHASE
B Company/19th Infantry
All we knew was that we had to hold certain positions for a certain length of time before we could fall back. A few of us just out of the hospital had a hard time keeping up with our retreating units; we just didn't have the physical strength. More than once I was almost left behind.

Once, while falling back, my buddy and I came upon the only survivor of a tank crew. He stepped from behind a boulder, a .45 pistol in his hand and shaking with fright. In my memory I can still see his eyes, bright blue and looking as big as saucers. When he saw we were Americans he started to cry. He told us he had decided to shoot himself rather than be captured. You had to have been there to understand the terror we had of being taken prisoner.

When I speak of this withdrawal, fall back, retreat, whatever, I do not mean to imply it was a disorganized rout. It was not! But even at our squad level, it came as a shock. Up till then we had been pushing the enemy back, slowly but steadily. Now it was our turn to be pushed back.

That night, while the rest of the company fell back to take up new positions, our squad was left behind to block the Chinese advance. It was pitch black and we could see nothing, but because we could hear him, we knew that the enemy was in front of us and getting closer. The Chinese and Koreans ate a lot of garlic, and that smell carried quite a distance. When we smelled them it meant they were really close, and this night we smelled them. None of us wanted a fight; outnumbered, we'd all be killed or captured. Suddenly, a shot rang out. Someone told us it was time to leave. A runner from the company had come back, and he now led us off. To this day I don't know what really happened to our squad leader. When we arrived back with the company, he was among the missing. On the way to the rear we were all scared and tense and thinking only of getting the hell away from there.

Cpl. VICTOR FOX
I Company/5th Cavalry

The company continued to give ground in face of massive Chinese attacks. Third Platoon wound up on a narrow saddle between two rising summits [the night of 26–27 April]. On the peak to the left were the 1st and 2d Platoons; on the right, our 5th Platoon made up of KATUSAs. It was around 11:00 P.M. A strong wind blowing from the west carried the scent of garlic and the faint noises of troops moving. The tense silence was broken by the artillery FO talking softly on the radio, giving map coordinates for supporting fire. We were alerted that the artillery would crash down right in front of our positions on the forward slope of the saddle. Everyone knew to keep his head down. Then, everything hit at once, including air bursts that sent shrapnel whining around our holes. It seemed these TOT [time on target] barrages arrived every five or ten minutes. The sounds of distant battle could now be heard to our left and right.

About midnight, word came for the company to pull back along the ridgeline on the left, which bent around to the east. Third Platoon pulled off the saddle, and 5th Platoon, protecting our rear, followed. The KATUSAs were almost clear of the saddle when the withdrawal stalled. My platoon was ordered back to the reverse slope of the hill that had been on our left; the KATUSAs were ordered back to reoccupy the high ground they had just vacated. The platoon and squad leaders seethed in silent anger. Everybody was apprehensive, out in the open as we were, but the KATUSAs got back into their old holes without incident. Time on target barrages and airbursts gave us continuous cover. The noise was absolutely deafening, and the aerial bursts with WP [white phosphorus] flared like a red-and-white hell.

Around 1:00 A.M. we again received orders to pull out, and this time we really did move off the ridge. We pulled back through a heavy machine-gun crew set up in a blocking position. A half hour later a terrific firefight broke out around the heavy machine-gun position. I never knew, or have forgotten, whether those men managed to get out.

[Once the enemy was across the Seoul-Kansong highway, he concentrated his full efforts on taking Seoul. On 27 April, Uijongbu was outflanked, and the U.S. 3d Division was forced to pull back again. The 1st Cavalry Division was pushed forward to cover its withdrawal.]

Sgt. F/C FRANK ALMY
E Company/7th Cavalry

As we boarded trucks and headed toward Uijongbu, I began to feel a little apprehensive about going into a fight with a new platoon. I'd been fighting with the 3d Platoon for nearly nine months, and old habits are hard to break. My 2d Platoon was full of men I'd never fought with before. They had a good record in combat, though, and the squad leaders had been handpicked by me. I also knew the platoon leader was one of the best you could have asked for. I believe part of my fear was due to the fact that many of my friends were no longer with the company and I missed them.

We arrived at our destination, a row of hills west of Uijongbu which overlooked the road northward. When I felt the platoon sergeant was taking too long to get the men in place, I took over the job myself. I assigned one squad to go down and set up along the road. The men didn't want to go, but I told them that if they saw or heard anything during the night, they could pull back to our position on the hill. I also placed a machine gun on the hill to cover the road. This satisfied them, and they went and took up their position. I don't blame them for being scared, I know I was. We kept hearing about outfits being surrounded and destroyed. The news was really bad at this time, and I fully expected to see a horde of Chinks pouring down the road chasing the 3d Division.

The night was cold and frustrating. Everyone had to stay awake all the time. Once the Chinese arrived, no one knew from which direction they would attack. One kid got so scared that he shook like a leaf in a windstorm. When I talked to him, I decided he wouldn't be much good in a fight and sent him to the rear. When a man's nerves give out on him—as I was to learn firsthand a month later— he's not much good as a fighting man. He actually becomes more of a threat to the other men than he is a help. There's no shame at- tached to being afraid—some people can handle it, some can't.

The day dawned gray and overcast. Our artillery to the rear be- gan firing. It looked to me as if the air bursts exploded when the shells hit the low clouds. Wasn't long before the men from the 3d Division began to go through our positions. The Chinese were close behind. We could hear the sounds of battle in the hills to the north. It took most of a day for the division to get through our lines, and once the men were clear, we were put on tanks and taken to some hills above Seoul where we were told to dig in.

Sgt. GLENN HUBENETTE
F Company/7th Regiment
Time seemed to drag. It grew very hot. We hopped a ride on some tanks. One of the guys put his bedroll on the tank's exhaust pipe, and it caught fire. The lieutenant and the tank commander began cussing at us; they were afraid the smoke would draw enemy fire. The guy and I stomped on the roll, but the fire wouldn't go out. Finally, we had to kick it off the tank.

Another time, the battalion commander gave us a pep talk from his jeep: We were going to stop soon and battle the Chinks, and he'd keep everything under control. Shortly afterward, the company got surprised around Uijongbu by the Chinese. An officer yelled, "Pull out! Get out! Every man for himself!" We panicked and bugged out. The new kids just ran, and we older guys couldn't get a hold of anything to slow it down. I saw rifles, BARs, ammo, and packs lying on the ground. I was trotting along the dike of a rice paddy when a GI named Menendez cut in front of me from another dike and jos- tled me. I nearly fell into the slop. "Hey," I yelled, "why'n hell don't you watch—" then the Chinks dropped a mortar round between us.

The concussion knocked me down and over. I heard Menendez scream, then I blacked out. When I came to, someone was kneeling by me yelling that I should get up and follow him. I recognized the voice of Sergeant Davidson. I was blind and couldn't stand. I shouted, "Get Menendez!" "He's dead. Nothin' to do for'm now." My sight came back. I made out Lieutenant Galt standing on the trail, helping men along. My head spun like a top, and the trail went from color to black-and-white to color, then faded in and out. There was a buzzing inside my head. I staggered down a slope and ran into a truck convoy. I heard a heavy machine gun ripping out long bursts of fire. I was picked up and thrown into the back of one of the trucks. It was hot. A great inner rage began to consume me. If I could ever find that officer who'd yelled, "Every man for himself!" I'd kill him. I knew enough not to get men running like a crazed mob. That man had screwed up and gotten good men killed.

I was finally hauled away in a jeep, and I never saw combat again. I had had it. Some call it "shell shock" or "battle fatigue"— whatever, I had it.

[On the 29 April, UN pilots caught nearly 6,000 enemy troops in the open as they tried to cross the Han, and cruelly punished them. When the Chinese were unable to keep up with their logistical demands or continue to shrug off their frightful losses, the enemy offensive blew itself out. Seoul would not be the Communists' May Day gift to the world, after all.

Meanwhile, Eighth Army, which had fallen back an average of thirty-five miles, took up a new line five miles north of the capital. This line, called in some places No Name line and, in others, line Golden or the Lincoln line, ran in a northeast direction across the 38th Parallel, thence to Taep'o-ri on the east coast. Van Fleet had, generally speaking, kept his major units in one piece and, during the week-long battle, traded some hills for Chinese lives. All things considered, the UN's forces were in rather good shape; the enemy's were not.]

Cpl. JAMES CARDINAL
Headquarters Company/3d Battalion/5th Cavalry

30 April

Dear Folks:

We are now on the northern outskirts of Seoul. The battle which
has been raging furiously for several days has subsided temporarily while the Chinese get their wind back in preparation for new
blows. Frankly, this is not as ominous as it sounds. We don't
frighten now like we did in November and December and there's
no talk of them pushing us out of Korea. Their losses . . . have
been almost beyond belief. Their dead are piled up in front of
our positions by the thousands. Sooner or later they'll realize
our firepower is too much for their manpower and agree to some
sort of truce. Just let's hope and pray it comes soon.

Of course, all this has its price. Four nights ago three companies in the battalion were overrun and K Company lost twenty-
eight men. My old I Company lost quite a few too, some of
them good friends of mine. For the past two days they've been
dragging the dead back into our positions. Right now ten of them
are lying in front of the medics. It's really a pitiful sight. Due to
the fact that it's hot now . . . decay sets in fast and the smell is
unbelievable. Flies cover the bodies by the thousands. GIs like
myself stand around dumbfounded, and have little to say. I think
often, there but for the grace of God lie I. One strange reaction
in me is that it gives me added incentive to live and return
home. A lot of times I get to feeling blue and not caring what
happens. Then seeing those poor guys makes me realize all there
is to live for.

Sgt. F/C FRANK ALMY
E Company/7th Cavalry

We were trucked again, and this time drove through Seoul. Toward
the end of the day we stopped below some hills the Marines had such
a hard time taking the preceding September after the Inch'on landings. From on top of these hills you could see practically the whole

city and, in another direction, the countryside for miles around. It was a beautiful view.

No one had to dig new foxholes, as there were plenty from the ones that had already been dug by the gooks and Marines.

The Chinks outnumbered us, but they didn't have near the capacity to outfight us. We'd made them pay dearly in lives for every foot of ground we gave up to them. When you can do that and pull back to fight another day, you've done what you're there to do.

Cpl. DONALD CHASE
B Company/19th Infantry

Eventually, we reached a spot where we were told to dig in and be prepared to stay. The days and nights now all blend together. We dug foxholes and connecting trenches, put up barbed wire, sewed mine fields and, at night, fought off Chinese probing attacks. We covered our fighting positions with logs, sandbags, and rocks, and hung empty C-ration cans with small stones in them on the barbed wire so they'd rattle when anyone tried to get through the wire during the night. The D Company [weapons company], with its heavy [.30-caliber] water-cooled machine guns, recoilless rifles, and mortars, was moved up and put right into the defensive lines. Every day we got stronger defensively, and each of us began to relax a little more. We began to feel that no matter what the Chinese threw at us, we could handle it.

The Air Force was busy every day, bombing and strafing any enemy they caught in the open.* The napalm bombs did fearsome damage, and terrible indeed were the sights of burned bodies. Some dead Chinese looked like over-grilled hot dogs. By keeping the enemy under cover by day, we knew he could only attack at night, so we were always ready for him. At one time flares were in short supply, so no one wanted to call for them unless absolutely necessary. But overall, when we needed something it was there.

One night the Chinese attacked the company to our left, and

---

*On 29 April, for example, Far East Air Force mounted nearly 1,000 sorties. Pilots claimed they had destroyed 800 buildings, 85 railroad cars, and 50 vehicles and caused 900 enemy casualties.

watching the battle was like looking at a movie. Tracers from both sides streaked across the night sky—ours were red; theirs, green. Exploding shells, especially the WP, made things look like a gigantic fireworks display. I watched this battle from my foxhole and shook the whole time. I thought our turn was coming. But the fight eventually died down, the enemy drifted away, and to my great relief, nothing further happened that night.

While we were in this defensive line, new replacements came in—so many, in fact, that to this day very few faces or names come to mind. One of the new men, who was twenty-eight or twenty-nine but looked fifty, never minded using the flamethrower when he came across what looked to be underground tunnels or spider holes. I remember another guy; he was so frightened he should never have been sent to a line company. One dark and rainy night he heard something in the next hole over and shot at it. Of course, it was one of our own men moving around. When the sun rose we discovered him half out of the foxhole, part of his head sliced off, his brains leaking out into the rain. The really sad part of this is that the fellow killed was due to rotate home in about a month. As for the scared GI who accidentally shot him, all that could be done was reassign him to a noncombat unit. These things happen and it's really no one's fault. Everyone feels bad when someone becomes a casualty, yet at the same time he's secretly glad it's not him.

Sgt. F/C W. B. WOODRUFF, JR.
L Company/35th Infantry

The first few days in our new position north of Seoul, we labored at still further improvements. We made minor changes to platoon and squad sectors, dug deeper, filled many sandbags, and put in much more barbed wire. We were issued additional light machine guns— up to three or four per platoon, instead of one. I remember assigning one of these to George Dunphy, a top rifleman from Ohio, who just about refused to take it. It was interesting how much pride and loyalty a man could develop toward his own occupation or craft, in the army as in civil life. The business of the rifleman is maneuver and close combat; that of the heavy weapons specialist is more static as he provides supporting fire. Rarely was a man good at both functions;

more interestingly, each tended to look down on the other's craft. To Dunphy, it was a demotion to be assigned as a machine gunner. Shortly afterward, regiment called for volunteers for a special reconnaissance platoon about to be activated. Dunphy volunteered, and I never heard from him again. (After the war my letters to his Ohio address were all returned.)

We also drew flamethrowers at this time, a weapon we had not had available previously. I believe they were issued, one per platoon. Another new wrinkle someone invented was to set out barrels of fuel—gasoline diluted with kerosene or oil—50 to 100 yards in front of the foxholes. White phosphorus or thermite grenades were taped to the barrels, and wires run back to the nearest foxhole. By pulling on the wire you could detonate the grenade and barrel of fuel. We never got a chance to try out these special and innovative arrangements, however. Despite their having been nipping at our heels as we entered the Lincoln line, the CCF never undertook a frontal assault on our sector.

The only enemy contact Love Company had during this period came one afternoon when a Chinese soldier came down the road carrying a dirty white "flag." We proudly sent him back for interrogation, supposing him to be a deserter. In light of later information, it is probable he was a trained Communist agitator, selected and ordered to surrender in order to get into our POW camps. Our Chinese prisoners then numbered many thousands. To the Communists, this was regarded as just another pool of available manpower. If they could no longer influence the purely military action, they could still influence the political and psychological warfare, which the enemy seemed to think more important, anyway. The objective was to get and keep all their own prisoners under close discipline, so that riots and other disturbances could be generated at appropriate times to take over the headlines in the American press. It was already becoming clear that some type of armistice negotiations would begin before very long.

[At General Ridgway's headquarters in Tokyo, the enemy's losses during what became known as the Chinese Fifth Phase Offensive were put at between 70,000 and 100,000. However, no one was fooled by these figures, for if nothing else, the Communists had manpower in abundance. The Chinese had not been decisively defeated, and it was believed they had seventeen fresh divisions available whenever they chose to attack again. Accordingly, General Van Fleet reshuffled his divisions to give the UN the strength to meet the next enemy offensive. In the west, I Corps comprised the ROK 1st Division and the U.S. 1st Cavalry and 25th Infantry Divisions, with the U.S. 3d Division and the mauled British 29th Brigade in reserve. Next in line to the east, IX Corps had the 28th Commonwealth Brigade (redesignated from the 27th), the U.S. 24th and 7th Divisions, and the ROK 6th and 2d Divisions in line, with the U.S. 187th Airborne RCT in reserve. In the center, X Corps was strengthened by the addition of the 1st Marine Division (now commanded by Maj. Gen. Gerald C. Thomas), which joined the U.S. 2d Division and the ROK 5th and 7th Divisions on the line. Farther east, defending the mountains, were the ROK III Corps (9th and 3d Divisions) and ROK I Corps (Capital and 11th Divisions). All in all, 269,772 Americans and UN troops and 234,993 ROK Army troops. Above them, the Chinese were believed to have 542,000 soldiers; and the still-dangerous North Koreans, 197,000 soldiers. In reserve, 750,000 Chinese troops stood poised north of the Yalu in Manchuria. No question as to where that advantage lay.

Before the enemy could make up his losses of late April, Van Fleet decided to capitalize on the lull and regain the initiative. On 4 May, he directed each of his divisions to establish a patrol base in regimental combat team strength in advance of its main position. From each of them, UN forces would carry the fight to the enemy's screening forces and, if all went as planned, keep the Communists off-balance.]

Cpl. VICTOR FOX
I Company/5th Cavalry
In early May, I Company found itself near the MLR, which was along the huge mass of mountains rising north and east of Seoul. We were in a wide gorge, or ravine, running east and west behind the front lines. Over the unimproved roads in the area there was a great deal of traffic, with equipment, supplies, communications, and men moving from one area to another.

The weather was warm, and Korean farmers were busy fertilizing the fields which ran along the ravine I Company was located in.

The stench from the human fertilizer permeated the countryside. (Come to think of it, the same stench could be smelled in Korean cities and towns as well.) A guy becomes tolerably immune to a lot of things, but rice paddies are not one of them. The stink got worse as the sun got hotter—shimmering, blazing sun, cooking the stench till it became unbearable. GIs that slipped—or worse, fell off the weak footpaths into the paddies—were avoided for days. Yet, on those occasions when a patrol came under enemy fire, no one hesitated to take cover by the paddy embankments.

A Korean farmer carried his human fertilizer (they are a thrifty people about everything) in two pots hung at the ends of a long pole which was carried on his shoulder. GIs called these pots "honey buckets." Occasionally, an innocent farmer carrying his pole with its honey buckets on either end would encounter a patrol of GIs on the road. The Americans would curse and shout at the poor feller, who would scamper off the road and wait until the GIs passed.

About this time our hot chow began to contain large portions of Korean-grown rice. We were assured the rice was safe to eat, and being always hungry, after our initial inquiry ("Hey, Sarge, ya sure this rice ain't been fertilized with shit?") we'd dig in.

Eventually, the company began to patrol northward from the MLR toward Uijongbu, and there ran into increasing enemy resistance. On one day, after finding the enemy in force to our front, we were ordered immediately back to the MLR. We hit the low hills which begin to rise steadily the closer you get to Seoul.

At night the withdrawal was very cautious, and we had strict orders to light no fires and make as little noise as possible. Around midnight the company was strung out on a ridge running along the side of a mountain. On the other side of the ridge we watched soundlessly as an ever-lengthening line of torches lit the way for the Chinese. It reminded me exactly of the "Night on Bald Mountain" scene from Disney's *Fantasia*.

At daybreak we neared the lines manned by one of the Cav's other regiments. Before we got to them, though, the Chinese caught up with I Company and began shooting up the rearmost platoon. The L Company became heavily engaged, too, but the enemy did not follow us into our lines. I remember the troopers we passed through were ready; they were actually eager for the Chinese to attack.

[*And attack they did, this time after darkness the night of 15–16 May. The drive, launched by twenty-one Chinese divisions flanked by three North Korean divisions in the west and by six in the east, was directed at the trackless, broken country defended by the U.S. X Corps and ROK III Corps. On the sixteenth, the Chinese crossed the Pukhan River west of Ch'unch'on and, late in the day, heavily engaged the ROK 5th and 7th Divisions along a twenty-mile front northeast of Inje. Trying to stop the Chinese was like trying to stop river rapids; the ROKs broke and fled. Van Fleet reacted at once to stabilize the front. The 1st Marine Division and the U.S. 2d Division, which had its right flank endangered, were ordered to swing eastward and cover the gap now swarming with Chinese and North Koreans. Then, the 15th RCT and the U.S. 3d Division, in reserve below Seoul, were rushed across the peninsula to the threatened area in a wild, seventy-mile night ride. The 7th and 65th Infantry Regiments immediately went into blocking positions at the southern terminus of the penetration. The situation turned critical when the Chinese and North Korean throngs nearly cut off the 2d Division, and attacked the Indianheads from three directions.*]

Cpl. DON THOMAS
K Company/23d Infantry
We spread out in a dry riverbed [8 May] and began to dig in. A few minutes later we were ordered to stop digging and get ready to move back on the ridge we'd just come from. We reclimbed the hill and again dug in. We dug and scratched on the rocky ridge for an hour or so before we heard we no longer had a right flank and would have to pull back.

While we were in the process of leaving, firing broke out on the road below us. I saw three or four Americans run across the road, with bullets kicking up around them. They made it safely to the draw in front of our ridge and climbed up to our position. The Chinese were on the other side of the road by this time, and had it under fire. A few minutes after this scrape, our company began to move up the hill. We reached the crest and entered the trees. We passed a group of GIs and ROKs carrying litters, which also included some walking wounded. This group eventually ended up at the end of our column. It began to rain. The column was now strung out for at least a mile.

The pace was fast. After a couple of hours my water was gone. We still had not been fired upon. We stepped over a small stream flowing out of an area of rice paddies. Most of us dipped our helmets full. It looked like clear rainwater. I drank it; so did most of the other guys. I never came down with anything.

We walked along saddles and down into valleys. A few mortar or artillery shells fell near my part of the column. I passed a GI; he was bleeding, and a medic knelt by his side. I could smell the acrid odor of the explosion. It sure spurred me on. I was wet clear through. My boots made noisy sucking sounds; my web belt and harness squeaked; the straps from the bandoliers and the field pack harness wore the skin from my shoulders.

I was far enough back in the line that at times I could see the rear. Later in the afternoon my part of the column cleared a narrow pass. I stepped out of line to take a break. I looked back to the rear and saw an officer pulling machine gunners and mortarmen out of the column. None too soon. The column had just cleared the trees on the far side of the small valley when the firing started. I saw the small group of litter bearers and walking wounded tumble down the slope. The machine guns and mortars from the column began to fire. I fell back into the line and kept moving. I had no idea how much farther I had to go. We received no artillery support or air cover at this time.

We moved fast until around eleven o'clock that night. We crossed a draw. It was very dark. All at once, "Who'n hell's down there?" came from the ridge on our left. With a great amount of relief almost everyone hollered, "K Company!"

A few minutes later we reached the defensive position of the 38th Infantry Regiment. Each squad in our platoon was assigned a tank. We dug in behind ours. C rations and water were given out. My partner and I managed to end up with one of the cases the rations came packed in. We split it open and laid it out over the mud. We lay on it and covered ourselves with a wet blanket and poncho. By morning my body heat had partially dried my clothing. Later in the day, we climbed on trucks. I started out still damp, but the sun soon dried me. On the trip another guy and I rode the top of a trailer between the bows. The canvas sagged like a hammock—it was very nice.

[The 2d Division held fast and, with an enormous concentration of UN firepower, broke the enemy's back.* After only four days, and after achieving only a narrow gap that could not be exploited, the Chinese second spring offensive came to a standstill.† The X Corps stabilized its front, and in the west the two U.S. corps easily stopped a feeble enemy push toward Seoul. General Ridgway recognized almost at once that the Chinese had overextended themselves, and he ordered Van Fleet to attack immediately. This sudden reversal in fortune caught the enemy by surprise. On 20 May, along the entire front, UN infantrymen left No Name line behind and began to move northward again, toward the 38th Parallel and North Korea.]

Gen. MATTHEW B. RIDGWAY
Commander, United Nations Command

. . . It was good sense to threaten and even to seize, if we could, the Iron Triangle, terminus of the formerly one good railroad from Manchuria and center for many good roads that kept the enemy's front fed and supplied. It was also vital to us to control the Hwach'on Reservoir, previously the source of water and electricity for Seoul and the heart of the enemy supply route. Consequently, the new offensive was meant to roll on over the 38th Parallel again, without our giving that line any further thought, and to destroy as much as we could of the enemy's potential.‡

Sgt. F/C W. B. WOODRUFF, JR.
L Company/35th Infantry

It was a relief when we got marching orders again. It was peculiar, but troops seemed to welcome a return to the line from a reserve or

---

* One field artillery battalion, for example, fired 12,000 105-mm rounds in twenty-four hours.
† For the week 17–23 May, Communist losses would be put at 90,000.
‡ Ridgway, 177–78.

other inactive period almost as much as they welcomed reverting to reserve after a hard tour at the front. Now it was back to business, to important work, to meeting those daily tasks and decisions that were so familiar. As a now-veteran outfit, we took this on with a practiced skill and a sure confidence in ourselves and our unit.

It was 20 May 1951 that we boarded trucks and moved north. Before many miles we off-loaded and set out across country. This time we took the Uijongbu road north from Seoul.

I had entered on this tour of duty in September [1950] just as school was starting. Most of my life I had spent in school of some sort, from September to May or June, year after year. It was now about time for school to be out. This year it had been a different kind of "school," but school just the same, for it had been one of the most intense learning and studying experiences I had ever known. When matters of life and death are involved, you study harder. It came to me that my service in World War II had been rather like college, and that what I had had in Korea was rather like a postgraduate course in war. I should now be about ready for my master's degree!

Had I carried this line of thought to its logical conclusion, I would have realized that I must first take and pass a final exam. In fact, though I did not know it, my "final exam" was already scheduled. It lay five days ahead, and would be conducted at a place called Hill 424.

Sgt. F/C FRANK ALMY
E Company/7th Cavalry

The company began to march through some of the country the Chinks had fought over in late April. They must have lost a lot of men, because there were graves everywhere along the side of the road. Some outfit—maybe the British—had really put it to them.

Our final destination was a large valley that the British [29th Brigade] had been trapped and lost a lot of men in. One day I climbed a hill and saw a lot of their dead lying where they had fallen. Another time, I found a place where a Bren gun outfit had been ambushed and annihilated. Corpses and trucks were strewn everywhere. Each time, I reported the findings so the British could go in and recover their dead.

Our men were put up in houses we'd taken from Korean civilians. The peasants were put into one house, and our men took over the rest of the tiny village. There were some nice-looking girls among the Koreans, and I had a feeling there might be some moonlighting if we let it. I sure didn't care. I figured the guys put their lives on the line each day, and they didn't need any nursemaids. They were tough kids, fighting a tough war, and deserved every break we could give them.

Sgt. ED HENDRICKS
F Company/5th Cavalry

We once had a West Point graduate officer lead our company. Here was a man who stood tall. There was no fear in the man; danger never bothered him. I remember once in the spring we were taking a hill and my, oh my, was it raining! Our captain got hit right in the jaw. A medic rushed up, splashing through the mud, and wrapped the captain's head and jaw to stop the bleeding. The captain put his steel helmet back on and stood up in the rain, then he started back up the hill. A little later he was hit again. This time, they carried him to the rear. God, how we respected that man. We'd have followed him through hell, which, come to think of it, we already had done. But of course, he didn't last too long. Shame.

Sgt. F/C C. W. "BILL" MENNINGER
2d Battalion/21st Infantry

As it is in every war, the army in Korea was constantly looking for second lieutenants. One day two friends, the battalion supply sergeant and the battalion S-1 sergeant, stopped by the CP. "Bill," they said, "have we got a deal going. Division is looking to make some NCOs lieutenants. This is our opportunity to get jobs back in the rear." Being wise beyond my years, and remembering a similar experience in the Second World War, I declined the offer to join them as officers and gentlemen. That same day they became second lieutenants. Within a week both were dead—one leading his rifle platoon in the attack, the other, while observing fire from his mortar section.

Cpl. JAMES CARDINAL
Headquarters Company/3d Battalion/5th Cavalry

24 May

Dear Folks:

It's late in the evening here and I'm writing by the light of a lantern. We are about thirty miles N.E. of Seoul but are not now in contact with the enemy.

You remember how I use to complain about the terrible cold last winter and how I thought I'd freeze to death. Well now I have another problem—the damned rain. It rains continuously, hour after hour and they say the rainy season is only starting, that it actually gets worse in June and July. God, what a horrible thing to look forward to.

You know, when I get out of here and start living like a civilized human being again and not like some dog or other beast, my days of looking for adventure are going to be over. All I want now is the comfort of a nice home and plenty of good food.

By the way, my buddy Jerry Emer is back again. He was in the hospital three months in Japan but now looks fine. I was sorry to see him come back as I was hoping he would be sent home and thereby spared more of this misery.

Sgt. F/C FRANK ALMY
E Company/7th Cavalry

Second Platoon was picked to capture some prisoners. We patrolled forward about three miles from base camp and stopped when we got to a river. It was late May and hot. Across from us we could see the Chinese on their hills and in the river. I'm sure the cool water must have felt good. Lieutenant Matthews wanted a prisoner real bad, and he took some men toward the river. I stayed with the rest of the platoon. Matt must have stepped on a booby trap, because I heard a muffled explosion. While I was trying to figure what had happened, a B-26 light bomber flew low over our position. He was looking us over, and I knew if he opened up with his machine guns, the platoon would be in a mess. I tried to reach him on the radio. When I couldn't get him, I began waving him off. Five times he made passes over us before being satisfied we were on the same side. You can't begin to realize what a relief that was. I knew right then how bad my nerves really were and recognized my breaking point wasn't far off.

Matt, who had been lightly wounded by the booby trap, returned a little time later with a prisoner.

Capt. LUTHER WEAVER
L Company/35th Infantry

The hill [424] gave everyone the jitters; we knew it was heavily fortified and defended by the Chinese. We knew a unit of the 24th Infantry had tried to take it before the enemy spring offensive and had failed. We were now in the vicinity of Ch'orwon and, after advancing 6,000 yards in the attack [24 May], were ordered to take Hill 424 the next day. Due to its configuration, the largest unit that could be expected to attack its summit was a company. The south flank was a sheer rock wall; the only approaches, therefore, were up the southeast side, along a couple of razorback ridges of which only one went all the way to the summit. Colonel Lee told me I could have whatever fire support I thought we needed. He informed me he'd have the 64th FA Battalion put some fire on during the night to prevent the Chinese from bringing up reinforcements. He also promised 4.2 mortars and two ack-ack quad .50 half-tracks, which would establish a base of fire until the company worked its way up the ridge far enough for us to use our small arms.

Before dark I sent a platoon-size patrol to check the area of our departure, which was a dirt road that led to the ridge. The patrol returned without finding the enemy but did notice some recently dug entrenchments. I established a platoon outpost in the area to prevent the Chinese from moving down on us before the attack.

We jumped off at 7:00 A.M. [on the twenty-fifth], with Sergeant Woodruff's 1st Platoon leading the way along the sharp ridge that rose to the peak of the hill. Second Platoon would advance along a shorter ridge, and when they could go no farther, they'd lay down a base of fire for Woodruff. Third Platoon would remain at the line of departure and be our reserve. I stayed at the foot of the hill with the 4.2 mortars so I could control their fire in front of Woodruff's platoon.

Sgt. F/C w. b. WOODRUFF, JR.
L Company/35th Infantry

As we entered the timber, about halfway up the side of the first rise or knoll, I heard firing up ahead and hurried toward it. I found Miller's squad prone at the crest of this knoll. Just over the crest, and ten to fifteen yards down the forward slope, his first scout lay wounded. Miller told me that when he reached this point he had drawn a sudden burst of automatic fire from the three knolls in front. Furthermore, when the scout was first hit he had yelled; the more he hollered, the more the enemy poured fire on him, until he had become quiet, apparently unconscious from multiple wounds. I remembered the scout, though I cannot now recall his name. He was a young regular who had been with us about two weeks and had seemed really gung ho; I figured he had volunteered for the first scout assignment. Now he lay seriously wounded or dead in his first action, within days of arriving at the front. The first thing to be done was to get him out.

I shucked my rifle and web equipment, then very carefully eased over the crest on my belly. Drawing no fire, I continued squirming down to the wounded man, who was unconscious but still breathing. The next question was how to move him. I resolved this by wriggling as close up to and under him as I could, then pulling one of his arms over each of my shoulders and crossing them under my chin. We were then both on our bellies, with him partially on top of me, and I was holding one of his wrists in each hand so as to keep his arms locked around my neck. Tied together like this, I squirmed and wriggled back to the crest, in part carrying and in part dragging him with me. At each instant I expected to be fired upon; the grass and weeds were nowhere near sufficient to conceal us from the higher ground to the front. Not a round was fired, however. The Chinese, I noted, had kept their record intact of never firing on a rescue effort.

When I had sent the wounded man off to the aid station and got my breath, it was time for a closer look at the tactical situation.

At first glance it seemed impossible. There were these three knolls to our front which were on a generally east-west line—actually three rises in one long ridgeline. The center knoll was the highest, and the one marked 424 on the map. This center knoll was about 600 yards distant; from it, another ridgeline ran generally south to our knoll. The four knolls formed a T, with us at its bottom, or base, and the other three knolls forming the top or crossbar of the T. The only apparent route northward from our location was along the ridge connecting us to the center knoll, or highest point, of Hill 424. The top of this ridge was no more than two feet wide, and along it ran the inevitable trail, occupying about a foot of its two-foot width. Both sides of the ridge fell off sharply. Jutting out from the top and sides of the ridge at intervals were rocky outcroppings and numerous large rocks and boulders. According to Miller's report, the enemy had automatic weapons firing from the center knoll directly down the ridge-line trail. They also had it in a cross fire from machine guns on both flanking knolls.

By this time Bressard and 3d Squad had come up to our left. I asked Bressard if he thought we could advance along the side of the ridge about six feet below its top, which would give us some degree of cover from the enemy on the center knoll, and good cover with respect to fire from the knoll on the opposite side of the ridge. It would, of course, have made us wide open to fire from the flanking knoll on our side of the ridge. He said we could try. About that time a heavy artillery concentration began falling on the enemy knoll to our left front; it was really being plastered. This decided the issue and gave us an opening. I told Bressard to move out along the left side of the ridge. I also told Miller, and I believe Lorenz, to stay where they were and to give us covering fire as best they could.

The artillery did a splendid job on the knoll to our left; we drew no fire from it thereafter. We accordingly made pretty fair progress scrambling along the side of the ridge. Bressard's scout was a former paratrooper named Royal, from North Carolina, who led the way. Bressard followed him, then me, then a rifleman named Bennett. Bennett was from Elgin, Illinois, and had just been married when his active duty orders came the previous fall, grievously disrupting his honeymoon. All three had been in the squad since last December when I had been squad leader, and I knew I was in good hands. The

rest of the squad followed single file behind Bennett, while White-
calf, as assistant squad leader, was in charge of the tail of the column. While we covered, Royal moved up five yards or so until he
reached the next boulder. Then each of us moved forward one at a
time, until it was Royal's turn again.

The first four of us, Royal back to Bennett, were all that I could
see most of the time. This is another example of how limited a rifleman's field of vision is. The company, then overstrength, probably
had 240 men; of these, there were 236 that I could not see, and I
had no idea what they were doing. That morning the success or failure of the company, maybe of the battalion—conceivably of the whole
35th Infantry Regiment with all its myriad firepower and manpower—lay in the hands of four men armed with M1 rifles.

We progressed without incident until the main height, or central knoll, of Hill 424 loomed over us no more than 100 yards away.
I closed up on Bressard for the umpteenth time, rested my elbows on
the top of a boulder, and settled into a position to observe and fire to
the immediate front. I nodded to Royal to begin the next move forward. I remember moving my head slightly to the right, cheek against
rifle butt, to better align my sights. This saved my life. At that instant, I was picked up as by a giant hand, rolled rearward, and slammed
against the ground onto my back. When I got my eyes into focus, I
was looking forward, aware that both Royal and Bressard had frozen
in place, both of them staring backward at me. I told them to get
their head and eyes to the front. Then, aware of Bennett's presence,
I looked back and asked him what they had done to me. He peered
intently, leaned forward, peered some more, and said, "Sarge, I believe they have shot you through the ear." What had happened was
that the bullet had just grazed my left cheek, passed about dead center through my left ear, and then struck the rear of my helmet from
the inside; it was the impact against the helmet that had upended
me. I reached up gingerly, taking my left lobe between thumb and
forefinger, and was gratified to learn that the ear was still relatively
intact and properly connected to my head.

Thinking that our present location was no place to camp indef-
initely and that we were too far forward to ever go back, I realized
our only hope was to move out smartly, which we did. The sniper

did not fire again. He had been smart enough to pick me out as the man in charge, and he was now smart enough to keep his head down.

Capt. LUTHER WEAVER
E Company/35th Infantry

As Woodruff's platoon began to move into position to assault the crest, I called a halt to the mortars and quad .50s, and moved with my runner, Private Haitz, and the SCR-536 up the ridge toward the battle. Halfway up, enemy machine-gun fire swept the razorback ridge. I slid off to one side, Private Haitz slid off to the other. He landed in an enemy foxhole that had been mined, and was killed. I radioed back to the company CP for medics, then I continued up the hill.

Sgt. F/C W. B. WOODRUFF, JR.
L Company/35th Infantry

We reached the base of the knoll, where the ridgeline widened and merged into the base of the last rise. I recognized we had another tactical problem. Somehow, in order to put maximum firepower forward and begin the final assault in a proper skirmish line, I had to get 3d Squad out of its present single file, or column, and into a line. I told Bressard as we came off the ridge onto the hill to do a column right and move to the far side of the hill, then to have the whole squad do a left flank. He looked dubious, but did it. I still have not found a textbook solution for this precise problem; ours was admittedly awkward, but it worked.

As we got our line formed and moving upward, one Chinese soldier darted from a dugout directly in front of me and ran for the crest. He did not make it. Then I spotted another hole; I called to Bressard to cover me and pointed toward the dugout entrance. I pulled out a grenade—my last; I had used two yesterday and failed to re-supply last night. This one I had been carrying a long time, and the pin had rusted to the cap. When I pulled, the ring broke off, leaving the pin intact. This was embarrassing from several viewpoints; I got rid of the now defective grenade and asked Bressard if he had one left. He did, so I covered him while he put it neatly into the dugout.

No more problem there. Then the advance turned up yet another dugout; Bressard saw movement inside. He called to us to watch out, and to the Chinese inside to come out. Three surrendered, hands up, two of them bowing and smiling, the third looking glum, ill-natured, and still defiant. Checking into the dugout to make sure there were no others, Bressard found a real antique—a heavy Russian machine gun mounted on wheels. We reached the crest. From off to our left there was a brief flurry of firing and a shout to watch out for counterattack. We maintained a sharp lookout, but there was no further action where I was. I looked at my watch. It was 11:30 A.M.; we had jumped off that morning about 7:30. I was conscious of being tired and hungry.

Capt. LUTHER WEAVER
L Company/35th Infantry

When I neared the crest, Sergeant Woodruff was moving back down the hill holding the bloody side of his face. We stopped long enough for him to tell me a Chink had shot him nearly point-blank. I said, "There should be some aid men down with Haitz." He told me, "I know there's at least one dead Chink up there."

First and 2d Platoons had meanwhile begun to move up the ridge. When I arrived at the top, 1st Platoon was mopping up. Some Chinese who were still able attempted to leave their firing bunkers.

We counted sixty-three bodies, and according to the eight POWs we captured, we wounded at least seventy-five more. The quad .50s and mortars had knocked them senseless, and when they lifted their heads, Woodruff and 1st Platoon were in amongst them. Ten enemy machine guns and two mortars had also been knocked out. Our own losses were two dead, seven wounded. A victory for firepower.

Sgt. F/C W. B. WOODRUFF, JR.
L Company/35th Infantry

By the time the doctors got through bandaging my head, I could not get my helmet on. They tagged me and told me to wait for the next truck back to the regimental collecting station. While waiting I read the tag, as this was my first experience with medical evacuation procedures, and I viewed them with some interest. The tag indicated the nature of my wound and was signed by the doctor. I do not remember his name, but I was struck by his rank—it was "Lt.(j.g.)" A navy doctor! I had heard that the army was so short of doctors that some navy surgeons had been given this kind of duty; it must have been a far cry from a shipboard dispensary.

A thirty-minute ride brought me to the collecting station, which was a small group of tents much like the sets for the "M.A.S.H." television program would later look. We were checked again and told to wait. I spotted a Lyster bag and went to refill my canteen. I passed a tent with an open flap. Inside was a sort of operating table; on it, lying face down, was the young scout of Miller's squad, our first casualty that morning. His shirt had been removed, and his pants pulled down to expose the base of his spine, where an enormous hole gaped. The doctor, with some instrument, picked up bunches of what looked like gauze, dipped them into a bottle filled with some solution, and inserted them in the hole in the man's back. I turned away, unable to watch. But I was glad he was still alive.

[Two days before Love Company's assault on Hill 424, the 1st Marine Division jumped off toward Yanggu, the vital road junction at the eastern end of the Hwach'on Reservoir. The route to their objective would take the Marines through some of the wildest, hilliest country in all of Korea.]

Pfc. PAUL MARTIN
Reconnaissance Company/1st Marine Division
Our first patrol went out over the same route we had traveled in early April. We stopped and set up on a ridgeline overlooking the southern shore of the Hwach'on Reservoir. Our first night passed without incident, as did the next day.

Around 3:00 A.M. on the second night, I was awakened by my buddy and immediately heard voices, even coughing, of troops heading toward us. How could the Chinese expect to infiltrate with all that ruckus going on? I rang the field phone three times before someone back at the MLR picked it up. I hoped they understood my whispered message and hadn't gone back to sleep. The Chinese passed close to where we lay; some carried their weapons on their shoulders, while others toted heavy packs. Then, a little way off, I saw another column of troops marching toward us. I began to worry that the rifle companies along the MLR wouldn't be ready for this attack.

A trip flare back toward the MLR exploded and lit up the night. The Chinese who had passed began to yell, while the ones closest to us fell to the ground. An amber cluster lit up the sky; the enemy never moved. Then the whole MLR erupted with small-arms and automatic-weapons fire, which was soon followed by the KA-RUMMP of mortar rounds landing. The Chinese lying near us pulled back. How odd, I thought; in the past they would have entered the attack and supported their own men. We stuck to our orders and did not open fire.

Around dawn we saw many small bunches of Chinese pulling back; they were everywhere. An artillery spotter plane appeared overhead and our big guns opened up. At which time, we too opened up on them with whatever we had. An air strike, I learned later, had been called in, but did not arrive until noon, when the opportunity had been lost.* Everyone was deeply disappointed at letting so many Chinese escape; they would be around another day and could kill us then.

When my patrol returned to the CP I saw plenty of Chinese prisoners. It seemed they were dispirited and discouraged.

Next morning [30 May] Recon Company was ordered to patrol the area in front of the MLR around Yanggu in jeeps with tanks attached [from 1st Tank Battalion]. We pulled out in a dense fog and met the tanks near the MLR. The sun came out and burned off the fog. We traveled for about an hour. After climbing a mountain pass, we discovered our outposts taking heavy fire from the ridges to their front.† We spent the rest of the morning futilely calling in artillery

---

* During this time the 1st Marine Aircraft Wing was under the operational control of the Fifth Air Force. Under this system, the Marine division did not enjoy the exclusive support of a Marine air wing, and never again in Korea would its close air support be as prompt or as certain as when it had.
† In late May the Marines discovered that the Chinese forces had escaped to the north and their places had been taken by the North Korean People's Army, which had been given the unenviable task of slowing down the leathernecks. Although not as well trained as the Chinese, the North Koreans would prove to be more determined in fighting defensive battles.

and air support. The planes did not arrive until the afternoon, and the artillery never got involved, as they were in the process of moving forward. Recon Company moved off to the west on foot and began looking for trails that might lead around the enemy. While doing so, we discovered a large cache of abandoned Chinese ammunition— bullets, mortar and artillery rounds, grenades, and HE. We got orders then to stop and cover this arms dump. Around midnight we left the cache and slipped across a rice paddy until we picked up a ridge that flanked the one defended by the North Koreans. (Another patrol went off and discovered a trail leading to the eastern tip of the Hwach'on). Three of us stayed behind while the rest of the platoon went back to guide the rifle companies up to our position. During the night I heard small-arms fire coming from the east. In the morning, fog socked in the area again, but the rifle companies appeared on schedule. Once the fog lifted we saw North Koreans moving in the open behind the ridge they were defending. Around midday Marine units took and secured the ridge, and the tanks which had been with us the day before clanked through the pass firing at anything that moved.

Pfc. DOUG MICHAUD
Headquarters & Service Company/1/5
This part of the war got very confusing. It was just one hill battle after another. You take a hill, and they try to take it back. Then you go fight a battle and take another hill. The hills all looked alike. You'd take a hill, but then there was another one to take, and another, and Korea has enough hills that this could have gone on forever. Endless hills, wherever you looked, forever and ever and ever. We were very busy—marching, plugging gaps, climbing hills, fighting battles, counterattacking, keeping our heads down—very, very busy. But we really weren't accomplishing anything. We got the feeling the politicians were playing chess with us. If they wanted to win it, why in the hell didn't they give us more people? Why didn't they throw in another Marine division? Rotation was the only help now. We had to take this, and we had to take that. . . . The only hope we had was putting in our time and getting the hell out of there.

What the hell, if you're not accomplishing anything, you might just as well be back home.

Pfc. PAUL MARTIN
Reconnaissance Company/1st Marine Division
Our next assignment reminded me of the battle of Quebec, when the British were able to find an unguarded trail that led them to surprise and defeat the French general, Montcalm. The company would try to find unguarded trails around the hills and ridges now so tenaciously held by the North Koreans.

We leapfrogged from one steep hill to another. Far to our left we could hear the sounds of heavy battles being fought. The hills we were on were thick with vegetation and trees, perfect for the defender. Once the lead platoon had climbed the forward ridge it would signal back to the next platoon in line, which would then proceed forward. Climbing down a hill can be as difficult, sometimes, as climbing up one. We had to continuously brace ourselves so we wouldn't slide or fall down. It was hot enough now to thaw out all the Chosin veterans. Everyone was too uncomfortable to think about being frightened.

At one trail junction the North Koreans blindly lobbed in mortar rounds, trying to prevent anyone from using it. We scaled a nearby hill and avoided the trails. Another time, on top of a ridge, we saw the North Koreans forcing a column of white-clad civilians, women and children, to carry heavy loads of ammunition and supplies. That night we set up along this trail, but a dense fog prevented us from seeing anything. We could hear the movement but not see it. Before dawn we returned to the top of the ridge. I learned one of our platoons had been sent to the rear—a curious development that puzzled me. The rest of the day was quiet, with only a few North Koreans coming down to a nearby stream and carrying back water to break the tranquillity. I couldn't imagine what purpose we were serving. My question was answered when the missing platoon returned with an endless column of Korean Marines [10 June]. They were briefed about what we had seen, and around sunset Recon Company returned to our CP. We heard the next day that the Korean Marines had surprised and defeated the North Koreans in a great night battle. I thought, Ahh ha, Montcalm bites the dust again.

Pfc. LYLE CONAWAY
F/1

A little north of the Hwach'on Reservoir, we got pinned down in a cross fire between two bunkers. The company CO, Captain [Goodwin C.] Groff, was one of the most "I-don't-give-a-shit" officers I've ever known. During this particular firefight, while our platoon leader, 2d Lieutenant Harry Randall, was calling for a machine gun to knock out one of the bunkers, Captain Groff, totally ignoring the Chinese shooting at him, walked up to Lieutenant Randall and began to discuss the use of rockets versus machine guns. At one point a bullet took out a large part of a tree Groff was standing behind. Randall ducked, so did I and everyone else nearby. Groff exclaimed, "Shit, Harry, if that Chink's CO saw how bad he was shooting, he'd send the bastard back to boot camp."

Later in the day we got some tanks to help us. Captain Groff, when he went up to one of them to direct its fire, was knocked on his ass by the cannon's back blast. When he picked himself up, he was really pissed. He rapped on the tank with the butt of his .45. The commander opened the hatch, and the captain told him in no uncertain terms what he would personally do to that tank if they ever fired again without warning him. The guy in the tank looked on in utter disbelief, then slowly closed the hatch. A short time later, as we moved up the slope of a hill, the tank fired three or four rounds toward a bunker higher up. I looked back at the tank, and at that very instant a Commie mortar round hit it. I couldn't help but wonder whether the tankers, just for a second, thought Captain Groff had had them clobbered.

[*While the Marines were making their final push on the Hwach'on Reservoir and Yanggu, the 35th Infantry, ten miles southeast of the*

leathernecks, was beginning to move toward Inje, which had been cap-
tured by the 187th RCT on 27 May.]

Cpl. DON THOMAS
K Company/23d Infantry
We lined up on the road to march into the Inje Valley, hot, dry,
and dusty, and keeping a ten- to fifteen-foot interval, as usual. Most
of us were low on water. After a mile or so, we crossed the Soyang
River on a pontoon bridge. Everyone topped off their canteens and
drank their fill. I dropped a purification pill in mine. We resumed
the march. The road forked left and right; we took the road to the
right. We marched next to the river for quite a distance. Around a
bend I saw three or four North Korean bodies hung up on a barbed-
wire fence that ran across the river. They had been there quite a few
days and were already bloated. I didn't see anyone dump out his
canteen. We were never sure when we might find water again.

We continued along the road. A Russian T34 tank was off in a
shallow draw just where the road made a hairpin turn. It looked like
it might have slipped off the road during a turn. It wasn't burned,
nor did it appear damaged. I saw quite a few dead North Koreans in
the draws that ran from the road.

Most of the huts in the valley were destroyed. There were a few
bodies lying around, also a few dead pack animals. I saw one that
had been rigged like an Indian travois, to drag wounded. The animal
and his wounded passenger were now dead.

We took up a position in reserve at the north end of the valley.
We set up our pup tents at the base of a ridge to avoid enemy artillery
zeroed in on the valley floor. There, we got a few days' rest. We hit
the shower point up on the river side of the valley, took off everything
except boots and dog tags, and washed up. On the other side, we dug
through clean piles of clothes until we found something that fit. No
one wore stripes.

We stayed for at least a week. Swam every day. In the evening
many of us walked the few hundred yards to the battalion HQ to
watch the movies. The "theater" consisted of benches in front of a
sheet held in place by two poles; the sixteen-millimeter projector ran

from a gas generator. I remember two of the movies—one was *Go for Broke*; the other, *Up Front, with Willie and Joe.**

The country-and-western singer Elton Britt performed in the valley while we were there. Most of us went to see him. During the performance I could hear distant artillery fire. You could see the people on the stage get a funny look when they heard it too. Didn't bother me, though—it wasn't falling nearby.

[Eighth Army made significant advances during the last week of May, and by Friday, 1 June, South Korea was again virtually clear of the enemy. The UN's line was nearly back to where it had been before 22 April, and ran now from Munsan-ni, through Yongp'yong to Hwach'on, thence, northeast to Kansong. The UN's casualties for May were put at 33,770—mostly South Koreans. American losses were 745 dead, 4,218 wounded, 572 missing, and 6,758 nonbattle casualties.

Many an infantryman writing home or in his diary at this time could have recorded, "Advancing steadily through heavily wooded terrain against harassing enemy fire. Raining now day and night, very miserable, no chow, am very tired."]

Cpl. DONALD CHASE
B Company/19th Infantry
During the fighting the adrenalin really flowed, and we did what we had to do. We'd hit them hard during the daylight hours, then dig in when the sun set and hope that during the night the enemy would not be strong enough to dislodge us during his counterattack. We prayed too—prayed that if we needed flares, they'd be there; prayed that the artillery would be accurate; prayed the radios would work; prayed we'd be alive when the sun rose.

There would be those times when the company got too far forward and somehow ended up on some mountaintop, surrounded by Chinese. Then we'd wait for the airdrops of water and ammunition.

---

* Both films were released in 1951. *Go for Broke* featured Van Johnson; *Up Front's* stars, David Wayne and Tom Ewell, played Bill Mauldin's famous GI cartoon characters, Willie and Joe.

The wounded would have to wait until another unit opened a road link to us, before they could be taken to an aid station.

There was no letup in the drive. After a while everyone was so exhausted we walked and talked like zombies. It was hard to tell what was real and what wasn't. I can clearly remember one morning, after a month of this, looking around at my buddies and seeing a bunch of ragged, bearded, dirty scarecrows. The scene brought to mind a movie I'd seen years before, about a group of men who'd just managed to survive a year of being lost in the jungles of Burma. Well, that's how we looked.

The smallest things were important. Getting a hot cup of coffee doesn't seem like a big thing, but what a lift it gave us when we learned 5-gallon cans of steaming coffee were on their way forward. The same with mail. Somehow, no matter where we were, or what circumstances we were in, the mail got delivered. Sadly, oftentimes letters from home arrived a day too late for some fellers.

The weather in early June was hot—very hot. There were four men left in my squad. We had begun six weeks before with twelve.

June 2 began as usual, with another attack. This time another company would take the first part of the ridgeline before we passed through them and took the crest. When it was our turn, we could see that the first phase of the battle had been costly to the Chinese. When we came through after the bombing and napalming, we stepped over badly burnt corpses and bypassed many severely wounded and disarmed Chinese soldiers waiting in their holes to be treated and taken to the rear. We were finally given the signal to take the crest. The ridgeline and hill were heavily wooded, with many of the trees shattered or down from shell fire. It was tough going. The Chinese were shooting at us from above. We charged, every man running and firing. It was impossible to aim at anything in particular—they were all so well dug in. Suddenly, my squad leader went down. I stopped for a moment and saw he'd taken a slug through the knee. I called for a medic. I raced ahead and took over the rest of the squad— two men. We reached the top and drove the Chinese off. The three of us lay huddled behind a fallen tree. Bullets flew overhead while I waited for my next orders. Something slammed into my neck. My mouth flew open, and a sheet of blood sprayed out. Having been shot before, I knew what had happened. Strangely, it didn't knock me out, but I couldn't move. I knew I was badly hurt but didn't want any morphine in case it put me to sleep. Casualties had been heavy, and there were no more litters. I was eventually put on a makeshift one, a poncho wrapped around two poles, and taken down the hill. *

Sgt. F/C FRANK ALMY
E Company/7th Cavalry

After the regiment came out of reserve, it received orders to push the Chinese in the Ch'orwon Valley. By this time I was just going through the motions, trying to hold on. Everything scared me now. After I'd been mortared [on 10 May] nothing again was the same. In early June I knew the real breaking point would come soon. And it did.

The company took the first hill in our path without any trouble. On top we didn't stop to congratulate ourselves; there were just too many more ahead for us to take the time. Each hill had to be climbed and checked. No one wanted to leave any Chinese in our rear.

We came to a hill [4 June], and saw the Chinese on its crest. An air strike was called in. The planes strafed first, then made their napalm and rocket runs. We knew by how low they flew whether the pilots were married or not. If a guy came down right on top of a hill, we always said he was single; if he made his run higher up, we said he was married. Artillery was also called in, and they pounded the hill pretty good. I watched one Chink making his way along the top of the hill. He crouched low each time a plane made its run, and was never hit. How they could miss him, I'll never know, but they did, time and time again.

It began to rain real hard. Some of the squad leaders went forward to look over the situation. We were in some trees and hidden from the Chinese. Returning, they reported a large enemy force in a ravine to our left, just waiting to counterattack. First Platoon, in front,

---

* Later, in a hospital in Japan, X rays showed a bullet in Corporal Chase's neck was lodged between the cervical vertebrae. Semiparalyzed, he was put in a waist-to-head cast to hold the neck in place. After hospital stops on Wake Island and Hawaii, he was flown to Massachusetts, where the bullet was removed. After a full recovery, Chase, now a sergeant first class, returned to Korea in late 1952, and as we will see, served as a platoon sergeant with I Company, 15th Infantry.

was pinned down. We couldn't move, either. Bullets flew all over the place. Several men were hit. The squad leaders went forward again to check on the situation. My breaking point caught up to me right then, and while they were away I removed myself from the platoon. It took hours to get to the aid station. If I hadn't had someone with me, with the rain and in my condition, I would never have made it.*

[Van Fleet's offensive advanced inexorably. Far East Air Force continued to fly hundreds of sorties in support each day. On 5 June, 500 buildings, 11 gun positions, and 80 vehicles were reported destroyed; 6 June, 970 sorties were flown, and 600 buildings and 75 railroad cars hit; 7 June, another 970 sorties which dropped 9,000,000 bomb fragments (the equivalent of 600 five-hundred-pound bombs); 8 June, 220 tons of bombs rained down on enemy positions around the Iron Triangle; 9 June, Eighth Army reported gains in the direction of Ch'orwon and Kumhwa, and in the Yonch'on and Hwach'on sectors; 10 June, 900 sorties were flown in rainy weather; 11 June, Ch'orwon and Kumhwa fell to the UN's forces, and FEAF flew more than 1,050 sorties.

One factor each infantryman must deal with, along with the fear, boredom, heavy work, and weather, is change. Gears on top of gears, wheels within wheels, all grinding, turning, spinning, as transfers, casualties, replacements, promotions, and rotations follow one another in quick succession. Some changes he ignores; others, he never notices. Then there are the other ones.]

Capt. LUTHER WEAVER
L Company/35th Infantry

While the 35th Division was in reserve, Colonel Lee called me to report to battalion headquarters [11 June]. The CO told me his S-4 [supply office] was rotating home the next day and that the job was

---

* Sergeant Almy spent several weeks in a hospital in Japan. He was eventually given a noncombat status slip before being sent back to E Company. He rotated home 13 July.

mine if I wanted it.* After some deliberation, during which I remembered that I had fought in combat in two wars for nearly 600 days, and that my good luck would some day disappear, I accepted the new job. I hated to leave Love Company, which I considered the best unit in Korea, but the new assignment was too good to pass up. †

M/Sgt. W. B. WOODRUFF, JR. ‡
L Company/35th Infantry

We were ordered to assemble the entire company, seating them on a hillside slope. My first thought was that we were to receive a briefing and be committed again. Not so. Captain Weaver got most of the way through an announcement that he was being reassigned and just wanted to say good-bye, then big tears flowed down his cheeks. What he had been saying had not really sunk in until that time. My vision became blurred. This symptom, I learned, was widespread; among the oldtimers it was universal. The captain cut short his remarks and quickly departed. I sat where I was in a state of shock.

We got a new company commander, a lieutenant from King Company. I counted up: 1st Platoon had undergone five or six changes in leaders, and the company had had four different commanders, in just six months. By contrast, my principal line unit assignment in World War II had lasted eighteen months, with service in Colorado, Louisiana, India, Burma, and China; when I left that unit, it still had the same commander and first sergeant as when I joined it. The situation in Korea promised to become worse. Rotation for the regular troops was in full swing, with men leaving every month, and the rotation program for reservists had been announced and would begin shortly.

I detected a distinct letdown in Love Company; the training program was lackadaisical. If the new commander conducted any

---

* In Korea, there was an unspoken policy in many infantry units that if a line company commander was still alive after six months and not eligible for rotation home, he would be offered a battalion staff job.

† Lieutenant Curtis Freeman was given command of the 3d Battalion's Headquarters Company at the same time; Lieutenant Schilling had been reassigned as battalion S-1 a little earlier. Command of L Company was given to 1st Lieutenant Roder, formerly of K Company.

‡ Woodruff had been promoted in early June.

meetings or briefings to get acquainted, announce his policies, or set goals and objectives, I do not recall them. I knew this period in reserve would not last forever, and began to feel some concern for our performance when we went into the line next.

During this time there was good news and bad news—mostly bad. One day, Crown, our machine gunner, and his assistant both came to see me. Crown's statement was to the effect that he believed he had done his duty in a tough assignment, but he had now found a new job open which offered hope of an easier and less dangerous life, and he was going to transfer. Somewhat defensively, he added that he wanted me to hear this news direct from him. Everything he said was true. I have often wished I had been more mature, and expressed to him my appreciation for his service to 1st Platoon, my congratulations on his new assignment, and my best wishes for his future. But the only thing that went through my mind was that 1st Platoon was losing a top-notch gunner and would have to begin trying to train some greenhorn in this critical job. What I said to him was to the effect that if he was looking for a soft job he had better hunt elsewhere, as we had none to offer in 1st Platoon. He left without another word, and I never saw him again. I never found out, nor did I make any effort to learn, where he went or what his new job was.

About this time also, Allen Lauhoff came to see me. He had been in the 2d Squad since December, under Baker, and was now assistant squad leader under Plunkett. I knew, from both my own observation and remarks by Baker, that Lauhoff had been the bravest of the brave. He was a tall, strapping youngster, blond and good-looking, with a big smile. I had more than once seen him under fire when he had not only stood and returned the fire, but laughed at the Chinese to boot. He told me that his reserves of courage were exhausted, and that he now lived with fear all the time. Moreover, the slightest hint of enemy action was enough to give him the shakes, and he explained that he could no longer control, nor be responsible for, his actions. One of his great fears was for the safety of other men in his squad, which might be jeopardized by an improper act or decision on his part. My heart went out to him, for I knew only too well what he was talking about. I suggested he might see the medics. He said he had already talked to them, and they could do nothing for him. He said I must find some way to get him out of a line company, at least for a while, to afford him an opportunity of recovery. He looked pale, and the smile I remembered was no longer present. After thinking for a minute, I told him rather sternly that there was nothing I could do, and that while he remained in Love Company he would be expected at all times to do his full duty. My concern was that if I had shown him the least sympathy, or done anything to get his hopes raised falsely, it might have contributed to his reaching a complete breaking point mentally. Being no psychologist, I was left to hope that I had handled this problem correctly. I never knew.

[There was a routine to it, and life went on—thousands of yards gained or lost; thousands of sorties flown; thousands of rounds of ammunition fired; thousands of men moved forward, or to the rear; thousands of hills climbed; thousands of beards that went unshaved and bodies that went unwashed; thousands of boxes of C rations eaten; thousands of orders issued and obeyed; thousands of letters to moms, wives, sweethearts written; thousands of oaths uttered, prayers murmured; thousands of. . . . And it rained nearly every day in Korea in June 1951. But there was a routine to it, thank God, and life did go on.]

Cpl. JAMES CARDINAL
Headquarters Company/3d Battalion/5th Cavalry

June 17

Dear Folks:

Right now where I am it's hotter than Hades. I'm sitting in a jeep writing this letter and the sun is beating straight down on me. It must be at least 95F. If this is an indication of what the summer is going to be like, I would like to leave right now. Have to go—will write later.

—Three hours later. I'm now at an outpost on a high mountain in North Korea overlooking the Imjin River. Behind I can see valleys and mountains, then, more mountains. The view from here must be one of the most beautiful in all Korea. Regardless of what you might hear people say, or what I may have written in anger, this country is really pretty. Mountains stretch out in all directions and everything is green and blue. The only discordant note right now is the rumble of distant artillery and these dratted flies.

Cpl. JOHN BISHOP
I/7

I had gone a little ahead of the other guys because I had to go to the head. All of a sudden, I saw a gook about thirty yards away, sitting under a tree holding his rifle. I fired my carbine and hit him in the face. He put his hands on his jaw, then fell backwards. I stood up to get a better view and saw two more of them a little to the right of the one I'd hit. I tried to duck down again, but something slammed into my hand. Wow, did it burn! When I was thirteen a firecracker had gone off in my hand. That's exactly how my hand felt now. I lay down. I was so scared. I thought, if I get up I'm going to get killed. It dawned on me then that they knew where I was, and I was more frightened than ever before. I began to crawl. Bullets hit the ground around me. I got up and ran like hell. A bullet whined past my ear. Luck and the Good Lord were with me. I got back to my platoon. A little later I was taken down to the road with another Marine, who'd been hit in the leg. There, an ambulance picked us up.

M/Sgt. W. B. WOODRUFF, JR.
L Company/35th Infantry

After supper I was ordered to report to the company CP. My memory is that a total of twelve men were there—all that remained of the first complement of reservist personnel who had joined the company in December. The CO told us he had orders to send three men home on rotation, and that they would leave in a few days; another three or so more would go in July. He then said that as he was new in the company and had not really known or served with us, he did not feel qualified to determine the order in which we would depart. His solution was for us to draw lots, unless someone had a better idea. No one did. He then placed twelve slips of paper in a helmet; the slips were numbered from one to twelve. Each of us would draw one slip and leave according to the number drawn. I drew number one. It was my first, and I think last, winning ticket in any drawing.

I do not recall any sort of ceremony within the platoon or the company on the day we left. However, when our truck stopped off at battalion, Colonel Lee announced that he wanted to see us. His message was brief, one of appreciation and best wishes. He moved through the ranks, shaking hands with each man individually. When he came to me, I asked if it were not a fact that he lived in Dallas. He said yes. I told him I was en route to Decatur, which is only sixty miles from Dallas, and was there anything I could do for him? He replied that I might call Mrs. Lee and tell her he was well; he wrote her phone number on a piece of paper, which he handed me.

The next stop was, once again, Yongdungp'o. At Sasebo, Japan, there was a delay of several days as we waited for our ship. Truthfully, as I waited, it was a question whether I was more homesick for Decatur or for Love Company.

[The UN's late spring offensive had carried the sobriquet Operation Piledriver. Line Wyoming, the bulge north of Kansas, was occupied, and the base of the Iron Triangle had been taken and secured. But although Piledriver had attained its territorial objectives, it had not caught or destroyed the enemy.

The fighting was temporarily overshadowed on 23 June, when the Soviet delegate to the United Nations, Jacob Malik, deputy foreign commissar of the Soviet Union, announced during a routine radio broadcast in New York City, that the "Soviet Peoples" believed the Korean conflict could be settled. "This would require," he continued, "the readiness of the parties to enter on the path of a peaceful settlement of the Korean question. The Soviet Peoples believe that as a first step, discussions should be started between the belligerents for a cease-fire and an armistice providing for the mutual withdrawal of forces from the Thirty-eighth Parallel." He believed such a step could be taken, provided there was a "sincere desire" to put an end to the fighting.

The next day, in Oslo, Norway, the secretary general of the United Nations, Trygve Lie, telephoned a message to UN headquarters urging that cease-fire negotiations "now be entered into at the earliest possible date." If a cease-fire could be obtained, the political issues could then "be appropriately discussed in the competent organs of the United Nations." The United States representative to the UN, Warren R. Austin, issued a statement that the UN would not withdraw or appease. It was always ready, he said, to negotiate, to "take the calculated risks for peace before engaging in the incalculable risks of general war." However, until the enemy was willing to "forsake aggression and conform to United Nations principles," we would fight. John Foster Dulles told the "Meet the Press" television program that if the Soviet Union was sincere, peace could be attained within a short time; but in view of past experience, he thought we should wait and see whether the Soviet Union proved its sincerity through deeds.]

Pfc. PAUL MARTIN
Reconnaissance Company/1st Marine Division

It came as a surprise that the Communists were proposing truce talks. I had the pleasure of telling the men. "Six months ago," I said, "the UN was pleading with the Chinese for peace, and was ignored. Thanks to their arrogance and the United States Marine Corps, the Communists are now asking us to stop the fighting." When I finished, a major who'd been standing nearby said to me, "Martin, you'd make a perfect political agitator."

What I didn't say to the men was that many times before, we had felt we had victory in hand only to see it disappear in defeat. I knew one thing: the sweet smell of victory meant I'd have to tighten my chinstrap one more time.

There were skirmishes near Yanggu, Yonch'on, and Kumhwa on 24 June; UN pilots flew 880 sorties, and there was a large air battle over Sinanju. Pilots claimed they had destroyed 65 vehicles, 1 locomotive, 25 railroad cars, 6 carts, 350 buildings, 1 supply dump, 6 ammunition and fuel dumps, 9 warehouses, 13 bridges, 44 pack animals, 2 tunnels, 1 railroad station, and 30 gun positions. Nine hundred British troops arrived in Korea, and the U.S. Defense Department listed 341 American casualties.

The next day was the first anniversary of North Korea's invasion of the South. Before first light on that rainy Sunday, the Communists had sent seven divisions and five brigades across the 38th Parallel. A

year later, both sides were dug in facing each other across a line running a little north of the border. The terrible seesaw battles fought
along the entire length and breadth of the peninsula had cost both
sides dearly. It was estimated 1,250,000 men had been killed, wounded,
or captured in battle—a million of them on the enemy's side. Another
two million Korean civilians had been killed, and three million more
made homeless—this, out of a total population of thirty million. In
actual territory won or lost, North Korea was on the debit side by
2,100 square miles.

ACES

The Air War

On the shoulder patch worn by the men of Far East Air Force, the five stars of the Southern Cross memorialized the organization's birthplace—Brisbane, Australia—and the Philippine sun symbolized its honor.

The old Army Air Corps had been driven from the Philippines by the Japanese in 1942, and the incorporation of the sun in FEAF's insignia had been a promise to avenge a national humiliation. The promise had been kept. As the tide of war had turned against the Japanese, and as American ground, naval, and air power advanced from island to island across the Pacific, FEAF's headquarters was moved from Hollandia to Tacloban, thence to Fort McKinley on Luzon. The Japanese surrender made FEAF's next projected move unnecessary. FEAF had been scheduled to move from Luzon to Okinawa, where it would have directed air support for Operations Olympic and Coronet, the planned invasions of the Japanese home islands.

In September of 1945, victorious FEAF relocated its command headquarters in Tokyo. Here, in the defeated enemy's capital, housed in the eight-story Meiji building overlooking the moated grounds of the Japanese emperor's palace, FEAF controlled the air phase of the occupation of Japan.

Through most of its existence, FEAF had been an offensive military instrument. As the major air component of General Douglas MacArthur's Southwest Pacific Theater of Operations, it had been used to wage aggressive war against the Empire of Japan.

In June 1950, on the eve of the North Korean attack on the South, MacArthur was still the American commander in the Far East. Indeed, he was virtual shogun of Japan. But the Southwest Pacific Theater of Operations no longer existed. In its place was a command designated U.S. Far East Command (FEC), whose primary mission was the defense of a vast area of operations including the Japanese islands, the Ryukyus, the Marianas, and the Philippines. FEAF had been incorporated into FEC, and its primary mission was to maintain "an active air defense" of the areas under FEC's military jurisdiction.

Secondarily, FEAF was commanded to provide, as needed, "an appropriate mobile air striking force" and "air support of operations as arranged with appropriate Army and Navy commanders."

The specific meaning of these directives was to be defined by General MacArthur as commander in chief, Far East (CINCFE), who in turn was expected to conform to the wishes of the president of the United States, as defined by the U.S. Joint Chiefs of Staff.

In April of 1949, Lt. Gen. George E. Stratemeyer relieved Lt. Gen. Ennis C. Whitehead as commander of FEAF. General Whitehead had managed the postwar force reductions ordered by Washington at the cessation of hostilities with Japan. He had, with some difficulty, contrived to reduce FEAF's numbers without too seriously curtailing its capacity as a fighting force. Thus, when Stratemeyer, a combat veteran of the China-India-Burma Theater of Operations, assumed command of FEAF, he inherited the benefits of General Whitehead's military prudence.

The largest and most powerful of FEAF's subordinated commands was Fifth Air Force, a fighting command born in Brisbane on 3 September 1942. In mid-1950 the Fifth's tactical units were deployed in defense of the Japanese islands. At Itazuke Air Force Base, on Kyushu, the 8th Fighter-Bomber Wing was supported by the 68th All-Weather Fighter Squadron. The 8th Wing was equipped with F-80C Shooting Star jet interceptors; the 68th Squadron flew F-86 all-weather fighters. At Misawa Air Force Base, on Honshu's northeastern coast, in position to defend northern Japan from the Soviet threat, was deployed the 49th Fighter-Bomber Wing, equipped with F-80C Shooting Stars. Yet Fifth Air Force's heaviest deployment was in the Kanto Plain of Honshu, around Tokyo. At Yokota Air Force Base were stationed the 35th Fighter-Interceptor Wing, 339th All-Weather

Fighter Squadron, and the 8th Tactical-Reconnaissance (Photo) Squadron. The aircraft at Yokota were F-80Cs, F-82s, and RF-80A photo-recon Shooting Stars. At Johnson Air Force Base was stationed the 3d Bombardment Wing (Light), with a strength of two tactical squadrons, flying B-26 Invader propeller-driven light bombers. The 374th Troop Carrier Wing and two squadrons of Douglas C-54 transport aircraft were situated at Tachikawa Air Force Base.

For the performance of its defensive mission, Fifth Air Force deployed several air-control and air-warning groups. The personnel of these groups were scattered across Japan manning radar and military air traffic control facilities.

On the island of Okinawa, Twentieth Air Force, commanded by Major General A. C. Kincaid, was headquartered at Kadena Air Force Base. Twentieth Air Force, whose B-29s had reduced Japanese cities to cinders in the closing months of the Pacific war, was now assigned to the defense of Okinawa and the Marianas. At Naha Air Force Base it deployed the 51st Fighter-Interceptor Wing and the 4th All-Weather Fighter Squadron. The 51st flew jet Shooting Stars; the 4th All-Weather was equipped with F-82 Mustangs. Attached to the Twentieth at Kadena on Okinawa was the 31st Photo Reconnaissance Squadron (Very Long Range). The 31st was a part of the Strategic Air Command on detached service at Kadena under tactical command of the Twentieth Air Force. The squadron was equipped with RB-29 photo planes— Boeing Superfortresses of wartime vintage, specially outfitted to perform strategic reconnaissance.

At Clark Air Force Base, in the Philippine Islands, was headquartered the Thirteenth Air Force—another command with a distinguished wartime record. Commander of the Thirteenth was Major General Howard M. Turner. At Clark were deployed the 18th Fighter-Bomber Wing (F-80Cs), the attached 21st Troop Carrier Squadron (C-54s), and a pickup provisional unit designated 6204th Photo Mapping Flight (RB-17s).

The fourth major command within FEAF was the Far East Materiel Command (FEAMCom), the organization assigned to provide logistical support for all United States Air Force units in the Far East. FEAMCom was stationed west of Tokyo, at Tachikawa.

FEAF also contained a number of scattered subsidiary commands, such as flights from the 2d and 3d Air Rescue Squadrons, the 512th and 514th Weather Reconnaissance Squadrons, and various unit headquarters squadrons. The British Commonwealth maintained a small air component in Japan consisting of the Royal Australian Air Force's No. 77 Squadron, equipped with F-51 Mustangs. This unit was available to General MacArthur if required, but was not officially a part of the American air command structure.

FEAF was officered almost entirely by professionals who well remembered how World War II began for Americans. Since 1949, when the Soviet Union detonated its first nuclear weapon, the officers and men of the United States Air Force had been obsessed by vigilance. But peacetime is a powerful soporific, and even the most willingly vigilant cannot maintain perfect alertness every day, every night, forever. The USAF was prepared for World War III; the term "brushfire war" remained to be invented.

On 25 June 1950, it was.

Once again, an aggressive enemy had struck on a quiet Sunday—but the enemy was not the expected one, and the attack had come where least expected. The North Koreans, in great force, had struck across the 38th Parallel in a divided country where American air deployments were negligible and the allied air force was weak and vulnerable.

General Stratemeyer was not in Japan. He had been attending conferences in Washington, and on the morning of 25 June he was in flight between San Francisco and Hawaii. His schedule called for a visit to Twentieth Air Force in Okinawa before returning to Tokyo. Stratemeyer's deputy, Lt. Gen. Earle E. Partridge, had been in temporary command of FEAF. On the twenty-fifth he was with his family in Nagoya.

In late June the weather in central Japan was hot, with scattered rainshowers. The summer monsoon season was beginning. Across the Sea of Japan, on the Korean peninsula, there had been several days of inclement weather. This had provided the cover needed by the North Koreans to position their troops along the 38th Parallel. No reconnaissance aircraft from Japan had detected these deployments.

At 0400 hours, the North Koreans had launched an all-out attack against the Republic of Korea. Long wary of their Communist countrymen to the north, the South Koreans had fortified the demarcation line and garrisoned it with their best troops. But their best were not up to the attack that fell upon them. By 0600 hours, columns of Communist troops, spearheaded by Soviet-built T34 tanks, had driven through the ROK lines and fortifications, and were approaching Kaesong in the west and Ch'unch'on, farther east.

The American Korean Military Advisory Group (KMAG) observers hesitated to report this as all-out war. An atmosphere of tolerance and restraint had permeated the Advisory Group. There had been dozens of cross-border attacks and raids in the preceding two years, and none of these had sufficed to alarm the commanders in the Pentagon or the politicians in Washington. The desire for peaceful coexistence with the Communist enemy had become a powerful argument for "restraint."

By 0900 hours, however, even the most cautious observers realized that the North Koreans were embarked upon nothing less than an aggressive war to subjugate the South. By 0930, Kaesong had fallen, and amphibious landings were being made on the east coast, south of Kangnung.

This was not the war for which FEAF had held itself in readiness, and FEAF's first assignment was curiously at variance with its fighting history.

As far as General Partridge knew, Far East Command had only one mission with regard to Korea. At the outbreak of war or any general domestic disorder—and only at the request of the American ambassador—Far East Command was required to provide for the safety of American nationals in Korea.

To accomplish this, or any similar mission, General MacArthur had charged FEAF to furnish such air transport as might be required to move United States citizens out of Korea.

But the professional military had not completely overlooked the possibility of trouble on the Korean peninsula. In an operational plan issued on 1 March 1950, the force structure required to perform the defensive function of evacuating American nationals from Korea was put in place. General MacArthur had ordered Fifth Air Force to be prepared to support an air evacuation with such offensive operations as might be required—but only upon his specific orders. The political climate in Washington was such that great care had to be taken not to provide the Communist adversaries with an excuse to expand a possible incursion into a full-scale war.

At Itazuke Air Force Base, the closest to Korea, General Partridge had designated the commander of the 8th Fighter-Bomber Wing as the air task force commanding officer. His instructions were to support the putative evacuation of Korea with what force might be necessary to assure its success. These plans were in place on the morning of 25 June 1950.

Throughout the afternoon and evening of the twenty-fifth, there was much speculation about what American policy would be toward the Communist attack on the Republic of Korea. Many officers of FEAF were of the opinion that the administration in Washington might simply carry out the planned evacuation of Americans and leave the peninsula to the Communists. To his credit, General Partridge refused to believe it. He was convinced that new policies would be forthcoming.

In Korea, events were forcing Washington to react with unaccustomed swiftness. The American ambassador, John J. Muccio, learned of the invasion at 0930 hours. He hurried to KMAG headquarters at once, where he learned that this was no simple incursion but a full-scale invasion. North Korean tanks had reached Uijongbu, and there had been several landings on the east coast.

At 1300, the North Korean air force made its presence known in the South. Two Russian-built YAK fighters buzzed Seoul and Kimpo airfields. It was evidently a reconnaissance, because no attack was made. But four hours later, more YAKs returned to strafe Kimpo, hitting the control tower, destroying a gasoline storage, and damaging a U.S. Military Air Transport C-54. More YAKs strafed Seoul airfield and damaged a number of ROK training planes. And at 1900, six more North Korean fighters returned to Kimpo and finished off the damaged American C-54. If there were any USAF doubts that the North Koreans were launching a serious invasion, these spoiling raids dispelled them.

On the morning of the twenty-sixth, General Partridge attended a staff meeting at Tokyo's Haneda Airport. Intelligence reports from Korea were optimistic. The American Korean Military Advisory Group reported that the ROK Army was showing "increasing steadiness" and that the invaders had been contained. So rosy were the KMAG reports, in fact, that FEAF released the transports at Ashiya (which had been prepared to begin the evacuation of Americans from Korea) to their regular duties.

But some signs of resolution were beginning to be signaled from Washington. MacArthur was empowered to send a delegation to Seoul to determine the amount and kinds of equipment needed by the ROK forces. He was authorized to ship this matériel and to protect the shipments from interference by the Communists. He was instructed once again to evacuate Americans from Seoul—and to use what force was needed to ensure their safety.

The Joint Chiefs of Staff also informed MacArthur that the Seventh Fleet, including the aircraft carrier Valley Forge, was proceeding from the Philippines to Sasebo, where it would come under the operational command of Vice Admiral C. Turner Joy, commander, Naval Forces Far East (NAVFE).

At the end of this teleconference, the Chiefs asked General MacArthur if he required further instructions. Characteristically, he replied that he did not.

As early as the morning of the twenty-sixth, when the first stages of the evacuation had begun, and flights of F-82 fighters were taking turns flying cover for the activity in Inch'on Harbor, a Communist radial-engined fighter dropped from the clouds and "bounced" the American planes. It was an attack of considerable insolence, since any one of the F-82s could easily have destroyed the North Korean airplane. But the stultifying effects of peacetime service on the American pilots saved it. They were actually uncertain as to whether or not they should return fire, and the flight leader chose simply to take evasive action. The Communist pilot escaped.

That single event, however, set a style that was to continue throughout the war. The North Koreans flew aggressively and with bravery. They, together with the professionals of the USAF, were destined to turn Korea into a fighter pilot's war.

It has been noted that the men of FEAF were, for the most part, professionals. They were also largely volunteers, and the aircrews— those who were not true professionals—were for the most part men who had previous experience of war in the air. Many were taken from civilian life as reservists, and had fought in World War II only five years before. There was much resentment of this, but the effect of the

Air Force's—and the Navy's—manning decisions made the air war in Korea unique.

For the first few months of the war, the North Koreans attempted to interdict first the evacuation of civilians, and later, all South Korean and American military movements, with aggressive attacks from the air. But they swiftly discovered that their YAK and Ilyushin-10 fighters were no match for even the obsolescent F-80 Shooting Stars that made up the bulk of the American air component in Japan and the Korean peninsula. On 27 June 1950, as the air evacuation began in earnest, the North Koreans attempted to attack the unarmed transports with eight IL-10 fighters. Waiting for the Communist pilots was a flight of five F-80Cs of the 35th Fighter-Bomber Squadron on air alert over Seoul. With a minimum of maneuver, the American Shooting Star pilots exploded four of the North Korean aircraft. The remainder turned and fled. When the Communist airmen returned to their base in the North, they carried with them the message that the Fifth Air Force was no longer uncertain as to how to respond to attack. The aggressiveness of the Air Force pilots over Seoul that day was to be typical of the pilots of the U.S. Air Force and Navy until the last day of the war.

Within a matter of months, the North Koreans were forced to replace their YAKs and Ilyushins with MiGs. These were met in turn by fewer American Shooting Stars and many more F-86 Sabres. Even before the term "MiG Alley" became familiar in the American press, the American professionals and "retreads" were inflicting heavy casualties on the Communist airmen. Even when the shock of the Chinese intervention sent the ground forces reeling back toward the 38th Parallel, the fliers of the United States Air Force and Navy continued to make the Communist pilots pay a heavy price for having challenged FEAF.

As in every war since aerial combat began, the pilots used a unique language to describe a unique kind of war.

Col. ROBERT BALDWIN
51st Fighter-Interceptor Group

We had three squadrons in each group. A squadron usually consisted of three flights of four aircraft. These flew in what we called a "finger four"—like the four fingers of a hand: flight-leader, wingman, then element-leader and his wingman. The flight tried to stay together, but that wasn't always possible in combat. The important thing was for the wingmen to stay with their leaders. The firepower of two airplanes together was more than twice as effective as the firepower of a single plane. It was the wingman's job to cover his leader's tail.

We went up as a group as often as we could manage it. Our mission was air superiority. We kept the MiGs occupied in the northern part of Korea, away from our ground troops.

We were right at the Yalu River every day. You couldn't just sit on your airfield and wait for an alert, the way the RAF did during the Battle of Britain. You had to be on the spot, patrolling. Each group was assigned a time on station. There were four working MiG Alley between the Yalu and Ch'ongch'on: the 8th Fighter-Bomber and the 18th Fighter-Bomber Groups, and the 4th and 51st Fighter-Interceptor Groups.

When the fighter-bombers first got their Sabres, they were allowed to mix it with the MiGs, but after things settled down to a regular routine, the fighter-bombers were sent back to their regular missions attacking ground forces. That left us with the two fighter-interceptor groups to handle the MiGs coming across the border from China.

That's not to say the fighter-bombers didn't sneak in a little air-to-air activity when they could. From time to time, we'd find some of them stooging around at high altitude looking for MiGs.

Keep in mind that I'm talking about really high altitude. We rarely engaged a MiG below 40,000 feet, and often they'd be up as high as 50,000.

That gave us problems, because the Sabre was designed to operate at 35,000. We'd see MiGs out of reach above us almost every day. So we decided to do something about it. We had a flight of four airplanes—called them the Hotshots—specially tuned for high performance. Any military jet is a hot piece of equipment when it is delivered, but there's no such thing as a machine that can't be improved.

We paid special attention to the engines on the Hotshots, got them to put out maybe 10 percent more thrust. Then we lightened the airframes by stripping out the armor plate around the pilot's seat, removing the back-up motors for the flaps—things like that. We even reduced the ammunition load and the fuel capacity. When we were finished, we had taken out about 2,000 pounds.

The trouble was that once you had an aircraft that would get to, say, 52,000 feet, you discovered it was almost impossible to maneuver at that altitude. If you lost any airspeed at all, you'd fall out of turns and be red meat for the MiG you were fighting.

Finally, I set Mach .83 as the minimum speed for a Hotshot above 50,000. If you couldn't hold that, you had to put the nose down and pick it up by diving. Of course, that meant that you lost all the altitude you had worked so hard to get. When a MiG went by at 50,000 or more, you had to grit your teeth and let it go. To do any harm, he had to come down eventually, and when he did, he got hammered. One way and another, we gave the Chinese and North Koreans a hell of a bad time. The quality of their pilots began to fall off early on. There was no shortage of airplanes for them, but we culled the North Korean air force right away.

There were plenty of Chinese, of course, and Russians, too. I know that's in doubt, but I remember a day when one of our people shot a MiG out from under one of their pilots, and he bailed out. I went over to have a look, and there he was, hanging in the risers, red hair just shining in the sun. I don't think there were very many redheaded Chinese or North Koreans.

By and large, the MiG was a good airplane. Lighter than a Sabre and a bit more maneuverable. But if you could hit it in the saddle-tank—which is kind of wrapped around the engine and the cockpit—the jet fuel would spill into the engine, and the MiG would go up like a torch, a lot like the Jap Zeroes in the big war. Sometimes the pilot managed to get out. Not always, of course.

The Sabre was tougher than the MiG, but it could be torched, too. I saw one hit in the left wing-root once. Flown by a Canadian, it was, an RCAF officer who was doing a tour with the 4th. I wasn't actually there; what I saw was gun-camera film from one of his squadron mates. It seems this Canadian and his wingman were patrolling the Alley when they were bounced by a MiG who squeezed in between the Canadian and his wingman and began firing. The wingman started shooting at the MiG at the same time, so his gun camera caught the MiG's cannon shell hitting the Canadian's Sabre at the root of the left wing. The aircraft exploded. It was all on the films the wingman brought back. The Canadian was blown clear, and somehow got his parachute open. He ended up as a POW.

We lost people, no denying that. But by the time we were well settled in, we were killing ten MiGs for every Sabre lost. And by the end of the war, the kill ratio was sixteen to one.

[The 1949 law intended to "unify" the armed forces of the United States fell far short of ordering anything resembling true unification. But it had its most beneficial effect upon the postwar careers of the men who fought in the air. The formation of the new and independent U.S. Air Force broke down many of the interservice barriers that had plagued the U.S. military since its beginnings.

The most radical, and seminal, change in military policy was that allowing aviators of the Marine Corps and the Navy to transfer "in grade" into the new service. It was a major change.

Even before the war in Korea began, pilots of the Air Force were allowed, even encouraged, to do tours with naval air formations. And Navy and Marine aviators were permitted to do the same with Air Force and Air National Guard squadrons.

One of the men to take full advantage of these changes was John F. Bolt, a Marine aviator who had done two tours in the Pacific, and who was a former member of Gregory Boyington's "Black Sheep" squadron of F4U Corsair fighters.

In the years immediately following the Japanese surrender, Bolt served in a number of places where he had the occasion to meet Air Force pilots and their growing jet force. An unabashed admirer of performance, Bolt managed to wangle exchange tours that enabled him to fly first the F-80 Shooting Star and then the pride of the Air Force, the Republic F-86 Sabre.

This experience stood him in good stead when he arrived in Korea in June of 1952. He flew ninety-two missions with the Marines; but it was as an exchange officer, at the controls of an F-86 Sabre, that he became the only Marine ace of the Korean War.]

Major JOHN F. BOLT (USMC)
51st Fighter Wing/USAF

I did ninety-two missions with Marine Air Group [MAG] 13. We spent our time on fighter-bomber tactics, figuring out ways for jets to keep from blowing themselves up with their own bombs when attacking ground targets. It was interesting work, but I hadn't had any chance at all for air-to-air combat.

At that time the Marine Air Group was permitted to keep two officers with the Air Force, and I already had over 100 hours of Sabre time, so it seemed to me that I was a logical choice for an exchange tour in the next cycle. I had flown with the Air Force before, back in the States, so I knew what they had for use against the MiGs. I spent two weeks with the Air Force in Korea when I first arrived in-country. Those two weeks were what I called "detached duty," and the personnel people at MAG 13 called "without proper orders."

So the group officer says to me, "John, you son of a bitch, I know what you're trying to do. You want to go north with the Air Force and spend another tour hunting MiGs. This time, you go by the book." What he meant was that Marines sent on exchange to the Air Force were selected about halfway through their tours, and I had already completed mine.

Well, I had some R and R time coming, so instead of heading for Tokyo, I hitched a ride down to Suwon, where George Rudell, an old friend from my days back at El Toro, had command of a squadron of Sabres. George had been flying F-80s when we first met. He came down to the Marine air station to talk to us and show us what the Shooting Star could do. We were still chugging around in old F4U Corsairs, and the F-80 made a tremendous impression on all of us. That visit of George's to El Toro probably had a lot to do with my getting the exchange time I had back in the States, flying with the USAF and the Air National Guard. When I learned that George had one of the 51st Fighter Wing's Sabre squadrons at Suwon, it made sense to go talk to him—particularly in view of the flak I was getting from MAG 13 Personnel.

I told Rudell that I was at Suwon on R and R, but that I had over 100 hours of Sabre time now, and would he let me fly a couple of times with his squadron?

George Rudell is a tightly strung guy, but admirable. He gave me a cockpit test on the Sabre, just to make sure I wasn't exaggerating my experience, and I passed it without any trouble. Then he let me do a couple of sweeps with his outfit, and it was great. I returned to MAG 13 absolutely convinced that I wanted one of the first available exchange assignments with the Air Force.

Personnel still hung in there tough. The personnel officer said, "I've alerted everybody at wing about what you're trying to pull, Bolt. The answer is no, and that's the way it is going to stay. We have other pilots who want a tour in Sabres." [It is supposition only, but the official attitude at MAG 13 might possibly have been influenced by the flamboyance of a former Black Sheep Squadron member's war record.]

So I went back to Suwon again. Rudell was having a few problems, himself. One of them was a fellow named Joe McConnell. McConnell was not allowed to fly combat because of some breach of flying discipline. But McConnell was raising hell with Rudell and getting on his blacklist by doing "test" flights and "training" missions, and all the while looking for MiGs very much against orders.

To keep McConnell occupied and out of trouble, George Rudell told me, "You go out and fly with this guy. Pick up some tactics. He's a pain in the ass, but he's sharp."

That was an enormous understatement. McConnell was absolutely fantastic. I loved flying with him. He was the best fighter pilot I have ever run into, bar none. Boyington couldn't hold a candle to him. The man was incredible. And the thing that is almost impossible to believe is that he was a B-24 navigator in the big war. The Army Air Corps classified him as "unsuitable for pilot training." But he never gave up. After he did his tour in B-24s, he put in for pilot training, and they finally gave him a chance. He turned out to be the best fighter-jet pilot in the Korean war.

He had absolute confidence in his own ability. I mean *absolute*. Rudell wouldn't let him look for MiGs, but flying with him was an education. I did a few flights as his wingman, and I learned something new each time.

I arranged things with Rudell so that when it was time for another Marine to do an exchange tour, he would ask specifically for me. Then I went back to MAG 13 and put in to have my stay in Korea extended.

Rudell got General Bart, commander of Eighth Air Force, to send a wire to the commanding general of the Marine Air Group saying that they were delighted to have Marine pilots flying with them, but that he hoped it was understood that any *inexperienced* pilot would always be a liability to the Air Force outfit saddled with him, and that the Marine Corps had a splendid opportunity to have the Corps represented by an officer named John Bolt, who just happened to have more than 100 hours in the F-86F (which was the only Sabre getting into action, now that the MiGs could top the E-series Sabre by 5,000 or 6,000 feet).

So my friend the MAG 13 personnel officer had to swallow hard and do what was necessary to keep things smooth with the United States Air Force. There were plenty of scowls when I picked up my orders and headed back again to Suwon.

George Rudell welcomed me with open arms, and assigned me to McConnell's flight. I flew eleven straight missions on McConnell's wing. It was a postgraduate course, even for a pilot as experienced as I was.

One of the marks of a really great fighter pilot is his absolute conviction that what he is doing is right, no argument. Sometimes that raises hell with regulations. That was McConnell's style. Maybe it was because of his experiences with the official way of doing things in World War II. After all, they did classify a potentially great fighter pilot as a navigator, and they kept him in B-24s when he could have been an Ira Bong or Don Gentile in a Lightning or a Mustang.

That's why when McConnell told us that we should run our engines at 100 percent power instead of the officially ordered 97 percent, we did exactly as he said. The orders said that we were not to drop our empty wingtanks unless we were actually heading into combat. McConnell's flight dropped theirs when they were empty, period. When we did find MiGs, there was no stooging around, no fiddling with this and that. And when McConnell's flight was up there on the river [the Yalu], and the MiGs tried to run away—well, you get the picture. Our radar coverage of the area wasn't all that great, particularly in between the mountains. When we had to bend the rules a little, we had a code for "strangling the parrot" [shutting down the IFF blip, which showed a flight's position on the UN radar sets].

McConnell would say on the radio, "Cedar," and I would respond with "Rapids." That would mean that our element would strangle
the parrot, and the second element would turn theirs on and veer
away from us. They would have the "squawk," and that would be
the signal the radar was getting.

Then, when we were sure of what was showing on the radar
back home, we'd go to 50,000 feet and head on north to hunt.

The first time I saw McConnell take a MiG under fire I wondered if, after all, I wasn't flying wing on a talented greenhorn. The
damned airplane was a speck in the distance. There was no way, I
thought, that McConnell could hit him. I figured all he would accomplish would be to spook the MiG pilot so badly he'd hightail it
for home.

In the fighting in the Solomons, we never fired until we were
300 yards or less from the Jap. If we could, we would close in even
tighter, to make an absolutely guaranteed kill.

But McConnell would start shooting at planes only he could
see. A thousand, twelve hundred yards off—range didn't mean a
thing to McConnell. He'd open up, and before you knew it he would
start getting hits. "If you get even one shot in on the turbine," he
would say, "he is going to start losing power. You might unbalance
his turbine fan. If you shoot off a blade, you've got him." So he
would crank his estimate of the range into the gunsight and rip off
ten or so rounds of .50-caliber. And more often than not, sure enough,
you'd see a flash, and a little juice would start leaking from the MiG.
McConnell would just kind of lob those shots in, a ripple or two at
a time, and somehow one or two of those shells would get home.
Then he would close in, and it was all over. For some reason or
other—chance, maybe—I never actually saw McConnell flame one.
I saw him get three in the eleven missions I flew with him, and not
one of them burned. They just went down leaking and smoking.

When there weren't any MiGs, we would head down onto the
deck and beat up the Red airfields, making what we called the Antone Tower Check. That was a stunt named after a guy who ended
up a POW. The drill was to dive in from 45,000 or so, roll over,
and hit the enemy control tower with a sonic boom. Then we would
back off a few miles, get right down on the deck, and buzz their
runways at about ten feet. It was a kind of challenge, an attempt to

tease some of them into the air. It seldom worked, but we did it as often as we could.

McConnell used to horrify me by keeping us out right to the bingo point—sometimes beyond it. The bingo point is the distance from home where you must turn and fly straight in, or risk running out of fuel.

No one could call it as close as McConnell. He would keep us out until we had only ten or fifteen pounds of fuel in the tanks—far less than you would need if you happened to get bounced by a MiG. Sometimes when we flew past bingo, we would have to shut down the engine and actually glide most of the way back to base. Mc-Connell led us on mission after mission when that sort of thing happened.

One day, after an Antone Tower Check, I was so low on fuel that when McConnell kept us out past bingo I was damned near hysterical. I got so mad, I threatened to shoot him. McConnell thought it was funny.

Yet he saved my life a number of times, just by being the superb fighter pilot he was.

McConnell knew how to use everything. Our Sabres had what is called a "flying" tail—that means the horizontal stabilizer and the elevators are mounted high on the vertical fin. The engineers had figured out that if the stabilizer and elevators were in the conventional position, at the end of the fuselage, the controls stiffened up when you went transonic. Sometimes it was so bad, the airplane became unmanageable. Some early fighters capable of breaking the so-called sound barrier actually crashed because of this.

The MiG was more maneuverable than the Sabre, but it had a conventional tail. So according to McConnell—and it turned out he was right—what you wanted to do if a MiG bounced you was go supersonic. Then you could maneuver and he couldn't.

Then there was the G maneuver. We had G suits that would keep us functioning at seven or eight times the force of gravity in turns and pull-ups. The Chinese didn't have G suits, so the trick was to get your MiG to follow you into a tighter and tighter turn. He would do that, because he knew the MiG could outturn the Sabre. But once you were pulling, say, seven Gs and just blacking out, you knew your MiG pilot was probably unconscious. What McConnell recommended was a quick rollout just as the tunnel vision sets in. And what do you know? Nine times out of ten, there would be your MiG, right under your guns, with a pilot blacked out.

There's a story that went around the 51st Fighter Wing's fields about the greedy Marine who stole one of the colonel's MiGs. It's funny as hell if you happen to know anything about fighter pilots.

The colonel in question is my friend George Rudell, who was a good pilot and a damned good officer. He was also one of the most ambitious officers in the Air Force. He wanted to make general more than almost anything—except becoming an ace.

George flew missions just like everyone else, but he had to take most of the jobs no one else in the squadron wanted, like escorting the fighter-bombers and doing all those things the brass wanted done just so, while McConnell and I and the others headed north to look for MiGs.

One night he called me over to his bunk in his barracks—it was just a cubbyhole with some plywood partitions around it; the Air Force didn't pamper their colonels much in Korea—and told me how badly he wanted just one more MiG so that he could have his five and go into the records as an ace. But he wanted to be a good officer, he said; in fact, he wanted to be a *model* officer and do what he was told. And one of the things he had been told, not once but many times, was that there was no hunting across the river. None. Period.

He knew damned well what McConnell and I had been up to, he said, and he didn't want to make trouble for us. But he wanted his fifth MiG even more than he wanted to be a general. Did I get his drift? I said I thought I did, and why didn't he join one of our hunts up north? He said, "You got it, John. *Way* up north, where you and McConnell have been getting your MiGs."

Without admitting, I said that we would be honored to have the squadron commander join us *wherever* we were getting our MiGs. After all, wasn't it George Rudell who made it possible for a Black Sheep Marine to fly with the Air Force?

So the next day the colonel announced that he was going to fly with some of the other flights, in a regular rota. I put a reliable man on his wing, and we gathered three flights to head north and look for MiGs.

Just to make sure the colonel made out all right, I put him to leading a flight, and I took the lead of the second element, where I could keep an eye on him. He already had four MiGs, but he hadn't had any air-to-air combat for a while.

We headed north to the Yalu through some beautiful weather. Blue sky and big patches of stratocumulus clouds at about 30,000 feet. And sure enough, when we reached the river there was a big fight going on. There were some MiGs down at 20,000, mixing it up with a gaggle of Sabres. The trouble was that whenever a Sabre closed in on a MiG, the Chinese would get very nervous and homesick. The Communist pilots at that time were already halfway to panic whenever they came south, and they made it a point to stay as close to the river as they could. They never came into our airspace if they could avoid it.

The Sabres already on the spot had scared hell out of the MiG pilots, who were turning for China. There were flak bursts in the air from the batteries on the north bank of the Yalu, and this was making it tough to zero in on the MiGs.

Anyway, George spots one below him and heads down in a steep dive with the rest of us following. Four Sabres on this one poor MiG. The pilot just about went crazy, jinking and taking evasive action as though his life depended on it—which of course it did. George slid in behind him and started blasting away. But he was so overeager that he let himself slide out of firing position. Meanwhile, the MiG pilot was hauling all-out for Peking.

The whole flight was lined up behind the colonel just like a firing squad, but we were about half a mile from the border, and I couldn't see letting the squadron commander fly into China, no matter what the arrangement was. The whole thing was taking too long. I kept wondering why George didn't shoot the damned MiG and be done with it, but he didn't, and finally I couldn't wait any longer, so I just opened up and shot the damned MiG into pieces. The rest of the squadron saw me do it, and from that day on I was known as the Marine who stole the colonel's MiG.

As it turned out, George didn't hold it against me too much. It seems that in all the excitement, he had forgotten to turn on his windscreen defogger, the glass had misted, and he couldn't see a damned thing.

By the time George Rudell left Korea, though, he had his fifth MiG, and three more for good measure.

[The advances in fighter techniques and equipment were not paralleled in bomber operations. The available targets for bombing were tactical rather than strategic—trucks and enemy concentrations rather than manufacturing centers for war matériel. These targets did exist, but by 1952 they were all in the prohibited country north of the Yalu River. UN bombers, mostly modified F-80s and obsolescent B-26s and B-50s, were extremely vulnerable to antiaircraft fire while attacking troops in the field in daylight. The decision was taken to fly most of these missions at night. Yet losses continued—mainly to enemy aircraft, which were themselves too vulnerable to UN fighter attack in daylight. Enter the night-fighter.]

Lt. GUY BORDELON (USN)
Team Dog/Composite Squadron 3 (Night)/USS Princeton

During World War II, some armchair hero came up with a catchy aphorism: There are old pilots and bold pilots, but no old, bold pilots. Anyone who has flown fighters will tell you that's absolute nonsense—loser talk. You have to be a hunter to be a fighter pilot, and thank God there were enough hunters to get the job done in Korea.

The Air Force was having an open season on the MiGs up around the Yalu, but it was taking some heavy losses farther south, mostly from ground fire. When they took their F-80s down on the deck to hit troops and trucks and tanks, they sometimes had to fly lower than the surrounding terrain, so that the Reds were actually shooting *down* at them on the bomb runs. And when they shifted to night operations—well, the Commies weren't stupid—they put into the air all the aircraft they didn't dare fly in the daytime and kept on shooting our people down.

I was in command of Team Dog on the *Princeton*. We had the Chance-Vought F4U-5N—a Corsair modified to carry radar and the other bits and pieces needed to operate at night.

During the period between early June and late September of 1953, we operated both from the *Princeton* and ashore, from a strip known as K-6 at Pyongt'aek, Korea. Usually, two 5Ns were flown off the carrier as barrier patrols to provide night security for the Seoul area. The rest operated on night "heckler" missions and air-intercepts from K-6.

Our 5Ns suffered the usual migraines to be expected in obsolescent aircraft. But, by and large, the old Corsairs did a pretty good job after dark. And as senior naval night-fighter pilot ashore, I wasn't about to let our mission fail because of any mechanical or technical problems.

Upon arrival at K-6, the first order of business was to equip our 5Ns for land-based, all-weather, night-combat operations. We also had to familiarize ourselves with the terrain. Flying over land in bad weather meant that most of the clouds had rock centers, so we had to become accustomed to a new set of rules for staying in one piece. Finally, we had to find out what our enemy's tactics might be.

In Seoul we got a briefing from the Air Force and discovered that they had had some disastrous encounters with the Communists. The enemy was flying old Russian World War II aircraft that, oddly enough, gave them an advantage for the kind of missions they were undertaking. They would fly low and slow, and the Air Force's all-weather jets were having a hell of a time with them. The Air Force people would try to make intercepts, but the Reds were so slow that the F-80s and Sabres would just overrun them and turn into sitting ducks. The enemy's "Washing Machine Charlies" had just destroyed some 15,000,000 gallons of aviation fuel and huge amounts of munitions stored at Inch'on. And when the jets went after them, they got into bad trouble at low altitude in the mountainous terrain.

We naval types had a major advantage over the Air Force jet pilots. We had been flying night intruder missions off our carriers with the 5N Corsairs, and flying low and slow was what we did for a living. Almost all our experience had been gained flying night attacks on trucks and trains resupplying the Commies through the mountains of North Korea.

The enemy had to use lights as they negotiated the steep mountain roads; and when they did, we could spot them. A set of headlights drew us down on them like bees after honey!

On one mission over Songjin, I sighted an enemy truck convoy snaking down a steep and twisting road between mountains. I immediately reduced power and reset the propeller pitch for a quiet approach. If you didn't do that, they would hear you coming and kill the lights so that there was nothing below but blackness—and hard-centered clouds.

As soon as I was in position, I started to strafe with 20-mm cannon, and made ready to drop my bombs on the lead truck. But as I closed, I suddenly encountered a regular fountain of tracers coming up out of the dark at me. I didn't want to fly through that kind of a steel curtain, so I pulled up sharply and turned—almost directly into a ridge. I don't know to this day how I missed it. It couldn't have been by more than a few feet. Night strafing could get very, very exciting.

The enemy had a clever trick of using smudge pots—just the way the citrus farmers used to do in Florida and California. Only, these smudge pots were used to create layer upon layer of smoke in the steep valleys. And if we dropped a flare to illuminate targets, the smoke turned everything into a milky-white smear. It could give a pilot vertigo. So usually, flares and lights were out. It was spot them, glide into position, and then go very low to hit them hard and fast. Hairy, but effective.

At least while we were stooging around over North Korea in the dark, we always knew who the bad guys were. Operating in the South from K-6, it got more complicated. At the JOC [Joint Operations Center] briefings we were told that it was absolutely necessary that we make positive identification of any bogeys we intercepted before opening fire. More than that, we were not, repeat *not*, to shoot before we had clearance from the JOC air controller. It turned out that every damned night there were friendlies flying about on unspecified missions—some of them with no flight plan, and some without even a verbal filing. This made for some very close calls.

On a number of occasions I was vectored onto a bogey, only to find myself bearing down on a UN transport plane flying blissfully unaware through our combat patrol area. And once, after having reported that I was zeroed in on one of our own aircraft, I was told by the JOC controller that there were no friendlies in the area, and to open fire at once.

On one nasty, dark night when—fortunately—I was not the pilot on combat air patrol, a Marine sergeant-pilot flying a night-configured AD-1 put a number of 20-mm cannon holes in a Piper Cub flying an unauthorized mission for a frontline artillery outfit. Very soon thereafter, a very large and very unhappy infantry officer showed at K-6 waving a .45-caliber automatic. He was ready to shoot the man who gave him what he called "a haircut."

Actually, he was lucky. The 20-mm rounds used by the night-fighter teams were all high-explosive incendiary. A hit on metal would have set them off. The fabric construction of the Piper Cub was too flimsy to detonate them.

On another CAP [combat air patrol] mission north of Seoul, I was vectored onto a target that my radar showed as barely moving. It was easy—too easy—to close on it. As soon as I did, it vanished. I tried everything but dragging my feet on the ground to slow down enough to get a visual sighting. All the while, the controller was telling me, "Shoot! Damn it, shoot!"

Finally, on my third or fourth pass, I caught the flicker of rotary blades. Our hovering bogey was a helicopter. I reported "helo" and "friendly" to the JOC controller, but he must have been in a very bad mood, because he kept ordering me to shoot. In desperation I suggested that the JOC typecheck to see if we had any air-evac helos in the area. Very shortly, I received an urgent message rescinding the "Shoot it down!" order. It was a Navy chopper flying wounded out to a hospital ship just off shore.

My first four kills were not nearly so exciting. There was moonlight, and a visual sighting was much easier. I was vectored onto a YAK-18 by the ground controller, and I closed to point-blank range before I fired. I hit him with all four of the 5N's 20-mm cannon, and he made an abortive turn to the left, then blew up.

The flash half blinded me, and I had to pull up and circle until I could see again. Then, only minutes later, I received another vector and closed the target for visual identification. It was another YAK-18, but this time the rear-seat gunner got off a long squirt at me. Tracers streaked past my canopy. Then I opened up with the twenties again. YAK number two exploded into a ball of flame.

I had had my problems with the radar officers on the ground, but this time they steered me straight to my targets without a hitch.

The next night's mission was a four-hour CAP from Inch'on north to the mouth of the Imjin River, and thence eastward to two bends in the river we used to call Marilyn's Left and Right Ones. That's where I was when the controller vectored me seaward of Inch'on, where I found two Lavochkin LA-9 fighters. I shot the wingman down almost immediately and then started for the leader, who headed north toward Kaesong, where the Reds had a number of anti-aircraft batteries. But I wasn't about to give him up. I managed to get in a good burst and watched him lose a wing and go straight into the ground.

After that, there was a long dull period during which the enemy decided not to venture too far south at night.

A week or so later, I was vectored onto a pair of Tupolev TU-2 bombers up to no good and heading for Inch'on. I hadn't had a chance to test-fire my guns because I had been flying over populated areas, and when I received permission to fire, the damned things wouldn't shoot. I tried everything, but no luck. So I told the JOC controller to send another airplane. Somehow, the message didn't get through, and they kept ordering me to shoot down the Tupolevs. So I pulled well ahead of the enemy aircraft, turned head-on to them, dropped my gear, and turned on my landing lights. I must have scared them to death, because they broke right and left and headed north at high speed.

Col. ROBERT BALDWIN
51st Fighter-Interceptor Group

One day, my flight ran into this flight of MiGs trapped under the overcast. For some reason—lack of training or the proper equipment—the MiGs seldom flew through heavy cloud cover, and when we found them down low, their weight advantage wasn't as useful to them.

The MiGs were trying to close in on another flight of Sabres, and they didn't see us until we were almost on top of them. I looked down over the nose, and there they were, a couple of hundred feet below us.

I couldn't just push the nose down and dive on them, because I didn't want to overrun them. And the dive brakes on the F-86 weren't always reliable: too much, and you fell out of the combat; too little, and you could slide out ahead of the target and get yourself killed. So I did a roll, a real sloppy slow roll to kill off speed and altitude. It wasn't pretty, but it worked. I just kind of *dished* out behind the last MiG in the enemy formation, and there he was, framed in my gunsight, about 200 yards away. There was no way to miss. I gave him a short burst and he started to burn. As I went by him I saw that he had a red dragon painted on his airplane, a big one. I thought: I have me a real honcho here. The honchos were their best pilots, and their best were damned good. The red dragon paint job was the giveaway. Only the hot ones were allowed to decorate their airplanes like that.

He was burning, but not all that badly, and I wanted to make certain he didn't get away, so I stayed with him as he headed down. He wasn't about to give up, either. The minute he saw that I was still behind him, he pulled up into the clouds, trailing this long plume of black smoke. The overcast had some breaks in it, and I kept following the smoke—like following the centerline on a highway—around clouds, through clouds, over and under clouds.

Then, all of a sudden, I find myself looking at the floor of my own cockpit; I can't sit up, my blast-shield [the device used to protect the pilot's face during a bailout] is down, and the controls will barely move.

It took me a little while to figure out what was happening. I had followed my honcho into a cloud, and we had both become disoriented. As my altimeter wound down through 12,000 feet, we came out of the clouds together, heading straight down at supersonic speed. At over Mach 1 in a vertical dive, you can use up 12,000 feet in one hell of a hurry. The ground looked like it was only inches away. I hauled back on the stick as hard as I could, just hoping the Sabre would stay in one piece. The airplane did fine, but I went black. When I could see again, my G meter had jammed at 10. My speed was down a little, but I was right on the deck, and there was this mountain ridge right ahead of me. I hauled back on the stick again and found myself heading straight up, back the way I'd come.

When I rejoined my flight, the fight was over. We formed up and started for home. I radioed to my wingman and asked if he'd seen what happened to me. "How close to the ground did I come?" I asked. "Awful damned close," was the reply. Then I asked, "What happened to my MiG?"

My wingman said, "He made a hell of a hole in someone's chicken yard."

The whole thing, from the time I opened fire until I rejoined my flight, took about two minutes—120 very long seconds.

Major JOHN F. BOLT, (USMC)
51st Fighter Wing/USAF

McConnell went back to the States, and I found myself leading a flight. A Marine Corps major leading a flight of Air Force hotshots.

The trouble was that suddenly things were not going right. Rudell let me lead the hot pilots, and I really screwed up my opportunities. It was embarrassing. On my very first flight as a leader, I totally fouled up a couple of bounces. Sure kills, and I didn't make them. I was in the depths of despair. I felt certain the flight was losing confidence in me. I thought about it very seriously, wondering if I just wasn't aggressive enough.

I'd had chances, plenty of them. The MiGs were there for the taking. They would come across the Yalu in strings, line astern, each one protecting the tail of the man ahead. What you had to do was break into that string, but it was risky business. The trick was to break in without getting your tail shot off—and I wasn't doing it. Twice I had let a whole damned string go by without breaking in for a shot.

I really began to agonize about it, and I decided that the next goddamned MiG pilot I encountered was going to be a dead man, or I was.

So on the next mission I was primed. We ran into a gaggle of MiGs almost right away, and I just drove on into their string, blasting away. But my MiG immediately started a series of high-speed scissors, and I couldn't get enough hits into him to slow him down. In the meanwhile, my wingman and I were really taking it from the MiGs at the rear of the string. There was a hell of a lot of shooting, but nobody was getting any hits to speak of. We weren't, and neither were the MiGs. It was terribly frustrating. You could almost see the big 37-mm shells they were lobbing at us from behind, and the rest of the people in my flight were yelling and cursing over the radio. Everything was in a state of total confusion.

Then, for some reason, my MiG goes into slow flight, hauling around to the point where I'm in danger of overrunning him and letting him have a clean shot at my tail. He might have managed it, too, except that he didn't follow through with his attack. Instead, he broke away and tried to climb away from me. Finally, I started hitting him. I could see the incendiaries flashing on his fuselage as he climbed up through 40,000 feet.

We were at 45,000 when he finally decided to pack it in. I had been shooting him to ribbons all the way up, but it wasn't until we were way the hell up there that he popped his canopy and bailed out.

I broke the famine that day. The funny part of it all was that, despite all the shooting and confusion, when my wingman and I landed back at the base, our Sabres didn't have a nick in them.

There were two Korean Wars. One was fought on the ground by men who suffered dreadful hardships and saw the death of their enemies close at hand. The other, the war in the air, was no less deadly, but as the airmen themselves describe it, it was a very different experience. As noted before, it was a war fought largely by professionals and those who had fought before. Whatever might later be said about the war on the ground in Korea, the war in the air was a victory.

ROUTINE

26 June-31 August 1951

After Mr. Malik made his dramatic proposal, both sides agreed the fighting in Korea would continue until a final truce was signed. A lull, nevertheless, fell over the front lines, as neither the UN nor the Chinese were willing to launch a major offensive while there was a chance to stop the killing. No day passed, however, without casualties as both combatants continued to probe and to consolidate their hilltop positions. The summer of 1951 was spent with regiments trying to seize slightly more defensible positions, and in small-unit actions designed to keep the enemy guessing. Patrols ventured forward, then withdrew, and artillery and air strikes pulverized Korea's hills and valleys. But in general, the various unit war diaries report the tempo of the war much reduced. The time had come when men were neither brave nor cowardly, when they no longer attacked or were attacked, advanced or retreated. The war was entering its first lengthy intermission. Fighting men, whether on land or sea or in the air, were suddenly and unexpectedly burdened with routine chores. Regular and more or less unvarying procedures crept into their lives. For the foxhole GI and the Marine rifleman, the business of daily life took over. This is therefore a good time to leave the outpost fighting and describe what life during the Korean War was like on a day when nothing unusual or life-threatening took place. Here are the ways some men in Korea spent a "normal" day, midnight to midnight.

Cpl. VICTOR FOX
I Company/5th Cavalry

The man coming off two-hour guard was responsible for making sure he was properly relieved. I had guard duty midnight to 2:00 A.M.; Bill Haltom had guard 10:00 P.M. to 12:00 midnight and had just awakened me.

"You awake, Fox? What's password?"

"Table—Show" [password and countersign]. Anything happen?"

"Nah. Usual stuff. Pretty quiet. Any scoop before you turned in?"

"Usual shit. Rush went out and tied in some more trip flares. Guess he wasn't satisfied."

"Yeah, saw that. He checked with me. Got everything tied in. A whole lot of stuff."

"Even a bug can set something off."

"That just about happened, remember? Gotta finish this cigarette. Who relieves you?"

"McAllister. Hope I don't spend half a night gettin' him up."

"Yeah. Sometimes he's a bitch to get out the sack isn't he? Let me know if anything happens, Fox."

"Will do."

It was a clear night, so I looked from the flanks to the front and back again. You never looked at anything long or it had a tendency to move. I never saw any animals, not even a field mouse. There were birds during the quiet times, and lots and lots of insects—especially mosquitoes. I made visual contact with the other squads' OPs on each flank. You never talked or visited them. The only time I moved was to relieve myself. The men in the squads alternated guard duty each night. The last man who pulled 4:00 to 6:00 A.M. went on guard duty first the next night, and did 8:00 P.M. to 10:00 P.M. This meant he got a full night's sleep. The squad leader normally did not pull guard. The assistant squad leader might not; it would depend on alerts, or if a squad member was ill.

I spent my two hours thinking about all the mundane things a nineteen-year-old thinks about—girls, booze, luxuries, R and R, and rotating home—but not necessarily in that order. I tried to figure out the immediate future, but didn't get too far except to know it was bleak; too many things happened suddenly or unexpectedly. I did some stargazing and had gotten pretty good about finding certain constellations. Except for some distant artillery fire, it was a quiet and uneventful two hours. I always worried a little that I'd screw up and fall asleep.

"Hey, McAllister. You awake?"

"Yeah, yeah. Two already? You sure?"

"Come on, McAllister. Ya gotta' get out of the sack."

"Jeez, it's cold."

"Hell, you always say that, even in winter."

"Don't be funny, Fox."

"What's password?"

"Table—Show. Anything going on?"

"Lots of artillery going on awhile ago, way over on the right. Machine-gun tracers way out there. Patrols, probably. Who relieves you?"

"Lesniewski. Yeah, Lesniewski, Ferris is down again."

"Okay, I'm gonna' turn in. Let me know if anything happens."

"I'll think about it. Damn, I really gotta' go. Here ya' gook bastards, piss on all you sons of bitches!"

"Shit. Take it easy, McAllister."

Off came my cartridge belt, jacket, and boots. It felt so good to get back into the sleeping bag and stretch my body. I went to sleep immediately.

"Okay, you guys, drop your cocks and grab your socks. Rise'n shine! It's a beauuutiful morning in Korea. Come on. Get a move on!"

Last man on guard duty—this day it was Lesniewski—went around the squad holes getting everyone up. I said to Haltom, "You know where he gets that 'beauuutiful day" crap? He's from Chicago, and a guy there says that on the radio whether it's a good day or not."

Haltom said, "Something like here, hey?"

The first thing everybody did was light a cigarette. Next, they got on their boots, then shook out their sleeping bags to air them. Someone set a little fire on the reverse slope, so we went to heat up water for coffee. We used small packets of soluble coffee and powdered milk and sugar saved from C rations or taken from the mess.

Sugar, in small packets, was always saved. Everyone found when climbing hills with water scarce that sugar was a good thirst-quencher.

Sergeant Blackie Furlan [squad leader, 3d Squad] went around and checked on his squad so he could fill out the morning report, probably the most important record the army keeps. It is a status report of all the men in the company present for duty. The sick call was also held by the sergeant. A guy really had to be a stretcher case before he'd be sent back to the battalion aid station. Company medic treated everyone else. All of us used this time to police the area and pick up refuse left from rations and cigarettes. "Let the enemy find you, don't show him the way," was the saying.

Sergeant Furlan called out, "Mess truck just pulled up below. It's my turn and Haltom, Fox, and Rush's to go down. Rest of you later." Half the men went down the hill for a hot breakfast. It took about a half hour to eat. This morning it was the old standby S.O.S., shit on shingles, otherwise known as creamed chipped beef on toast. Thermos cans were used to serve the food hot. If eggs were served, it was powdered eggs scrambled for the thermos cans. There were also individual packages of dry cereal and watered-down powdered milk set up on a table for us.

This morning the mess crew brought up three 50-gallon clean new garbage cans, a sure sign we were in a fairly stable area of the MLR. They were filled with boiling water. One of them was used to dip your mess kit in before going through the chow line; the other two were used to dip the mess kit in after chow. Each of these 50-gallon cans used a gas-operated immersible hot water heater, which brought the water to a boil. Even when ignited correctly, these water heaters were tricky and often gave off loud explosions.

The deuce-and-a-half truck which brought chow also towed a 300-gallon water trailer; Sergeant Huber, the supply sergeant, did the same with his truck. From these we filled our canteens and every available 5-gallon can we could lay hands on for use the rest of the day.

Breakfast was the best time of day because we were all glad to see the light of a new day, and it meant exchanging "the scoop," or news, with the mess cooks from the rear. We also exchanged the scoop with Huber and his crew. Everything possible was checked out. If it was rumor, it was stated as rumor and not fact.

At breakfast, C rations were given out by the mess crew. They would be our noonday meals.

While we were at chow, I saw either the company commander or his exec. No one ever approached these officers—didn't want to get known as a brown-nosing kiss ass. Also, nobody wanted to be unduly brought to the attention of the CP people, especially 1st Sergeant Mitchell, who would figure a man had better things to do with his time than bother the company CO. However, the captain, or his exec, would circulate amongst us to get a feel of our dispositions.

Breakfast chow never ran over half an hour; the other half of the company was anxious to come down off the hill and get their hot S.O.S.

Around 8:00, depending on orders from the CP, a squad would be sent out 600 or more yards in front of the company to man the outpost. These men took C rations and a basic load of ammunition, and spent the day on this duty. The OPs, if possible, never used the same location twice. Changing the location, however, was severely limited by the terrain. There are a finite number of places on a hill where holes can be dug which overlook routes the enemy might take to the top of the hill.

My squad was not sent out this day, so until noon the men cleaned their weapons. I helped one of the machine gunners clean his gun. Unless done carefully, this could be a hazardous job. In reassembling the MG, if the powerful main operating spring was not given a last locking turn, it could get away from you and put a hole through someone.

If cleaning patches were not available, scraps of old T-shirts, which actually worked better, were found. BAR men nearly always wrapped the delicate trigger housing of their weapons with a T-Shirt to prevent it from becoming jammed with dirt.

After I finished helping with the MG, I cleaned the barrel and firing chamber of my rifle. The bluing had worn off the barrel, and not wanting it to reflect light, I rubbed the metal with charcoal. Plain old dirt worked well, too. The M1 Garand rifle, the basic infantry weapon, was incredibly reliable and durable. It could be dragged in mud, laid out in the rain, dropped, or run over by a truck, and it would still come up firing.

The squad broke out its boxes of C rations around noon. We looked first to see what brand of cigarettes was contained in them. Most men preferred Lucky Strikes or Camels; no one cared much for Chesterfields. Some bets or past favors were settled at this time with favorite cans of food, such as franks and beans, hamburgers, mashed eggs and bacon, and so forth. A few Second World War veterans were forever telling us youngsters how lucky we were to have this kind of ration, which had not been available in that war. Everyone reminisced all the time about his mom's home cooking and kicked himself for having been so fickle at the dinner table.

Five-man C-ration cartons were occasionally distributed to the men. We guessed the stockpile had gotten too big, and considering that no one liked them much, the rear-echelon types dumped them off on us line troops. Sometimes the company mess kitchens took these five-man rations and made a really decent hot meal out of them.

It was pretty dreary to be on line for days on end when nothing happened. But when action began, I kicked myself for ever thinking that I'd been bored with inactivity.

The afternoons were spent doing many things. If a man could nap, he would, but never openly.

I must mention singing, which went on all during the day. I don't know about other units, but Item Company sang a lot. Most of it was led by the southern boys, especially the guys from North Carolina. We sang mostly what we called "hillbilly" songs—the term country and western had not been coined yet. Very few contemporary hits were sung unless they were country tunes. My buddy Haltom was a wonderful singer. He and his North Carolina pals sounded very professional to me. In reserve they'd find a guitar, maybe even a fiddle; then we'd have real concerts. One particular man in the company had a hair lip, but this didn't stop him in the least from belting out a tune. This afternoon I started "I'm Always Chasing Rainbows." Haltom joined in, and our harmony stopped everyone cold. It was just surprisingly good. We never again sang that well together, but on this afternoon we were good!

Many men used the afternoons to write home. The writing paper and envelopes were supplied by the Red Cross, Salvation Army, or the U.S. Army. To mail them, all we needed to do was write *free* where the stamp would go, add *via Air Mail*, then hand them to the supply sergeant, who would arrange to have them shipped out.

I spent time bullshitting with the guys. Actually, it was "man talk," and it went on all the time. For the most part we were truthful and honest. In some cases we got to know each other fairly well. You could tell someone your deepest secrets and never fear he'd tell someone else. To sit around and just shoot the bull with your buddies just gave us a good old time. If a guy got carried away too much, someone would always parody Army radio talk: "Bullshit One, this is Bullshit Two. Over."

We often talked amongst ourselves about whether to tell war stories when we got home. Second World War veterans told us civilians would not be interested. We thought they might be if they read them in a book, or were told them by a publicly acclaimed hero. The consensus was, If people could see us now and what's happening to us, they still wouldn't believe it, so why go out of our way to tell them after the war?

The guys decided that because a feller was a great brawler or lover, he wouldn't necessarily have the stuff to be a hero. We had already experienced a few guys where the opposite was true. Nobody could ever define bravery. It appeared to me that in actual combat relatively few men ever made the difference between success or failure. I often thought about other nineteen-year-olds I knew back home and wondered whether they could put up with all the crap I went through. Hell, I figured, a guy proved he had courage by just being in combat. At times we talked about how screwed-up politics could get. Some guy would remind us that the Germans fought the Communists in World War II, and we'd fought the Germans. Now we were doing what we'd fought the Germans for doing, except we were doing it in Korea. Most frontline troops were conservative in their politics. That's just the way it was. Any kind of liberal or idealistic leanings seemed inappropriate; they seemed simply not to fit in with death and destruction. Liberals in the company just kept quiet about it; so did our one atheist.

Another subject we talked often and long about was what we would do once we got out of the army and returned to civilian life, ". . . that is, if I make it" [out of Korea]. In expressing our ambitions and desires, we often forgot that being filthy and in constant danger made our dreams seem a bit incongruous to everyone but ourselves. Talk of future plans might not always ring true; nevertheless, we believed in them. Being right there on the front lines made most talk of the future seem like wistful fantasy, but the men had to believe they were going to leave Korea, and that some day they would have a future somewhere else.

Most grudges did not last long. The provokers usually got the message in the bull sessions to lay off. We all had to live and die together. It was understood that anyone could be in a position to save your life someday. The one leveler was the teamwork necessary within the squad and platoon; everyone shared the good and the bad. If a guy did not have the backing of his squad, he was very much up shit creek. Resentments and feuds went on but, for the most part, were borne in silence, forgotten, or settled at another time. Everybody went through their good days and their bad days in Korea. Some arguments erupted into fistfights, but these were embarrassing to everyone. As men said, "Christ, knock it off. Somebody could get hurt!"

Most profane talk was exchanged with squads and men in other platoons, rather than in the immediate unit a man was assigned to. Within the squad there was surprisingly little swearing, except for *shit* and the omnipresent *fuck*. Frequent use of profanity proved to be quite boring. One thing I was amazed at was how certain ideas and words could be combined with expletives; I had never heard in civilian life, for example, "Jesus fucking Christ!" I also marveled that, as a man progressed up the NCO ranks—staff sergeant, sergeant first class, master sergeant—his barracks vocabulary grew more refined.

The squad on outpost duty was called back at 5:00 P.M. When they returned to our lines, they reported seeing a combat patrol, sent in the morning from K Company, return. Everyone wanted to know how these men had made out, whether they had run into fights or ambushes or anything else. On this day the OP in the rear remained in position, for some reason, until after the mess vehicle left.

Supper chow, the second hot meal of the day, arrived at the bottom of the hill between 5:30 P.M. and 6:00 P.M. Since Sergeant Furlan, Haltom, Rush, and I had gone down to breakfast first, we went to supper last. Tomorrow we'd rotate that order.

Hot supper was some kind of roast meat with boiled potatoes, vegetables, biscuits, and hot coffee the way only the Army can brew it.

Occasionally, at this time, the Chinese laid artillery and long-range mortar fire on the company. They knew our habits. If we began receiving fire, we would take cover behind the reverse slope of the hill. There was no fire on this particular day, however.

Once in a while, before the rear-echelon GIs returned to their camp after delivering the chow, one of our guys would sober them with the thought "Remember, you guys, if the Chinks get past us, you're next!"

We filled our canteens for the last time until the next morning. Then we filed back up to our hill positions.

Mail call was done at supper time. Everyone looked forward to this. Letters containing good news and photographs were ones we treasured the most. I once received a letter containing a pair of homemade socks. I was very appreciative, even though they lasted only two days. Mail call could be a cheerless time for men not receiving word from home. Sometimes the news from the States was bad. One Second World War veteran I remember got a "Dear John" letter just before the company attacked Hill 174 [on 14 September 1950]. I heard he ate the letter. He also perished on Hill 174.

One thing I came to realize as being true was the saying "Don't believe everything you read in the newspapers." After mail call we read newspaper clippings about the war that parents had sent. It was a different war. Some guy would say, "What'n hell are they writing about? Where's that war?"

The sun began to set, and Sergeant Furlan filled us in on the frontline situation—this for about the third time that day. Most of it was repetitious but necessary—likely avenues of approach by the enemy; where our artillery and mortars were registered; when and how often flares would be fired; any changes in company positions or fields of fire; information on friendly patrols likely to cross our zone; what units were on our flanks, behind, and below us; scoop on medics; last check on ammo, grenades, and water; settling any bitches bothering anyone except for wanting to get the hell out of there. "Tonight," Furlan told us, "the password is *Bleach—Lilac*. Try having a laundryman say that."

At this time Sergeant Furlan mentioned that his 3d Squad (us) had outpost duty the next day.

We broke down into small groups. The last bullshit sessions began; familiar voices gave encouragement. It grew darker. Voices grew softer. GIs climbed into their sleeping bags; outdoor living made one sleepy.

The sun's last rays, far to the west, speckled the tops of the highest hills. Third Squad lay in their bags and in the gloom looked at what they could see of Korea. The distant hills, where the enemy lay, were wrapped in purple haze. Below our perimeter the setting sun glinted silver off a nearby river and the surrounding rice paddies. The clouds above reflected a soft orange and red. Suddenly, it was dark. I hoped the night would pass uneventfully and quickly.

I took off my web equipment, and having worn it all day, I felt undressed. Next, I took off my jacket and boots. Haltom and I in our two-man hole arranged our bandoliers of ammo and our grenades. We both thought, Hope no one screws up tonight, and the perimeter guards stay awake. My thoughts then drifted toward home—lots of good, hot home-cooked food, loving girls, warmth, security. . . .

Pfc. DAVE KOEGEL
B/7

Awoke at 6:00 A.M. It had rained all night, and the squad's light .30-cal machine gun covered with a waterproof bag was the only item in sight that hadn't been soaked.

After pulling on squishy boots, we determined who would remain on the hill and who would be the first to go down to the road for chow. This day we were in luck. Instead of the watery mass of powdered eggs "scrambled" in a 20-gallon vat and the greasy concoction of corned-beef hash with diced, dried potatoes, we were served pancakes, bacon, and real eggs scrambled on a grill. At the end of the mess line was a table with jam, sugar, and cans of condensed milk. A few months earlier the jam and milk would have been frozen to a slushy consistency, and when stirred together would make a passable ice cream.

Back at our positions on top of the hill, I found my sleeping bag was a soggy mess; the overcast sky promised no easy drying. I draped

the bag over my shoulder and trekked down to the small Korean
village at the base of the hill. Smoke from one of the huts promised
a good fire. In the farmyard an obliging older Korean man interpreted my pantomime and took the bag inside to dry. In an adjoining
shed, two nubile girls were treading on a crude lever mechanism that
pounded grain into meal. Despite our innocent interest in the prim-
itive process, the old man gave an abrupt order and the girls disappeared. After a short time the sleeping bag appeared, dried and rolled
up.

At this time we were in close contact with battalion headquarters, and some men had taken the time to check in at sick call with
various complaints—the "trots," colds, and, in one case, piles. The
latter sufferer figured he was good for some minor surgery in Japan.
The doc's diagnosis was far simpler: "Well, son, be sure to take better
care of yourself. Try not to sit on the ground. Just remember to take
your pack off and sit on it."

When all the gear was squared away, word came that there would
be a work detail assigned to pick up parachutes from the airdrops that
had kept us supplied. We marched down the valley and looked up to
see clusters of brightly colored red, green, blue, and gold chutes flut-
tering down; at the end of each harness were 55-gallon drums of
gasoline. I thought, Just our luck, nothing to scrounge. Some of the
chutes did not open fully, and the drums burst on impact, spraying
gasoline all over the muddy rice paddies.

As soon as the planes cleared the area, we dashed out to retrieve
the chutes. The mud made everything more difficult. But this morning we were in luck; there were ration cans buried in the muck—the
leftovers from the last parachute-retrieval detail. We stuffed the filthy
cans in the bulky pockets of our dungarees and field jackets, then
proceeded to load the various colored chutes onto waiting trucks.

Back at the company position, we were happy to find mail and
some long-anticipated packages awaiting us. The luckiest of us received a carton of food: tollhouse cookies, olives, and bitingly salty
anchovies. Letters received contained such improbable questions as
"Are you learning anything in the Marines that you will be able to
use when you get back?" Some letters also contained marvelously
distorted newspaper accounts of past actions.

With no specific duties assigned, I dug into my pack for some precious stationery I'd been hoarding for just a day like this. These few sheets had been given out some time back, and bore the logo of a World War II outfit, the 5th Field Service Supply Depot, FMC Pac. Underneath was a small watercolor sketch of a palm-lined sandy beach. A few sprays of exploding shells near a landing craft were the only indications in the sketch that a war was going on. Conscious of the need to keep up morale on the homefront, I ignored any recent combat and focused my letter on the good breakfast chow; the recently scrounged extra rations; and the word, which had just arrived, that a portable show had been set up down on the road. A local farmer wandered by, and I invited him to jot down some words for the benefit of the folks back home. He declined. Only later did it occur to me that he may never before have held a writing instrument of any description, let alone an American pencil.

The trip down to the showers proved a disappointment. At the end of my fifteen-minute hike was an hour-long wait as a huge line of dirty men stood in front of the one tent. The sun came out and the day began to warm up. A few of us in line decided to wash in a nearby stream. The water was cold, and I didn't stay in long enough to get more than a little of the grime off.

On the road back to the hill, I learned my brother's outfit, Dog Battery, 11th Marines, had set up its 105-mm howitzers just a few miles away. Leaving my buddies, I hitched a ride on a passing six-by-six truck. At the sight of the snubbed-nose 105s, I hopped off and located my brother in the squad's pyramidal tent. Ah, I thought, the comforts of the artillery! We sat on the classic folding wooden cots and filled each other in on our activities since our last meeting, which had been at the Bean Patch [Masan] after the Chosin withdrawal. A few random 75-mm rounds from a well-hidden enemy gun began to fall nearby. "Hey," I said, "back on the hill, we haven't heard hostile fire for several days. Do I need this? No thanks. See 'ya soon Brother, dear."

Back in the relative safety of Baker Company, I noticed replacements had arrived and were sitting around swapping scuttlebutt. The stocks of the new men's weapons had a high luster which showed meticulous rubbing with linseed oil. Of particular interest in this group

were the Negroes, who had, up till a few months before, been assigned to Combat Service Group, the ghetto where many black Marines had been assigned before the enlightened view that frontline
troops could come from any color or race. In my squad one of the
new Negroes was assigned to share a hole with an Alabaman. Knowing looks went around. They were for nothing; the two men soon
became fast friends.

On this particular day, news from the battalion mess was not
good; dinner would feature the much-abhorred pork and greasy gravy.
Private Ortega, a farm boy from New Mexico, offered a solution. We
agreed willingly to his plan and gave him whatever 1,000-won notes
we carried. He went down the hill and bought an old hen from one
of the farmers. That afternoon we learned the difference between
frying chickens and stewing chickens. Our bird might have responded
to a long simmering in a steel helmet hung over a slow fire. But
done hobo-style, as we did it, on a spit with only a little rock salt for
spice, the bird proved to be a stringy challenge to our molars. We
finished the meal with some of the C rations we had gathered earlier
from the muddy rice paddy.

After dark, a few venturesome Marines drifted down to the village, where one of the huts was home to a number of "unattached"
girls. During the evening's activities, the house accidentally caught
fire. The girls, whose livelihood was threatened, grabbed their douche
pans and attacked the fire with vigor. We left the area shortly afterward, so I never learned how quickly the ladies brought their establishment back to full operation.

I slipped into my sleeping bag and looked up to see bright stars
twinkling in the heavenly dome above me. Happily, there would be
no rain that night. I began to drift off; four hours of sleep before I'd
be awakened for the midnight watch. I thought fondly of the few
original members of the regiment who had received orders to return
stateside under the rotation plan. I began counting the members of
the outfit who had seniority over me—it was better than counting
sheep.

Capt. HENRY MARQUART *
Company Commander/Eighth Army

Shortly after first light, each platoon sent forward a squad-sized patrol to recon some 500 yards in front of our position, to ensure that the enemy had not crept in close during the hours of darkness. While this happened, platoon leaders dispatched several small teams of three or four men to occupy designated observation posts [OPs] 500 to 1,000 yards beyond the company's position. Two-man wire teams accompanied them. Once the OPs were occupied, the teams laid wire back to the command post [CP]. During this time the company was on full alert. The men in listening posts [LPs], who had been providing outer security during the darkness, would now be relieved and return to the company area, rolling up their commo wire as they came in. Once back, the men would report to the CP to be debriefed. Although the LPs would do a commo-check every fifteen to thirty minutes during the night, I thought it a good idea to have them talk to me about the activities of the night. Sometimes, I found men were somewhat reluctant to report activities for fear of being accused of "crying wolf," and this brief chat with me in the morning gave them the opportunity in a relaxed setting to tell their story. More than once I would detect a sheepish look, which clued me that it was possible they had gone to sleep while on duty. I could then launch into my little spiel about the importance of maintaining security and how their buddies depended on them, without accusing anyone of dereliction of duty. This time with the men also gave me an opportunity to look into their eyes and they into mine—equally important—to size up one another and our determination to get the job done.

While I was doing my thing with the LPs and checking that the OPs were in business, the men in the company area policed their respective areas, relieved themselves, washed, shaved, and got chow.

I then generally moved out to the battalion HQ to learn what I could about the overall situation and what battalion was up to. If time permitted, I'd fit in a visit to a nearby company and a chat with its CO. We were all friends, and it was good to exchange small talk and try to figure out what really was going on. We also used this

---

* A pseudonym, as this account is based on several sources.

time to discuss problems and our solutions. Depending on the distances involved, this generally consumed several hours.

Back at my own CP, usually for noon chow, I'd end up at my field desk dealing with administrative matters with the supply sergeant, the mess sergeant, company clerk, and XO. During the few minutes I spent at this desk, I devoted my time to confirming promotions, writing up recommendations for decorations and awards, and writing letters to next-of-kin [NOK] of men who had been killed in action or wounded, or who had excelled in some manner or another. The toughest administrative duty I performed—no question— was the NOK letter on a KIA. The family had already received the telegram from the Army but had not been given any details. Sometimes a close buddy also felt compelled to write. I would urge these men to exercise great constraint, to remember that in some cases their letters would be resented by the families of the dead men—the simple truth was, Why should one man live and another die? Families asked this question and resented the men who were still alive. As a result, I think I wrote most of the NOK letters. I had never received instructions on how to write such a letter nor been ordered to do so; it was simply something one did. I felt I owed it to the dead man.

Following time at the field desk, I generally walked about the company area talking to the men as I came across them—getting better acquainted with the new men, reminiscing with the older ones (older to the extent we'd been together longer).

Midafternoon, I'd head for one or more of the OPs and spend several hours observing the surrounding terrain, determining the extent and necessity of patrol activity and confirming defensive fire registrations, particularly if the supporting weapons had been moved, or I had adjusted any of the company positions.

An hour before dark I'd return to the company area. If we were in a strictly reserve position, I would simply walk the position checking on the men, then return to the CP to get chow. If, however, we were in an on-line position, then this period was particularly active. The OPs would be brought in and the LPs sent out. Night patrols or ambush parties would be dispatched, and fields of fire verified.

During the night I would be up on the radio all the time a night patrol was out or anything else important was going on. Once the night patrols returned and I talked to the men, I would try and turn to for a bit of sleep. The XO simply caught his sleep when I was awake, for when I was asleep, he was awake. Sometimes, when we were both so exhausted we couldn't stay awake at night for more than fifteen minutes at a time, we'd alternate shaking each other awake so one of us could shut his eyes for a couple of minutes more. Sleep was a big thing all the time. You never got enough of it and always needed more. Men thirsted for it; some men died for it. I think sometimes guys welcomed a wound that didn't pain too much, because they felt that back in a MASH they could sleep for days. I know on more than one occasion I felt that several days of uninterrupted sleep in a hospital would be just compensation for getting a hole in my side and bleeding all over my clothes.

Sgt. F/C JIMMY MARKS *
A Battery/61st Field Artillery Battalion
We have just moved to a new position and it has begun to rain—hard. The chief of firing battery, Master Sergeant Lacost Murdock, then tells the six chiefs of section where he wants their [105-mm] howitzers dug in. Once the howitzers are pulled off the road, the cannoneers hop to it. When the trails are spread and the panoramic telescopes are in place, the aiming stakes are put out.

The weapon currently in my charge is an old war-horse left over from the Second World War, but if properly cared for, very reliable. Manufactured by the Vilter Manufacturing Company, our piece is an M2A1 with gun #2923 and carriage #2033. It weighs 4,980 pounds and has a muzzle velocity of 1,550 feet per second with a range of 12,500 yards. When pushed, my section can deliver fifteen to twenty rounds per minute. At night the gun fires at prearranged coordinates, such as an intersection of two highways—or more properly, two dirt roads. The harassment and interdictory fire, called H & I, is done at random to keep the Chinese on their toes. We did not fire H & I's last night because the battery was being moved to a new location. The gun crew—we have eight at this time—is split between me and

---

* Marks had become chief of 1st Section in January, and had been promoted to sergeant first class on 1 April.

Sergeant Dial Miller, the cannoneer. The routine at night is divided into two six-hour shifts; Miller takes 6:00 to midnight, and I take 12:00 to 6:00 in the morning. Of course, if the battery receives a big fire mission, the entire section is rousted out.

While the aiming stakes are being placed, the battery commander is busy at the aiming circle, plotting in the direction the guns will fire. Once the battery is laid in, the backbreaking work of digging parapets for the guns begins. Once the original dirt wall is constructed, it will gradually be reinforced with sandbags and ammo boxes. If there isn't a fire mission to answer, we dig foxholes and erect a tent for the crew. The longer we stay in one position, the more comfortable our "accommodations" become.

While we are digging and building, the wire section is busy laying telephone lines between each of the battery's six guns. It doesn't take long, perhaps just minutes, before all the chiefs of section report to the FDC [fire direction center] that they are back in business and ready to fire. The rain has let up a little, but the day is still dreary.

The battery commander suddenly calls with a fire mission he has received from an air observer flying nearby. The battery has been given four targets of opportunity: an enemy AAA [antiaircraft artillery] gun, a CP, and two antitank guns. The order from the battery FDC comes down to me over the field telephone, "Fire mission! Battery adjust—shell, HE; fuse, quick." Direction and range are quickly adjusted. The gunner lines up the cross hairs of his panoramic telescope with the two aiming stakes. The number one man, Lou Iglesias, sets the elevation. The other men have removed some of the seven powder bags from the shell casing. The number two man, Private Elmer Blankenship, rams the projectile home. Iglesias slams shut the breach block with a loud clang and waits for my command to fire. Orders from FDC continue to come down to me, "Battery, three rounds—fire at will." Six chiefs of section shout almost simultaneously, "Fire!" The guns crash together, then two more times each. In less than a minute, eighteen rounds fall on the four enemy targets. The spotter waits for the smoke and dust to clear, then reports, "All targets destroyed."

The bore of the gun is then cleaned until the thirty-six lands and grooves shine like a new silver dollar. Work on the parapet then picks up where it left off.

The field kitchen has arrived during the firing mission, and the mess crew begin setting up. Because of our frequent moves over the past few days, we have been eating nothing but C rations. Today we will have our first hot meal in quite some time. In a little while the mess sergeant calls that chow is ready. I let a few men go first. The line is pretty spread out. We have learned the hard way not to bunch up. Some units have had frightful experiences of infiltrators getting into the line and opening up with burp guns or throwing grenades. The first group returns and reports the hot meal this day is "stewed rats"—stringy roast beef. The rest of us groan. But at least the cold stewed tomatoes, peach halves, and a slice of bread are edible. We all pray that the next day the cooks will have had more time and the food will be better.

Once the parapet is as strong as I want it, the men pitch their pup tents. Each man shares a shelter half with a man on the other shift; that way, only one man at a time has to occupy the cramped space. If we find we are going to spend more time in one location, we build more-elaborate structures out of discarded ammo boxes, tarps, and any Korean woven mats we can lay our hands on. Some of the men have already begun to boil water in their helmets to shave and bathe with, then wash some clothes in. If we are lucky, someone might find an old chicken which will make a good stew.

Late in the afternoon there is a lull in the activity around the gun pit. Iglesias takes his shoes off and writes a letter home. Bill Peterson, the number four man, and our truck driver, Ric Myers, are in deep conversation with Odell Giles, Jerry Griffith, and Herb Pugh, the other section members. We hoped to get some mail on this day, but realize it won't catch up with us because of our movement. Maybe tomorrow, we all hope.

Another fire mission is called for. Everyone runs for the gun. Peterson sets the time on the fuse; Odell Giles hands the heavy shell to Blankenship, who rams it home with his gloved fist. Herm Daniels cuts the charge and takes out two of the powder sacks from the shell casing. The target this time is a hill held by a well-dug-in enemy unit, and we'll fire TOT. When the command is given, the six guns in the battery fire simultaneously. Each piece fires eighty-eight rounds; the mission lasts about twenty minutes.

After dark, Miller's crew tries to get some sleep; they will have to get up at midnight and relieve us firing the H & I's. Because the second watch is preferable to the first—no one has trouble going to sleep after midnight—the routine will be rotated. All night long, A Battery, 61st Field Artillery Battalion, harasses the Chinese. Maybe we'll keep them awake too.

Sgt. LEONARD KORGIE *
Headquarters Company/21st Infantry Regiment
The regimental headquarters was situated about ten miles behind our line company's, and my section was set up in a big squad tent complete with folding cots, blankets, desk, switchboard, typewriter—even mats on the wooden floor. It was a beautiful early summer morning. Wildflowers in abundance grew everywhere, and the trees were covered with green leaves. I got out of the sack around 6:30 A.M., having slept through the night, put my boots on, and woke the other three men in the tent—a clerk/typist and two field men; then I went and woke up the CO, Captain Wolpert.

Breakfast was the usual powdered eggs with spam in one of several forms—sliced, diced, or chunks. On nice days, and this was one of them, we ate around the mess tent; on rainy mornings we took the food back to the tent and ate there. We smoked after chow and talked, mostly about the latest rumors of the military situation picked up around regimental headquarters, or fantasized about rotating home. With all the replacements I was seeing, I had to believe they were in Korea to take the places of men who were going home. With the fighting beginning to slow down, I began to think that someday somebody was going to arrive and take my place. But before I would get totally carried away, I remembered the red-hot rumors of October '50—the ones reporting we'd all be home by Christmas.

After chow I went about my "toiletries." No entrenching tool and muddy field here, as I had been used to with the line company; now it was a board to sit on, over a hole. We even had toilet tissue. I appreciated these luxuries and went about my morning business

---

* Korgie was assigned to the 21st Infantry Regiment's Civil Assistance Section and became its chief clerk and operations sergeant in mid-March.

leisurely and carefully. I filled my helmet with cold water drawn from a central supply bag—pure, clear water—and washed my body from the waist up. Next, I slowly shaved, then brushed my teeth. Never before in Korea had I seen so many razor blades or tubes of shaving cream or toothpaste. I began to get a little vain about my appearance, even grew a little mustache—that is, until an officer gave me a hard look. I spent a long time in front of a mirror. I hadn't seen my own face for months and now enjoyed the image. I sewed chevrons on my sleeves and, since someone issued it to me, began wearing my combat infantryman's badge. I hated wearing my helmet; it mussed up my carefully combed hair. I regularly polished my boots and washed my clothes. I was well fed and rested; ten miles behind the MLR I felt tough as hell. My smile broadened and my step grew more spirited. I almost bounced when I walked. God, was this a long way from Taejon and the Pusan Perimeter!

With my grooming activities out of the way, I helped clean up the tent. I wrote up my reports and had the clerk type them. Once Captain Wolpert signed them, they were sent to Lieutenant Colonel Daniels up at division headquarters.

About 10:00 I put the clerk on the switchboard for the day, and the captain, his driver, and I drove north to visit some Korean villages. We brought with us two truckloads of rice, DDT, medicine; two Korean doctors; and about thirty South Korean policemen.

The UN Command was much concerned about the welfare of the civilians caught up in the combat zone, and my job was to assist in administering the help these poor souls were given.

We set up a minigovernment in every village. The man with the most education, or the one we thought the most intelligent, no matter his age, was appointed mayor and put in charge of food distribution.

Wounded or sick civilians were funneled back to our aid stations for treatment. These units, not now treating battle casualties, cooperated beautifully.

The policemen doused everybody with DDT and maintained order. In some villages the doctors found typhus; these huts would immediately be burnt to the ground.

Prostitutes were a daily problem. Some of our battalions used Korean boys to help out in their mess tents. Sharp operators would

smuggle girls in, and with their hair cut short and wearing oversized
fatigues, they were hard to tell from the boys. Our doctors had the
responsibility of trying to separate one from the other. At one time I
had as many as sixty prostitutes locked up in a jail guarded by our
policemen. I never wanted to know what went on in there, as I was
afraid I'd find the women beating hell out of the cops.

On this particular day we drove through our 2d Battalion's area,
and I ran into old buddies from the 34th Infantry.* I was very glad
to see my former company CO, Lieutenant [William] Syverson. He
was a major now. When we met we smiled and the message was,
What a hell of a long road we've both traveled.

About 4:00 P.M. our convoy returned to the regimental headquarters area. My notebook was filled with data on all the food distributed, patients treated, and DDT sprayed. I checked on phone
messages and planned the next day's itinerary; then I washed up and
went to chow.

Ham in all its forms frequently appeared at dinner, and when
coupled with mashed (powdered) potatoes and peas, it was solid food—
filling and delicious. Dessert was either apple or peach cobbler. The
meat was washed down with black coffee and finished off with a
cigar. Man, this was living.

At night I heard the distant sound of artillery. None of the guys
in my outfit, or officers, had served in a line outfit as I had, and they
could not understand my utter disdain for this fire. Shit, I knew it
was outgoing and faraway. I just considered it a nuisance.

Eventually, I slipped off my boots and made a pillow of my
sleeping bag. The guys in the tent bullshitted until we fell asleep. I
always kept a .45 under my pillow. A lot of Chinese had been cut
off during our May offensive, and they occasionally came down out
of the hills, hungry as hell, looking for food scraps we'd thrown away.
I'd been ambushed too often to let it happen again.

---

*After the 34th Infantry had been nearly destroyed trying to stop the North Koreans in July
1950, it was reduced to paper status in late August. At that time the 187 survivors of the
regiment were transferred to the 19th and 21st Infantry Regiments. Korgie had served as a
rifleman in L Company, 34th Infantry, until the transfer.

Cpl. HERMAN VOELLINGS
Headquarters Company/1st Battalion/5th Cavalry

Being a cook sounds easy, and if you were experienced, as I was, it was; unfortunately, most of our cooks weren't. When I was being processed into the battalion I was lucky enough to be asked if I had any cooking experience—I had. The sergeant then assigned me to the battalion headquarters kitchen. This, of course, was my life insurance; the two other men who were processed with me were assigned to rifle companies and later killed.

My day began around 4:30 A.M., when the baker or mess sergeant woke me. Often, I would have spent two hours on perimeter guard duty, and I felt more like going back to bed than getting up to put in another day in the kitchen. Artillery fire and sporadic, distant rifle or machine-gun firing during the night put me on edge, and I often had difficulty falling asleep. I'm not ashamed to say that there were times I was so scared I shook myself to sleep.

We received our food from the division quartermaster's stores. It would be broken down then into regiment, then battalion, then company supplies. It was a big operation. Whenever our food distribution system was disrupted, the units reverted to eating C rations. A master menu was printed out, and on a given day the same meal was served throughout the division. Each company would send its mess sergeant each week to a breakdown area, where he would pick up his company's rations. At times I know we were shortchanged and the battalion was not given the proper amount of rations required to feed the troops. I heard via the grapevine that a black-market scheme had surfaced, and some officers at division were skimming food and selling it elsewhere. We considered these officers as bad as the rats we put up with.

I know we ate well in battalion. We had steaks until they came out our ears. We also had roast beef, pork, ham, chicken, and hamburger. Some of our fresh vegetables came from Korean farmers who grew them in nearby villages.

I cooked on a regular field-kitchen range made of lightweight aluminum, with a gas-operated burner. One of our jobs was to keep the pressure constant in the gas tanks so the heating element, the flame, remained constant. Grilling was done by using the covers to the cooking pans. The ranges were built in levels, so the one closest to the flame cooked food faster than the one farthest away. Portable containers kept the food hot while it was transported to the troops on the line.

Every day I took hot chow or coffee up to the MLR, and often it was a risky trip, as we did not know what we'd meet along the road. Someone always rode shotgun and looked out for ambushes. One day a cow blocked our path. I thought, Here it comes. But fortunately there were no Chinese hiding nearby.

The most unpleasant task I had was in the evening, when we went to blackout conditions. Then, ventilation flaps at the top of the tent, along with the entrance flaps at both ends, were sealed. Battalion was always afraid that light would draw enemy artillery or mortars. With the tent sealed, the cooking gases had no where to go, and we cooked with teary and stinging eyes.

One evening I was assigned to guard two prisoners, one of whom I was told was Chinese, and the other, North Korean. They were tied back-to-back, and I don't know who was more scared, them or me. I began to think, What if they're so important their comrades come and try to free them? The night was quite black, and I was very glad to see the sun come up next morning.

Capt. LUTHER WEAVER
3d Battalion/35th Infantry

My day began after breakfast with a battalion staff meeting called by Colonel Lee for anytime between 7:00 and 7:30 A.M. At this meeting each of the staff officers reported on significant events that had taken place during the preceding twenty-four hours, and the CO would update us on what had happened at the patrol base.* Then, each staff officer would voice specific requests; in my case, it would be for more logs [for building emplacements], sandbags, tactical wire, pickets, or for the resupply of clean fatigues, socks, boots, underwear, and so forth. Once the meeting came to a close, if nothing urgent

---

* The patrol base was situated six miles forward of the MLR and the Turkish Brigade, on Hills 717 and 682.

needed my attention, I checked on the status of our supplies and transportation. I always found that some items required by battalion through supply channels were not forthcoming. In order to speed delivery of these items, my driver and I would drive back to the nearest supply depot that stocked the items I was looking for. I always found depot personnel very cooperative with combat units. Once I found what I was looking for—assuming they had it—all they required was a signature and the name of the unit the items were going to. If the items were more than my jeep could handle, I'd dispatch a truck from battalion to go back and retrieve them. I usually had everything under control by 4:00 P.M.

There would then be approximately two or three hours of daylight before dark, and I would use this time to scout the area on foot for pheasant, of which there were many. Sometime in July, Colonel Lee had given me custodianship of an old Remington 12-gauge automatic shotgun, which had found its way to Korea from the 25th Division Special Services. Apparently, when the division had been hastily moved from Japan to Korea the year before, a few of these shotguns had been at battalion, where I assume they were being used for skeet shooting. Anyway, one day I found two of these guns with a few boxes of shells in one of the battalion supply trailers. Colonel Lee was quite delighted with my find, as he believed the guns and trailer had been lost several months before in a Chinese ambush. He decided to keep one of the shotguns for himself and to give me the other. I discovered that after a year of bumping around in the cold and heat of Korea, the shells had become too swollen to fit the shotgun's firing chamber. I solved the problem by peeling two layers off the shell casing. And that's how I ended up with a single-shot automatic which, if lucky, fired two shots before it hung up.

The Kumhwa Valley was a rather fertile farming area. Rice paddies were surrounded by patches of soybeans, peas, and maize; the adjoining foothills were covered in scrub brush. The war had pushed the Korean farmers off the land, and ringneck pheasants were enjoying more than anything, or anyone, the spoils of war. Even with faulty shells it was not unusual for me to bag three or four in an hour or so. In a matter of several weeks, I supplemented the battalion mess with about forty pheasant.

On one particular afternoon in late August, just prior to dusk, I walked back in from my usual round of pea patches and bird-flushing, and noticed I was approaching the Love Company mess tent. The company was all in line for evening chow. Of course, I recognized nearly everyone. One boy hollered, "How many did you get, Cap'n?" At that precise moment two big cock pheasant near me flew up in a roar. In unison the men shouted, "Shoot 'em! Shoot 'em!" I instantly realized I better not miss, or my name with that audience would be mud. One bird veered to the right, away from the mess line. I snapped the gun up and fired. Down went the pheasant. A big roar went up from the men. "Same old Cap'n Weaver," they shouted. "Never misses what he shoots at." No question, this was my most memorable pheasant kill. To have as spectators my old company which I admired so much made that shot really special. After much handshaking with many of the men I knew by name, I gave Joe Wlos, the mess sergeant, the birds I had with me and told him to treat Love Company to a pheasant dinner.

A few days later, the battalion patrol base and most of my hunting ground would be in Chinese hands, I would lose the shotgun, and most of the men in Love Company would be missing or dead.

FLARE-UP

---

1 September–30 November 1951

During August, the 35th Infantry Regiment had been in a quiet sector of the war and in division reserve.* The men of the regiment had spent a cheerless and uncomfortable month erecting and strengthening defensive positions in the monsoon rain that fell nearly every day. The routine for the regiment's 3d Battalion changed somewhat on 26 August, when it was ordered to establish a company-size outpost north of the main battle position of the Turkish Brigade in the vicinity of Tangwon-ni.

The advanced patrol base, as it was officially known, was maintained on Hill 717 and the adjacent Hill 682, ground which dominates an entire system of hills and ridges north and west of the Hant'an River and south and east of the hamlet of P'yonggang. The base was occupied by one reinforced company, which was rotated between the battalion's three rifle companies every three days.† On 1 September it was King Company's turn to live in the bunkers and trenches dug on Hills 717 and 682.

Across the swollen Hant'an, the Chinese occupied Hill 1062, a prominence some distance to the east, overlooking the patrol base.

---

*The regiment had been one of the earliest units committed in the war, and had arrived in Korea between 13 and 15 July 1950. On 1 September 1951, the 35th Infantry had been in action for 416 days, suffering battle casualties of 106 officers and 2,514 enlisted men.
†A heavy machine-gun platoon and a 75-mm RR platoon from M Company were attached to whichever company was on duty at the base.

From there, they watched the activities of the American rifle compa-
nies with great interest. An enemy reconnaissance unit patrolling the
wooded countryside around Hills 717 and 682 had also been assigned
to keep an eye on the GIs. The information the patrol returned with
would be used soon by the Communists with deadly efficiency.

The K Company was relieved by L Company on 3 September. It
would be Love Company's turn now to watch and wait at the patrol
base, and to be watched by the Chinese on Hill 1062.

Capt. LUTHER WEAVER
3d Battalion/35th Infantry
At the daily battalion staff meeting [5 September], our new battalion
CO, Colonel Jones,* who, incidentally, had not been in combat yet,
lectured us rather sarcastically, I thought, on our responsibilities of
getting out to see what the troops were doing. In that the staff was
made up of ex-company commanders, we all thought his remarks
were slightly uncalled-for. Nevertheless, without hesitation, Captain
Don McGraw, the battalion S-3, and I spoke up and volunteered to
walk to the patrol base [on Hill 717] the next day when Item Company relieved Love.

6 September
Battalion S-3 [McGraw] and S-4 [Weaver] departed assembly area
at 0730 to inspect patrol base. I Co. moved out of assembly area
to relieve L Co. on patrol base. Both companies will remain on
base overnight.
EXECUTIVE OFFICER'S UNIT JOURNAL, 3D BATTALION/35TH INFANTRY

Capt. LUTHER WEAVER
3d Battalion/35th Infantry
The trail sloped upwards, then, after several miles, grew steeper as it
neared the peak of 717.† The infantrymen from Item carried three

---

* Lieutenant Colonel James Lee had been reassigned to G-2, 25th Division, on 23 July.
† Hills 717 and 682, about 1800 meters apart on a roughly east-west line, are the highest points
of a ridge complex that rises abruptly from the Hant'an River Valley. Major spurs of this

day's worth of supplies, and the 200 Korean laborers we had with us lugged A-frames stacked with rolls of barbed wire, sandbags, ammunition, 5-gallon water cans, and so forth. The going was quite slow, and we did not reach L Company's position [six miles in front of the battalion CP] until around 5:00 P.M. McGraw and I went directly to the sandbag CP bunker that was used by all the companies and met Lieutenant Roder, Love's CO. He talked continuously of his fear that the Chinese would attack the OP that night. I thought he appeared rather nervous. Enemy artillery occasionally hit the hill, and around dark three men were wounded and taken care of by the medics. McGraw and I decided we had better find ourselves a fighting hole, just in case Roder was right. We decided on two emplacements some thirty or so yards from the company CP and the artillery FO's bunker. The next thing we did was try to find weapons for ourselves. McGraw had a .45; I did, too, plus I carried that old Remington automatic 12-gauge shotgun and five shells for it. I had carried it to the outpost in the event we were "attacked" on the way by pheasants. McGraw and I found a couple of M1 rifles, which we put in our fighting holes.

Hill 717 was the peak of a small plateau; to the north, forward of the artillery FO's position, the hill dropped precipitously. On the west, a gradual slope led to a draw covered in scrub timber; to the east, a saddle connected 717 to Hill 682. Our defensive positions ran around the rim of the plateau, then along the saddle to 682, where one of L Company's platoons was dug in. A small finger of land led in a northwesterly direction from the plateau and was covered by a section of light machine guns. Wire and radio communication connected the platoons with the company CP. Item Company was dug in on the reverse side 717 and would remain there until the following morning when L Company was to be relieved. That was the plan, anyway.

---

complex extend to the northeast, northwest, and south, with lesser spurs projecting in all directions. The ridges are high and steep sided. No valleys approach the ridge complex from the north, east, or west; on the south, however, two valleys approach the area from the main valley of the Hant'an River.

6 September

1940 Arty still coming in on 717; estimated 76-mm howitzer or
       larger. L Co OP on Hill 717 lost communications by wire
       and radio with 682. Another 8 rounds have been received.

                     S-2 JOURNAL, 3D BATTALION/35TH INFANTRY

Capt. LUTHER WEAVER
3d Battalion/35th Infantry

Around 8:00 P.M the enemy artillery intensified, and it appeared they
were zeroing the hill. McGraw and I remained with Roder in the
CP. Just before midnight, incoming artillery increased to heavy shelling. McGraw and I ran to our fighting holes. Somehow, I found
time in mine to scribble in the diary I carried everything that would
happen in the next six and a half hours.

Midnight Heavy shelling. A lot of men wounded. All wire
          communications knocked out.

0030   Artillery lifts. Alert for an attack.

0035   Outpost on 717 under attack by enemy small-arms
          fire. Enemy troops firing colored flares. Can be heard
          moving in for attack. . . . Outpost withdraws back to
          perimeter defense. Hill 682 also now under attack.
          Enemy troops very noisy and now attacking from all
          sides.

0200   We redistribute ammunition, plug holes [with Item
          Company] and prepare for another attack. All com-
          munications out. Many men wounded. FO killed and
          radio out. Have lost contact with 682.

0245   Enemy renewed attack and we are completely sur-
          rounded. Killing enemy trying to get through barbed
          wire. Ammo running low.

0330   Enemy reorganizing again. We have many dead and
          wounded.

0400   Enemy makes fanatical banzai attack from all sides,
          screaming, yelling, cussing Americans. Now killing
          Chinks right on our emplacements. Lord, give us
          daylight soon. Some Chinese in our lines and are in
          the Korean laborers' holding positions.

It was at this time, when the ammo for my M1 was nearly exhausted, that I grabbed the 12-gauge shotgun. The enemy was coming through gaps in the barbed wire. The first shot hit two Chinks on my left and dropped them; they screamed like wounded animals. Due to all the dirt and debris in the shotgun I had difficulty reloading it. I did manage one more shot and stopped another enemy soldier. Then the blasted thing hung up again. As a last resort I began using my .45 pistol.

Someone jumped into the back of my hole. I turned and tried to break his neck. I felt hot blood run down my neck and side. (After it got light I saw, to my sorrow, that what I thought had been a Chink had in reality been a wounded Korean laborer who tragically jumped in my hole to escape the attack.)

0530 Some daylight beginning to come through. Enemy flares go up and enemy begins to withdraw. We still hold the hill. Many dead and wounded Chinks just below our emplacements, plus several inside the perimeter. We have many wounded and dead, including a number of Korean laborers, who were not armed.

0630 Reorganize what we have left and redistribute ammo— what we can find. Daylight has saved us.

[At 8:30 A.M., K Company, the 3d Battalion's only uncommitted rifle company, was ordered to the patrol base to support L and I Companies. On Hill 717, repeated attempts to supply the survivors by air drop were unsuccessful, owing to the smallness of the drop zone and the sharp ridges of the base.]

Capt. LUTHER WEAVER
3d Battalion/35th Infantry
Captain McGraw, now in command on the hill, gave me one of the two remaining SCR-300 radios and asked that I try to get the wounded out. I began at once to organize the walking wounded and to gather the severly wounded and litter cases.

[At 9:45 A.M., K Company, rushing northward, reported back to the battalion CP that it had come under small-arms and mortar fire. Like the curtain rising slowly on a theatrical tragedy, the gravity of the situation around the patrol base gradually became apparent to the 3d Battalion's staff officers. If the enemy was between K Company and Hill 717, he must also be in the valleys through which Captain Weaver's group of wounded and the other survivors of the night battle would have to pass.]

Capt. LUTHER WEAVER
3d Battalion/35th Infantry

Around midmorning I began moving my group and a few riflemen who would give us some security down the back of the hill. McGraw and I agreed we'd stay in touch by radio as long as we could.

Near the base of 717 I spotted an enemy force digging in several hundred yards to the south. I reported the situation to McGraw, who told me to hold where I was, as he had just heard that a friendly force [K Company] was on its way to relieve us. I put all the wounded I could in old dugouts and holes and waited to be rescued. We had no medical supplies left, and during the morning two of the wounded died. I put out a screening group so we could watch enemy movements.

[As the day advanced, K Company, still far to the south of Hill 717, was joined by F Company, 35th Infantry. When the two companies found themselves unable to advance against stiffening resistance from what was estimated to be a reinforced Chinese regiment, they formed a defensive perimeter and waited for the night. Meanwhile, at the patrol base, the situation grew even more precarious. Toward late afternoon enemy fire on the hills picked up tempo.]

    1470 Elements on Hill 682 returning to Hill 717 are receiving arty fire.

    1445 Hill 717 receiving small arms and artillery fire.

S-2 JOURNAL, 3D BATTALION/35TH INFANTRY

Capt. LUTHER WEAVER
3d Battalion/35th Infantry
Some of the wounded from Hill 682 began to come into my area.
The hills were being repeatedly attacked, and the newly arrived
wounded reported that the Chinese were closing in. With the artillery and mortar fire growing heavier, I decided to move my group of
wounded and try to get away from it. Before we started, a group of
men from Item Company with Captain Burkhart, their CO, came
by. He was wounded badly in the face but still able to walk. These
men reported that there were many more wounded still up on the
hill. I started my group to the rear with Captain Burkhart and his
men. Leaving my radioman at the foot of the hill with instructions
to wait for me, I climbed back to the top of 717 with the intention
of picking up whomever else I found wounded.

*[What Luther Weaver could not know was that, moments before he
decided to return to the patrol base, a vigorous enemy infantry assault
had driven the remaining defenders from Hill 717.]*

Capt. LUTHER WEAVER
3d Battalion/35th Infantry
I noticed enemy troops all over the peak and plateau. Apparently L
and I Companies had been forced off. I hurried back down to the
foot of the hill, but then could not find my radio operator. I figured
he had joined one of the small groups of men who were now trying
to make their way back to battalion. I picked up an M1 and a clip of
ammo which one of the wounded men had left behind. There was
no doubt in my mind that I was surrounded. My plan was to catch
up to the wounded group and Captain Burkhart. I hoped to do this
before it got dark. The time was now about 5:00 P.M.

   I moved along a narrow, winding trail that cut through a deep
draw, and had gone several hundred yards when I suddenly ran head-
on into a Chinese patrol. I dashed off the trail and down a steep
embankment into a ravine covered by heavy brush. I fell into a deep
ditch and lay covered in warm water and black muck. The Chinese
fired into the ravine, but I was not hit. Fortunately, they did not
choose to climb down and look for me. After a while they moved

off, and their yakking faded away. In the late-afternoon quiet I took stock of my situation. The M1 was only going to get in my way in the heavy brush, so I threw it away. This left me with just a .45. Next, I chewed and swallowed the battalion radio code call signs printed on onionskin paper which I carried.

I moved out of the ravine. Near the trail I saw someone walking toward me from the direction of the patrol base. I could tell at a distance from his clothing he was not Chinese. When he arrived near where I lay, I whistled softly and showed my face. The man immediately jumped off the trail, and together we slid down the embankment. He was Chong Lee, an ROK soldier I knew from my time as L Company's CO. Together, we crawled and crept along a concealed gulley that led up a small hill or knoll. About then we heard firing coming from our right, and the cries of Koreans. Lee said the Chinese were shooting Koreans. I knew there were Korean laborers with the wounded group helping to carry the litters. I decided then that Lee and I would wait until dark before we tried to break out. Before it got too dark, I knew I'd have to get on some high ground to see where I wanted to go. Some Navy fighters flew over and placed an air strike on 717. They circled and made another run on the hill. I heard several explosions and saw black smoke rising above the trees.

It was time now for Lee and me to make our move to a hill that rose several hundred yards to the south. We assisted each other up its steep, brush-covered slopes. I had not heard any more gunshots and assumed the group of wounded had been either murdered or taken prisoner. From the top of the hill, Lee and I saw Chinese patrols moving all over the area. Off to the right, a large group of Chinese, maybe 100 or so, were digging in on a hill. Just at twilight an enemy squad began to climb the hill on which Lee and I lay. Even though we had hidden under leaves and branches, there was no way they could miss finding us. They climbed closer; my heart pounded like a drum. This was it. All of a sudden, the Chinese on that other hill began whistling to the patrol. This saved us for sure. The Chinks laughed and made their way back down the hill and joined that large group doing the digging.

The sun set. It grew quite dark and quiet. Chong Lee and I raked the leaves and dirt off each other and sat up. He pointed to my neck and back and told me there was a lot of blood on them, was I hurt? "No," I replied. He said, "Not many GI get off hill. Went that way," and he gestured to the east. Every now and then a few artillery rounds went over. Hills 717 and 682 were being plastered again. Now it was our side that was doing the plastering. I hoped our artillery wouldn't decide to blast the hills in our area, and especially not the one we were on. The Chinese on the next hill were quiet, and except for some patrols they'd run along the trail, I thought they would probably stay that way.

I explained to Lee as best I could what our plan would be. Earlier, I thought I had heard in the distance the sounds of tanks, and figured they must be part of a rescue force. [A tank-infantry force sent out at 3:30 P.M. had made its way along a valley trail and was in position near the village of Chungmoksil. Around 6:30 P.M., when Weaver heard the tanks, they were withdrawing, having accidentally been raked by friendly artillery.] Lee and I would make for a tiny village near where I believed the tanks would be. I told him he was not to fire his carbine or pistol unless it was a matter of life and death.

At 10:00 P.M. Lee and I quietly left the hill. We then followed a small stream bed until it crossed the trail. There we waited, and sure enough, a Chinese patrol eventually walked past our hiding place. We waited for it to pass again before we crossed. Lee and I were soon making our way through a heavily wooded area. Keeping the trail on our left, we walked as quietly as possible through the forest. From my trip with Don McGraw to the outpost on the sixth, I knew that the trail would lead to the village [Chungmoksil]. Both of us kept our weapons cocked. We moved, stopped, listened, moved again. After traveling in this fashion for several miles, I felt we should be nearing the village and could risk walking along the trail. It was now about 2:00 A.M. Stealthily, we approached the village. If it was occupied by Americans we would hear some noise; if it was occupied by the enemy, we wouldn't. Lee and I waited. When we didn't hear a sound, we cut off the trail and found a stream, along which we worked our way past the village. Beyond the village we returned to the trail and continued toward our own lines. Shortly afterward, I discovered fresh tank tracks. They had to be ours. Our spirits skyrocketed. We walked more quickly now, more confidently. Suddenly a real crisp, "Halt!" rang out. I hollered, "Captain Weaver, Captain Weaver. Blue Four," my radio code name. A man I recognized stepped out of the darkness. He had been with Love Company a few months earlier, before volunteering for the Provisional Raider Platoon of the 35th Regimental Headquarters Company. [This platoon, along with a company of Turkish infantry on loan from the North Star Turkish Brigade, was guarding a forward aid station set up near a concrete bridge that crossed the Hant'an River near the village of Chongyon-ni.] I'm not sure who was more happy to see whom. He wanted to know how I got through the village. According to him, the evening before it had been "crawling with Chinks."

Some U.S. tanks blocked the trail a little ways farther along. It was now 4:30 A.M. and still dark. The tank commander wanted us to remain with him, but I decided to go the extra mile and report to the battalion forward CP. The sky in the east was growing lighter. Lee and I made our way across open ground along a footpath. High weeds grew along the bank of a stream. It was 5:00 A.M. WHAM! A slug fired almost point-blank parted my hair. Lee and I fell to the ground. "Americana!" I yelled. "Americana!" A guy came up, his M1 ready. "Me Turk. Me Turk." I was really shook. I finally said something to the effect of "Take me to your CO." A Turkish sergeant in charge of the outpost gave me permission to continue our journey. Lee and I moved about 100 yards and ran smack into a mine field which had not been there when McGraw and I walked to Hill 717 forty-eight hours before. Back of it, I knew, should be a barricade of barbed wire fences covered with machine guns. I told Lee we'd wait in a ditch until the sun was fully up.

About a half hour later, Lee and I carefully picked our way through the mines. I would hold a trip wire for him to step over, then he would hold one for me. Before we came to the double-apron barbed wire, we encountered an area covered with ground fog. Rather than take any more chances, I hollered a couple of times, "Americana, Americana." Someone shouted, "Okay. Okay." We approached the fence and used a pass-through gate to get around it. When we finally crossed to the south side of the stream, I felt like getting down and kissing the earth. A few hundred yards farther, and we reached the battalion forward CP tent.

I walked in and found on duty a lieutenant I knew real well. When he saw me, his surprise was so great he nearly fell out of his chair. I must have looked a mess—bloody, muddy, wet, and damn near exhausted. A call was immediately made to battalion rear, "Captain Weaver's back." Reports that had come in the night before had me missing in action. All kinds of conflicting stories were told about me—one had me firing a machine gun, half my face shot off. "Surely, there's no way Captain Weaver could make it back."

[*The patrol-base survivors led by Captain McGraw, who had been driven off Hill 717 late in the afternoon of 7 September, had scattered into small groups and made their way safely through the spurs and ravines south of the patrol base and arrived at the battalion's MLR around midnight.*

The group of wounded men including Captain Burkhart had also made it back to friendly lines. By the time Luther Weaver arrived at battalion, these men had all been evacuated to MASH units in the rear.

On 9 September, after fourteen hours of ferocious fighting, much of it hand-to-hand, the 2d Battalion, 35th Infantry, recaptured Hill 717. The regiment's 1st Battalion did not secure Hill 682 until the next morning. Both battalions then searched the ridges and draws around the patrol-base area, recovering bodies of men killed on the seventh and collecting abandoned weapons and equipment. Among the weapons gathered up was Luther Weaver's pheasant-hunting 12-gauge shotgun. The stock had been blown off, probably during one of the friendly artillery and air strikes which ripped Hill 717 on 8 and 9 September.]

11 September
Companies L and I were reequipped and moved out to an assembly area. The 3d Battalion was reorganized. Muster was taken to get an accurate count of casualties and KIA.

12 September
Battalion commander requested fifteen NCOs from 1st and 2d Battalions be transferred to 3d Battalion due to heavy casualties on Regimental Patrol Base.
EXECUTIVE OFFICER'S UNIT JOURNAL, 3D BATTALION/35TH INFANTRY

[*Losses to L and I Companies were put at 46 KIA, 130 WIA, and 36 MIA. Enemy losses were estimated to be well over 600.*]

Capt. LUTHER WEAVER
3d Battalion/35th Infantry
Shortly after the patrol base was recaptured, the bodies of men found on the hill were brought in to be identified and processed by Graves Registration personnel. At this time the stark horror of that battle really hit me. I had known many of these men by their first names.

The first few days after the battle, most of the survivors were in a state of shock and disbelief. I found it hard to think about visiting Love Company or ascertaining the status of some of the individuals I knew well. A few days before the battalion was pulled back in reserve, I managed to find the courage to visit the company. I arrived while the men were having their evening meal. Other than the mess sergeant and a couple of cooks, I found very few faces that I knew. About 40 or 50 men out of the 160 that had been on 717 before the battle made up L Company now. I had a deep feeling of loss when I realized that this was all that was left of that great rifle company I had led a few months earlier. To me, they were still my L Company, and I could not have been more proud of them.*

[*Most of the solid fighting of September 1951 erupted after the Communists walked out of the summer's ongoing truce talks. Once the preliminaries had been settled, the UN delegaton, headed by Admiral C. Turner Joy, had held its first meeting on 10 July with the Communist truce team, led by North Korea's vice-president, Maj. Gen. Nam Il. The negotiations, held in a once-fashionable, but now abandoned, teahouse on the outskirts of Kaesong, had gone on throughout most of July and August. The daily sessions, best described as chilly and inimical, were marked by Communist delaying tactics. Once the battered Chinese armies had been given enough time to regroup and reequip, the Communists concocted an incident that gave them an excuse to leave the talks. A charge was leveled that on the rainy night*

---

* Luther Weaver rotated home in early November 1951.

of 22–23 April, UN planes had bombed an area near the neutral conference site. Although no substantial evidence of this "attack" was ever produced, the talks were immediately recessed.*

The UN Command decided at once to make tactical use of this interruption in the peace process. Eighth Army was ordered to resume the offensive with a major effort along that part of the eastern front covered by Maj. Gen. Glovis E. Byers's X Corps. There, the U.S. 2d Division and the 1st Marine Division were ordered to improve the UN's positions north and east of the Hwach'on Reservoir in the area of that dismal and forbidding volcanic crater known as the Punch-bowl.† The leathernecks, with a regiment of ROK Marines [KMC] attached, opened the drive on 31 August and at first encountered only light to moderate opposition. The next day, against stiffening North Korean resistance, the advance slowed, then stopped.]

Pfc. TROY HAMM
Antitank Company/7‡

There was one particular bunker [on Hill 602] that we fired at all day. Artillery and air strikes were called in to help. Again and again, we destroyed this bunker; and again and again, the North Koreans rebuilt it. By sundown it had been leveled to the ground, and we could no longer see it. That night the North Koreans rebuilt it again: When the sun came up, the bunker was back on that hilltop as good as new.§

I was an ammo carrier, and along with the other humpers we would go down daily to the resupply point, pick up ammo [for a 75-mm recoilless rifle] and pack it back to our gun position.

---

*In October, the negotiating site would be moved to the tiny hamlet of Panmunjom, on the main road five miles east of Kaesong and about fifteen miles west of Munsan. Talks would resume on 25 October.

†The 1st Marine Division's strength, including the KMCs, was reported on 1 August as 1,386 officers and 24,044 men. On the twenty-sixth the division's regiments were disposed as follows: the 1st Marines, near Chogutan; the 5th, around Inje; the 7th, close to Yanggu; and the 1st KMC Regiment, at Hangye. The 11th Marines remained attached to X Corps's artillery.

‡Antitank Company/7 was attached to B/7; Pfc. Hamm's squad was assigned to a platoon led by Lt. Eddie LeBaron, the future quarterback of the Washington Redskins and Dallas Cowboys.

§Hill 602 was finally taken by 3/7 the morning of 2 September.

One day after many trips, I was very weary. The North Koreans began to hit our path to the supply point with mortars. I was knocked down by the concussion. When I picked myself up, I discovered a hole in my hand. I wrapped the wound and continued down the hill to pick up more ammo. The enemy fired on us the whole way. At the resupply point I smelled exploded powder and an odor that was new to me. An incoming round had made a direct hit on one of the guys, and pieces of him were scattered over the area.

[Four days of heavy, uphill fighting brought the Marines to their initial objectives, and on 4 September they were in full possession of line Hays, a series of ridges overlooking the entire northern rim of the Punchbowl.

Orders were then cut for the second phase of the attack, the advance to another ridgeline 4,000 to 7,000 yards forward of the Marine positions on Hays.]

9 September*
1st Marines—to be released from X Corps reserve near Hongch'on to Division control; to be prepared to pass through the 7th Marines, when that regiment secures its objectives, and continue the attack to seize Objective CHARLIE, the ridgeline leading northwest from Hill 1052.

1ST MARINE DIVISION OPNO 23-51

Pfc. LYLE CONAWAY
F/1
One night when we were in reserve, most of the battalion gathered in a rice paddy to see some movies which were projected on a sheet stretched between two posts. Afterward, the CO [Lt. Col. Franklin B. Nihart] stood on a small stage and gave us a pep talk. "Men," he said, "I don't know where we're going, and I don't know when, but I'm sure it will be soon. One thing I do know, there will be a lot of

---

* It was on this day, seventy miles away in the west, that the 2d Battalion, 35th Infantry, recaptured from the Chinese the regimental patrol base on Hills 717 and 682.

Purple Hearts given out. I know you're as anxious as I am to get going." Everyone stood and sang "For He's a Jolly Good Fellow"; that was followed by the Marine Hymn.

The next morning we struck our tents, policed the area, had roll call, and were issued ammo and helmets. Then we boarded trucks and were taken north.

Pfc. FLOYD BAXTER
Weapons Company/1/1

When we entered the valley, a young guy named Brun, who had married just before coming to Korea, was in front of me in the column. There were tanks lined up on our right. I should have known then that we were in for trouble. Tanks almost always drew fire. We went down the road some ways when all hell broke loose—enemy seventy-sixes, at regular intervals, came screaming in. One of the first blasts knocked my helmet off. I thought, Now I've got no place to hide. Then it was run and hit the deck, run and hit the deck. A shell exploded to the left. I looked up, Brun was already on his feet and running. I jumped up and followed. I ran about ten steps when I heard another shell coming in. This one didn't whistle; the sound was more like someone blowing between his teeth. Brun dove to his right, I jumped to my left. He never knew what hit him; the blast caught him full in the chest. The Marine behind me went to pieces. I believe he finished his tour in a rear-echelon administrative job.

Pfc. TROY HAMM
Antitank Company/7

We moved out early [10 September], wet and cold. All night long it had rained like I'd never seen before in my life. We sat in a wide open field all night. The old ponchos we wore funneled the water down our spines and out the seat of our utility trousers. To add to this misery, when we moved out, we carried the weight of our packs— a packboard with two cased 75-mm RR rounds, a waterproof bag containing our winter and summer sleeping bags, three days' supply of C rations, and extra boots and utilities. I also carried an M1 rifle and plenty of .30-cal ammo. The load was so heavy that when we stopped I had to position the packboard above me on the side of the hill so I could get under it enough to stand up without falling backward.

As we got closer to Hill 673, the sounds of firing grew louder. The roar of artillery—ours and theirs—and frequent air strikes marked our progress forward. By now I was so keyed-up, I forgot the weight of my pack.

Late in the day, five of our M26 tanks came up and supported us. Just their appearance and the noise they made boosted our morale.

That night we moved into an area where the tanks had fired rounds of willie-peter [white phosphorous]. We were all afraid to dig into that smelly white stuff.

We began our assault on Hill 673 early the next morning [11 September]. Our guns were to knock out a large enemy machine-gun bunker. This particular gun was in such a strategic location on the hill that if it wasn't knocked out we would lose a lot of men.

My squad was ordered to move up as close to the bunker as we could, then set up and fire on it. Without warning, the machine gun opened up. I flattened out like a lizzard. I was only 150 yards away from its muzzle.

A Marine above me on the hill was hit by the first burst. He was already on the ground when the rounds ripped down his back and whistled over me. Our squad leader yelled, "Ammo up!" The gun had been set up and was ready to fire. Before we could move, another squad farther back fired at the bunker; its first round went right into the bunker. A flamethrower was sent forward and finished off the position. When I walked past it, I saw it had been constructed of twelve layers of logs, plus about ten feet of dirt, which is why the artillery and air strikes had not been able to neutralize it.

When we took the hill, we found some Marines who had been captured. They had their hands tied behind them, and had been brutally murdered.

We moved up the hill and learned quickly to walk on the trails that the North Koreans had used; the rest of the hillside was covered with land mines and booby traps.

That night we sat our gun on top of the skyline in a bomb crater. Five of us moved back to another large hole. There were no trees, bushes—not even twigs. The whole mountaintop was bare; the soil, from the pounding it had received, was like silt.

We began catching incoming rounds. We heard the POP in the mortar tube, then along the ridgeline to the right, POW! We began to count the explosions and soon realized they were coming closer; the North Koreans were walking the rounds toward us. We hunched as low as we could get. The next round hit to our left. The one after that exploded to our right. They had bracketed our hole. The next round would land on top of us. We prayed out loud. A round hit next to us. One guy screamed and began to run. The section leader reached up and tripped him. We held the man down. I held my breath and waited. CRASH! A flash of light. I could smell and taste the powder. We lay in a heap for I don't know how long. A lieutenant had been hit. He had shrapnel in his back, head, and legs. We lay in that hole all night. It was very difficult to evacuate the wounded.

We got word later that we would be relieved by the 1st Marines. We had lost too many men to effectively resume the attack in the morning.*

[The relief of the 7th Marines by the 1st Marines on Hill 749 took place the night of 12–13 September. The 1st and 3d Battalions, 7th Marines, then went into division reserve at Wont'ong-ni. The regiment's 2d Battalion, however, continued to be pounded by accurate North Korean mortar and 76-mm fire the morning of the thirteenth, and its relief was delayed.]

S/Sgt. JAMES IEVA
F/7

In the morning [13 September] the CO [1st Lt. Don Phelan] was called back to the battalion CP. Before he left he said, "Gunny [Ieva was the acting gunnery sergeant], look after things till I get back." Later, three men went forward to reconnoiter. They were stopped by heavy enemy cross fire and returned. The FO requested mortar fire on a group of North Koreans coming up the hill. I thought, I haven't

---

* Marine casualties on 11 and 12 September were 22 KIA and 245 WIA.

had a chance to use my Thompson [submachine gun]; I'll make up for it now. Mortar rounds continued to fall around us. I contacted our 81-mm mortar section and asked for another fire mission. Five rounds landed on a group of gooks; a sixth round landed short. We took no casualties, which is more than the North Koreans could report.

Lieutenant Phelan returned before noon; he had with him a company from the 1st Marines which relieved us.

[Fox 7 was relieved by the 2d Battalion, 1st Marines, late in the morning of 13 September. It took another twelve hours of bitter battle on Hill 749 before the 1st Marines was able to relieve 2/7's other two rifle companies. By nightfall, the leathernecks were finally in position on 749. Colonel Thomas Wornham's 1st Marines continued the battle for Hill 749 on 14 September. Enemy bunkers hidden among the trees on the northern slope had to be taken one by one. By dusk, the regiment's advance had netted a mere 300 meters.]

Pfc. FLOYD BAXTER
Weapons Company/1/1

The enemy covered their foxholes with grass and leaves and whatever. Once we had run past their holes, they'd pop up and hit us from the rear. This is why we lost so many men. Even after we secured our objective and our mortars were set up behind Charlie Company, we still found gooks hidden in small holes. Many of them elected to fight, and they died in their holes.

After everything had quieted down, we sat around our eighty-one [mortar]. Suddenly, we were sprayed by a burp gun. Fortunately, only one man was hit. The gook doing the firing had lain in his hole for a day. He came screaming up the hill at us. A shot from the M1 of one of the ammo carriers stopped him; his head seemed to explode. Needless to say, we sent out a couple of patrols then to find and destroy any remaining gooks.

Hospitalman JOE HAVENS (USN)
D/1

Marine humor, no matter what the situation, never failed to amaze me. The first North Korean I saw was a dead one. Left so we new-comers would see him, he was propped up in a sitting position in a bend on one of the trails on Hill 749. He held in one hand a dead man's poker hand of aces and eights.

Pfc. FRANK O. HART
D/1

The second night we spent on 749 [14–15 September] was quite chilly. September evenings were growing cooler, and this night was the chilliest I'd known in Korea. Our packs had been left behind when we were ordered to attack the hill, and all Tom Hull and I wore were our utilities. We were happily surprised when Mike, the platoon leader's runner, jumped into our hole and produced a bottle of Canadian Club. "The lieutenant says to have a swig." No better medicine could have been prescribed. Not only did it help the chills, it also boosted our morale.

[Unit diaries report that on 15 September* the 1st Marines spent a quiet day, relatively speaking, on the slopes of Hill 749.].

Pfc. LYLE CONAWAY
F/1

Late in the morning [15 September] Colonel Nihart came up and told a group of us to go back down the hill along the path we had used earlier and gather up all the ammo and stretchers we could find. Around 8:00 A.M. we'd received word that we were to continue the attack on Hill 749. While we waited, it had been a strain to have that black hill looming over us. We knew it was going to be tough.

---

*On 15 September the previous year, the 1st Marine Division had stormed ashore at Inch'on.

I remembered over and over, Colonel Nihart's words "a lot of Purple Hearts. . . ."

I went down with four other people, one of whom was named McGee. He and another man explored an area near a burned-out bunker, and they both stepped on land mines. They sat in a state of shock, staring at their smoking feet. Immediately afterward, we took about ten rounds of mortar fire. The other two men with me were hit by shrapnel, both in the stomach. McGee and the other guy tried to move but kept falling over. I yelled to them to stay where they were, then dragged the two wounded men nearest me under some pine trees. Up the hill about 200 feet were some engineers clearing mines. I shouted to them to come down and give me a hand. They glanced at me and continued their work. I knew they had to be rear-echelon types. A corpsman named Hoover and another guy carrying a stretcher ran up. The three of us went over to McGee and lifted him onto the litter. We took a few steps when the man with Hoover stepped on a mine. The blast hit Hoover in the arm and eyes, and rattled me. I shouted again to the engineers to come down and help us. They didn't budge. I tried something that usually works in combat: I *ordered* them down to me. They never moved. Now I was really pissed! I fired my rifle; the round hit between them. That was a real mistake; they just took off running in the opposite direction.

I was caught now between being very angry and scared stiff. I told Hoover and McGee to wait until I returned. I walked to the path, making marks in the earth which told me how to get back without stepping on a mine. Then I made several trips back until I got all the men out. Eventually, stretcher bearers arrived and carried the six men down the hill.

Later in the day we lost another corpsman, and a Mexican-American kid named Contreras took over his duties. He was a very brave person, and I saw him several times that day treat people while exposing himself to mortar and sniper fire. Later that afternoon I found myself in a hole with him. "Well," Contreras said, "the cops in Omaha will be glad to hear that Lefty [Edward] Gomez is dead." I asked, "When? How?" He said, "Yesterday—flung himself on a grenade. Strange, Lefty told me a couple of days ago he was gonna win the Medal of Honor." I knew Contreras was telling the truth, because a week or so earlier I was with Lefty while we thumbed through an issue of *The Leatherneck* magazine. When we got to the page listing all the medals awarded, he said, "I sure hope they don't run out of these things before I have a chance to get one." *

Around 5:00 P.M. there was an air strike on our objectives. We were ordered to move forward. The fight the gooks put up was very fierce. I was up with Joe Vittori. The enemy pounded us with machine-gun and artillery fire. Then two Corsairs made a pass right on us. One guy stood up and waved an air panel. He was hit and went down. Vittori yelled, "Whose side are those bastards on?" One of the aircraft was so low I actually saw the bomb shackle open to release the bomb. That bomb sailed over our heads and exploded in a shallow ravine. It was too hot to wonder where the Corsairs went, but they did stop strafing us.

Then a lieutenant was hit in the thigh and began to yell, "Pull back! Pull back!" Here we were, nearly to the crest, and we were ordered back. We pulled back to our previous positions [of the night before]. It was still light. Everyone was confused. I saw our captain [Frederick A. Hale, Jr.] going from person to person. "What happened? What went wrong?" He had an anguished look on his face. "Why did you come back?"

We dug in, knowing the gooks would counterattack. It got dark. Word came down, "Get Vittori's BAR and a rifleman forward." I could see our squad leader in his hole about forty yards away. I shouted the message to him. Then I yelled that I'd go with Joe. In a few minutes Vittori came by. I strapped on ammo and stuffed my pockets with grenades. I also had a Thompson submachine gun, as well as my M1.

It was quite black by the time we got to the point. I made a mental note that the heavy machine gun was seven holes away. In between were some light machine guns and BARs with riflemen. Up toward the heavy was the artillery FO's position.

The moon came out and lit the area. I remember, too, there was a wind blowing.

---

* Private Edward Gomez of E Company, 1st Marines, was awarded the Medal of Honor post-humously.

We began to get probed, and so as not to give away our positions by firing, we threw grenades. Word was passed back to get more grenades up front. They were promptly delivered by Sergeant Kesler, our platoon sergeant, who missed us and walked into no-man's-land. We shouted for him to come back. Someone said, "Hey, S'arnt, whose side 'ya on?" Everyone laughed.

A cloud covered the moon. We heard the North Koreans moving toward us. The wheels on a machine gun squeaked as they rolled it forward. A gook officer issued orders, then it seemed to me, he began to curse. I clearly heard their troops grunting when they tried to move something heavy. We got into a shouting match with them. I had picked up some gook curses when I served in China in '46. I called them "turtles," which is supposed to be as insulting to an Oriental as calling an American an SOB. I shouted, "Hey, you rickshaw-pulling turtles, stick your heads out so I can knock them off!" From the darkness down the hill, someone screamed, "Marine, fuck Harry Truman and John Foster Durres!" Vittori laughed. I asked him, "Who in hell is John whats's-name?" Up till then I didn't know who Dulles was.

Our FO yelled for us to get down because he was going to bring in a barrage in front of us. CRASH! CRASH! In it came. I felt good knowing we could get the gooks when they were between the lines.

Once it was over I looked over the rim of the hole and saw the flash of an enemy 76-mm gun. The shell hissed toward us. It exploded in the treetops above and showered us with shrapnel. The fourth round exploded near the FO's hole. A kid nearby yelled, "He's dead! He's dead!"

A spotter plane flew over and called in artillery. The 76-mm stopped firing.

Clouds floated across the sky. Sometimes the moon was out and it was bright; other times the moon was covered by clouds, and it was pitch black.

I no longer have an accurate sense of when certain events on that night took place. I know Joe and I decided each of us should try to catch some sleep. I took the first watch, but after only ten minutes Vittori sat up and told me to try to get some rest. Damn, I fell asleep. Next thing I knew, Joe was shaking me and saying, "Here they come! Here they come! Look at 'em. Look at all of 'em!" I couldn't see shit,

I just couldn't wake up. My eyes wouldn't open. Then it broke loose. Everyone began firing at once. The area was engulfed in flames. All I could see were flashes. I fired at muzzle blasts. Two or three Chinese crawled toward our position. I fired at them. One of them raised up and threw a grenade; I couldn't see it, but I recognized the gesture. It exploded on the lip of the hole, and the concussion blast caught me in the face. I raised up instinctively and caught a couple of slugs in the shoulder. I fell back heavily and was now really disoriented. Blood from wounds on my scalp and forehead flowed over my eyes, nose, and mouth. The noise was tremendous. You had to shout to be heard. Joe looked at me, then yelled, "Corpsman!" I knew where I was, but not how badly I'd been hit. I knew I wasn't blind. I moved my right arm, but it was stiff and numb. I barely heard Joe's yell, so I knew no one else could. I really didn't expect any help to get through that hell. Joe leaned down and shouted that I should try to get over the ridge. When I looked in that direction I saw enemy fire sweeping it like a broom. I concentrated my entire effort now on getting back into the fight. I located my rifle by the edge of the hole. When I tried to fire, I found it had jammed. Joe kept yelling, "Look at them! Look! They're all over! Help, throw grenades!" I pulled the pins with my right hand and threw with my left. I managed to throw them far enough so we weren't splattered by our own shrapnel.

I heard the splat that a bullet makes when it hits flesh. Vittori sort of slumped. I was really frightened, because his fire had been so effective and kept the gooks off us. He straightened up in a kneeling position and rubbed his chest. I could see it was wet. He said, "Load my empty magazines. Don't load 'em backwards like Pete did." The two machine guns on our left fired steady streams of bullets. Joe got his BAR back into the fight. The scene looked as if it were lit by a barn fire. I saw men running and firing. I alternately loaded magazines and threw grenades. The machine gun farthest away took a grenade, and the gun tumbled on its side. Its red-hot barrel ignited some leaves and grass. Then the gun pit next to us took a couple of grenades. Both guys fell over. One of the guys, Blankenship—I recognized him because he was very stout—got up and began firing the gun again. He leaned over, his face nearly touching the red-hot barrel. He was hit again and fell on the barrel. His hair caught fire.

Normally, the enemy ran out of ammo after twenty minutes,

and the fighting would stop until they were resupplied. Not so, this night. The longer it went, the worse it got. I had a tough time breathing—just too much smoke; the smell of cordite made me cough. The gooks tried to organize themselves, but fortunately they could not hear each other. The noise was deafening.

Joe began firing over my head; I ducked as low as I could. The muzzle of the BAR was only inches from my ears, and the muzzle blasts felt like my eardrums were being pierced. About then, I was overjoyed to find my Thompson at the bottom of the hole; I'd clear forgotten about it. Joe shouted, "I'm gonna go get the machine gun." He crawled over to Blankenship's gun. I began firing the Thompson. Joe pulled the body off the gun, but when he yanked the gun toward him it fell into the hole. I'm not sure, but I think about then, Vittori got hit again. He doubled up. I knew if he went down, we'd be overrun. It would then be just a matter of time. I saw to my right everything had been knocked out, even the heavy machine gun. I think the guys in the FO's hole held out for a while, but then they, too, were silenced.

Suddenly, everything grew quiet. No more noise. A few whistles, but no more firing. It was totally unreal. Joe said, "We can't hold 'em—have to get back. I'll cover you, go ahead. I'll cover you." I could hear many sounds now; the gooks were giving commands and trying to pick up their wounded. I heard moans.

A group of about eight gooks came out of somewhere and walked up the hill. I believe they thought we were all dead. I hoped Joe would begin firing soon. If he waited too long he'd be in my line of fire. Joe opened up. Then I did. My shoulder hurt and was still numb. We really splattered them. Another group behind the first opened fire on us, then faded into the night. Joe got into a kneeling position. He said again, "Gotta get back to the ridgeline. You go, I'll cover for you." A rifle cracked. Splat. Joe's head snapped back. He grabbed his face and fell over. When I got to him, I saw steam coming from the blood running down his face. I fired one more clip, then scrambled up the hill toward the ridgeline. Looking back once, I saw my canteen glinting in the moonlight. I did not know then how much I was going to miss that water; if I had, I might have gone back for it.

I stumbled over the top of the ridge and fell into a foxhole.

When I looked up I was facing the business end of a .45. My face was so swollen and bloody, they didn't know who I was.

Reinforcements arrived. I showed them where our positions were.* This done, I started walking south.†

[A little after first light, the 1st Battalion, 1st Marines, passed through the battle-dazed leathernecks of 2/1 and took the fight to the Communists. This passage of lines was made difficult by accurate enemy mortar fire. The North Koreans, their backs now to the wall, continued throughout the day to battle the Marines for every foot of ground.]

Pfc. FLOYD BAXTER
Weapons Company/1/1
We had our version of Bloody Ridge [a ridge leading to Hill 749], a place where men reached down in themselves and did the impossible—they survived. When the objective [Hill 749] was finally taken, we began to dig in our eighty-one. A guy by the name of Jack and I were filling sandbags. Enemy mortars began to fall around us. Jack found a shallow foxhole. A round landed about ten yards away. The blast didn't hurt him, but he was so wedged in the hole, I nearly had to pry him out of it.

I believe Hill 749 will be remembered by men who were there as the battle that was won with bayonets and rifle butts—and on a couple of occasions, with bare hands.

[The 1st Marines finally secured Hill 749 at 6:00 P.M. on 16 September; it had cost them 90 dead and 714 wounded. Enemy losses were 771 known dead (1,400 were estimated KIA) and 81 taken prisoner.

Thirteen months before, to the day, the Marine brigade (5th Marines) had been preparing to assault another well-fortified position held by the North Koreans; then it was deep in South Korea, along the Naktong River on Obong-ni Ridge. At the time, their losses—66 dead,

278 wounded—had seemed astronomical. In the hills around the Punchbowl, those figures would have seemed like just another firefight. Although Hill 749 had been taken, another four days of savage fighting would take place before the battle for the Punchbowl would end.]

Pfc. FLOYD BAXTER
Weapons Company/1/1

Hill 1052 is where the gooks were heavily armed and solidly dug in on a hill that looked right down our throats.* It was nearly straight up, and the Communists had built bunkers and trenches all over it.

It rained hard just before we jumped off [18 September], which made the going very slippery. You might say 1052 was taken by crawling instead of charging. There were shoe mines [a wooden box with an explosive charge in it] everywhere.

Charlie Company had made the initial assault, and we were bringing our gun up for the next action. An ammo carrier and I went back down the hill to get some more ammo. We thought the path we had chosen for the trip had been cleared of mines, but we were cautious, nevertheless. I stepped over a body which had been burned by napalm. As an afterthought, I turned to warn the man behind me to leave the body alone, as it might be booby trapped. The butt of a burp gun stuck out from under the blackened body. Before I could speak, I saw the guy reach down for the gun. I yelled! It was the last thing the man heard. The concussion knocked me down, and the blast blew the other guy's hand and most of his face off. †

[For nine days the Marines had slugged it out with the North Koreans, the last battle taking place on 20 September. Three of four objectives in the Punchbowl had been secured, but only after frightful losses on both sides. The Marine division's last objective, a ridgeline northwest of Hill 1052, had yet to be attacked when orders brought the fighting to a sudden stop.

---

* Also known to the Marines as "Luke the Gook's Castle," or simply, "The Rock."
† The 1st and 2d Battalions, 1st Marines, were relieved by the 5th Marines on 19 September.

The Marines were directed next to extend the boundary on their right by taking over a rugged mountainous area controlled by the ROK I Corps. Because of its wild and isolated location, Maj. Gen. Gerald C. Thomas, CG of the division, decided that a large-scale operation using rotary-wing aircraft would accomplish the mission more easily and faster than a fifteen-hour backbreaking march. Operation Summit, the first helicopter-borne landing of a combat unit in history, was scheduled for the morning of 21 September.]

Pfc. PAUL MARTIN
Reconnaissance Company/1st Marine Division
We were transported at dawn through a heavy fog to the helicopter loading area. We waited for the fog to burn off. Finally, around midmorning, we lifted off, and after one year of keeping my head down I got an opportunity to really see the Korean landscape. I'd always thought how nice the airmen had it, each night able to return to a secure base for a hot meal and a good night's sleep. Now I thought how nice it would be to be back on the ground, where you could always find some cover. I couldn't wait till I reached the LZ [landing zone]. No doubt, this helicopter lift saved us a lot of discomfort and energy, but hiking and hill-climbing make one too tired to be scared.

The helicopters reached Hill 884 in about twenty minutes. I was glad to see ROK troops waiting for us below.* Ropes were dropped. I slid down one. I dropped the last five feet and moved a short distance to an area which the engineers began to immediately prepare for a helicopter landing. In less than an hour, the LZs were completely leveled. Shortly after that, the rest of Recon Company was moved by helicopter to the hill. Once a helicopter landed, five men from the company jumped out, and the chopper lifted off to get another five.

The entire lift ended with a 'copter laying a wire from the hill back to the 1st Marine's CP, about eight miles to the rear.

The landing took place without any enemy interference, but later

---

* The ROKs, once relieved, climbed down Hill 884 and marched back to their own corps area.

in the day, when a chopper circled overhead, we drew enemy artillery fire. Thanks to the sheer drops on both sides of the hill, these shells whistled overhead and fell in the chasms below. I said to my sergeant, "Our names are on those shells." He answered, "That's okay, they've got the wrong address."

When the shelling stopped, I looked around and in the distance made out the blue of the Sea of Japan, which, after seeing nothing but hills for a year, looked great.*

[*Three weeks before, at the beginning of September, as the Marines jumped off to seize their objectives around the Punchbowl, the U.S. 2d Division found itself in its own buzz-saw of a battle, and one as ferocious as any since those of the Chinese spring offensives. The Indianheads were just west of the Punchbowl, in an area of looming, jagged peaks that rose sharply from the So-ch'on River Valley. The division had been ordered to clear a large, heavily fortified North Korean force from a hill mass dominated by three peaks—the highest of which would soon be known as Bloody Ridge. It was a battle of attack and counterattack; knife-edged ridges changed hands frequently, often several times a day.*]

Cpl. BEN JUDD
F Company/23d Infantry

We continued on down to another part of this hill, a part of which was known as Bloody Ridge. We reached our positions and dug in. I had two men in my squad who decided to take over a foxhole that had formerly been owned by the Chinese. A day later one of those boys came to me complaining. "There's a terrible smell in this hole," he says. I says, "There's a terrible smell all over this bloody ground we walk on. There's blood and flesh mixed in with the dirt and in the sand and all around us." "No," he says, "I'm quite sure there's a Chinese in our hole." Jokingly, I says, "Well, dig back there and find out." I never expected him to. However, he and his buddy dug

---

*Three days later, the division reconnaissance company was relieved on Hill 884 by units of the 1st Marines.

back, and sure enough, there was a Chinese corpse buried in there. The boys reburied the soldier and moved to a hole they dug themselves, one which had better ventilation.

During this time, we were under frequent mortar and artillery attack. We found a fresh water hole; the trouble was, the Chinese, if they chose, could drop a mortar round directly into it, the hole being no bigger than two square feet. Nevertheless, it was a supply of fresh water, and it was only 300 yards from our fortifications. Many men were injured going to supply their units with water. As I considered myself no better than anyone else, I too went back to get water. On the return leg one day, I was caught by artillery firing white phosphorous. Smoke was all around me. Amazingly—and it may have been due to my exceptional speed of movement—I was never burned.

There were many firefights, all too painful to recall in particular or detail. The hill was attacked continuously, and we lived in bunkers and holes. These "homes" were made of logs, rocks, and dirt. I remember one bunker built by men in my squad. I remarked to them, "I believe your hole may be too large." "Well, we do want comfort, if we can have it," they said. "We have little else here."

Several times during the many artillery attacks we endured, our bunkers were hit directly and repeatedly. My assistant and I had a hole barricaded with solid rock dug in the side of the hill. I remember six direct hits on those rocks, and I wondered each time whether they would collapse. My assistant was an old hillbilly from the mountains of Kentucky who knew how to build log cabin chimneys from stone and rock. He built our bunker well.

[The North Koreans, weakened by an estimated 15,000 casualties, withdrew suddenly on 4 September, and the next day the U.S. 2d Division climbed and seized Bloody Ridge.]

Cpl. BEN JUDD
F Company/23d Infantry
From positions we occupied on the ridge, we ran what I called "suicide runs," which traveled toward an area eventually named "Heartbreak Ridge" by the newspapers. We traveled light—one belt of ammunition, one canteen of water, and our weapons. We were or-

dered to keep radio silence. The patrols were to draw enemy fire but not return it. September 10 my squad made this patrol. We encountered small-arms fire and returned to our lines. We learned the company had pulled back, and all that waited for us was our assistant platoon sergeant. I felt a little surly. Where would the help have come from that we'd been promised had we needed it? Surely this one assistant platoon sergeant could not have come out to rescue us. We were escorted back to transportation and taken to an area where we regrouped.

At this time, Sergeant Reed, who had come to Korea with me, was transferred home on rotation. I, myself, had a few days to go before I too would be sent home.

[General Van Fleet immediately ordered X Corps to follow up its victory on Bloody Ridge and seize the next hill mass to the north. The task of taking Heartbreak Ridge, as it would soon be called, was given to the 2d Division.]

Cpl. BEN JUDD
F Company/23d Infantry

We readied ourselves for an advance which we knew was to come. There was very little talk in the unit. I had never heard the men so silent. Someone remarked lightly that I should stay behind, as I was to leave soon. My answer was that I would not be leaving Korea on rotation or standing up. Somehow, I knew this. I think others felt this way about themselves, too; it would account for the moody silence that seemed to surround the company.

We left the jump-off area early in the morning [of the thirteenth] and proceeded up hill and down valley, ending on this one particular ridge where, along about midday, we were called to halt. Immediately, everyone scattered out and sat down to wait. For no particular reason, I began to get somewhat apprehensive. I asked the platoon sergeant, "Shall we dig in?" The word was, "No need to, we'll be going forward in minutes. We're awaiting the arrival of the Ninth Infantry Regiment." Little did we know the 9th Infantry would not arrive—not this day, anyway. It strikes me as strange now to have asked about digging, for I was one not prone to making holes. In any event, time would not have permitted us to, for within minutes of my question, enemy artillery came down on us like rain. "Scatter out!" I shouted. My words were unnecessary; the men needed no urging. But there was no cover anywhere. Within seconds the shelling stopped. Around me I heard men calling for the medics. Four men in my squad, two excellent BAR men and two riflemen, had been hit, all above the waist. I asked them, could they walk? They said yes. I advised them to start for the rear, the medics would be too busy with others. Just as quickly as the first, another fearful barrage hit our area. Shells fell over the entire company. There was no place they were not falling, and there was no place to take cover. We sat like ducks in a hailstorm of fire.

I had known that morning my time was coming; I could sense those things. I thought it would be a bullet, swift, clean. It came instead with all the force of an explosion, one so close I think I could have reached out and touched it. Flashes of black and red spun in my brain. I had never before felt force like that, and I had worked the iron and steel industry; I knew power. It lifted me off the ground; it shook me like a gigantic dog shaking a rabbit. The flesh of my body and the brain inside my head vibrated like a tuning fork. My life, my feeling, was in my bones, not my flesh. I fell heavily and lay flat on the ground. I was not stretched out enough, though. Another shell landed, exploded. No jar this time, but I felt the burning of molten steel. It tore through my left shoulder and foot and burned into my right leg. More shells fell. Then they stopped. I said, "My God, I've been hit!" I yelled for a medic. Someone close said, "Hush, there's men hurt worst than you." I yelled, "I'm gone." Two men rushed up and helped me off the hill to the medics. Before I left, I told the two remaining men in the squad to see the first sergeant and join another squad. Then I said, "I'm leaving." *

The last man I was to see in Korea from Fox Company was the medic, an old friend named Whitey. I said, "Things are gonna get rough up there, so watch out." "I will," he said. "I've been there, you know."

---

* On this same day, at about the same time, a few miles east on Hill 749, F Company, 7th Marines, was being relieved by the 2d Battalion, 1st Marines.

In Japan, in the hospital, sometime later, I found one of the men who'd been in my squad. He'd just been brought in and was badly wounded. He told me the outfit had taken a terrible beating.

[*It wasn't until the morning of 13 October, when the French Battalion, attached to the 23d Infantry, stormed and captured the last peak, that Heartbreak Ridge finally fell to the 2d Division. The costs in the month-long battle had been fearful for both sides. The Indianheads had suffered over 3,700 casualties, more than half of which were sustained by the 23d Infantry and the French Battalion. The three North Korean divisions and the Chinese division that had held out for thirty days lost an estimated 25,000 men. Ammunition expended in taking the granite ridge was tremendous: 547,000 rounds of artillery, 119,000 mortar rounds, 18,000 recoilless rifle rounds, and millions of rounds of small-arms ammunition had been fired.*

With the last ridge secured, and the 2d Division consolidating its hard-won gains, it is appropriate to shift our attention from X Corps and the east central sector, to I Corps and the western front. While Marines and soldiers battled in September for control of the hills around the Punchbowl, I Corps's efforts south of the Imjin River were characterized by company-size tank-infantry raids and counter-raids, combat patrols, and outpost engagements similar to the one fought by Love Company on Hill 717. This pattern of passive patrolling changed dramatically in October—the dry weather of early fall was always thought of as being a good time to attack. In late September, General Van Fleet explained his strategy. "My basic mission during the past four months," he wrote, "has been to destroy the enemy, so that the men of Eighth Army will not be destroyed. . . . In prodding the*

---

* In mid-September Eighth Army had fourteen divisions from four corps committed along a 125-mile front across the peninsula. United States I Corps, defending a broad fifty-mile front in the west, comprised the ROK 1st Division, British 1st Commonwealth Division, and U.S. 1st Cavalry and 3d Infantry Divisions; U.S. IX Corps, in the west central area, had the U.S. 25th Division (Turkish Brigade attached), ROK 2d Division, U.S. 7th Division (Ethiopian Battalion attached), ROK 6th Division, and U.S. 24th Division (Colombian Battalion attached); X Corps, dug in along the east central sector, was made up of the ROK 8th Division, U.S. 2d Infantry (French and Netherlands Battalions attached), ROK 5th Division, and 1st Marine Division; the eastern zone was anchored by the ROK 1st Corps. UN strength in September was put at 607,300; enemy strength was estimated at 600,000. The Communists, however, had a numerical advantage of at least four to three on the firing line.

enemy in the deep belly of the peninsula we have taken many casualties. . . . It is mandatory that we control the high ground features, so that we can look down the throat of the enemy and thereby better perform our task of destruction. . . . As we open our autumn campaign, the enemy potential along the front line has been sharply reduced by our hill-hopping tactics. The Communist forces in Korea are not liquidated, but they are badly crippled." *

Van Fleet proposed now to cripple them even more. Early in October, four divisions from I Corps and one from IX Corps launched a limited offensive which, it was hoped, would advance the west central front three or four miles and establish a new line, Jamestown.† Operation Commando, as it was called, jumped off along a forty-mile front on 3 October. From the banks of the Imjin northeast of Munsan-ni, to Ch'orwon, all but one of the divisions met light to moderate resistance and had little trouble taking their objectives. The exception was the 1st Cavalry Division. Across its line of advance, in the eight miles of hills connecting Kyeho-dong with Kamgol, parts of two Chinese divisions waited in heavily fortified bunkers reminiscent of those being found on Heartbreak Ridge.‡ For sixteen days the Chinese would make the Cav pay dearly for every foot of ground they gained.]

Sgt. DARRALD FEAKER
I Company/5th Cavalry

The hills and the fighting just went on and on and on. One hill we eventually bypassed—just went around it. It was so steep, we just spun our wheels trying to climb it. Supporting fire was bad because the trees caused premature shell detonations that sprayed shrapnel over us. I don't know how many assaults were staged on that hill. Seemed like every time a unit went up, only half its men came back. One company, which had watched our futile attempts, refused when

---

* Eighth Army Command Report, October 1951, 5–6.
† The four divisions were, west to east, the ROK 1st, British Commonwealth, U.S. 1st Cavalry, and U.S. 3d and 25th Divisions. The Commonwealth Division had been formed on 28 July from 28th Commonwealth Brigade, 29th British Brigade, and 25th Canadian Brigade.
‡ The 139th and 141st Divisions of the Chinese 47th Army.

it became their turn. Some guys just decided they wouldn't go, and refused the order. The way I remember it, MPs were sent forward to put those guys under arrest. It was a tough hill, a real bad one. The Chinese had bunkers and trenches all over the place. After one particular attack, a guy from my squad named Louie told me he had found a gook in a trench who was no older than a kid. "I couldn't shoot him," he said. "Well," I asked, "what did you do?" Louie shook his head. "I just kind of backed down the hill and threw a hand grenade. I don't know—it's his tough luck he didn't get out of there. He was just a kid, couldn't have been more than twelve."

On another hill, it looked suddenly like we were going to be overrun. Everybody began to bug out. There was a lot of bugle playing and their artillery fell all around us. Captain Watke ran down the hill with his .45 in hand, yelling—screaming for everyone to stop and get back up that hill. "Get up there! First guy past me, I'm gonna shoot! Get back up there, start firing! I don't care shit what you fire at, just get back there and fire!" Everyone climbed back on the hill and, by gosh, we hung on all night.

Next morning, when it got quiet, Watke spoke to some of us. He didn't say, Well, you guys are sure a bunch of cowards. Instead, he laughed and said, "Aw, I couldn't have shot anybody if I'd wanted to."

A day later we took a ridge and found a large number of Chinese who wouldn't surrender hiding deep down in one of their bunkers. An interpreter was brought forward, and he told the Chinese what we would do if they didn't surrender. We heard them talking to each other. It was no use, they didn't come out. Explosives were sent up, and we blasted the bunker shut. Buried the Chinese alive.

That same night, a lieutenant sent me out forward with a guy from my squad named Powell. We were to go along a finger that was attached to the ridgeline. The lieutenant said, "There could be an attack tonight, and we want you on a listening post. Soon as you hear something, come on back."

On the way down the path, Powell and I picked up a can of corned beef hash somebody had dropped. We ate it in our hole. It was turning dark and we munched quietly. We were very alert, watching and listening.

Without warning, one of our own mortar rounds crashed in nearly on top of us. It was either a short or the lieutenant, not realizing where we were, had called in a registration round. I'm not sure if it hit in the hole or next to it, but next thing I knew, I was in the air, stretched out parallel to the ground. I fell heavily on my back down in the hole. When I opened my eyes, powder and smoke and dust were blowing around me. My whole body was numb. I didn't know if I'd been blown apart, or what. I heard Powell gagging. I looked to my side and saw a jagged hole in his neck. I knew he was on his way out. I was still numb and trying to feel myself to see if I was all there. I couldn't feel anything. When my body finally stopped buzzing, I realized I hadn't been hit. I looked at Powell again and thought there was nothing I could do for him, the hole in his neck was big. I picked myself up and raced back to the platoon to get a medic to go back with me.

When the medic and I got back to the hole, Powell was lying where I'd left him. The medic took one look and said he couldn't help him.

I ran back along the finger and up to our company positions. When I found the lieutenant who'd sent Powell and me out on the LP, I called him every name in the book. I asked him why he had sent us forward and then called mortars in on us. The lieutenant said to a man standing nearby, "Get him out of here. He's in shock."

The next morning I thought more about the incident and learned that there had been two machine guns covering the area where Powell and I had had our LP. I could never figure out what we were supposed to do. It wasn't much of an idea, in the event of an attack, to have men out front of machine guns. The whole business was ridiculous, but I didn't pursue it. I knew I was wrong to call an officer names. It was something you were never supposed to do. But I couldn't help it, I did it anyway.

There were lots of air strikes on the hills we assaulted. It was something scary to see. The jets flew over and actually released their canisters above our lines. The napalm floated over our heads before exploding in orange flame on the Chinese-held hills. When our jets strafed, their 20-mm cannon casings rained down on us. I picked one of them up, but it was so hot I dropped it quick. There was so much brass around, I thought, What a waste.

We used tanks to pull 155s up some hills. Some of the big guns were practically bore-sighted on the Chinese bunkers when they blew them to smithereens.

I was in a group that once went up a hill with a tank. Even though we were a weapons platoon, we were often used like infantry. Near the top of a hill, along a ridge, a little Chinaman with a bazooka stepped out and BAM! disabled the tank, setting it afire. Black smoke swirled around. The tankers jumped out, and one of them yelled, "Bug out!" We all went back down the ridge. I thought about this later. I'm sure there were just a few Chinese on the hill then. When we left, it allowed the enemy to reinforce the hill, because later we had a lot harder time taking it. It went through my mind, Why the heck hadn't we just grabbed some people and run up and taken out that one bunker?

We were in a bunker another time and getting shelled real good. I read later nearly 4,000 rounds landed in our area. I was with four other guys; the shelling was so heavy, we couldn't leave—couldn't even get out to find food or water. We were there a long time. We drew straws to determine which of us would act as guard near the mouth of the dugout. We didn't want to get caught in there during a Chinese attack—one grenade and we would have been finished. Their mortars were all over us. I just knew we were going to get it. I figured the enemy could see us, or at least knew exactly where we were. I told Louie, "I don't know. I might crack up." I don't remember what he said. But, anyway, I didn't.

Only when losses in men and supplies forced the enemy to withdraw did the 1st Cavalry Division take possession of its part of line Jamestown. On 19 October the Chinese were forced across the Yokkok-ch'on to their next line of defense. Estimates of enemy losses during the sixteen days of Operation Commando placed the total at more than 21,000. The I Corps, too, with its 4,000 casualties, three quarters of whom were in the 1st Cavalry Division, had also been badly scourged.

In the lull that followed Commando, General Van Fleet did some creative housekeeping and found places to rest a few of his exhausted divisions.* One other change took place at this time that should be noted. On 1 October, the all-Negro 24th Infantry Regiment was inactivated, and the 14th Infantry Regiment replaced it as the third regiment of the 25th Division. There had been a gradual shifting away from segregated units in the Army following the Second World War, and the Korean War offered a solution to the entire racial problem. When, in early 1951, Eighth Army began to receive black replacements in its heretofore all-white combat organizations, the fears of diminished performance and open hostility between whites and blacks proved to be largely groundless. These favorable experiences convinced General Ridgway that the time had come to integrate Far East Command as a means of improving the overall combat effectiveness of his forces. Department of the Army approved his plan, and when the all-Negro 24th Infantry was inactivated, its personnel were distributed among all-white units in the Command. Several other all-Negro units were also broken up. The blacks in the 3d Battalion, 9th Infantry, were absorbed throughout the 2d Division; and those in the 3d Battalion, 15th Infantry, were taken in by other infantry units of the 3d Division. In other cases, integration took place with a simple exchange of personnel.†

Eighth Army's limited offensives petered out in late October, just as the negotiators returned to the peace talks. The character of the war reverted to the stagnation of July and early August, and a policy of live and let live settled over the front. While not conclusive, the grueling battles for dominating terrain fought in September and October had kept the Communists off balance and, more important, established a line the UN would consider satisfactory if a cease-fire should be agreed upon.

In November the UN relaxed the military pressure on the North Koreans and their Chinese allies. Those few words spoken on that

---

*The U.S. 2d Division, with its French Battalion, was transferred to IX Corps, where it went into reserve; and the U.S. 7th Division, with its attached Ethiopian Battalion, was shifted to X Corps. The ROK 5th Division in the X Corps was exchanged with the ROK 3d Division in the ROK I Corps. In the British Commonwealth Division, the 1st Battalion, Royal Ulster Rifles, was relieved by a battalion of the Royal Norfolk Regiment and prepared to return to Hong Kong.
† When the Korean War ended in July 1953, 90 percent of all blacks in the Army were serving in integrated units.

Sunday in June by Jacob Malik had finally paid off. On 12 November, General Ridgway instructed Eighth Army to assume an "active defense," limiting offensive operations to the capture of outposts, while being ready to exploit targets of opportunity. Eighth Army would continue to organize, construct, and defend positions along the MLR, but it could not attack with a force larger than a battalion (about 1,000 men) without prior consent of the UN commander. Offensive action would be limited to establishing an outpost line not more than 5,000 yards ahead of the front lines.

The White House and Pentagon did not believe that with the forces available the UN could win. The politicians, and for that matter the Joint Chiefs of Staff and General Ridgway, believed further gains would not justify their losses, and that the MLR as it existed in November 1951 could not be greatly improved without undue casualties. It should also be mentioned that 1952 would be a presidential election year in the United States.

Across the MLR, aerial reconnaissance photos clearly revealed that the Communists had built a system of interlocking fortifications more intricate and formidable than anything since Verdun and Flanders. It was obvious the Communists had switched their tactics, from one based on movement to one based on defense in depth. But if the enemy now was unwilling to start a fight, he certainly did not go out of his way to avoid one.

November 1951 brought an end to the slugfest; from this point forward it would be jab and counterpunch. This is not to suggest that the fighting was over; in fact, some of the bloodiest engagements of the conflict were still to be fought. The war's most famous battles— the Pusan Perimeter, Inch'on, Seoul, the Chosin Reservoir—would be soon forgotten and replaced by battles on obscure ridges and outposts that carried names such as Old Baldy, The Hook, Bunker Hill, Porkchop Hill, Esther and Dagmar, Reno and Vegas. And the killing would go on without interruption for another twenty months.

In November 1951, snow, fog, and clouds the color of gunmetal rolled down from Siberia and blanketed the MLR all the way from the Yellow Sea to the Sea of Japan. An uneasy stillness settled over Korea's snow-covered hills; the second winter of the war was beginning.

TRUCE TALKS
AND POWs

By November 1951 it had become apparent to friend and enemy alike that the war—begun as a United Nations "police action"—was one which would never be won. Not that the means were lacking. The blunting of the Communist offensives of spring and summer, which had taken a heavy toll of Chinese and North Korean lives, had made it plain that Communist war aims in the Korean peninsula were thwarted. But in the opinion of the politicians, victory in the traditional sense was too risky to seek. There remained the specter of Russian involvement and the wider war that would entail. And there was the political damage that still more American casualties could do the administration with an election year just over the horizon.

In April, the inevitable clash between General MacArthur and Harry Truman had finally come.

MacArthur had never been in favor of limiting the war to the Korean peninsula. He had smarted for months under the onus of his error in judgment concerning the willingness of the Chinese to intervene in the war, and the precipitous (and costly) retreat it had caused.

The general had never made a secret of his displeasure with the political constraints placed on his military options by the exigencies of the Cold War.

On 20 March 1951, MacArthur wrote to Representative Joseph W. Martin (R-Mass.) expressing his dissatisfaction with the political conduct of the war. It was in this letter that he expressed his now-famous dictum that "in war there is no substitute for victory." That *a serving officer should bypass the chain of command and bring his arguments directly to bear on a member of the Congress was, while not unknown in American history, unwise, to say the least.*

Representative Martin, an opponent of the Democratic administration, lost no time in making MacArthur's letter public. President Truman was furious.

In this connection it is well to correct the views that revisionist historians have attributed to MacArthur. He did not advocate the use of nuclear weapons against the Chinese homeland, nor did he envision an invasion of mainland China by United Nations troops. He did advocate air and naval attacks on the Communist bases and sanctuaries in Manchuria. He also proposed to "loose" Chiang Kai-shek and his idle Nationalist armies on the mainland.

General MacArthur was convinced that the Soviet Union would never intervene on behalf of China. He believed that the natural rivalry between the two Communist giants—and Russian fear of United States nuclear superiority—would keep the Soviets at a wary distance. It has been suggested (though never proved) that MacArthur felt that if the Russians should, by some miscalculated chance, respond militarily to his initiatives, the time to deal with them would never again be so propitious for the United States.

He went so far as to make contact with the Chinese commander in Korea and called upon him to surrender or face the condign punishments mentioned above.

It was too much for Harry Truman, and he exercised his constitutional authority as commander in chief to rid himself of Douglas MacArthur once and for all.

General Matthew B. Ridgway, a competent officer but a far less overbearing figure, was appointed UN commander in Korea.

These events were, of course, critical to the conduct of the war. By what amounts to political fiat, the idea of victory in Korea was in effect declared not only impossible, but undesirable. The historical results of this decision are dealt with in the summary section of this book.

Now, with 1951 drawing to a close, the fighting lines stabilized near the 38th Parallel. Enormous amounts of blood and treasure had been expended, only to return the military situation very nearly to the status quo ante July 1950.

MacArthur's return to the United States after so many years of absence was, at first, the occasion for an emotional binge of remarkable proportions. He was asked to address a joint session of the Congress and did so. It was on this occasion that he made his statement "Old soldiers never die . . . they just fade away."

In point of fact, the general had no idea of "just fading away." He had been encouraged by many in the United States Congress to believe he could become president. Despite his glittering military record, however, this was never a real possibility.

He was asked to testify—along with many others—before a committee of Congress investigating the conduct of the war. But if there indeed was a "MacArthur position" on the war (and any future wars), it was heavily undermined by the testimony of members of the administration—supported by members of the Joint Chiefs of Staff.

Throughout the hearings the question of possible Russian involvement in the war was a recurring theme. General Hoyt Vandenberg, the chief of staff of the Air Force, gave the senators of the committee a short course in the strategic use of air power. The Air Force, said Vandenberg, could conduct a strategic air campaign against Russia or China, but not against both simultaneously. SAC, he declared, could level the cities of China, but he could not promise that such a campaign would be conclusive, because nothing in war was conclusive.

Most important of all from the Air Force perspective was the need always to keep the Strategic Air Command intact for striking, if need be, at the heart of the Soviet Union, which was where the strength of the Communist world was concentrated. Implicit in Vandenberg's arguments was the clear message that the Congress had kept SAC and the U.S. Air Force on short rations by withholding the money needed to make it what it could and should be. The Air Force, sixty-eight groups strong in 1951, would have to be twice that size before MacArthur's plans could even be contemplated.

In Vandenberg's opinion, the only proper task for the Air Force in Korea was the one it was now performing: the interdiction of the supply lines between the Yalu River and the fighting front.

Vandenberg was backed by Major General Emmett O'Donnell, who had commanded Far East Air Force Bomber Command for the first six months of the war in Korea. O'Donnell contended that it was "a bizarre mission" for his B-29s to be "blowing up haystacks" in a land without any targets of strategic value.

There was a time, O'Donnell testified, when SAC could have hurt the Communists in Manchuria very badly. But now (in mid-1951), any strategic bombers venturing over China could expect heavy opposition from the MiGs of the Chinese Air Force. To expose SAC to such attrition would compromise its main mission: the attack on the Soviet Union, for which the force had been designed.

All of this was duly reported in the national press, and General MacArthur's position (always suspect, even to the hero-worshiping public) was eroded badly. The administration's plan for ending the war—which was actually no plan at all, but a gradual cessation of hostilities and a return to the status quo—began to look good by comparison.

Secretary of State Marshall was asked many times how the war would be ended. Marshall told the senators, "[We must] inflict terrific casualties on the Chinese Communist Forces. If we break the morale of their armies, but more particularly if we destroy their best-trained armies, as we have been in the process of doing, there, it seems to me, you develop the best probability of reaching a satisfactory negotiatory [sic] basis. . . ." What this, in fact, indicated, was that the idea of conducting the war with a clear victory as its aim was no longer (if it had ever been) a possibility.

There was more testimony before the committee, much of it expert, and all of it intended to show that, in General Omar Bradley's words, Korea was the "wrong war." Bradley, like almost all the American military establishment, was a soldier dedicated to the defense of Western Europe. To him and the others at the Pentagon, a showdown with the Communists in Asia could not be contemplated.

History was to vindicate their position to a degree, but the real effect of their statements that summer of 1951 was to reinforce the limited war aims of an administration with an increasingly unpopular war on its hands.

After the hearings, General MacArthur returned to New York and a round-robin of highly political speeches. But the high-water mark of his popularity had been reached and passed. At a ballgame he attended, complete with recorded seventeen-gun salute and the playing of "Old Soldiers Never Die," some voice in the crowd was heard to shout: "Hey Mac, how about that Harry Truman?" The sally brought forth roars of laughter. This was regarded as a sign that the MacArthur boomlet had spent its force. The Democrats in the Congress breathed a sign of relief and set about seeking a compromise to end the war.

On 29 June a directive had been sent to General Ridgway which ordered him to send the following radio message to the Communist commander in chief: "As commander in chief of the United Nations Command, I have been instructed to communicate to you the following: I am informed that you may wish a meeting to discuss an armistice providing for the cessation of hostilities and all acts of armed force in Korea, with adequate guarantees for the maintenance of such an armistice. Upon receipt of word from you that such a meeting is desired I shall be prepared to name my representative. I propose that such a meeting take place aboard a Danish hospital ship in Wonsan Harbor."

It is of passing interest that until a reply to this message came from Kim Il Sung (as supreme commander of the Korean People's Army) and General Peng Teh-huai (as commander of the Chinese People's Volunteers), the UN Command had not known even the identity of the Chinese commander.

Instead of the Jutlandia at Wonsan, the Communists proposed that the meeting take place at Kaesong, in the no-man's-land west of the Imjin River and some three miles south of the 38th Parallel.

On the morning of 8 July 1951, a United Nations Command helicopter carrying three liaison officers—Col. Jack Kinney, USAF, Col. James Murray, USMC, and Col. Soo Young Lee, ROKA—circled the ruins of Kaesong and landed on the designated field outside the town. After a few very tense moments, the UN officers were taken to a former teahouse, to be met by a Colonel Chang, of the KPA; a Lieutenant Colonel Kim, also of the KPA; and a Lieutenant Colonel Tsai, of the Chinese People's Volunteers. Arrangements were made for the main delegations to meet, two days hence, in the same location.

In Washington it was thought the armistice discussions would take about three weeks. Thirty-six years later, they are still going on.

The Communists were now, in fact, unable—and the West was unwilling—to seek a victory on the Korean peninsula. More fighting and dying remained to be done, but the battles were not for victory. They were intended to improve positions at the truce table.

The Communist offensives of spring and summer 1951 had cost the Chinese and North Koreans upwards of 70,000 casualties. They had ample reason to agree to the preliminary truce meetings at Kaesong. But they never ceased to probe and patrol, and whenever and wherever they sensed that advantage could be taken, they conducted operations in force.

The Eighth Army dug in at the Punchbowl and in the Iron Triangle, meeting the Communist probes with resolution. Meanwhile the Communist negotiators, indulging a penchant for incivility that remains intact to this day, took every opportunity to insult and badger the men of the UN Command, whom they saw almost every day across the green baize tables. In late August the negotiations stumbled and came to a halt.

The war had, of course, never ceased; now the tempo of battle picked up. Between August and November there were a number of sharp encounters which bloodied the Communists badly. Their supply lines were overextended, and their troops had not recovered from the reverses of spring and summer.

On 12 November the truce negotiations began again, this time at Panmunjom. On the same day General Ridgway ordered all offensive operations stopped. The military parameters of the United States' first truly limited war were established.

Preeminent among UN Command concerns was the matter of the treatment and exchange of prisoners of war. This concern was merited. Both the Chinese and North Koreans dealt with captured United Nations troops in what can only be considered a barbarous manner. Many POWs had already been held for more than a year in atrocious conditions. Worse was to come.

Pfc. LAWRENCE BAILEY
C Company/32d Infantry
I was captured on December 2, 1950, at the Chosin Reservoir, where we had been surrounded for three weeks by Chinese infantry. Our

supplies ran out and there wasn't much else we could do but surrender, and that was what we did.

The Chinese formed us up and took us back over some of the ground we had fought for weeks before. There were still Chinese and American dead everywhere you looked—frozen corpses, some of them sitting up with their eyes open. It was a terrible sight, very depressing.

The Chinese broke us up into groups. I was with eleven other people at first, men from other outfits captured at the same time as we were. We didn't know where we were going, and of course the Chinese didn't bother to tell us. Even if they had tried, we wouldn't have understood a word. There was no interpreter. We guessed the Chinese didn't care, because it was cooperate with them by walking, or drop out and die.

We kept picking up other prisoners along the way. We marched all night and then, during the day, we had to hide under the brush because there were American planes overhead all the time.

Our captors didn't give us anything to eat during the daylight hours. At night they fed us one at a time as we marched. Maybe *fed us* is too strong a way to put it. What they gave us was a handful of soybeans which we could put in our pockets and eat as we went along. Oh, yes, we got a cup of hot water to drink, for which we were grateful because of the awful cold.

We were on the march for about ten days, moving through territory we had fought over on the way north. It made us all feel very depressed.

After about eight or nine days, we had twenty or thirty in our group, most of them casuals picked up along the line of march. Many of the men were wounded—some of them badly—and all of us were suffering from hunger and frostbite. But you didn't want to drop out of the column, because when someone did, a guard would stay with him until we were out of sight, and then you would hear rifle shots, and the guard would catch up with us.

My feet were frozen, and my boots felt like pieces of wood. It was very hard to walk, but I kept moving because I knew what would happen to me if I didn't. When I did fall down from time to time, a guard would stand over me and stick the tip of his bayonet into my back to get me moving again.

We finally reached a place we all called Death Valley because so many of the POWs died there. The Chinese kept us in a group of small Korean huts. There was no heat, but we kept warm because there were so many of us in the huts that the only thing we could do was lie on the floor squeezed against one another. When one person wanted to turn over, everybody in the hut had to move and get into another position.

In Death Valley the Chinese turned us over to the North Koreans. They took those Americans who could still walk with them when they left. We never did find out what happened to them.

The North Koreans seemed to want to show us that they could be stricter than the Chinese. For rations we got a boiled potato—one per man, per day—and for water we got the muddy stuff the potatoes had been cooked in. We began to get desperate because we were literally starving. After a month or so in Death Valley, people who had frozen body parts actually started pulling them off—toes and fingertips and ears—and putting them in a pot the Koreans left in our huts. I don't know what the Koreans did with those rotting parts of human beings. I do know that some of our people were talking about eating them. I hope no one ever did, but I wouldn't be surprised if one had. You get a little crazy when you are starving. I lost all the toes on my right foot and four from my left, and I lost the little finger of my right hand.

By the time we had been in Death Valley for a month people were dying, two and three every night, mostly from starvation and untreated wounds. But there were deaths from other causes, too. The lice were thick, and we had cases of what must have been typhus. It was hard to be sure. There were no medics with us. In a way, the dead helped the rest of us stay alive. We would keep the bodies covered up for as long as we could so that we could collect the dead men's rations.

In April, I think it was, the North Koreans decided to move us, and they put us on carts because even they understood we could no longer march. We rode those damned carts for ten days, sometimes heading south but not always. We ended up at a place the Koreans told us would be called Camp Number One—just as soon as we helped to build it. We couldn't have been much use to them because we were on our last legs. Half of us, or more, had died in the months since Chosin.

When the camp was built, the Chinese came back and took it—and us—over from the North Koreans. Rations improved a little. They gave us a cup and a half of rice each day. It had worms in it, but we ate them without any complaints.

It was at Camp Number One that some of our people really fell out with the Chinese. They would argue with them and get beaten for it. The Chinese called people who gave them any kind of trouble at all "reactionaries." That was when they decided that we would have lectures on communism every day. The lectures were in Chinese, and the interpreters were not very good, but we had to sit and listen to them, and then afterward we would have "discussion groups." We were supposed to talk about the advantages of communism. Some of the POWs got pretty good at it.

Cpl. JACK BROWNING
M Company/34th Infantry

I was captured in a small village near Taejon, about thirty miles south of Seoul, on July 8, 1950. I was with a soldier not from my regular outfit, by the name of Roy Rogers. Who could forget that name?

Well, Roy and I had taken cover in a house in this village when the North Koreans overran our position and called on us to give up. We were out of ammunition and cut off, so we did as we were told. We came out of the shot-up hut straight into a bunch of North Koreans who wanted to know if the people they had killed—there were bodies all around—were *Americansiki*. I told them that they were, and it seemed to please them very much. One Korean knocked off my pot helmet with his rifle, nearly knocking me off my feet. I began to understand right away that we were not going to get particularly good treatment.

They put us—Roy and me—in a jeep (made in the USA and probably a gift from the Russians) and drove us back, away from the lines into the rice paddies. I was afraid they were simply going to shoot us, but instead they took us to a house just under the brow of a hill. It was a miracle it was still standing after all the fighting that had been going on in the area. But it was, and it was shelter of a sort.

They fed us a bowl of horrible-tasting rice that I managed to get down because I had a pretty good idea they were not going to feed us any more than they had to. It turned out I was right. That rice was the last food we had for over two days.

We spent the night in the hut, lying on the dirt floor, with our hands and feet trussed up behind us. Then, in the morning, they started us out toward a village called Pengyong. It took a day and a half to get there. We got assimilated into a large column of prisoners—a sad sight—and by the time we reached the railhead the Koreans had collected about 750 of us. We had to cross the Namihan River and it was filled with floating corpses. Even so, many of our people were so thirsty after a day and a half without anything to drink that they rushed down to the banks and sucked up that muddy water in spite of what we all saw floating in it.

Of course no one told us, but we were being sent to P'yongyang, by train. As soon as we were jammed into boxcars, we all began to pray. Our fighter pilots were all over the place, and trains were their favorite targets. But somehow we made it to P'yongyang without encountering a Mustang or Corsair.

The trip was bad enough without opposition. I think the Koreans took us the long way around so that they could show off all the *Americansiki* they had captured. They never did feed us, and it took them at least forty-eight hours to get around to giving us water. When they did, it was in buckets we were expected to pass around. One poor fellow just couldn't make himself stop drinking. I don't know how long he had been without water, but the water he drank that afternoon killed him. He cramped so badly that the water—in addition to whatever else was wrong with him—just killed him.

In P'yongyang they kept us in an old schoolhouse for several days. We were there when our air force made the first raid on the enemy capital. The North Koreans were storing ammunition in some of the houses in the city, and I don't know whether or not it was an accident or good intelligence, but they hit these buildings, and they went off with a terrible explosion and then secondaries. The bombs dropped within a half mile of where the POWs were being kept, and we all prayed a lot.

Everyone was really scared. The North Koreans were, and so were we. After the planes left, the North Koreans got some of us out and made us work with mops and brooms to clear up the plaster that had fallen inside the school building from the concussion.

We stayed in P'yongyang for about another week, and then the Koreans decided to move us again. So it was back onto the train and the fear of being blown up by our own air force. While we were traveling, we got *two* meals a day. That is, we got two little balls of rice and a cup of dirty water.

On the second day out of P'yongyang, our luck ran out. One of our pilots came over, spotted the train and made a pass. He just riddled it from end to end. The miracle was that we had stopped for one of our two meals, and were not actually aboard when he came over. But two men did get hit anyway, and we buried them in shallow graves right there by the railroad track. I often wonder if their remains were ever recovered. I suppose not.

The train carried us north for two more days, then we had to get out and start marching. We were afraid we were going to end up in China. We reached the Yalu River and turned east along its banks. The food we got was a handful of soybeans, but we did manage to catch some fish and eat those. I had never seen fish like these in the Yalu. When you cleaned them, the maggots would roll out. But we ate them, just the same. We were beginning to lose people to malnutrition and dysentery. Almost every day two or three men died.

Roy Rogers was still with me—until the day we heard some small-arms fire and had to run for it. We never did find out what the firing was about. We were a long way from the United Nations troops. Perhaps there were bandits or guerrillas up there near the Yalu. But we had to leave the temporary camp where we were staying, and a lot of our men were too sick to travel much farther. Roy was one of these. A Korean officer made a great speech and told us that the men who could march would be moving into a comfortable camp; the ones who couldn't would stay behind and go into the hospital. I was very suspicious of that, and I tried to warn Roy, begging him to come with us, no matter how hard it was to travel. He said that he couldn't make it and would only be a burden to those of us who could. So he stayed. I don't think he ever saw the inside of any hospital. I think the North Koreans killed him.

Our Korean officer was so mean, he was called The Tiger. It made him angry to have to be on the move all the time, and he seemed to imagine that we were not following orders. So one morning he decided to give us a lesson in Communist discipline. He picked out one of our officers, Lieutenant Thornton, put a blindfold on him, and just shot him through the head as an example.

One of our sergeants had been on the Bataan Death March in the Philippines. He said that our march was tougher and that we lost more men per mile than the people in the Philippines did. I don't know about that, but I do know that they seemed to want to keep marching us around North Korea until we dropped. Plenty of us did. And those who just dropped out of the line of march, they shot. I remember one day they killed thirty-one of us for dropping out exhausted.

[There is a great deal more to Cpl. Jack Browning's account. By the time he had been in captivity for one year, half of the 700-odd POWs in his original group were dead. Many had fallen to sickness and starvation, but many others had been murdered out of hand by their Chinese and North Korean captors. Browning's and Bailey's experiences were far from unique. And there were thousands of United Nations prisoners in Communist hands. Little wonder that the plight of the prisoners of war and their early repatriation was a prime concern at the truce meetings now being held at Panmunjom.]

Rifleman Pvt. LEONARD JONES
1st Battalion/Royal Ulster Rifles

It was after the fight at the Imjin River on 22 April that I was captured. The Chinese had attacked the British Brigade with waves of tanks and infantry, and the Gloucestershires were rather too far forward and we were surrounded and cut off.

We held the line for almost three days, until we ran out of ammo and were reduced to fighting off the Chinese with rifle butts and entrenching tools. But on the night of the third day, we received orders to make a fighting withdrawal and save what we could. The Chinese were all around us, and so it became a matter of every man finding his own way out if possible.

We came down out of the hills in groups of two and three into a place called Happy Valley. As we reached the floor of the valley our artillery opened up, trying to support our withdrawal; but a great many of the rounds fell short, and a lot of the lads were killed by our own guns.

The Inky Pinko were on the hills above us and on both sides of the valley. Some of them had even gotten in position ahead of us.

Some of the lads were too tired to keep moving through the rice paddies in the valley, but I knew it would be suicide to stop and rest. Even so, crossing those paddies, I knew we weren't going to make it. We used the few magazines of ammo we had been able to collect from the dead, but soon that was gone and the Chinese kept closing in on us.

It was about this time that I joined up with a group of four other men from the battalion who had been hauling a Bren gun. There were only two magazines of shells for it left.

We fired off what ammo we had, and then realized that it was all over as far as fighting went. We had nothing left to fight with. So we smashed our rifles and the Bren gun, and then went to ground, keeping low and hoping that the Chinese would just bypass us. But that was not to be. They spotted us and were on us like a swarm of bees, yelling and screaming and beating us with their rifle butts. We were prisoners of war. What followed was something I shall never forget.

They marched our small group into a ravine between the mountains, where they had collected most of the Gloucesters they had captured. They kept themselves and us under cover because the Sabre jets were howling through the valleys looking for them and dropping napalm.

That night we moved back across the river. We were still in tropical dress—shirts, shorts, and top-hose—and the temperature dropped to freezing. We crossed by wading in that icy water up to our chins, and with the Chinese screaming and beating us with their rifles as we struggled to climb the banks. I don't know how many of the lads were lost during the crossing. There were quite a few, of that I am certain.

We marched twenty miles that night, dripping wet, of course, and without food or medical attention for the wounded. When daylight came we had to take cover again from the American jets. When the planes came over, the Chinese would go crazy, beating and cursing us. They hated and feared those daylight raids by the fliers.

That was the pattern for the next five weeks. We would march all night and hide all day from the jets. We ate what we could find, and that was not much. People began to die of malnutrition and dysentery on the march. To drop out was a death sentence. If you fell and couldn't rise, you were shot and left behind, unburied.

As we marched through North Korean villages, the people would come out and throw stones at us and curse us. The Chinese thought this was amusing. They never made any attempt to protect us from the civilians. After the war, Colonel Carne of the Gloucesters was given a V.C. [The Victoria Cross is Britain's highest military honor.] On that march north the colonel was very ill, and many of us took turns in helping to shoulder him along so that he wouldn't drop out and be killed. We all had a small part in winning that V.C. for him.

We had other officers with us. Captain Farrar-Hockley of the Gloucesters gave us all a fright when he told one of the Chinese who had pulled him into line to "keep his filthy hands off the King's uniform." We fully expected the Chinese to gun us all down on the spot, but somehow it didn't happen.

At the end of the march, which took us 400 miles into North Korea, we arrived at Ch'ongsong prisoner-of-war camp. I can't even guess how many men died along the way—far too many.

I spent two years and four months in that hellhole. I expected to face pain and death in the Army, but Ch'ongsong was like nothing I had ever imagined.

There were Americans in the camp, as well as British. Men died every day from lack of food and medical care, and from executions. We called the graveyard "Boot Hill" after the burial places in American cowboy films. But Boot Hill was frozen for a third of the year, and so the dead just lay out there in the open. It looked like a battlefield.

The Chinese seemed to think it was very important that we all study Mao's little red book. Some prisoners actually turned Communist—or at least, claimed to have done so—because it meant better treatment from the Chinese. But most of us used the book for cigarette papers (you could smoke the pages with dried leaves rolled in them), or for toilet paper. The Chinese got very angry when they found anyone doing something like this, and the punishment was a severe beating and even less food than we ordinarily got.

I remember an American soldier being punished (I don't know what for) by being put into a shower in the middle of winter and kept there until he began to freeze. They waited too long to take him out, because he lost both feet to frostbite and gangrene. That was the sort of thing that happened at Ch'ongsong. The Chinese told us that the American was lucky that the camp medical staff was there to care for him.

My time at Ch'ongsong isn't something I like to remember, even after all these years. But I guess others had it just as bad, or even worse. It was that kind of war.

> "A" Company and part of the O Gp [orders group] got onto the road by B Coy position and joined some tanks of 8 H [Hussars]. The road south . . . to the RV was considered safe by all, but the reverse was in fact so, and many were lost as the tanks, out of ammunition, ran the gauntlet.
>
> WAR DIARY, 1ST BATTALION/ROYAL ULSTER RIFLES

Cpl. LAWRENCE DONOVAN
Medical Corpsman/25th Division

On the morning of November 27 [1950], I and four other men from my company were taken prisoner by the Chinese. We had taken cover in a deep ravine into which the Chinese troops were throwing concussion grenades. We fought until our ammunition was exhausted, and then surrendered.

The Chinese were apparently infuriated by our resistance, because immediately that we dropped our weapons, they were on us, screaming and beating us with their rifle butts.

As a medic I carried medical supplies. But the moment I was taken, these supplies were stolen from me and scattered all over the mountainside. Morphine and bandages that might have saved lives were simply thrown away.

One of the men from my company must have particularly enraged our captors, because he was taken immediately just out of sight and shot to death. It was a fair indication of the treatment we were going to receive from the Communists.

We were marched down the valley to a kind of shed, where others of my company were being held prisoner. We were all rather ashamed of having been taken prisoner. It didn't fit in with our picture of proper behavior for American soldiers. What I didn't consider was the possibility that for the next thirty-three months I would be fighting just to survive.

When we began to move, the Chinese would only march at night. They were terrified of our planes. So during the daylight hours we huddled in caves and ruined huts and sheds—whatever cover was available.

Since the enemy had destroyed all of our medical supplies, within a day or so the wounded began to suffer horribly. We carried them in rice mats slung between bamboo poles. It was very difficult and extremely painful to carry the weight on our shoulders, because they immediately became lacerated and infected.

The Chinese seemed to delight in inflicting unnecessary suffering on us. When we encountered frozen streams filled with rocks and broken ice, our guards would force us to remove our shoes and wade barefoot. Then, on the other side, we would find our shoes and boots in a pile. Since we moved only in darkness, we had to grope, hoping to recover our own shoes—which was impossible, of course. We never ended up with the same pair of shoes twice. It was a peculiarly nasty thing to do to helpless men, and many of our people paid for our captors' "little joke" with frostbitten and frozen feet.

We marched up high, ice-coated mountain trails in the dark and cold. Not one night passed but there were shots—executions of the prisoners too weak to go on. The wind was like a knife, bitter and cold. But we kept walking because by now we understood that to fall out of the line of march was a sure way to get a bullet in the neck from the guards.

Ten days after being captured, we arrived at the place that was to become known as Death Valley Camp. If there is such a place as hell on earth, then Death Valley has to be a contender for that terrible honor.

The day we straggled in, bearing our surviving wounded,

exhausted and near to starvation, was my twenty-first birthday. I remember thinking that here I was, and I had never even had an opportunity to vote.

The huts that were supposed to give us shelter were so flimsy the wind blew straight through them. There were no blankets. We slept in what we had on us, which wasn't much in that Korean winter weather. Our diet, if you can call it that, consisted of boiled corn and millet (and very little even of that). There were no eating utensils, so we were forced to eat with our hands. My weight began to drop. All of us began to look skeletal. Dysentery hit us at once, and we were soon passing blood and mucus. There was no way to keep clean, and so we quickly infested with hog-lice, nasty creatures that soon laid eggs by the millions in our hair and clothing.

To me, as a medic, one of the worst things about Death Valley was the total lack of any medical care or supplies. The Chinese had such things, but they never used them on us. Our quarters reeked of infected wounds and dysentery. Men died every night. Men who could have been saved with just a modicum of civilized treatment.

A thing I shall never forget is the death of Father Capon, a Catholic priest who somehow had been put in with the POWs at Death Valley. He was a truly religious and saintly man who did his best to make life in the camp bearable for the sick and wounded. I'll never know what the father did to enrage the Chinese, but one night they took him away and beat him to death. A group of prisoners claimed the body and buried it with what prayers they could remember. The Catholics in the camp, myself included, felt that Father Capon was a saint and a martyr.

Late in January 1951, we were moved to Camp Five near P'yoktong, North Korea. We were marched through the streets so that the civilians could spit on us and beat us with sticks and fists. Then, when we reached the camp, the Chinese informed us that our conditions would be much better because they now had facilities to take care of the thousands of UN prisoners they had taken.

Conditions did not improve as promised. If anything, they grew far worse. In Camp Five we got only one meal each day. The death rate soared, and that first winter we buried 1,600 fellow prisoners. The camp was on the south bank of the Yalu, but we were forced to ferry what seemed an endless procession of dead comrades across the river so that they could be buried on the north bank. I am certain that this was done so that if the day of reckoning ever came, no one in the outside world would ever know how many men died at the hands of their Chinese captors.

[Of particular, if secret, concern to the UN truce negotiators was the new and pernicious campaign to enlist suffering POWs in the Communist cause by offering them preferential treatment in the prison camps. With conditions so atrocious, it was feared that the subversion of prisoners—"brainwashing" was the term invented by the press— was succeeding. In fact, the prisoners who allowed themselves to be seduced were few, but the danger was real.]

Cpl. JACK CHAPMAN
D Company/31st Regimental Combat Team

[Corporal Chapman, stationed in Japan when the North Koreans invaded the South, arrived in Korea with the units supporting the landings at Inch'on. Within a matter of weeks, the North Koreans were in flight northward, followed by victorious UN troops. By October 1950, a second amphibious assault was planned for Iwon, ninety miles north of Wonsan, North Korea. This was to be a thrust into the North Korean heartland—a fatal blow to the Communist cause in the peninsula.

Meanwhile, scattered and somewhat disorganized and unsupported troops were pursuing the North Koreans, who were in headlong retreat. Some United Nations Command forces had reached the Chosin Reservoir. Talk of peace was in the air. UN troops were being cautioned not to cross the Yalu River.

Corporal Chapman's unit received orders to march north to the Chosin Reservoir. It arrived early in the evening of 28 November. By midnight, the Reservoir and the Marines and soldiers in position there were surrounded by seven divisions of the Chinese People's Volunteers. China had changed the character of the ci-devant "police action" completely.

On 29 November, after a bitterly fought action against superior numbers, Corporal Chapman—wounded in the arm, leg, and head— was taken prisoner.]

Immediately after I was captured, the Chinese found the 75-mm recoilless rifle we had been using. There was a single round left for the piece, and it was in the chamber. I had put it there for one last shot, which I never had a chance to fire. One of the Chinese picked up the weapon and started to play with it. No one warned him there was a round in firing position. He hit the firing circuit and the piece fired. The backflash seriously injured several of their soldiers. I was going to hear about that, much later.

The Chinese made no attempt to treat any American wounded— and there were plenty of them, including myself.

We marched exclusively at night because the Chinese were afraid of our planes. They stripped us of all personal possessions, such as wallets, jewelry, papers, and photographs—we later learned how they used such items—and they also relieved us of our overcoats and field jackets. This caused great suffering because the weather was bitterly cold.

For nineteen days we marched on frozen feet—north, then west. My wounds were troubling me badly, untreated the way they were. We helped one another as much as we could, but even so, there were men dropping out of the column every night. When that happened the man was always shot and left to freeze there by the side of the road or trail. I personally saw a Marine who had been wounded at Chosin Reservoir murdered by one of the Chinese soldiers. The Marine had a bad leg wound and couldn't keep up. He died for that.

The group we were with was small, ten or a dozen men, and getting smaller all the time. One of the troops had saved a can of C rations, and that was all we had to eat for the first two days—one can shared out. The Chinese gave us nothing. When we stopped, we couldn't always find shelter. When it was like that we would just drop in the snow and try to sleep.

I was luckier than many. I was helped by some of the others and by a British Marine that the column had picked up somewhere—I couldn't be certain where, because by this time I was feverish and half-delirious.

When we finally arrived at Kang-gye, we were given shelter of a sort. The huts were of mud, with thatch roofs, but of course there was no heat of any kind. The temperature by this time was below zero every night.

We stayed in Kang-gye only a couple of nights, and then we were moved on through the town to some old buildings where the Chinese were concentrating prisoners of war.

As soon as we arrived, we were made to stand at attention in the snow while a Chinese officer—smiling and gloating—told us that the Chinese Volunteers had pushed the United Nations troops into the sea. This meant, he said, that escape was impossible for us, and we had better take his warning to heart. On the other hand, he said, they had what was called the "Lenient Policy" for prisoners who made a sincere effort to behave themselves and to learn all the things that the Chinese had to teach them.

The speech was a long one, and we were half dead from hunger and cold and fatigue, but the officer made it very clear that he was not concerned with such petty matters. We needed help, he told us, and he intended to see to it that we received it.

When we were finally released to go to the miserable huts allotted to us, we found them no better than those we had suffered in during our march. They were just as cold, just as crowded, and just as filthy.

We heard rumors about Red Cross packages several times, but if there were any delivered, the Chinese kept them for themselves. When we asked about parcels, the guards told us the Red Cross was a "running dog of Imperialism." That didn't stop them from confiscating whatever came—if anything ever did. Food was scarce, and people were actually starving. I was lucky enough to get some little care from my fellow prisoners, and though it took a long while, my wounds healed, more or less.

Shortly before Christmas Day, 1950, some Chinese political official let it be known that they were going to give us a party to celebrate the season. We could hardly believe what we heard. They were going to start their new Lenient Policy. That meant better food, blankets, medical care, maybe even heat in the huts where we shivered all night.

But first, we were told, there would be a lecture in one of the bigger buildings where we could all gather to hear something very important. What was so "important" was an appearance by that same Chinese political official and a half dozen brainwashed POWs who made odd-sounding speeches, using all the same words the Communist used, about how we were fighting a "millionaires'" war for the profit of "big business." One of the POWs told us that we had "innocent blood" on our hands. Another one said that he had been a prisoner of war in Germany, and that the Chinese were far more humane in their treatment of prisoners than the Nazis had been.

They accused the United States of bad faith, cheating on agreements, spreading germ warfare, and trying to stop the march of progress.

All the talk lasted until the early hours of the morning; and when the turncoats had finished addressing us, the so-called party was finished. That was all there was to it.

It is possible the Chinese thought they had made a good impression, because for Christmas dinner they gave us some rice with slivers of pork in it—the first meat we had tasted in months, except for some dog we were given on the march. After Christmas they gave us a drum of water and allowed us to heat it by building a fire in the snow so we could bathe. It was the first bath any of us had had for months—twenty of us, all using the same single oil drum of water.

Every day we were lectured. It was part of the Lenient Policy. We were told that we could be home with our loved ones if the capitalists who ran America hadn't sent us off to fight an unjust war. They knew quite a lot about the people at home. Those pictures and letters they stole when we were first captured were used to keep them informed about what our home life in America was like.

There was a camp newspaper, called *New Life*. It was filled with articles saying how wonderful life was under communism, and how terrible it was in the capitalist world.

There were some in our camp who were willing to do what the Chinese wanted so that they could get the "lenient" treatment the Communists promised.

My own sergeant wrote several articles for *New Life*. Then there was that POW who claimed to have been a prisoner of the Germans. He somehow found out I had been the gunner on the recoilless rifle that had injured those Chinese soldiers when I was captured. He told me that I should have admitted that to the camp officers. I said that I was not going to admit any such thing. But a few days later I was called into the camp headquarters and questioned about the incident.

They didn't believe me, but I stuck to my story. People were punished at Kang-gye for much less than that.

When we didn't all respond to their Lenient Policy they started to make things hard again. Like many others I was beaten with rifle butts on several occasions—mostly during work details, gathering firewood for the Chinese barracks. My wounds were more or less healed, but I couldn't really get around fast enough to please the guards.

One day, during a lecture, the Chinese official in charge informed us that we were all going to sign an appeal to the United Nations to get out of Korea.

We were very worried, but we refused to do any such thing. Yet things must have been progressing at the truce talks, because there was no physical punishment for refusing to sign the appeal.

There were prisoners who only pretended to go along with the Communists in the camp. They said that it would make life easier for all of us. The trouble was that some of these people actually got better treatment, and they made no attempt to hide it from the rest of us. That made it very hard to take.

The Chinese worked on the prisoners in small groups of ten. Many of the "instructors" spoke perfect English. Some were graduates of American universities. It made us wonder what they had been taught there.

Maybe the Chinese just got fed up with not having as much success with their "leniency" as they thought they should have. In any case, on a February night in 1951, we were awakened by the Chinese screaming at us and beating us out into the snow. We began a series of terrible forced marches to what seemed to us to be nowhere. Many of the men were in rags by now; some had no shoes; everyone was weak from malnutrition. The temperature fluctuated from twenty degrees above in the daytime to well below zero at night. One of the Marines in our group died on that march. We couldn't bury him. We had to cover him with snow and leave him.

We arrived at another camp in North Korea, but we didn't stay there long. Every few weeks we were rousted out and marched off to someplace else, and there was never any medical care or adequate food. Some of our noncoms suggested that they were just marching us around Korea so that the people could see how ragged and sick we were, and how many prisoners they had taken.

Corporal Chapman's account of his experiences as a prisoner of the Chinese and Koreans was neither worse nor very different from the accounts written by many others. The fact is that the men who were taken prisoner were treated with abominable brutality. Cruelty and neglect were the norm. United Nations Command intelligence knew it, and eventually the press learned of it, but this was not a moment for outrage, and coverage of the savage treatment of prisoners was not given wide distribution. In any case, there was little the negotiators at Panmunjom could do about it. The United Nations Command had been instructed to hold what the troops had taken, but to take no further aggressive action. From this moment it became apparent to the negotiators, all of them, that the administration in Washington wished for one thing only: to end the war on terms the American People would accept.

ROTATION

The ways for a man to leave Korea during the war and return to the United States were for him to be rotated, severely wounded, be a victim of sickness or accident, or be killed. Men deemed too badly wounded or ill to return to the front were usually sent to Japan, where they were treated at the Army hospital at Fukuoka or the naval facility at Yokosuka. Depending on the nature of his wound, a patient might be flown to the continental U.S. by the way of Tripler Hospital in Hawaii. Once in the States he was taken to either the Navy Hospital in Oakland or Letterman General in San Francisco. When a patient was considered ready, he was transferred to a hospital near his home.

In mid-February 1951, the Army and the Marine Corps began to rotate home men who had been selected on a basis of combat time, wounds received, and length of service. The first soldiers sent home were GIs from the 24th Division who had survived the terrible battles of July 1950, when the outcome of the war hung in the balance. The 1st Marine Division also rotated at this time 5 officers and 600 veterans of the Marine brigade, which had arrived in Korea in early August and had been immediately thrown into the fighting around the Pusan Perimeter. One of the Marines to rotate in February was newly promoted Maj. Gen. Edward A. Craig, who had led the brigade throughout its short, illustrious life.

Later in 1951, to qualify for rotation, a man had to have nine months of duty at the front or a total of thirty-six points. Four points were awarded for each month served at the front; two points were

given for service elsewhere in Korea. From the summer of 1951 on-
ward, an increasing number of men became eligible for rotation, and
during the fall and winter of 1951–52, between 15,000 and 20,000
soldiers were rotated home each month; the Marine division returned
2,066 officers and men in early November, and another 2,468 in late
November.

Returning to the United States was accompanied by emotions
boxed between relief at one end, and guilt at the other. Cut loose
from battle, the men's feelings raced giddily between being anxious
and bored, hyperactive and lethargic, manic and withdrawn. They
were surprised to learn that life in the U.S. had not stood still while
they were away, but had changed. Things were somehow different.
But their greatest discovery was understanding that their country, their
towns, their loved ones had not changed nearly as much as they had
themselves. As one of the men explained, "War will stress any man to
his max." When they were in their homes, surrounded by family, the
battles were over, but as the men were slowly to realize, in their atti-
tudes and emotions, the Korean War would go on. The memories of
confronting Russian-built tanks with rifles at Taejon, clambering over
the sea wall at Inch'on, walking amongst thousands of rotting corpses
around Chipyong-ni or below Gloster Hill remained; the stench of fear
and death just would not go away. It was the stuff that silently binds
combat veterans of any war together and makes them members of a
fearful fraternity that, fortunately, most civilians will never under-
stand.

Sgt. F/C LEONARD KORGIE
*Headquarters Company/24th Division**

When my rotation date was set, I just couldn't believe it. I was going
to make it! The night before I left the company, the guys in my
section and some of the medics threw a party. The medics supplied
some potent alcohol, which we cut with grapefruit juice. Now, I was
never much of a drinker, didn't much care for the taste, and if I
drank at all I handled it pretty well. That night, however, I got really

---

* Korgie had been transferred from the 21st Infantry Regiment in June 1951.

snookered. I eventually stumbled back to my cot. It was my custom
before going to bed to pop the clip out of my .45, then point the
weapon over my shoulder and squeeze the trigger to make sure it was
clear. This night I forgot to pull the clip. PLOWEE! I nearly blew
out my eardrum, and did succeed in blowing a hole in the side of
the tent.

Cpl. VICTOR FOX
I Company/5th Cavalry
By the time I was due to be rotated home, I was very hard to get
along with. I was disgruntled, discouraged, and "dis-" everything else.
One evening at chow a grinning Lieutenant Cadman came up to me.
"Fox, what are you mad about? You're going home tomorrow. Catch
the breakfast jeep." What a wonderful sense of relief! I sincerely thanked
the lieutenant for telling me the news. When my squad went off that
night on a patrol, I was told to stay behind. In fact, I was allowed to
sleep through the night.

     In the morning, I gathered up my M1, equipment, and bedroll
and went down to the breakfast chow line. I shook hands and wished
good luck to everyone I met. The jeep took me to Regimental Rear,
where my processing began. That same day a clerk told me I might
have to stay in Korea for a few days to testify at the general court-
martial of an I Company soldier accused of desertion. Nothing could
discourage me, just knowing I would never again go up to the front
lines was enough to keep me happy. In the evening I received word
that I Company was under heavy attack. A clerk told me to get ready
to return to my unit. A senior NCO told the joker to lay off. The
next morning I learned that the deserter [Cpl. Jefferson D. Brown,
Jr.] had been given eighty years at hard labor and a DD [dishonorable
discharge]. I knew the guy well, and had for a long time. This was
an example of a tough guy who turned out to be a coward in combat. *

     At Inch'on I was surprised to run into a good buddy, George
Blossingham, who was also rotating home. With five Purple Hearts,

---

* Brown had deserted in March after Chipyong-ni. His term was eventually reduced to twenty-
five years.

I thought he'd have left L Company, 5th Cav, long before. I'd known George in Camp Carson, Colorado, before the battalion left for Korea. While we waited at Inch'on for transportation, we reminisced about that time. I clearly remembered going in to see the company CO, Captain Allen, and asking him to put me back on the list of men due to be shipped to Korea. Somehow, my name had been removed. Later, Captain Allen told me what he was thinking at that moment: "Poor bastard, doesn't know what he's volunteering for. He sees adventure and challenge where there is nothing but dirt, shit, horror, fear, hunger, mangled bodies, and death." Captain Allen was proven correct.

Sgt. F/C LEONARD KORGIE
Headquarters Company/24th Division
The embarkation base at Inch'on was set up to handle hundreds and hundreds of men. The first thing we did was give up our weapons. Damn, was that an experience! No one wanted to part with his, especially the guys who had just arrived right off the front lines. When you sleep a whole year with your "honey," whether it's a rifle or carbine, you don't let her go easily. It was our security blanket. I felt like they had taken my right arm.

That night, "Bed Check Charlie," a North Korean biplane which dropped mortar rounds out of the cockpit, flew over. The rear-echelon types ran around. Some guy yelled to us, "Out of your bunks. We're being bombed!" Most of us didn't budge. The hell with Charlie.

The next morning we sailed for Sasebo, Japan. For the first time since I arrived in Korea, which was right after Taejon, I felt a sense of relief. It was finally over.

Pfc. PAUL MARTIN
Reconnaissance Company/1st Marine Division
Two LSTs [landing ship tanks] brought the replacement draft in. As the new men marched ashore, a voice on the loudspeaker announced, "The Tenth Rotation Draft dedicates this song to the

Fourteenth Replacement Draft."* Music floated over the beach: "My heart bleeds for you, cries for you. Please come back to me."

We climbed aboard the ship. Before the ramp was raised, a guy nearby said, "Take your last look at Korea, guys." I looked behind me and saw an old Korean man leading a small boy by the hand down a hill. The ramp clanged shut. Once we were underway, I went topside. It began to rain. In the distance I could see the blurred outline of snow-capped mountains. For some reason I flashed back and remembered vividly the last LST I had been on. It had been mid-September, the year before, and Recon Company was going ashore at Inch'on.

Sgt. F/C LEONARD KORGIE
Headquarters Company/24th Division
We received the royal treatment in Sasebo. What a surprise. Everyone there was considerate. We slept in clean bunks and enjoyed a night of uninterrupted sleep. In the morning we were awakened by music piped over the PA. No one moved or made a move to go to breakfast.

Later in the morning, we assembled and were ordered to strip off all our clothing, including boots, and to leave it where it lay. We put our personal belongings into a paper bag. Then guys went around and in a nice way took away all the Russian and Chinese weapons men were bringing home as souvenirs. I learned later Navy and rear-area Army types picked these weapons up, and because they were processed differently, these men were able to bring them home. "Look at this Russian pistol, sweetheart. Took it off a dead gook." Shit!

We then were issued new clothes. I didn't know my size; I had lost so much weight, and my feet were flatter. I have to credit the Army though, they did a good job. We gave a clerk our names and serial numbers, and he issued us summer khakis complete with decorations and ribbons. In nearly every case they were right on the button.

---

*The 14th Replacement Draft, 2,756 Marine officers and men, came ashore on 7 November. Within hours, 2,066 officers and men making up the 10th Rotation Draft were detached from the 1st Marine Division.

The government owed me six months' pay, which I went and collected. Then I went and took a long, hot shower and got my hair cut. God, I began to feel human again.

We were not kept in Japan long. Some of the guys who'd been stationed in Sasebo before the war knew where the girls were. After chow, the Army moved everyone aboard a ship. I was finally going home.

2d Lt. EDMUND KREKORIAN
C Battery/3d AAA AW Battalion (SP)/3d Division

Most of us had left Korea with only well-worn fatigues, combat boots, and a few other items of clothing. We had no dress uniforms, shoes, caps, etc. In Sasebo we went wild. I bought two tailor-fitted dress uniforms and all the associated equipment. The greatest luxury was a dozen sets of white underwear. All we had to do now was to wait for the ship to take us home. The serenity, the lack of danger, the boredom was almost maddening. Some of my friends went to town every night, including the night before we were to leave. I had taken up with several officers who, like me, had been newlyweds when torn from their brides and shipped to Korea. We were a rather staid group of twenty-three- and twenty-four-year-old lieutenants. We spent our two evenings at the Sasebo Officers' Club stuffing ourselves with steak, fried chicken, and shrimp as we relived the war and played "Can you top this?"

At last our ship was ready. I had been anticipating a troopship like the one in WW2 which carried me, as an enlisted Marine, to and from the South Pacific. Then, our bunks were stacked six deep in the hold of the ship. There was so little space between bunks that one could hardly turn in his bunk without disturbing the man above and below. Meals were twice a day and abominable; at midday we were given an apple. I was also very seasick going and coming. I hated ships. When I boarded the ship at Sasebo, I was delightfully surprised by the accommodations. I was assigned to a room with four double-decker bunks and an adjoining latrine. There were even portholes which could be opened for ventilation. The greatest luxury of all, however, was the meals. There were three of them each day, served family-style on tables with clean white tablecloths, china, and silver. After nine months of C rations, K rations, reduced rations, or no rations, it was like *Alice in Wonderland*. The meals were the great events of the day. We lived from meal to meal.

If there were any positive aspeects of being confined aboard ship for three weeks after nine months in a combat area, it was the almost unlimited opportunity to ventilate one's experiences with one's peers. It was a sort of forced emotional catharsis. It was forced in the sense that there was nothing else to do on board ship, and the war was the only subject we could discuss intelligently. I was with officers my own age whose experiences in war paralleled mine. Some had endured situations which made my tour seem like a picnic. By the time we reached the United States after three weeks at sea, most of us had been drained of any meaningful hangups.

Some of the stories I heard were very funny. One involved me. We were in our bunks one night; all the lights were out except for the red emergency ones. A lieutenant in the engineers was relating an incident in which he was required to use his engineer platoon as infantry. He admitted he knew very little about infantry tactics, and his platoon knew less. When briefed for the attack, he was told he would be given close support by a self-propelled automatic-weapons platoon: half-tracks with four .50-cal machine guns and M24 tanks with twin 40-mm cannons. Although I had been almost asleep at the beginning of the narrative, I came to full alert at the mention of self-propelled automatic weapons. My platoon had been made up of these awesome weapons.

The lieutenant continued: As his platoon jumped off in the attack, the close-support fire began. He and his men were shocked at the large volume of fire snapping five to ten feet over their heads and impacting only several hundred yards in front of the lead elements. They were convinced the rounds would soon drop into them, cutting them to pieces. He tried to radio a plea for the fire to be lifted, but the radio failed. "What did you do?" asked a voice in the dark. "What do you think we did? We hugged the ground and prayed that dumb-assed ack-ack lieutenant knew what he was doing."

I chuckled, for I recognized the operation as one my platoon had supported. Our weapons were high-velocity, flat-trajectory, direct-fire weapons. The entire platoon could collectively fire up to 8,000 rounds of .50-cal, and 800 rounds of 40-mm, per minute. It was a scary support, even for experienced troops. I could well imagine the response of uninitiated troops.

I felt obliged to defend my platoon and myself. "Come on," I said. "You were supposed to be given close-support fire, and that's exactly what you got. It would have been a lot closer, except for a message that advised I was supporting green troops and not to panic them with any of my fancy fire."

Sgt. F/C LEONARD KORGIE
Headquarters Company/24th Division

There was an enormous amount of gambling that took place on the ship. Everyone had just been paid, and the dough was burning holes in guys' pockets. The men on my deck went at it day and night. I saw one pot for $12,000. Some guys lost everything; others cleaned up. Mess stewards bringing us coffee and sandwiches were given ten-dollar tips. You know, they brought us food as often as possible. I ate and slept my way across the Pacific.

Sgt. F/C FRANK ALMY
E Company/7th Cavalry

The weather during the voyage home was beautiful. Although I was on my way to the States, I was still as nervous as a cat on a tin roof. I knew how a man on death row must feel when he gets a reprieve. That's the way I felt. It took some getting used to, to sleep through the night, to not always be on the alert, to not worry about a gook slipping up on me while I was asleep. I also began to feel a great loss. Sure, I was out of it, but what about all my friends who were still fighting? I had been with the Cav for almost a year, and only once had the enemy beat us in a firefight and run us off a hill. I was company proud and platoon happy.

The ship made a stop in Alaska, but because of a measles epidemic no one was allowed ashore. At least I could say I saw Alaska. Next stop, Seattle.

I loved the Army, but being infantry, well, I wasn't sure what the future held. I decided, therefore, that when the time came, I'd get out of the military.

We slipped down the west coast of Canada and eventually docked in Seattle. Boy, what beautiful country. All I could think about, though, was getting home to the wife I had married two days before shipping out to Korea.

2d Lt. EDMUND KREKORIAN
C Battery/3d AAA AW Battalion (SP)/3d Division
Our ship entered the Straits of Seattle. We were the first ship carrying Korean War returnees into Seattle. Everyone was up on deck soaking up the sight of our beautiful country. Some of us had at times despaired of ever seeing it again. An uncontrolled wave of grief and depression came over me. I could no longer repress the memories of the men I'd known who had been killed. I felt overwhelming guilt that I had survived. While I wallowed in remorse and sorrow, the ship was jumped by a flight of Marine Corsairs. They made a series of dry gunnery runs, flying so close we saw the pilots waving and saluting. They put on a superb airshow escorting us into the harbor. They flew off doing a series of victory rolls. I thought, What a beautiful gesture of appreciation. God bless the Marine Corps.

Once we were in the harbor, fireboats arrived spraying fountains of water. Dozens of private motorboats and sailboats blowing horns and whistles and ringing bells escorted us to the pier. We were overwhelmed, as no one had anticipated any kind of a reception, especially one like this. We felt honored, appreciated, and recognized for our efforts.

There were hundreds of people on the pier. Flags, division crests, and pennants hung everywhere. A large sign read, "Welcome Home, Defenders of Freedom." Miss Seattle with a bouquet of flowers met the ship, and a band played the National Anthem. It was too much for me. The tears slipped over my cheeks. I wiped at my eyes as though clearing an irritation. I ended up laughing. There were dozens of others wiping away eye irritations.

Pfc. JACK WRIGHT*
G/5

Just before we arrived at the pier in Oakland, we were told if our parents were at dockside we could go with them, but that we had to return to the base at Treasure Island by 6:00 P.M.

When we tied up, there was a band playing and a platform of Movietone cameras cranking away. The first ashore was the highest-ranking officer in our rotation draft, the next man was the most decorated Marine. About that time I spotted my mom, stepdad, and girlfriend down on the dock. The ship's PA announced that Marines with two or more Purple Hearts could leave and not wait for their own group to disembark. I jumped on the gangplank, and my mom started running for me. We met at the foot of the gangplank. It was a good thing the Marine sentry got out of our way. I got one arm around my mom and the other around my girl, and shook hands with my dad. I looked about fifteen years old, and my uniform was too big for me. The newsreel people must have thought I looked cute. Someone stuck a microphone in front of me. I said, "Jesus *bleep bleep*. Christ, it's good to be home. Holy *bleep*, this *bleep bleep* country looks *bleep* great." My language wasn't the type you spoke around your mom, but I forgot where I was.

My dad asked me, "What's the first thing you'd like to do now you're home?" That stumped me. I couldn't think of a thing, so we just got in the car and drove all over Oakland and San Francisco. When we eventually got up to the gate at Treasure Island, who should I see but my BAR buddy, Private Rose, a guy that had been hit during the battle for Seoul. I stuck my head out the window, "Rosie, you *bleep bleep*! What the *bleep* you doing here?" He looked. "Wright!" Next thing I knew, we were hugging and slapping each other. Traffic backed all the way up to the bridge before I said good-bye to him.

We stayed at Treasure Island for about four days. Everyone was forced to stand in long lines in a big gym. We had physical examinations and were given shots. At one table we got a blood test; at another, a urine test; at another, we were asked to do something in a

---

*A veteran of the Marine brigade, Inch'on, the battle for Seoul, and the Chosin Reservoir, Wright was one of the first Marines to rotate home.

box. About every twentieth man was pulled out of line and told to go see the talking doctor. During World War II, we were told, men returning home refused to talk about their experiences. This caused them mental problems. When we got home we should not be afraid to talk. If someone asked us what had happened overseas, we should go ahead and tell him.

[The novelty soon wore off, and after the first ships docked, the ones that followed were welcomed routinely. It wasn't long before ships arriving from Korea were treated as business as usual.]

Pfc. FLOYD BAXTER
Weapons Company/1/1

As the troopship passed beneath the Golden Gate Bridge I really didn't know what to expect. Sitting in a freezing cold foxhole at a place called Mago-ri I had just turned nineteen.

When the ship nosed into the pier, I looked over the side and asked myself, Where are all the people? I thought there'd be bands and confetti like at the end of World War II. I was in for a rude awakening. On the dock there were a few relatives of the guys who lived in or around San Francisco, and the usual Red Cross workers with hard donuts and cold coffee. That was it. Believe it or not, most people I talked to the next day or so wondered where I'd been.

That feeling passed. I was just so glad to be back home in the States. I called my mother. We could only talk briefly; I had to hang up, my emotions just took over. The many letters I received from her in Korea were nothing to actually hearing her voice again.

On the train from San Francisco to San Diego I thought, I survived, I'm alive. What more could I want?

Sgt. F/C FRANK ALMY
E Company/7th Cavalry

All the guys were given a choice of how they could get home—they could fly, take a bus, or ride a train. I wanted to see some of the country I'd spent a year fighting for and be comfortable doing so. I therefore chose the train.

It wasn't a troop train, but there were a lot of Air Force MPs riding it. Right off, one of them jumped me for having my collar unbuttoned and my tie loose. I felt like throwing the SOB off the train but, instead, just removed the shirt and tie and sat around in a T-shirt, sort of civilian-like. I met some very nice people interested in the war, and I talked a great deal.

In Chicago I had to change trains. With five hours to kill before I left for Hopkinsville, Kentucky, my buddy and I found a bar. The owner, who was the bartender, was having a birthday party, and the place was packed with the guy's friends. When we discovered this, we started to leave. They would have none of it, made us stay, told us our money wasn't any good there. We had all we could eat and drink on the house. Just like World War II.

When I finally got home to Hopkinsville, it was nothing new. If I hadn't just come from it, I would never have known there was a war going on in Korea.

Pfc. FLOYD BAXTER
Weapons Company/1/1

It was 12:30 A.M. when the train pulled into T&P Station on Market Street in Shreveport. I had left from the same station more than a year before. I saw my mom first. My brother Charles, eighteen months younger, and his girlfriend, Pat, were also there. He shook my hand and said he was glad I was home; then he and Pat left, said they had some place else to go. I guess it dawned on me then that things would never be the same again.

One of the first things I did at home was sit in a tub of hot soapy water; did it for hours. The dirt and grime of Korea was still in my pores and embedded under my fingernails. I had to soak it away.

Mother and I talked then for a while about what had happened while I'd been away. My mind drifted back to my buddies still in Korea, and I wondered what they were doing at that moment. I was safe at home and they were still there. I broke down and cried. My mother told me to let it out, that she understood. I answered, "No! You, or anyone else who was not there, can never understand what it was like."

I didn't sleep much that first night. I couldn't stop thinking about my buddies. I loved them so.

Pfc. LEONARD KORGIE
Headquarters Company/25th Division

I got off the train in North Platte, Nebraska, in the middle of the night, hours before my parents expected me. Except for the usual railroad people moving around, the depot was deserted. I walked up and down the platform, trying to adjust to my new hometown. (The year before, my parents had moved to North Platte from Columbus, Nebraska.) I found a taxi and drove to my family's new home. It was beautiful. My dad had opened a grocery market, self-service, and our home was next to it.

My parents were overjoyed to see me. They kept telling me how good I looked. Our cocker spaniel, Susie, would raise holy hell whenever a stranger knocked on the door. She hadn't seen me in three years, but she didn't let out a peep. She just go so excited and ran around the house knocking things over. My old fishing buddy, she hadn't forgotten me. For an hour or so, Susie jumped in and out of my lap and licked my face. She wouldn't let me out of her sight. Damn! She hadn't forgotten me.

2d Lt. EDMUND KREKORIAN
C Battery/3d AAA AW Battalion (SP)/3d Division

I made my flight in Seattle—a Boeing Stratocruiser—with ten minutes to spare. As I boarded, I recognized some officers and NCOs from the ship. There was an abundance of vacant seats; we had no difficulty sitting together. We were fatigued from the exciting anticipation of actually being on the last leg home. Most of us fell quickly asleep. The throb of the engines was soporific; few could resist. I'm sure we all gained a sense of comfort and security from being together. We were special. We had met "evil" and triumphed—or at least, survived.

In Chicago all my comrades from the ship departed. The vacant seats began to fill with civilians. They looked, acted, and talked strange. I felt I had very little in common with these people whose primary conversation was limited to baseball and the movies. They seemed to know very little about the war and cared less. Several attempted to start conversations with me. Small talk was never a strong suit with me. I allowed these attempts to degenerate into silence. These people were boring; I missed my comrades. I was no longer secure or comfortable. I fell asleep trying to imagine what my wife looked like.

The bump of the plane as it touched down in Atlanta awakened me. By the time it was parked at the terminal and the door had opened, I was wide awake with my heart rate in the danger zone. Patricia saw me about the same time I saw her; then she was in my arms. I held her close and closed my eyes. The misery of Korea and our separation was behind us. It was time to continue with our lives, together.

Pfc. JACK WRIGHT
G/5

I was so keyed up from Korea, I was restless as hell. When I got home on thirty-day leave I found the folks in Hanford [California] getting ready to give me the "conquering hero" welcome. When I was in Korea, down on the Perimeter, or at Inch'on, or up at the Chosin, the local paper would run stories about me—local boy makes good, and all that. Well, I wasn't really interested in a parade or any fuss made over me. I didn't want to be put in front of a lot of people and showed off like some kind of freak. I politely let my folks know, and they passed the word on.

At first I prowled the streets at night, couldn't sleep. I did have some dates, but as far as girls were concerned I was very inexperienced. One day I went up to my high school to see some old buddies. The principal greeted me and said I was welcome to go to all the dances and games. I thought that was pretty nice of him. Then I visited my old English teacher and his class. I brought with me a dud hand grenade I had from Korea—no powder and no detonator. The teacher, a World War II infantryman, asked if I would tell the class about it. I explained its explosive radius, and how it could really do a job on you. "One thing about a grenade you should know," I explained, "never try to run from it. Always pick it up and throw it back. That way, you might live." I glanced over at the teacher and I swear he knew what I was going to do next. I pulled the pin. "See, nothing happens as long as I hold down the spoon." I began to reseat the pin and—"oops!"—I dropped the grenade. It rolled down one of the aisles. A kid sitting near an open window went through it headfirst. It took the rest of the kids about a second to clear the room. Later in the day, the school counselor told me I was welcome back any time, but I should leave my souvenirs at home.

The girls were very nice. There was one special girl. She was the only one that seemed to have grown up a bit and really knew how I felt. Maybe later we would have ended up getting married, but at the time I didn't understand all the changes that had come over me.

Before Korea I had meticulously planned out my future and saved every dime I made. When I came back, life was too short. I lived life to the hilt and spent every penny I'd saved. Then I borrowed more from my parents. My dad had just bought a new Studebaker. At the end of my leave it was a pile of junk. He never said a word. He would see me sitting, and he'd walk up and drop the keys in my lap. He was one hell of a good man, my stepdad.

When I'd gone through my back pay, like I said, I went through my savings. My mom went to the bank with me. I took the pen and began to fill out the withdrawal slip. My hand began to shake. I took a deep breath and tried to write again. I began to shake again. I looked up, and the cashier and everyone in the bank was watching me. I couldn't stop trembling. My mom signed the slip and got the money for me.

After my thirty days were up, I reported to Barstow. When I got back with other Marines I settled down and began to feel comfortable around people again.

Pfc. FLOYD BAXTER
Weapons Company/1/1

Time passed. I saw several of my high-school friends. Some asked what I'd been doing since graduation and, as they hadn't seen me around, where I'd been. I gave them a brief summary and left it at that. Somehow, I felt I had nothing in common anymore with these guys; I couldn't relate to them. We were the same age, but they seemed younger than me.

One of my relatives asked me how many Chinese and North Koreans I'd killed. How do you answer that question? I mumbled, "I didn't keep count."

At night I woke up and wondered whether I was really home. Many a night I got up and walked around the house; I'd jump up and down to make sure I wasn't dreaming.

Pfc. HERBERT LUSTER *
A/5

While taking some liberty at the Oak Knoll Navy Hospital [in Oakland], I met a lot of men who apologized for not being able to go to war. Some had been in accidents, some had been in the pen, everyone had a good reason why he couldn't fight. Some of them really wanted my forgiveness, and I always made them feel as good as possible. Once, while I was waiting for a local bus, a guy came out of a bar; and when I wouldn't go back in with him so he could buy me a drink, he talked for ten minutes straight about why he wasn't in the military. A lot of men told me they had fought in the "Big War." People asked my opinion about Truman firing MacArthur. I had to find an opinion, even though I'd only been a private and knew little about the political infighting going on while I was fighting the war. I recalled I had taken an oath to serve the United States and to obey the orders of my commander. Since Mac had once taken the same pledge, I was forced to agree with the president, even though I was all for going right to Moscow to bring the war to an end once and for all.

---

* A veteran of the 1st Provisional Marine Brigade, Luster had beeen severely wounded on the slopes of Obong-ni Ridge the morning of 17 August 1950. His right arm was amputated the next day.

2nd Lt. EDMUND KREKORIAN
C Battery/3d AAA AW Battalion (SP)/3d

While I was in Korea, Patricia taught art in an Atlanta high school. Her term had another five days to go. On each of these days I drove her to school about 8:30 A.M. Until 4:30 P.M., when I picked her up, I was on my own. There was little to do. I drifted around Atlanta noting how different it looked from Seoul or P'yongyang. I usually made one or two trips to Fort McPherson [3d Army Hq] just to be in a military environment. I was incredibly bored; my mind drifted back to Korea. At times I recognized a crazy longing to return to the front. Fortunately, I was always able to suppress those pathological thoughts.

When Patricia's term finally ended, we slipped away to New Hampshire and the White Mountains. I love these mountains; I've climbed them since I was fourteen. They are for me, beautiful, unchanging, and permanent. They reaffirmed the enduring nature of certain basic values. On them I felt close to God, and I loved sharing them with Patricia. We had spent part of our honeymoon backpacking and hibernating in the Randolph Mountain Club huts. In fact, this activity on our honeymoon may have saved my life by delaying by several weeks my arrival in Korea. In early July 1950, the Korean War was going very badly for the U.S. forces. Lieutenants were desperately needed. While Patricia and I were camped at timberline on Mount Adams, the Army was trying to notify me that I was on orders to depart immediately for Korea. The orders were rescinded when I could not be located. There were many lieutenants on those orders, including the West Point class of 1950. A frightful number were killed in action—as I might have been, had I gone at that time.

During our last few days in New Hampshire, we stayed at an old hunting lodge which belonged to some dear friends. They had recently been given two bear cubs to look after by the game warden. Someone had shot the mother bear out of season. This seemed like murder to me. Patricia and I fell in love with the cubs; they adopted us. We fed them their bottles of milk, brought them ice-cream cones, and played with them. I experienced an inner glow as we cared for these orphaned, helpless animals. Ironically, this quality was shortly to conflict violently with qualities I had acquired in the war.

In New Hampshire, Patricia presented me with a .22-cal Colt Woodsman automatic pistol. She had bought it for me several months

after I had been in Korea. I had written that some of my friends had
their own side arms; a few even had fast-draw holsters. She decided
to send me a pistol for added protection. The post office refused to
accept the pistol for mailing. She put the pistol up to give me after
my return. In my mind guns were for killing. I quickly bought some
ammunition, loaded the pistol, and went out looking for something
to kill. A harmless porcupine moved clumsily through the foliage. I
killed it with three quick shots. Patricia was horrified, not only by
the senseless killing of the porcupine, but by the depersonalized manner in which I had shot it. I was suddenly frightened myself, for I
realized I felt no remorse or other emotion. I felt guilt at feeling no
guilt. I defended my act, "For Christ's sake, what in the hell did you
think I was doing for the last nine months?"

This marked the beginning of a crisis in our short marriage. I
insisted on sleeping with the pistol in bed. She balked. That was a
stupid and dangerous practice. Besides, there were no Chinese Communists or North Koreans in Jefferson Highlands, New Hampshire.
I tried to justify an overwhelming anxiety I was experiencing that
could only be satiated by the physical presence of a weapon.

When the Chinese Communists entered the Korean War in late
1950, it was their practice at night to slip into an area where UN
troops were sleeping. They quietly killed any guards, then proceeded
to kill as many troops as they could before being driven off. We were
warned repeatedly of this practice and were advised to sleep with
weapons in our sleeping bags. To me and some of my friends this
advice seemed a bit extreme. The last thing any of us young lieutenants wanted was to go home with a self-inflicted wound, particularly
if the wound might impact on our masculinity. We decided we would
place our .45s and holsters alongside our sleeping bags. We were
reasonably confident we could deal with any enemy from that configuration.

I tried to explain all this to Patricia. All I succeeded in doing
was convincing her that she had a problem on her hands. We reached
a sort of loony compromise. The pistol could stay under my pillow,
provided there was no round in the chamber and the clip was not
fully seated. This practice continued for several months. Each morning I admitted to myself that I was engaging in a stupid, silly, and
dangerous practice. If I had any willpower, I would get rid of my

lethal teddy bear. Each night I would reach under my pillow to feel the reassuring bulk of the pistol. One night an incident took place which eventually ended the problem. I dreamed I was jumped by three North Korean soldiers; though outnumbered, I fought valiantly. I somehow hit Patricia on the shoulder. We both woke up immediately. When I saw what had happened, I started laughing. She saw nothing at all funny and proceeeded to tell me she had had it with this war veteran stuff. I noticed the pistol under the pillow. I thought, My God, what if I had grabbed it and started shooting? The pistol went to the bed stand, then to the closet. Eventually, it was disarticulated and hidden in various parts of the house.

Fusilier PETER FARRAR
1st Battalion/Royal Fusiliers
One strange paradox of the Korean War was that many soldiers went down with malaria for the first time when they arrived home. I met several in the Hospital for Tropical Diseases at St. Pancras, in London. Like me, they had been told that taking Paludrine tablets regularly would prevent malaria. Consequently, when several weeks—or even months—after leaving the Army they felt ill and feverish, they thought it was influenza and went to bed. Some were slow to notice they had a very high temperature every forty-eight hours. I was initially given penicillin by a puzzled doctor, whom I assured I wasn't carrying any tropical diseases I'd picked up in Korea. On the sixth day, feeling better, I shaved but cut myself. My sister, a medical student, took a slide sample of my blood and had it examined by a specialist. He declared a malaria parasite could be seen.

At the Hospital for Tropical Diseases, I had the good fortune to have the mystery explained by Sir Neil Fairley, an Australian who was the world's leading authority on malaria. He told me I had benign tertian malaria. Paludrine, unless taken with unfailing regularity, would not stop parasites from finding a safe "dug-out" in the liver or spleen. In such cases, the Paludrine simply suppressed the onset of malaria for as long as it was taken and for a time afterward. Luckily, there was a new drug [Primaquine] which quickly cured my malaria. I informed the Army authorities about my experience, who said the matter would be passed on to the Medical Directorate. If subsequent drafts returning from Korea were warned of the dangers, then my initiative was the most useful thing I ever did as a soldier.

Pfc. HERBERT LUSTER
A/5

With my first leave from hospital, I decided I'd visit the East. After I got to Little Rock, I hitchhiked all over with only a ditty bag, a set of greens, and a few dollars in my pocket.

One night, I found myself in a car with a businessman who was so interested in our talk, he did not know he was speeding until a trooper pulled him over. The man got very nervous. Once the patrolman saw my uniform he stopped talking to the driver and looked me over. He recognized immediately my Purple Heart ribbon. The trooper then thanked the driver for giving me a ride and warned him to watch his speeding.

In New York City I paid a visit to a VA hospital. A few old vets asked me questions about the new war and seemed to appreciate my answers. The old-timers looked at me with searching and dreamy eyes. I wondered what they were thinking about or, more important, what they were trying not to think about.

A few days later I was in Washington, D.C. As it was Sunday evening I went to services at a local Baptist church. Afterward, some kids who were supposed to be my age took me to play miniature golf. I made four holes in one. The boys had other things on their minds and did not care to play another round. They pointed me toward 8th and I Streets and the Marine barracks where I was staying. There, a quick inventory told me I did not have to return home yet; I still had twenty bucks in my pocket. I figured I'd go south.

When I was leaving Washington, the car that picked me up got caught near one of the Potomac River bridges in bumper-to-bumper traffic. All of a sudden I heard someone outside calling my name. I looked out the window and saw Corporal Dale Ellis hopping up and down on his one good leg. Dale had been my fire team leader on Obong-ni Ridge. The traffic began to move, so I could do no more than smile and wave at him. My driver could not believe the coincidence that that one-legged civilian had been the very man who shot the gook who had shot me. I had a hard time believing it myself, but it really had been Ellis.

I traveled both day and night. The gas stations where the truckers stopped were ideal locations for getting rides. Some drivers were worried about an inspector seeing a rider in the cab, and I was often asked to duck down. The drivers of these big rigs seemed to be well informed about the Korean War. Some guys really raged about Truman's handling of the war but always listened to me; I was often able to calm some of these men down.

In Georgia one day, a farmer picked me up after dark and invited me home. The farm family was very warm toward me, and that night I slept in the room of their son, who was in the Army. I thought of all the dead soldiers I'd seen in Korea and wondered if the boy in whose bed I slept would someday be killed. In the morning I ate a hearty breakfast and polished off everything put in front of me. I was hungry, as milk in gas-station stores had been my main diet for several days. Still, even that was better than combat.

I found colored folks more friendly than in the big cities up North, but they seldom gave me rides. When they did, I discovered they knew very little about the war or anyone fighting it.

One rainy afternoon a trucker offered me his shotgun seat. I accepted, and we headed for Miami Beach. When we reached West Palm Beach, the rain was so heavy the driver could not see out his big windshield. He pulled over, and we both took a cat nap. We woke to a quiet, steady rain. The radio warned of more. At the next gas-station stop I decided to change directions and return to California.

I took a bus to Los Angeles. When I arrived, I had less than five bucks. Somewhere around Hollywood and Vine a soldier stopped me to ask a question, only to learn I knew less about the city than he did. A middle-aged woman asked us if we were interested in seeing a radio quiz show, "Double or Nothing." She handed us two tickets. A line had already formed outside the door when we got to the studio. Because we were both in uniform, the soldier and I were immediately shown to the head of the line. Inside, once everyone was seated, Walter O'Keefe, the MC, came out and began looking for contestants from the audience. I was surprised to find everyone pointing to me. I was quite elated to be there; now imagine my feelings when I was chosen as a contestant. Mr. O'Keefe told me not to worry, I couldn't lose. On the air I said my favorite Campbell's soup—the sponsor—was Chicken Noodle, and when asked my pet peeve answered, "People who complain, but do nothing about their problems." Since I was unmarried, I was asked what I was looking for in a girl. I had never thought about it that way before but said, "I'm looking for a girl who is looking for me." The audience roared. The jackpot question was something I knew nothing about. After the show, the program gave me four new ten-dollar bills. I was rich.

It was the holiday season, and I heard the news from Korea, which was bad. My old unit [A/5] had been trapped in the snow around some reservoir in North Korea. I figured when I got back to the naval hospital in Oakland I'd find out what was going on.

I arrived in Oakland one afternoon a little late for evening chow, but someone fixed me up with a snack. When I got back to my old amputation ward, 42 A, I was surprised to find it flooded with new patients flown in from hospitals in Japan. Since I could walk, I was told to go to another ward. This one was quiet and nearly empty. What got my attention was the nurse on duty; she was beautiful. I was so overwhelmed by her looks and charm, I could not carry on a conversation with her. She finally gave up on me. The next morning when I woke up, I was relieved to find a more acceptable-looking nurse on duty. It was real nice to see an American girl, but a guy could lose his senses around too much beauty and charm. I had never been overwhelmed like that before, and would not be again until the following September, when I first laid eyes on the woman who eventually became my wife.

2d Lt. FRANK MUETZEL *
A/5

I can't say enough good things about the treatment the Navy gave me at Oakland. The Navy personnel—medical officers, nurses, and enlisted men—simply couldn't do enough for me and the other guys

---

* A veteran of the Marine battles around the Pusan Perimeter, Muetzel was severely wounded the day following the Inch'on landings. When gangrene set in two weeks later, his right leg was amputated.

like me. They bent the rules, entertained and sympathized with us, wined and dined us. I made an ass of myself a million times, and no one took offense. While other patients left for hospitals closer to home, I remained there for nine months as the only officer amputee.

The first full day I was a patient in the hospital, three nurses who lived off base threw me a welcome-home party. They smuggled me out of the hospital, and when I arrived at the apartment I found the entire Sick Officers' Quarters waiting for me. Mike Shinka * was there pouring drinks into the hole in his face where his mouth had been by bending backward over the sink. John Tobin † was in a body cast, and Ed Emmelman ‡ had a concave depression in his skull where he'd been shot. It was a weird group, but we'd all served with the brigade and I was very glad to see them. The key to that evening's hilarity was the fact we were all extremely happy and slightly amazed to still be alive. Later in the evening, when it became apparent I couldn't make it back to the base, the nurses put me up on their sofa.

During the time I was on the ward, there was never a cross word or an argument. We didn't take much guff from the staff, but we did it with a laugh and they never complained, even though they had good cause. The pressure was off; we'd made it back alive. There would be no more death or destruction, no more friends killed in front of us, no more guilt for the death of others. During the day the ward was a noisy place. The nights were quiet as the ghosts in our memories walked the halls. In the darkness there were nightmares, insomnia, and just plain hurt.

We did our own thing together and ignored the outside world. We often made a shambles of the officers' club, and the Navy not only let us, they joined in the fun. Many months later, after I left, with the war dragging on, I heard the Navy put the club off limits to patients — but it was sure fun while it lasted. One of the nurses gave

---

* A platoon leader in D/5, Second Lieutenant Shinka had had his chin shattered during the attack on the summit of Obong-ni Ridge, 17 August 1950.

† Captain Tobin commanded B/5 until wounded by Communist machine-gun fire below Observation Hill, 17 August 1950.

‡ Second Lieutenant Emmelman was wounded in the head while pointing out targets on Hill 342 to a Marine machine gunner, 8 August 1950.

me a key to the nurses' quarters, and I was in and out of there at all hours of the day and night. The surgical team let me scrub and sit in on an amputation so I could see what had been done to me. The physical therapy department took special pains with me because I desperately wanted to walk well. And they let me off the hook when I absolutely refused to go to occupational therapy classes to learn how to make wallets and tool leather. I really wasn't a very good patient, but I didn't hurt anyone else, and I didn't play games with the female staff. They were just too nice to play that kind of trick on.

But the really good treatment ended at the hospital main gate. Off the base, it was as if there was no war taking place. While very few civilians were consciously rude or offensive, it became quickly evident the man on the street just didn't care. The war wasn't popular, and no one wanted to hear anything about it. Here's an example of what I ran into in the civilian world: To hold down inflation the government had tightened credit regulations. A car loan could not be for more than twenty-four months without special sanction. I went to the main office of the Bank of America to see about a new car. Mine was a straight-stick '49 Ford, which was being financed by B of A. I wore my uniform with ribbons and hobbled in on my crutches. I was kept waiting and no one thought to ask me to sit down. When I finally talked to the loan officer, he told me that as I was obviously going to have to leave the Marine Corps I could not qualify for special treatment. He added, "I see you want to go back to school. You won't need a car there, anyway." I never dealt with B of A again, although I resided in California for eleven more years.

I can't say I was badly treated; it was just that no one seemed to care. We had all arrived at the hospital bursting with our experiences—Pusan Perimeter, Obong-ni Ridge, the Naktong Bulge, Inch'on—but we learned in a hurry to clam up. I guess the American People couldn't stand the thought of two wars so close together. When newcomers arrived in the ward in the same frame of mind we had had, we called them "The Men with the Message"—the message no one wanted to hear.

Even the Marine Corps got into the act. The reserves had been called to active duty, and many administrative types couldn't accept the way we regulars felt about the Corps. I had known Lieutenant General [Graves B.] Erskine, the commanding general in San

Francisco, when he had been CG of the 1st Marine Division at Camp
Pendleton. He had verbally okayed my request to retire from a Marine base, but not a hospital. When the time came for me to leave
the hospital, General Erskine was out of the city. I therefore reported
to a major at Marine headquarters. I was in full uniform and used
my artificial leg, as I could walk well with it. He asked how long I'd
been back in the States. I told him. When I next told him I wanted
to go to the Marine base at San Diego, he exploded—told me he
didn't take instructions from junior officers, and that he was going to
send me to a replacement draft for return to Korea. I should have
accepted the orders. I finally got across to the jerk that General Erskine had approved my request. I was on my way to San Diego in
half an hour.

I was on the staff at MCB, San Diego, for six weeks, and they
treated me right.

My orders to retirement were cut in Washington, D.C., on June
30, 1951, and I received them by mail in California three days later.
The paymaster refused to pay me for the three July days. Now, he
didn't have to go out of his way to do that. It's just an example of
thoughtlessness carried to an extreme. Then I had to walk from one
end of the base to the other and have privates attest that I hadn't
stolen library books, athletic gear, and laundry. The disbursing officer got in his licks; he told me I looked awfully young to retire. I told
him I had enlisted when I was six, and to just pay me and keep his
comments to himself. He took offense at my attitude, but by this
time I was past caring. The crowning blow came when I returned to
the BOQ and received a message that the post housing officer wanted
to know how fast I could vacate my room. I called the assistant base
commander, Brigadier General Reginald "Bull" Ridgely, and told him
what was happening. I had worked for him in the 2d Marine Division, and we liked each other. Everyone backed off in a hurry. I was
told to stay as long as I wanted, and that there would be a retirement
ceremony in my honor the following Friday—which is all I wanted
in the first place.

I now had a little time to digest my feelings at being separated
from the Marine Corps. In a word, I was shattered. I had been a
Marine since 1944, and my only training was as a rifle platoon leader.
The separation from old friends and the life I'd chosen and loved

came as a tremendous blow, made no less so by the fact that I knew it was coming.

I took the review on the parade ground at the Recruit Depot, where I had been stationed in 1945, and again in 1947. I knew that for the recruits who marched by, this was the beginning of a new way of life, and for me, it was the end of one. The dress blue uniform and the drums and bugles never meant more to me than they did on that hot summer's day in 1951. It was one of the bleakest days of my life.

The Navy had earlier taken its best shot at me. I returned to the hospital in Oakland after a party in San Francisco and found the Silver Star medal on my bed with a cover letter which read, "Delivered with appropriate ceremony."* They just didn't, or wouldn't, grasp why anyone was crazy enough in the first place to join the Marines.

A month after retirement, I escorted the body of one of the members of my platoon killed at the Second Naktong to his home in Tulsa for burial. I used him as a token for all of those who did not return alive. Through him I tried to do what I would have liked to do for all of them. I felt I owed it to them, but after the ceremony I couldn't get out of Tulsa quickly enough. I have kept in touch with the family over the years, and each September, on the anniversary of the boy's death, I send a note reminding them I haven't forgotten.

Sgt. F/C LEONARD KORGIE
Headquarters Company/24th Division
The first week of my thirty-day furlough I spent fishing, just Susie and me.

I couldn't get over how luxurious and clean everything was. Living was so easy—Korea had been such a struggle. A great number of people came over to meet me and to talk. I wanted to wallow in all this happiness, but somehow I just couldn't. I began to notice I had a hard time talking to people. I put a shield between myself and my friends. I felt anxious about everything but didn't know why.

---

*The medal was awarded for the action on Obong-ni Ridge the night of 17–18 August 1950.

My family and friends were concerned about Korea, but more important, they were confused about it. They couldn't understand the losing, the winning, the losing, the winning. What were these tremendous casualties all about? What kind of a police action was it that had dead and wounded reported in small-town weekly newspapers? That had local boys dead, or home with missing arms and legs? "What the hell kind of Army have we got over there? We plastered the Krauts and Nips in World War II, and now you guys can't do shit against North Koreans." I kept my mouth shut. They would have to learn about limited conventional warfare themselves. They would have to get the drift without my help. How could I explain it? I didn't understand it, myself.

What really surprised me was how many of my relatives and friends couldn't believe Korea was a "real war," that I had actually been in combat. In fact, some of them were very puzzled by the ribbons I wore on my uniform. A combat infantryman's badge, why? Before the war my folks told neighbors I was stationed in Japan, at the war criminal prison at Sugamo, and playing a lot of baseball. When I got home in 1951, one of my friends remarked, "Lennie, what'd you get the Purple Heart for, get spiked stealing second?" Damn, that hurt. I was introduced once to a Marine who had been at the Chosin Reservoir. We didn't say much to each other. Didn't need to, we both understood.

One evening I went over to a local bar and tied one on. I didn't know why. My sister brought me home. That night when I went home I checked to see where my M1 was. Oh hell, I thought, what do I need a rifle for, the war is over for me.

When I had left my parents' home to join the Army, I had been a mild-mannered, soft-spoken, extremely patient person. I wouldn't have said "shit" if I had had a mouthful. I returned from Korea an aggressive, rough, short-tempered guy, whose language was full of expletives. My dad was the first to notice the difference. One evening, a little before closing, my dad came up to me in the store, where I was helping out. "Leonard, if anyone tries to rob us at gunpoint, don't do anything stupid. Give him the money." I think he felt I wouldn't. I know I wouldn't have. I had developed this streak. One day I got sick, thought it was flu. It was August and I was sweating and shivering. My family got real scared. I was rushed to a hospital, where I learned I had malaria. I was able to return home a few days later. Since I was still in the Army, I had the medical bill sent to my next post, Fort Riley, Kansas. Well, what a mess that was. When I got to Riley I was told to report to some first lieutenant. He lit into my tail like a buzzard, "Why'n hell didn't you come into the post hospital?" I shot back, "I was three hundred miles away from this damn place, flat on my back—what'n hell was I s'pose to do, die?" I looked like I wanted a fight. He looked me over very carefully, calmed me down, and dismissed me. Outside in the hot sun, my combativeness scared the wits out of me. I'd never spoken to any officer like that before. I began to realize I had to watch myself; hell, keep up that way, and I'd be in the stockade before I knew it.

I began to have nightmares. Three occurred again and again and again. I have them to this day.

The first: I'm jumped by the gooks at close range. I can see them busting through the bedroom door. I scream, "Shoot the sonovabitches!" Sometimes I am awake enough to hear the words come out of my mouth. At other times my wife shakes me until I wake up.

The second: This one has to do with securing a defensive perimeter. In July 1950, and in the early days of the Perimeter, the North Koreans were able to go around and come at us from the rear. In my nightmare I'm always making sure the Perimeter is secure. Suddenly, I yell, "There's one over there! Shoot the bastard!"

The third one is strange. At Fort Riley, when I was there in 1952, there was a rumor that combat-experienced sergeants would be sent back to Korea. I don't remember paying too much attention to it. It sure got into my subconscious, though. I dream I'm pleading with an officer: "How the hell can you send me back? I've already been there. Look at all the guys around this camp who haven't gone. Send them. Don't send me back to Korea! Please don't. Please."

Replacement drafts filled the gap left by rotation. During the winter of 1951–52, between 16,000 and 28,000 men were sent out from the United States. In early November the 14th Replacement Draft added 2,756 officers and men to the 1st Marine Division. A month later 2,316 more leathernecks arrived at the front. Plans had also been finalized for the transfer of two new U.S. infantry divisions to Korea. For some the war was over; for others, it was just beginning.

TALKING AND FIGHTING

As the truce talks began at Kaesong, General Ridgway wrote to the chief of the UN delegation, Vice Admiral C. Turner Joy:

> To Communists the use of courtesy on your part is synonymous with concessions and concessions are a sure indication of weakness. I suggest that you govern your utterances accordingly, employing such language and methods as these treacherous Communists cannot fail to understand, and understanding, respect.

Later he was to say, "For Westerners who have never been exposed to Communist negotiating tactics . . . it is virtually impossible to conceive in advance the extent to which truth is perverted and facts distorted. A tax is placed on patience that even Job would have found all but unendurable."

When the talks commenced, the city of Kaesong was in Communist hands. The UN suggestion of a meeting aboard the Danish ship Jutlandia *had been ignored, and the city of Kaesong demanded as a site. Despite the understanding that General Ridgway's letter to Admiral Joy clearly indicates, the UN Command got off on the wrong foot immediately by conceding to the Communists the choice of site.*

Within days it was necessary to suspend the talks. The grounds around the Kaesong meeting place were understood to be "demilitar-

ized." But upon these grounds there suddenly appeared a strong Chinese unit, heavily armed with submachine guns and 60-mm mortars.

Admiral Joy protested at once, and was told that the offending unit was a company of military police. To ask the UN delegation to believe that a unit armed as only assault troops were armed was a company of MPs was not only absurd, it was insulting.

On General Ridgway's orders the talks were immediately halted. Ridgway broadcast the statement that the meetings would resume only after the Communists conformed to the agreements previously made about demilitarization of the truce area.

The Communists held out for five days, then capitulated. But Ridgway was informed that though the English-language broadcast account from P'yongyang had spoken of a Communist request for a return of the UN delegation, the Japanese-language account beamed at Japan had reported a demand.

Ridgway therefore announced that the Communist response had been unsatisfactory, and that he would not authorize resumption of the talks until it was "clarified." This brought a slightly more civil request and a small measure of agreement.

But agreements at Kaesong were few and difficult to achieve. There were repeated incidents—not all of them perpetrated by the Communist side. On 17 August 1951 a Chinese security patrol near the neutral zone was fired upon by South Korean irregular forces. The Communists demanded an apology. Ridgway refused. Five days later the Chinese insisted that a UN liaison officer come at once to verify "an unprovoked attack" on the neutral zone by an American aircraft.

In a drenching rain, USAF Colonel Andrew Kinney and his aides accompanied the Chinese to the site of the supposed attack. There, Kinney found some holes in the ground that appeared to have been made by small buried explosive charges of hand-grenade size, some bits of metal that might (or might not) have once been part of an airplane fuselage, and an empty auxiliary gasoline tank from an air-craft. There was no cratering, no scorching (as there would have been in the case of a napalm attack), and no damage. There was only a story of an attack at night by an aircraft that approached with land-ing lights on and fired rockets at the grounds of the Communist dele-gates.

No UN aircraft had been in the area that night, and the

evidence was equivocal, to say the least. But the Chinese demanded an immediate "confession," to be followed by an apology that would make clear to the world the "guilt" of the United Nations Command. The Chinese and North Koreans were obsessed by apologies.

Their demands were once again refused, and once again the talks were suspended. When they were eventually resumed, General Ridgway refused to allow the UN delegation's return to Kaesong. He insisted that any further truce negotiations be held at Panmunjom—a village in truly neutral territory and closer to the United Nations lines.

The Communist delegation began the talks by demanding that the truce line be set at the 38th Parallel. The UN Command insisted that the lines be established more in keeping with the military realities. This quarrel was to continue through all of 1952 and into 1953. Meanwhile, some of the bloodiest battles of the war were being fought.

General MATTHEW B. RIDGWAY
Commander, United Nations Command

Another area the enemy held dear was an ancient volcanic crater we named the Punchbowl, about twenty-five miles north of Inje, and the same distance from the east coast, near the zone boundary of the U.S. X and ROK I Corps. Its rim was nearly knife-sharp all around the edges, rising abruptly several hundred feet above the crater floor, and thickly wooded on every side. The enemy was solidly entrenched on the rim here and well armed with mortars and artillery. Much blood was to be spilled in the coming months to win control of this area. In the Eighth Army's possession, it would shorten the line, provide better observation, and lessen the chance of strong enemy surprise attacks in that quarter. Once we had seized it, we never gave it up.

[By 6 July 1951, the long battle for possession of the Punchbowl had begun.]

Pfc. JAMES ANDERSON
Heavy Weapons Company (81-mm Mortar)/1/1

On 6 July, at about 0400 hours, we were loaded into trucks and driven out of the Reserve Area. At 0800 the trucks dropped us off where the 11th Marines were emplaced. Then we started walking. We were soft from being on stand-down, but the road was flat and the surface good, so we made fairly decent time. Then the NKPA artillery started shelling us from the high ground, and we were pinned down.

When the barrage lifted, we got up and started to hustle down the road. A couple of minutes later—more incoming. Shells hit the road embankment and tore things up pretty badly, but by some miracle we hadn't yet taken any casualties.

The officers had a conference. The question was to decide whether or not we kept on going. While that was going on, the enemy artillery opened up on us yet again. This time one round hit directly between Sections One and Two. [There were two guns to a section; three sections made up a mortar platoon.] It was a near thing, but still no casualties. So we started moving up as fast as we could, trying to get ourselves out of the area the enemy obviously had well registered.

We veered off to the north, where we saw the results of some earlier barrages by the enemy guns. There were mules and other pack animals lying about, all dead. I hated to see that.

After a few minutes' rest, we were ordered to start up a steep hill. I think it was the side of the crater they called the Punchbowl, but you couldn't be sure. All I do know was that the climb was a killer. The terrain was rough and the weather was *hot*. We stopped about thirty yards below the ridgeline. Then we had to wait for a drink until the Koreans we had with us packed the drinking water up to us. Some of the troops used heat boxes [alcohol and jelly packs] to warm up their rations. I didn't. I was already too hot and thirsty.

We dug in right there below the ridgeline and set up and registered the guns that evening. We had apparently settled into the 2d Battalion's old spot, a place the officers were not really happy about. That night Baker Company sent out a patrol to see if we could move, but they ran into NKPA or Chinese and had a firefight that killed one and wounded two. They didn't know whether or not they had inflicted any casualties on the enemy. We stayed in place.

On 8 July, early in the morning, all of a sudden all hell broke loose. Patrols went out from Able and Baker Companies and guns five and six (mine) started firing missions over the ridgeline.

I don't know what we hit, but we must have hit something the NK cared about, because we immediately started getting counter-battery fire.

There were Marines up closer to the ridge. A Navy corpsman who was with them had been sunbathing on his sack when the counterbattery fire started coming in. One round landed a few yards from him, and he was badly wounded. But he was lucky, even so. If he hadn't been on his belly sunning himself, he would never have survived.

The same round that wounded the sunbather put a piece of shrapnel right into my cheek. It hit me just as I was bending over the sight of Number Six mortar. It was like being punched in the cheek.

As soon as the wounded corpsman had been taken care of and my gun secured, I went to find the remaining medic to see about taking care of my face. He started to lay out his tools: plasma, knife, forceps, and sewing kit. He looked like he was getting ready to take out my appendix. I didn't like the looks of it. So I asked him for the loan of his forceps and a mirror, and pulled the fragment out myself. It didn't hurt because the whole side of my face was numb.

The CO told me to get on down the hill to an aid station, but I kept thinking about that badly wounded corpsman—the sunbather—and then I thought about going all the way down and having to come back up here again in a week or so. So I walked about fifty paces down the hill, stopped, turned, and headed for my bunker.

I couldn't smile for a couple of weeks, but what the hell, there wasn't much to smile about there on the ridge, anyway.

On the ninth it rained. To get even, we fired some missions and drew counterbattery again. One round landed twenty feet from the bunker I shared with a Marine named Barratt. The Chinese fired in two-round salvos. One round would hit, and a split second later, another. We had one man wounded, and Dave Laque's shelter half got shredded.

It poured down rain on the tenth, so hard that Barratt and I had to move. We got a good bunker reinforced with logs and sand-filled ammunition boxes.

Larry Millson's gun, higher up on the slope than mine, fired all day without drawing any counterbattery fire. No one ever knows whether the enemy will hunker down and take what you throw at him, or if he'll get mad as hell and start trying to knock out your guns.

All the time we were up on the ridge, there was fighting going on for the Punchbowl. On the eleventh, at about 0630 hours, the battery commander yelled for Gun Number Six to stand by for a fire mission. I flew out of the rack and tore the camouflage off the gun, but nothing more came through for us until 1130 hours. Then we started firing, and we kept it up intermittently until almost 1800. The lieutenant said we were shooting anything that moved and could be seen by the people at the command post or by the forward observers. The Punchbowl fighting was getting hot.

That night, Able Company's 2d Platoon went out on a patrol in force. When they got back they had lost four KIA and two wounded. When morning came we started to get NK incoming, a lot of it. My good bunker took a round and was totally destroyed. We got two replacements to make up for the four people Able Company lost.

The next night we fired steadily, one round every few minutes, for about three or four hours. I never did know what we were trying to hit. From time to time, the NKs fired back. Able Company had two casualties—the two replacements who had arrived the night before.

On 14 July, our line was supposed to be attacked by "at least five battalions of NKs," so we were out of the rack at 0500 hours, getting the guns ready, and breaking out 81-mm ammo.

Nothing. No attack. To make up for it, battalion sent up a few gallons of ice cream. Then the NKs started shelling our right flank as though they owned all the ammunition in the world. That night Baker Company sent out a patrol that wound up in a mine field. Three KIA, four wounded.

On 15 July it was wet and rainy. No fire missions, only rumors that we were going to be relieved by some troops from 2d Division. Usually, rumors are just that, but sure enough, on the sixteenth we trekked down the mountain again and went into reserve an Hongch'on.

Pfc. LYLE CONAWAY
F/1

We were holding the ridgeline, and two miles to the north was this mountain held by the enemy. They were using it as an observation post for their artillery, which was laying a steady stream of harassing fire on us.

We had an air forward observer with us. He was only a few yards from where I was, and I could hear what he said and what came back over his radio. He called in an air strike, and pretty soon two Corsairs appeared to start making passes at the enemy position.

On the third or fourth pass, one of the Corsairs was hit by small-arms fire and it started trailing black smoke. The pilot was really upset. He kept asking the FO about whose lines he was over. There was no way in the world that pilot was going to get himself captured. The smoke kept getting worse, and the FO started telling the pilot to bail out, that it was okay, he had friendly troops all around him. But the pilot said no, he was going to stick with his airplane and try to get back to his base.

It was like a football game. Some started yelling for the pilot to bail out, and others for him to stay with it. We even started making bets about which it was going to be.

All of a sudden, while he was right above us, his engine just belched out a huge puff of smoke, and engine parts went flying— you could actually see them exploding from the airplane's nose. The pilot yelled, "It's getting damned hot in here. I'm getting out!"

He rolled the Corsair over on its back and dropped out of the cockpit. His parachute opened up almost immediately, and all the troops that were betting on a bailout started cheering.

But the next second, everybody, including the FO, was scrambling for cover as that Corsair—still loaded with napalm and bombs— came diving down on us.

At the last minute it seemed to level out, and it bored into the hillside about a half mile from us.

The pilot landed okay, but he wasn't too popular for having almost landed his Corsair right on top of us.

I have often wondered what the Chinks on that hilltop—those the pilots had left alive—thought about the whole performance.

2d Lt. RALPH HOCKLEY
37th Field Artillery Battalion

The Punchbowl is not far from the 38th Parallel, which is what made it worth all the fighting, I guess.

There's this flat area, almost like a football field, running approximately north and south, with hills and ridges all around it.

The 1st Marines occupied the southern part of the position, but there was plenty left over for others, believe me. Sometimes to hear Marines talk, you would think that the Punchbowl and Heartbreak Ridge—and, for that matter, the whole damned war—was some sort of a purely Marine operation. That just isn't so.

I was forward observer with the 23d Infantry Regiment when we took the lower slopes of the mountains north and east of Heartbreak Ridge. We had to drive the NK and the Chinese out of deep bunkers to do it. And after we had taken the position, you could count on a firefight of some kind every night.

When they pulled us out of the line and moved the 2d Battalion—the one I was FO with—back into reserve, it didn't exactly mean what you would normally expect when you say "reserve." The troops in the so-called rest area got the job of night patrolling. What we did was load into trucks and drive up the east side of the hills surrounding the Punchbowl. Then we would dismount and walk— patrol—through the ravines of the northern perimeter, where the NK were trying to infiltrate back into the area, until we reached the road on the west side of the position. The 38th Infantry was holding the line there.

After we came off reserve, we moved directly into the Punchbowl and actually bivouacked right there with the enemy looking down our throats from the high ground. I don't know what military genius thought of that one.

The company commander took off and left us there to hold the position. I was an artilleryman, not an infantry officer, but we were short of officers and so I decided I had better take charge of some of the outposts. I went the rounds every night to see to it that the sentries were staying awake, and in the process got into some pretty bitter arguments with one of the unit's sergeants. He was taking it pretty damned easy, considering our tactical situation, and I chewed him out for it. I said, "Look, you can't just send the men out without any supervision. If they screw up and fall asleep, or anything like that, the next thing you know, we'll have a patrol of gooks carving us up. I want you out there with your men, and I want enough of them out there on the perimeter so that if some *do* fall asleep, there will still be someone awake if the enemy decides to come at us."

It didn't make me popular, but it may have kept us alive.

The French Battalion was there at the Punchbowl, too. After the position on the floor of the Punchbowl was relieved, I was reassigned as FO with the French. I speak French—that was the reason for the posting—but I imagine some of those infantry noncoms who were shirking their jobs were glad to see me go.

When the push to actually take Heartbreak Ridge came, we were ordered up the steep slopes flanking the enemy positions. During the assault we lost quite a few Frenchmen—about thirty-nine or forty killed or wounded. The fighting was at close range, sometimes hand-to-hand.

The first attack on the ridge got badly bloodied, and we were pulled back to sit on our hill to the east for about ten days. Military doctrine said that we were not supposed to fire artillery on targets we couldn't actually see—that is, keep under observation. And yet the country all around us was mountainous, which made it almost impossible to handle artillery by the book.

The Chinese and the North Koreans were masters at digging in on the backsides of hills—what you call "in defilade"—and in getting their artillery pieces up to the tops of these damned mountains. They'd haul a field piece or a heavy mortar out of its sheltered position, hump it up to the top into firing position, let go a few rounds, and then haul the whole thing back into its hole.

There were NK and Chinese on the next hill from us, and we could actually hear them grunting as they moved their pieces. Sometimes we could even hear the clunk as they dropped mortar rounds into their tubes.

I spent days trying to convince my headquarters that they should allow me to fire at these enemy positions. I could call in fire from 105s, 155s, and 8-inch howitzers, and my sergeant had control of a 4.2-inch mortar outfit—we had all the firepower in the world. But since I couldn't tell my people that I actually could *see* the enemy positions, they wouldn't let me call them in as targets. I was getting very frustrated. Another assault had been launched at Heartbreak Ridge, and the situation had gotten very nasty. There were artillery forward observers with the assault troops—people I knew, friends of mine. The FOs were taking casualties. Artillerymen were being wasted.

One day, after we had been in this crazy situation for about eleven or twelve days, I overheard the battalion commander complaining over the radio to my battalion CO back at the guns. He was very angry, and he was telling my CO, "I want you to tell your FOs to fire. *Mon dieu!* What are they waiting for?"

Instead of saying that we FOs had been begging for permission to fire, he just said meekly, "Yes, Colonel. I'll see what I can do about it." I was furious. But pretty soon we did get permission to fire, and I took full advantage of it. I pulled out my maps with all the targets I had registered over the last week and a half, and really let go on them. I must have had the guns firing for three hours. I plastered the area. We even hit the Chinese we could hear on the next hill—practically right next door.

I heard later that the real reason they let us fire on defiladed targets was that one of the Chinese or NK mortars had laid a few rounds into the rear areas and killed the commander of one of the 23d's heavy weapons companies. His regimental colonel had got on the telephone to the artillery battalion commander and ordered him to "get those bastards." We got them.

Apparently the artillery strikes we called in loosened things up and got everyone moving again. Within a day we received orders to leave our hill and join the attack on Heartbreak Ridge.

Pfc. FRANK J. DAVIDSON
Heavy Weapons Company/1/1

We approached the line at night, and we could see flashes and hear explosions nearby. My stomach was knotted. This was my first experience in actual combat, and I had no idea what was happening or what we could expect.

With all the noise and the explosions so near, I had a mental picture of incoming enemy artillery. The night just seemed full of it. Until we got close enough to see the guns, I didn't realize that we were moving up through our own artillery positions, and what I was hearing was our own guns firing.

We set up temporary positions just short of Hill 749, a part of the Punchbowl battle line. There were tanks—ours—firing over our heads at the North Korean positions on the ridgeline.

Marines were always digging in and expecting to stay a few days, only to have the gunny come along, usually within hours, with the order "Move out!" This is what happened to us a day after we went into reserve below Hill 749.

We started moving up through an open valley. Gunny Hamilton got us lined up and ordered us to keep a five-yard interval "because we will be under direct enemy observation." That made us pay attention, no mistake.

We reached the center of the valley before the North Koreans saw us moving up, carrying our mortars and ammunition. They immediately started shelling us with 76-mm artillery. One of our platoon gunners caught a ground burst a few dozen yards ahead of me. He just seemed to come apart. It was a terrible thing to see.

There were a couple of Inch'on veterans in our outfit, men who were about ready to go home. They were more nervous than the new men because they knew what it was like, and the last thing they wanted to do was go into another action only days before they were due to get on the boat for Japan and the States.

The shells were raining down in earnest as we slogged across that open valley, and Gunny Hamilton, acting like a Marine in a John Wayne movie, just strolled along the line urging us, "Get a move on, Marine, you're falling back." He was a veteran of Tarawa, and a typical Marine regular.

[Whether or not this is the same action as described by Pfc. James Anderson is uncertain. If it is, their recollections vary somewhat.]

I don't think I'll ever forget Hill 749. We mortar ammo carriers were used to filling in holes in the rifle company lines when we weren't humping mortar rounds to the guns. It was almost better than carrying ammunition up the slopes of Hill 749, which seemed almost vertical.

The enemy really didn't want to give up the Punchbowl. The

hills around it were valuable—the highest ground in that part of Korea. So there were counterattacks on our line almost every night. And when there were no counterattacks, we were shelled by their biggest mortars.

One night I watched from my gunpit as a friend, Mickey Healy, ran from one hole to another while the rounds were falling. There was one enormous bright flash and I saw Healy flying through the air, his arms and legs flailing away at nothing. I thought surely he was dead. But he fell near my own hole and promptly crawled in with me. He hadn't received a scratch. A miracle.

Our casualties were heavy, but we held on to our hill, and to the Punchbowl as well. We stayed in the area for a couple of months.

In March we were taken out of the line and marched back to a rest area on the west coast near Panmunjom. Even in the rest areas, we were not exactly safe. There were always incidents. So we dug in again to wait for whatever came next.

From our positions we could see the barrage balloons in the air over the truce village near Panmunjom.

Pfc. FRANK O. HART
D/1

Before we relieved the 7th Marines on Hill 749, we were pressed into service as stretcher bearers for them. I was helping carry a stretcher with a man who had a serious leg wound, and as we were carrying him we kept getting stray rounds of small-arms fire. A spent round hit the wounded man's good leg and just dropped into the stretcher without doing any damage. I thought at the time how ironic it would have been for this poor guy to get hit in his good leg just as he was being carried out, presumably getting out of harm's way.

After we secured Hill 749—we gave it our own name, Bloody Ridge—in the late afternoon of September 13, we had to dig in to receive the expected counterattack from the gooks. My bunkie, Tom Hull, and I had a long discussion about where we should dig. I was sure I had just the perfect spot. A huge hemlock tree had been uprooted by artillery fire, and I was trying to tell Tom that this was the A-1 spot because we could use the tree trunk as a natural parapet.

But Tom was adamant and kept insisting that we dig in about twenty feet behind the uprooted tree.

I just couldn't understand his reasoning, but after arguing about it for ten minutes I gave in—mainly because he had been in Korea for two months, and I had just arrived.

Five minutes after we started digging, two Marines from our platoon came along and spotted that big uprooted hemlock, and *they* said, "That's the perfect spot" and started digging.

About an hour after we were all dug in, a gook artillery barrage began. These two Marines who had "my" hemlock tree took a direct hit from a mortar. One of them was killed outright, and the other was barely breathing when we dug him out. I doubt he lived. I just thank the Good Lord for giving Tom Hull the persistence to talk me out of it.

The gooks were artists with mortars. They probably had that hemlock tree registered and were just waiting for some Marines to move in.

The Secretary of the Navy
Washington

The President of the United States takes pleasure in presenting the PRESIDENTIAL UNIT CITATION to the

FIRST MARINE DIVISION, REINFORCED

for service as set forth in the following CITATION:

"For extraordinary heroism in action against enemy aggressor forces in Korea during the periods 21 to 26 April, 16 May to 30 June, and 11 to 25 September 1951. Spearheading the first counteroffensive in the spring of 1951, the FIRST Marine Division, Reinforced, engaged the enemy in the mountainous center of Korea in a brilliant series of actions unparalleled in the history of the Marine Corps, destroying and routing hostile forces with an unrelenting drive of seventy miles north from Wonju. During the period 21 to 26 April, the full force of the enemy counteroffensive was met by the Division, north of the Hwachon Reservoir. Although major units flanking the Marine Division were destroyed or driven back by the force of this attack, the Division held firm against the attackers, repelling the on-slaught from three directions and preventing the encirclement of the key center of the lines. Following a rapid regrouping of friendly forces in close contact with the enemy, the FIRST Marine Division, Reinforced, was committed into the flanks of the massive enemy penetration and, from 16 May to 30 June, was locked in a violent and crucial battle which resulted in the enemy being driven back to the north with disastrous losses to his forces in the number of killed, wounded and captured. Carrying out a series of devastating assaults, the Division succeeded in reducing the enemy's main fortified complex dominating the 38th Parallel. In the final significant offensive action in Korea, from 11 to 25 September 1951, the FIRST Marine Division, Reinforced, completed the destruction of the enemy forces in Eastern Korea by advancing the front against a final desperate enemy defense in the "Punchbowl" area in heavy action which completed the liberation of South Korea in this locality. With the enemy's major defenses reduced, his forces on the central front decimated, and the advantage of terrain and the tactical initiative passing to friendly forces, he never again recovered sufficiently to resume the offensive in Korea. The outstanding courage, resourcefulness and aggressive fighting spirit of the officers and men of the FIRST Marine Division, Reinforced, reflect the highest credit upon themselves and the United States Naval Service."

Appended to this citation is a substantial list of other units of the Fleet Marine Force, and an even longer list of units of the United States Army. One must first negotiate the picket line of adjectives and the heights of hyperbole usual in such documents before one can examine what it really says. The awards officer who wrote this citation (richly deserved, to be sure) speaks of the "destruction of the enemy forces in Eastern Korea," the "liberation of South Korea in this locality," and the "decimated" enemy who "never again recovered sufficiently to resume the offensive in Korea." This would come as a surprise to the men who fought so desperately and died in such numbers in the hundreds of engagements, large and small, that were fought between September of 1951 and 1000 hours (Korean Time), 27 July 1953, when General William K. Harrison of the UN Command and General

Nam Il, acting for China and North Korea, signed the truce documents that stopped the shooting.

The exasperating and unbelievably tedious goings-on at Panmunjom tended to occupy the attention of the American home front. And except for some dramatic and well-publicized encounters, such as Heartbreak Ridge, Porkchop Hill, and a few others, it appeared that the war was at a standstill. This was far from the case. Most of the next eighteen months' battles would be harsh, bitter contests for hills and high ground few people save the participants even bothered to name.

THE WAR FOR
THE RIDGES

The truce talks at Panmunjom dragged on, acrimonious and ill willed, and their overall effect on the conduct of the war was enormous. A political decision had been reached to seek a resolution of the war on what amounted to a status quo ante basis. General Ridgway's order for the cessation of offensive operations had been intended to reduce casualties in the expectation that the talks at Panmunjom would soon bear fruit. This did not happen. The disagreements between the negotiators at the truce village were deep and vexing.

If no further military advance was to be sought, no ground could be lost to the Communists, who remained active and as aggressive as their resources would permit. The war became one of position, and all along the MLR the UN and the Communist forces found themselves involved in bitter firefights for the high ground.

Cpl. MALCOLM H. DOW
K Company/45th Infantry

For us the winter of 1951–52 was relatively quiet. We did a few patrols that didn't amount to much, though we heard that other outfits were having it a lot tougher. But after the first of the year, business began to pick up, and we were in a number of sharp firefights.

Then we were sent to occupy Hill 191, replacing Item Company. We received replacements the afternoon we were scheduled to move up. The new people didn't even have time to undo their packs.

They just rested a few minutes and then moved into action. I felt sorry for these new men; no one knew them and no one was really looking out for them. They weren't old familiar faces.

On the first night we occupied the right side of Hill 191, and one of the other platoons occupied the left, where most of the action was going on. Then when morning came, we switched sides to give the other platoon some relief. There was an area on our side of the hill—the left side was ours now—that no one walked through. The enemy artillery had it registered, and it was worth your life to let the gooks see you moving around there.

There was so much preliminary activity that I was certain we were going to be hit the next night, so I put a lot of effort into preparing my hole. I dug straight into the side of the hill and then made a left turn. My hole was a work of art.

A brand-new lieutenant who had come up the hill with us thought that I'd gotten carried away with too much originality in preparing my hole. He dug his straight down, in the traditional, good old Army way.

That afternoon an artillery FO joined us, and I invited him to share my hole. He was glad of the company, and we enlarged my hole by turning the L into a T. The lieutenant just watched, acting disgusted.

The artilleryman and I spent the late afternoon calling in concentrations to establish a ring of fire around Hill 191 in preparation for the night's activities.

Sometime just before dusk, an enemy soldier on the next hill appeared in clear view, calmly set up a recoilless rifle, and began to shoot at us point-blank. He blew the stub of a tree right off the top of our hole without even dropping any dust inside. I knew the hole was a good one then, regardless of the lieutenant's opinion.

We tried to call some artillery in on the gook sharpshooter, but to no avail. We were told that he was in an area in front of an ROK division. I guess that made him their target property. Anyway, our artillery wouldn't take him as a target, and we had no way of contacting the ROK artillery. That's the military mind at its finest.

As soon as it was properly dark—around 2100 hours, it must have been—the enemy started his attack. Incoming shells started bursting in front of our position, and the enemy came charging right through their own artillery, blowing bugles and screaming.

We tried to call in some artillery of our own, but we had no better luck this time than we had that afternoon. The artillerymen told us over the radio that we would get fire support when we could actually see the gooks. We yelled at them that they were damn near on top of us, but by that time it was too late. We were not going to call in artillery on our own positions.

The gooks were all over the hill. The lieutenant with the regulation foxhole was the first man hit. One of the gooks dropped a grenade in the hole with him. He was knocked out and hurt, but not mortally wounded or anything like that. In fact, he woke up after a few minutes and yelled at me, "Get him!" I asked "Where?" and the lieutenant said, "Damn it, right behind you!" And sure enough, I looked and there was an enemy soldier standing practically beside me. I ducked back into my hole and tried to ease a grenade onto him, but it went astray and the son of a bitch shot me four times, three in the arm and another through the tip of my thumb. And I couldn't see where he had gone. He just vanished.

The gooks began to fall back, but they didn't completely abandon the position, so we were in a kind of stalemate, scattered all over the crest of Hill 191.

The wounded lieutenant got to feeling pretty bad. He would drift off into unconsciousness and then wake up and moan. The minute he did that, the gooks would start tossing grenades at him out of the dark. He lost his helmet when one of them exploded almost in his face. I gave him mine.

Later in the night, one of the enemy managed to lob a grenade right into my own specially constructed hole. The T branches saved the artilleryman and me, though I took a bit of shrapnel in the forearm, and the FO got a piece in the calf. We didn't have any way of being very effective in getting the gooks off our hill, so we just sealed off the entrance to our burrow with the FO's radio and settled down to wait for morning.

When the sun came up I eased out of the hole and looked around. The ground was littered with dead and wounded enemy soldiers. It was quiet when a platoon from Item Company came up the hill to relieve us.

I retrieved my helmet from the lieutenant, who was being patched up by a medic, and started down toward the aid station to get my wounds taken care of. I didn't think they amounted to very much, although they were beginning to give me quite a lot of pain. Back in the company area I told the captain that I would man a rifle for him if someone would bandage my thumb for me—which was what was hurting me most of all. But the medic told me to keep right on walking until I reached the battalion aid station.

They looked me over there and put me first on a jeep and then later in an ambulance. By this time I was feeling pretty bad. At noon I was in a field hospital with doctors carving up my arm. When I woke up the next morning, I knew I wouldn't be returning to the company anytime soon.

I eventually ended up at the Swedish Hospital in Pusan. There were twenty-eight men from my company there, all of them wounded on Hill 191.

[*All along the MLR, probes and patrols sought—and found—the enemy as both sides maneuvered for position. More often than not, position was obtained only after bloody fighting. What follows is an account of a night patrol and firefight. The troops involved were members of a recon company of the First Marines; the objective, Hill 591. It could have been almost any body of frontline troops, almost any hill along the MLR. It was vital to take the high ground that would give command of the valleys below and so establish a claim to territory now under discussion at Panmunjom. But it was a costly business.*]

Cpl. BARRY A. MURPHY
Reconnaissance Company/1

We arrived at Hill 591 by helicopter, about 1500 hours on a cold, windy, really beautiful winter afternoon. We were briefed on the objective and on a route through the valley below.

My buddy Corporal Bruce Warner and I had a discussion about what we would do if the patrol was hit badly, or if we became separated. Warner had a good head for terrain. Pointing, so I could follow what he was saying, he said, "Meet at the bottom of the ridge that extends into the valley. Or, if we miss one another, follow the riverbed"—more pointing—"from there up to the lines, no problems." Like I say, Warner was good at not getting lost.

When it got dark, the squad started down the ridge from the crest of Hill 591. We went in single file—Indian file, Warner called it.

The main body of the squad went on ahead, down into the valley, leaving two fire teams as a rear guard to follow at an interval.

We hadn't gone very far before we realized that the ravines on both sides of us were crawling with gooks. You could see them silhouetted against the snow. We stopped and made a perimeter, holding our fire because the gooks hadn't seen us.

All of a sudden a flare burst, and the whole scene was as bright as high noon. We froze—didn't move a muscle—until the flare went dark again. Somehow, the main body of the squad had made it down to the floor of the valley without encountering the gooks.

Word came from the CP to drop off the last fire team as a rear guard, then to hold in position until the patrol returned from the valley. But it was obvious that the operation was not going to go as planned. Warner and I had a whispered discussion about it and decided to move a little bit farther down the ridge to see if we could get through the gooks the way the rest of the squad apparently had. Not that there was much hope of that. There were just too many of them. It was a miracle they hadn't seen us yet.

About 100 yards farther on, we stopped again. We could hear Chinese all around us below the ridgeline on both sides. It was plain that our plans were fucked up and we had somehow eased ourselves into a very dangerous position. There was no way in hell we were even going to get to the valley floor.

Having left the second fire team behind us, there were only four of us remaining. We formed a defensive circle, digging into the snow as quietly as we could, figuring that maybe the gooks would move on. Warner was on my left, the other two Marines behind me, facing down the hill.

There was only starlight, but it was so clear and windy that the visibility was perfect. We could see the Chinese moving around, dark shadows against the pale snow. There seemed to be a great many of them, and they showed no sign of moving off.

Warner was facing up the slope. Suddenly he hit me with his elbow and rose to a crouching position; he said, "Look out, Murph!"

Not more than a couple of feet from Warner, a dark shape loomed up and shouted something in Chinese or Korean. Then there was a crash of gunfire and the muzzle flash of a burp gun just over my head.

I rolled right and came to a sitting position, firing my M1, but I must have missed, because the Chinese started to run back down the hill. At the same time, I heard an agonized scream. I knelt and fired again at the running enemy soldier. He fell, tumbling down the steep hillside in the snow.

When I had a chance to look around me, I saw that Warner was dead. He had taken that burp-gun volley right in the face. The scream had come from one of the other Marines behind me. He had caught some of the bullets, and both of his arms were broken.

There was a flurry of shooting down in the ravine to our right. It was impossible to tell what the gooks were shooting at. The firefight had startled them, and they were shooting at anything that moved.

Then, as quickly as the shooting had started, it stopped, and there was an eerie stillness. Using Warner's body to shield my movements, I crawled to where I could look down into the ravine. The gooks weren't moving around any longer, but they were there. You could hear them jabbering to one another.

I don't remember being particularly afraid of dying there on the ridge. But what did scare hell out of me was the thought of being captured. In my mind's eye there appeared a statue of the Virgin Mary, like the one in the church back home. I said a rosary. More than one. The wounded Marine behind me was moaning and getting some first aid from his buddy. But my buddy was past help. I think I prayed for him. I hope I did.

We stayed like that on the ridge for what felt like hours. Below, in the ravine, the Chinese stopped talking, and pretty soon you could hear them withdrawing. They had no idea how many of us were up on the hill, and the firefight must have confused them into thinking there were more of us than there were.

Then the most remarkable thing happened. The main body of the squad, which I was sure must have run into about 1,000 gooks, came slogging up the ridge. They had heard the shooting, but they hadn't seen any of the enemy at all.

I told the corporal in charge that Warner was dead, and we had time to make a stretcher out of saplings and spare clothing for him. I helped carry him back to the company position—the first leg of his journey home.

The really rotten thing about it was that both Warner and I were eight days from rotation back to the States.

[One of the ironies of the war at this stage was that the existence of the truce talks, ostensibly intended to bring the fighting to an end, had the opposite effect. The Communists, as well as the UN Command, were constrained by the character of the negotiations to seek in every way possible the improvement of their military situation along the MLR. Late in December 1951, UN intelligence believed that the North Koreans intended to send heavy reinforcements down the east coast of the peninsula by rail and by boat to give Communist forces more punch along the MLR. The accuracy of the intelligence was questionable, but any such North Korean activity could not be ignored. Spoiling raids by British Royal Marine commandos were laid on.]

Lt. Cdr. LEFTERIS LAVRAKAS
Commanding Officer, USS Horace A. Bass (APD-124)

I had been in command of the *Bass* since October when the orders came in instructing me to conduct clandestine operations in North Korea with the Brit 41st Royal Marine Commandos.

A young UDT [Underwater Demolition Team] officer named Teddy Fielding was on board for a visit when the radio messenger delivered the TS board to me. Fielding "just happened" to steal a look at what was on it: orders to the CO, USS *Bass*, to take charge of landing the 41st Commandos in North Korea and assist them in disrupting planned troop movements by the Communists.

Fielding begged me to take him along, and as it happened *Bass* was short of officers. I needed help in planning the raid and making a number of operational decisions even before picking up the British troops, so Fielding got recruited.

Besides my regular duties as commander of USS *Bass*, I was also designated commander of the task element, which was to include the British Marines, my ship and crew, the amphib boats the Marines would use, and finally a fire-support destroyer—quite a responsibility.

Actually, I stopped by the flagship in Sasebo [Japan] before getting under way, hoping to get another officer or two, but I was told none were available. I had been lucky to have Lieutenant Fielding as a volunteer.

We picked up Lieutenant Colonel F. N. Grant (his men all called him "Chips") in Wonsan and spent several days getting the Royal Marines squared away on board and then conducting a couple of rehearsals for the North Korean raids. I was anxious that things go right. Not only were their lives involved, but this was my first chance at independent command and I wanted it to go perfectly.

The night before our departure from Sasebo, a journalist had come aboard. And although I didn't know it at the time, while we were putting the operation together, our "secret" raid became headlines in every newspaper in the States. Evidently the stalemate ashore wasn't generating enough news, and here was a joint operation by Americans and Brits. The magic words *commando raid* were all it took, apparently. What shocked me when I heard about it later was that CHINFO, the UN Command press office, actually cleared the story for release. The release of secret information which could have been so damaging was not, in the end, serious. I guess the Communists hadn't yet learned to study the American press for military information.

Twenty-four hours after our task element left Wonsan I received a message that put Colonel Grant into a tizzy. I was informed by Naval Command that my ship and landing boats were needed on the *west* coast of Korea. It was an informational dispatch, not an order.

However, it implied that I should debark the British Marines at any convenient spot and proceed at best speed to the island area off the Taedong Estuary and put myself under British operational control to intercept "thousands of assault troops missing at Chinnamp'o."

To steam from our present position around the peninsula to Chinnamp'o would take about two and a half days, not counting replenishment. Then I would have to rendezvous with a British cruiser to pick up armed naval personnel to man the patrol boats.

I discussed this with Colonel Grant, and he made a very good case for not complying with the informational dispatch. There were, he said, many good things to be learned if we stuck to our original plan and did the raids as scheduled. We had put a few troops ashore the night before and then recovered them, and we had fresh intelligence which would, according to Grant, "almost guarantee a significant outcome to our operation." The plain fact was that Grant and his men *wanted* to do the raids, and so, frankly, did I.

In the end I made a kind of military compromise. I sent off a radio request for clarification of the informational dispatch I had received. What I was asking was, did they really mean that I was to abandon my mission and take on another on the far side of Korea?

The reply to my message was that my request had gone to the blockade commander for a decision. Grant and I waited. The day waned. No reply. So I took the next step. I told Grant I would apply to the senior naval officer back at Wonsan and see if *he* would make a decision.

As the sun set—at what Colonel Grant called "the crepuscular hour"—the word came back: *Complete your operation.*

There was one more task to complete before heading north. I had to report aboard the British flagship. (The whole operation was under the overall command of the senior British naval officer, due to the involvement of the Royal Marines.)

Waiting for the message from Wonsan had made me late reporting to the flagship. When I came over the side, the British commodore was on the quarterdeck, sword in hand, waiting to receive me. As I stepped onto the ladder, that sword was pointed straight at my Adam's apple. "You, Captain," he said, "are late. May we now get the war under way?"

That night *Bass* and *Tingey* steamed north about 130 miles, and when we reached the designated target area, we put the Royal Marines ashore in two landing boats. Young Fielding made himself useful by doing a solo reconnaissance in a Brit kayak before the landing proper.

Unfortunately, either our intelligence was faulty, or the North Koreans were more alert than we expected. They had prepared the high ground behind the beach very carefully, and defenders were there in force. Grant's men made a number of tries to reach the railroad, but were repulsed with several casualties. After two attempts to get past the beach, Colonel Grant decided to withdraw back to the ship.

In the morning we met at sea with the USS *Wisconsin* and transferred the wounded to the battleship by high-line.

The next night we were off shore from our second objective, and we repeated the operation of putting the commandos ashore in the landing boats. But the second raid's scenario was almost a repeat of the first. Resistance was heavy, and the Marines found themselves pinned down on the beach again. There was no possibility of reaching either the railroad or the tunnel we had been told was unguarded. Once again, Grant was forced to pull his men back. Heavy explosive charges were placed on several underwater obstacles defending the beach, and the Marines were loaded onto the boats.

From the ship we could see the charges on the beach going off as the boats began to turn and head back to us. It was then that Lieutenant Fielding performed an act of really remarkable bravery. Colonel Grant told me about it later.

As our last boat cleared the beach, it backed onto a sandbar close aboard one of the mined obstacles. The obstacle had a large charge fastened to it, one with a three-minute fuse.

There followed some really frantic efforts to get the boat clear, but progress was very slow and time was ticking away. Teddy Fielding, our "volunteer" UDT man, earned his passage by slipping over the side—by this time the charge was about a minute and a half from detonation—and disarming the fuse.

Colonel Grant said it was one of the most courageous acts he had ever witnessed.

U.S.S. HORACE A BASS (APD-124)
c/o Fleet Post Office
San Francisco, California
Rear Admiral George C. Dyer, USN
U.S.S. PIEDMONT
Dear Admiral Dyer:

This is to thank you very much for the admirable way in which all arrangements were made for our current operation. I had everything I needed. Excellent up to date air photos came promptly from TF77 and were dropped on our front door at WONSAN. The USS TINGEY furnished us with prompt and remarkably accurate fire support.

In particular the USS HORACE A. BASS has done a wonderful job. The boats were in tip top order (I wish mine were like them) and the crews were competent and cool under fire. The CIC vectored us on the nose on every occasion. Nothing has been too much trouble and we have had wonderful cooperation. I feel the ship and my unit really worked as a team. We shall be sorry to say good bye to such good friends.

On each occasion of landing I pulled my men out when the opposition got serious. I did not consider a ten-foot bridge worth serious casualties. Our main aim—that of keeping up the threat to the [enemy] coast—was achieved. Our difficulty ashore on each occasion was similar. The Gooks in good positions rolled grenades down the steep slopes on which we were climbing. Nonetheless we reached the top on both targets. We could have maintained ourselves there but only at a cost not commensurate with the value of the target.

The UDT officer aboard the BASS (LT. FIELDING, USN) was of the greatest assistance and on each occasion went in with my swimmer/canoeist and reconnoitered the beach. A daring officer who had to be restrained from going ashore to wage a two man war.

I have come to the conclusion that given an APD for two weeks, a small UDT party and occasional support from a DD we could raise quite a little hell up this coast. Sampan hunting, snatching sentries, beating up the beach and carrying out small landings. We were unfortunate on this occasion in that the only locomotive which appeared did so when the canoe party were on the beach and we could not fire. But I am sure that ship's gunfire directed from a craft 500 yards off shore would have destroyed it.

I will in due course submit these ideas to you formally when I have worked things out in more detail.

I have a firm conviction that an APD with a troop of mine on board could really be a thorn in the NK flesh. I know that Commander Lavrakas agrees with me on this, and I sincerely hope I will again one day be able to place myself under his direction.

F. N. GRANT
LTCOL RM

[*One of the most persistent troubles plaguing military thought is the tendency of planners to attempt to fight today's war with yesterday's tactics. Despite Commander Lavrakas's and Lieutenant Colonel Grant's understandable efforts to make them appear so, the Royal Marine Commando raids on the North Korean coast were not a resounding success. Lieutenant Fielding, however, was eventually awarded the Navy Cross for his bravery in handling the underwater explosive charge.*]

S/Sgt. RICHARD TURNER
C Company/23d Infantry

You don't really realize what you look like. There's no mirrors. You can't go and look in the water and see a reflection. There isn't that much water, anyhow—mostly muddy rivers.

We advanced as far as this small town—a village, really—and then we were ordered to pull back into the hills and bivouac there. The weather was good, though in Korea all that means is that there isn't snow on the ground.

We were in winter uniform, of course, woolens and parkas. Our big dream about that time was to get an A-frame—the *right* A-frame, that is. Understand that an A-frame is a wooden pack frame the Koreans use. We were always looking for a small one we could put our sleeping bags and gear on. The U.S. Army pack just wasn't the thing. Now, what I wanted was one that was just right—small, that would ride high on my shoulders, with woven grass ropes. That was my dream, to find a really nice one. And some rope. I needed the rope, too.

So I was sitting up there on the hill, watching this little town and wondering if I could find a piece of rope down there. After a long while in combat, small things become very important.

So as we were sitting there relaxing, this swamp-water sergeant in our outfit comes up and he says, "Hey, Turner. They're going to shell that town." And I say, "Yeah, too bad. There's probably a lot of good stuff down there." And he replies, "Well, you got a couple of hours. Why don't you run on down there and see what's what"— or words to that effect.

The plain fact is that we were not supposed to go down there. The place was suspected of having NK in it, or they wouldn't have decided to shell it. But suddenly I wanted to go down there and look for rope and maybe that perfect A-frame. So I talked a couple of members of my squad into going down with me.

The first thing we did when we got there was to tell what people were still around that they had better bug the hell out of there because in about three or four hours the whole place would be flat. We had some propaganda pamphlets with us, and we handed them out. Mostly, the few people in the place just ignored us. Most of the village had been evacuated, anyway.

I was still fixed on finding rope, so I went up to this house and, you know, used the old movie search method: Kick through the door, swing your rifle around at the ready—hardcase soldier at work. There was no one in the room, or, I thought, in the house. Except that suddenly I heard something through the rice-paper wall, something in the next room. So I went carefully and slid the wall back, and there, all huddled together, were about a dozen women and little kids. When they saw me they started screaming and howling.

I calmed them down, you know; I said, no, they didn't need to be afraid of me. I slung my rifle to show them I wasn't going to shoot them. I might even have taken the ammunition out of it, I don't remember. Anyway, I got them all quiet and calmed down.

And then over on the wall, I see this really nice length of woven grass rope—just exactly what I had been looking for. I thought, How about that? How lucky can a guy get?

So I took my bayonet out to cut me a piece of this great rope. And the minute the women and kids saw me with this great, huge blade in my hands, they started howling again. They were absolutely terrified, sure that I was going to cut them into pieces.

I went over and cut myself a piece of the rope I wanted, and then I backed out of there, just hoping that one of them didn't get so desperately frightened she would try to put a knife into me. Those people were just terrified.

Well, I could understand that, you know. Because in the main room of this house there was a mirror. And as I backed away from the women and children I caught a glimpse of myself in that mirror. Lord, what a sight! It wasn't a full-length mirror—and I guess I was grateful for that—but it showed me from the waist up, and let me tell you, if I had seen something that looked like me, I would have screamed and yelled, too. I hadn't washed or shaved for sixty days. Whatever food you eat goes right down the front of you. Your skin begins to look crusty and sick. You stink something awful. It's just tough. There is no way to clean up. We didn't wear our helmets, because it was so cold; we used those terrible pile caps instead. All in all, I looked like the wrath of God. I tell you, it was frightening to see what I looked like.

2d Lt. MARVIN MUSKAT
H Company/160th Infantry

I was flown over from the States as a replacement. I rather think the Army was running short of company-grade officers in Korea. They were in a hurry to keep the ranks filled.

In Pusan, at the replacement depot, I was assigned to the 40th Division depot outside of Ch'unch'on. I traveled by train, and the accommodations were about what you would expect of a troop train in a war zone.

As we went farther north, we could see that the hills became steeper and steeper. It was obvious that this was going to be rugged country to fight in. By the time we reached Ch'unch'on, we were almost within range of the enemy artillery. You could hear our own guns firing, too. The northerly horizon would light up as though there were heat lightning flashing over the mountains.

A jeep from regiment came down to Ch'unch'on and picked me
up. When we reached the regimental CP, I reported to the adjutant
and was told that we were in what was called a "four-point zone."
Korea was all carefully divided up into point zones so that each soldier would accumulate points for rotation according to the point rating of the zone in which he served. A four point was the highest
rating there was. Anyone lucky enough to last nine months in a four-
point zone automatically had enough points for rotation.

Thirty-six points was the score needed for rotation. Everyone
knew this, and the result was that there was a real tendency to just
keep one's head down, take no unnecessary risks, and collect points.
It wasn't like World War II; you knew there was no big push coming,
no fighting until the enemy surrendered. This was a war that was
going nowhere. No advances. General Ridgway had specifically ordered that there should be no offensive action, so the line was supposed to be static. But it wasn't exactly that way. As soon as I reported
to the 160th, we were involved in what was called "aggressive patrol
action." It wasn't intended to take ground, only to kill enemy soldiers.

The first real action for me was being ordered onto Heartbreak
Ridge. We had taken the Punchbowl, but the ridge always seemed,
somehow, to be in contention.

I had heard about the place. I heard about it the minute I landed
in Korea. People told about hand-to-hand fighting, trenches, guns
frozen into the ground. The newspapers called it Heartbreak Ridge,
but we had some other names for it. Sandbag Castle is one, because
the high ground was a real madhouse of bunkers and trenches all
lined with sandbags.

The 160th Regiment was in corps reserve at Ch'uch'on, and the
word came down that we were going to take over Heartbreak from
the present tenants—I think it was the 24th Division.

We were told to remove all insignia that would identify our unit.
The enemy might guess we were coming, but they were not to know
who we were. We moved into position at night. Not a shot fired. We
were patting ourselves on the back, telling ourselves what a wonderful
job we were doing. We took over the forward command post, then
the observation post and the rear CP—that was my post. I shook
hands with the officer I was relieving, kicked him out and told him

he was relieved—to go on home now. The relieved troops withdrew, headed to the rear—a perfect relief. We're not talking squad or company movements here. Two rifle companies up, one in reserve. A battalion reserve and the Heavy Weapons Company supporting the front. All smooth as silk and quiet. Keep the enemy guessing, right?

All of a sudden loudspeakers open up all along our battalion front. *"Welcome!"* In perfect English: *"Welcome to the officers and men of the 160th Infantry Regiment. Welcome, Colonel Benjamin Turnage!"* Good God, we had just had a change of command and they even had the new colonel's first name right.

The effect on the morale of our troops was devastating. Our people realized immediately that the Chinese had seen the whole relief and had calmly allowed it to go on, knowing they could have blown most of us to pieces any damned time they wanted to.

They even mentioned a few of Colonel Turnage's staff officers and got all *their* names right, too.

Only an hour or so later, all hell broke loose. Screaming and yelling and blowing their damned bugles, they attacked us. We turned them back, but casualties were high.

[As winter gave way to the cold and sullen Korean spring, there were intervals of relative quiet for the men holding the positions along the MLR. The truce talks at Panmunjom continued, but progress was slow. The Communist negotiators resisted anything resembling a genuine move toward ending hostilities. The South Korean government of Syngman Rhee added its own dollop of recalcitrance. Meanwhile, the troops in the line fought and rested and behaved as soldiers do.]

Sgt. F/C C. W. "BILL" MENNINGER
2d Battalion/21st Infantry
When we had time on our hands, we would end up doing anything. For example, the Air Force guys were so hungry for war souvenirs, we poor old infantrymen decided we'd use a little American know-how and help them out.

On our way out of the line and into the reserve area, we had come across a gook arms cache that was wall-to-wall Russian pistols. The place had been napalmed, and the weapons were badly damaged. We collected them and then sent off to Sears, Roebuck for bottles of bluing. When they arrived, we sandpapered the worst of the blisters from the Russian weapons, blued the steel, whittled new grips from ammo boxes, cut some M1 springs to the right length and installed them. When we had done, we had working weapons of a sort—though I wouldn't have liked to be within 100 yards of one actually being fired.

We sold the whole lot to Air Force people for two fifths of whiskey or fifty dollars each.

2d Lt. MARVIN MUSKAT
H Company/160th Infantry

When things were quiet, we took pictures. I must have taken a thousand slides. You see, you fought in Korea with guns and with cameras. Every officer and soldier seemed to have a 35-mm camera. Everyone—bar none. Because most of the fighting took place at night, during the day you took pictures. I have pictures of Heartbreak Ridge that show every foxhole, every trench line, every broken tree stump, every sandbag castle.

RESTRICTED
Security Information
Section II
Training Bulletin No 4

ARMOR EMPLOYMENT IN KOREA

Tanks in Korea are principally used for strengthening infantry positions along the MLR, for raids to inflict casualties and destroy enemy positions, and for counterattacking. Their aggressive and skillful employment, despite the adverse terrain, has been a powerful factor in the successful defensive operations conducted.

Since the MLR across the Korean front is, in most cases, located on steeply sloped ridges, special roads have been constructed to enable tank emplacement. The majority of these tanks remain in defilade. When targets of opportunity appear, a tank may move as little as forty feet to a prepared position on the ridge. A few tanks remain in a fixed position atop mountains and are consequently visible to the enemy. These are normally dug-in hull defilade and are well sandbagged. A protective trench leads to the escape hatch which is used as the entrance. Tanks are also employed in valleys, where such valleys intersect the MLR, primarily to block enemy armor which may use those routes.

Tank units of varying size frequently move forward of the MLR to raid enemy positions. Prior to a raid, an intensive intelligence study is made in order to locate mine fields, obstacles, anti-tank weapons, and profitable target areas. Ground and air reconnaissance and aerial photo study supply most of the required information. The low incidence of mine damage on raids is attributed to precise intelligence information. Whenever possible, commanders and other key personnel are briefed at a point where they can observe their target areas.

RESTRICTED
Security Information

Cpl. CRAIG KOETZLE
72d Tank Battalion/2d Division

Before each tank probe behind enemy lines, it was common practice for the people involved to do a reconnaissance by L-5 [Piper aircraft used for liaison and general utility by the ground forces]. The idea was to get a first-hand look at enemy bunkers, tank traps, things like that.

This was to be my first airborne mission, and I must admit the adrenaline was flowing when I reached the airstrip. It was carved out of the side of a hill, paved with metal mesh sections, and it was neither straight nor very long—about a city block's worth, I would say. Parked in the mud to one side of the strip stood two Piper L-5s and a shack made of wood and tar paper with a sign, FLIGHT OPERATIONS, nailed on the door. Inside the shack were two very young 1st lieutenants wearing Army flight wings.

I was briefed by my pilot, who informed me that we would patrol at 2,500 feet "in order to overfly small-arms fire." Since only a day or so before I had seen an F-80 on a napalm run shot down by ground fire, his comments weren't exactly reassuring.

Outside, two crewmen had hauled the Piper to the end of the runway, and we walked out to the plane. It was cold, and I was wearing a parka and my thermal boots—the ones the line troops called Mickey Mouse boots because of the way they make your feet look. I also had an Ernie Pyle cap on under my steel pot, and I was carrying a .45-caliber pistol strapped to my waist.

The crewmen helped me into a parachute, so that by the time I was ready to climb aboard I must have weighed 250 pounds. Then they pushed and hauled me into the rear seat of the tiny airplane. I had never flown in anything this small. It looked as though a good shake would make it all fall into pieces. It was nothing but skinny rods and fabric, like a kite.

The pilot climbed aboard and twisted around to instruct me on how to fasten the safety belt and shoulder harness. By the time I got through, I felt like a mummy.

He explained to me that if we were hit and forced to bail out, I was to go first. My only thought was, Where are the crewmen to undo me and shove me out the door?

As the young lieutenant warmed the engine for takeoff, I was very unimpressed by the length of the runway ahead of us. The engine sounded like a loud motorcycle, and the Piper shook and rattled as though it were going to disintegrate on the spot.

When the pilot was finally satisfied with the RPM, he released the brakes and we began to roll down the steel mesh runway. We didn't actually get into the air off the end of the runway. Instead, we sort of flew off the edge of a steep downslope and dove into a shallow valley until we had flying speed. My silent prayers were answered only after we started gaining altitude.

The strip was about a mile from the MLR. As I looked down on our positions I was shocked to see how exposed and vulnerable our troops looked from a mere 1,000 feet. I hoped the Chinese emplacements would be as visible once we crossed the line.

But from 2,500 feet, I was really dismayed to see absolutely nothing. No enemy troops, no gun positions. I was wasting my time and the pilot's, looking from this height. So I tapped him on the shoulder and pointed down.

I could sense his reluctance, but he nodded and banked into a slow descent. I could scarcely move to use my field glasses. So I unwisely unfastened my harness and shifted my weight to the banking side of the airplane.

The ground came closer, and our spiraling descent became a real dive. I wondered why the pilot was doing this, but I figured he knew what he was about. Meanwhile, I began to spot gun flashes on the ground. That showed me where the enemy guns were, and from that I could begin to make out the trenchlines and emplacements. I was feeling pretty good about finally doing what I was supposed to be doing on this mission.

As we descended faster and faster, I could see tracers coming up and zipping past us. I began to get nervous again, particularly since the pilot didn't appear to be ready to pull out of his spiraling dive, and the ground seemed to be getting awfully close.

My next sensation was a sharp rap on the side of my pot helmet, and I looked away from the Chinese positions to see the pilot turned in his seat and yelling at me to move my damned foot. The Piper had dual controls, and though the stick had been removed, the rear-seat rudder pedals had not. My foot, huge in its Mickey Mouse boot, was resting on the low rudder pedal—I was doing my unwitting best to fly us straight into the ground. I yanked my foot away as though I had stepped on a red-hot coal, and the pilot regained control, shaking his head. We were what looked to be only yards from the ground.

Then we were gaining altitude in a steep climb, with the throttle pushed right up against the stop. I heard a couple of slapping bangs behind me. I didn't know what caused them, but I had a nasty suspicion it was bullets.

We returned over our lines again and headed for the airstrip. From the air it looked even smaller than it had on the ground. I thought to myself, In a minute this baby first lieutenant is going to attempt the impossible—landing on that postage stamp.

With full flaps, and the engine howling with the propeller in low pitch, the L-5 seemed to be hanging in the air. Then we pitched over into a forty-five-degree descent that had my heart missing a few beats. The end of the steel mat passed under the nose, and *bang!* we were down—but not stopped. We rolled on and on, with the pilot standing on the brakes until we stopped about nine or ten feet from the end of the mat and the drop-off into the valley.

The lieutenant unstrapped and exited the plane. I sat there, unable to move. The ground crewmen looked inside and saw that I couldn't reach the buckles on the safety harness. I would have had a great time trying to bail out!

Next, they wrestled me out of the airplane and stood me up. My knees were so shaky I could hardly bear the weight of all my gear. The crewmen were understanding—maybe they had flown with the lieutenant. I walked none too steadily to the wooden shack and sat down to a cup of hot coffee. My pilot was nowhere to be seen. The ground-crew people wheeled the L-5 past the shack. One of them leaned in the door, grinning. "Hey," he said. "There are four bullet holes in the fabric right behind the rear seat. Want to have a look?"

I was so glad to be sitting on terra firma drinking coffee!

Within the hour, I headed back to our tank positions, reports in hand. My platoon leader went over my findings. He particularly wanted to know if the Chinese gun emplacements really were where I had noted them on the map. I asked him if *he* wanted to go back to the airstrip and inspect the bullet holes. He thought I was joking.

Sgt. EDWARD GABRIEL
I Company/31st Infantry
We made our way up Sandy Hill as far as we could, and Lieutenant LaSasso told us to dig in. We were already getting heavy fire from the Chinks on our front. The Navy planes were being a help; they kept coming in every few minutes, strafing the enemy positions and making them keep their heads down while our 2d Platoon deployed.

As the name suggests, the soil on the hill was very sandy and loose. It took a long time to get a good foxhole dug; and all the while, we were taking fire from the Chinese on the ridge above us. They kept lobbing grenades down at us—stick grenades, they were, with a wooden handle about a foot long. Several of our guys were wounded by these things. The only good thing about it was that they were not very powerful, nothing at all like the Mills-bomb style of grenade we had.

But despite all the help we got from the Navy planes, the Chinese were hanging onto the high ground, and they kept us pinned down all day. They also had a sniper, a good one. Lieutenant LaSasso made the mistake of standing up to look around and shout an order, and this sniper hit him with a shot right in the head. He died instantly.

My buddy Jerry Styles was shot by that sniper. His hole was farther down the hill than the lieutenant's, but in the same line of fire. I heard the shot, and then I heard people behind me yelling "Medic!" When I looked back I could see them kneeling by Jerry's foxhole. Only a few minutes before, I had been back there looking to see how he was doing with his hole-digging. It was during one of those intervals when the planes were keeping the Chinks down.

I called over to Lee Young, asking him how bad it was with Jerry. He said he didn't know, so I crawled back to see for myself. The medic was working hard on Jerry, but when I asked how he was doing, he just shook his head. But he did call for some help to get Jerry down off the hill and on the way to the hospital.

Later, they told me he had died while they were dragging him down the hill.

We stayed in our holes all that night and most of the next day, until we were relieved. Our platoon was hit hard. Sergeant Jackson was wounded, and so were Mac and Trigg; and of course, Lieutenant LaSasso and Jerry were killed. The Chinese didn't even try to hold on to Sandy Hill. During the night they retreated, leaving their dead and wounded behind.

S/Sgt. RICHARD TURNER
C Company/23d Infantry
Sometimes, when they had been hit badly, the Chinese would bury their dead right in their foxholes, in the spot where they died.

It's dangerous to let an enemy know how weak you might be, so they would try to conceal their dead. If they had time, they would haul them away, but if not, into the ground they'd go, right in their fighting holes.

Our platoon was on a conditioning march through some country that had been fought hard over, though it was quiet enough at the moment.

The walking was tough and then easy and then tough again. A nice outing for us, and for a change no one was shooting at us.

It came time to stop for chow, and we dispersed over this gentle slope that had been churned up by fighting only a couple of weeks ago. I took my squad to the top, and we settled down there to eat our rations.

I notice that where I was sitting, the ground felt kind of spongy. I stood up and pushed at the earth with my boot and this kind of weird, grayish liquid came oozing out. It gave me a bad feeling. Of course, what had happened was that I had been sitting eating my C rations on top of a shallow Chinese grave.

RIOT

As the tide of war swept up and down the Korean peninsula, the forces of the UN Command accumulated a truly staggering number of prisoners of war. By January of 1951, the UN armies had taken more than 140,000 North Korean and Chinese prisoners, and their care and confinement had begun to be a source of concern to General Ridgway, then Eighth Army commander.

On 6 January 1951, Ridgway wrote to General MacArthur expressing his anxiety about the resources that were being diverted from the fighting front to feed, house, and control this growing mass of inconvenient prisoners. MacArthur replied that he had recommended removal of the prisoners from Korea to the United States. They could not be moved to Japan for two reasons: The location of prison camps there would almost certainly expose Japan to a charge of belligerency, with its attendant risks; and in the climate of long-standing enmity and prejudice between Koreans and Japanese, the presence of the prisoners was likely to enrage the Japanese population.

But no decision on removal was forthcoming from Washington. This was the first evidence of a naïveté in dealing with the Communist enemy that was to grow into near-disastrous proportions in the following months.

Eventually plans were made to remove the prisoners from the compounds on the peninsula and confine them in camps on the islands off the southern Korean coast.

The first site selected was Cheju-do. But the problems were im-

mediately apparent. To situate the prisoners there, together with the personnel required to guard and maintain the compounds, would more than double the population of the island. Without an enormous expenditure of manpower and money—both in short supply—the island simply could not tolerate such an invasion. Therefore, General Ridgway urged that another way of solving the dilemma be found.

The solution—which in the event was no solution at all—was to move the prisoners to the much smaller island of Koje-do, a scant few miles southwest of Pusan.

Koje-do was mountainous, rocky, and inhospitable. There was little flat ground for the dispersal of the necessary compounds, and as a result, the island was soon jammed with human beings forced to live in abominable conditions. The number of prisoners increased steadily, as did the military and civilian personnel required to guard and administer the camps.

Though it should have been foreseen, the conditions on Koje-do were perfect for the breeding of a prisoner mutiny.

In his personal account of the war General Ridgway writes:

> Besides the increasing thousands of prisoners, there were hundreds of guards and other custodial personnel, with many more prisoners in the compound than was desirable for proper oversight and discipline. In consequence the Communists found it relatively easy to execute the plans of which we were then wholly unaware—the fomenting of mass demonstrations, riots, mutinies, and breakouts, and the subjugation of non-Communist prisoners. *The personnel we could spare to take charge of the camps was not of a quality to ensure the alertness needed to detect these plots or to identify and isolate the ringleaders.* [Italics added.]*

It is significant, and of a piece with the naïveté mentioned earlier, that as late as mid-1952 no inkling of the troubles brewing in the POW camps had reached the UN authorities. But the UN

---

*Ridgway, p. 206.

Command was soon to be facing a pattern of Communist behavior as alien to Western political thought as the language of the bees.

There were four barbed-wire enclosures built on the island, each intended to hold 6,000 prisoners. But by the summer of 1952, the POW population had vastly outgrown the accommodations on Koje-do and now had to be expanded to another southern island, Pongam-do, as well as to the site originally rejected, Cheju-do.

Trouble was brewing in the camps, but nothing really significant took place until the truce talks began. This was the moment chosen by the Communist High Command to set in motion a series of incidents intended to shame the United Nations Command among the people of Asia.

The Communists had established a tight system of communications and control in the POW compounds by the straightforward expedient of having hardcore Communists cadres surrender in order to establish leadership in the camps. Once inside the compounds, they distributed messages by the simplest and most obvious methods: stones wrapped in written instructions were tossed from compound to compound, orders were sung and chanted, and "trusted" prisoners carried Communist directives from camp to camp.

High-level conferences were held in hospital wards among prison leaders who reported themselves ill. The ease with which the POWs were able to organize themselves into a solid mass of resisters was, in retrospect, dismaying. General Ridgway's comments about the quality and alertness of the camp supervisory personnel can only be interpreted as an understatement.

Within the compounds, discipline was maintained by the Communist cadres through the device of kangaroo courts operating under a disciplinary "code" which invoked various punishments for infractions, including even the death penalty. Western POWs in other wars and under far more vicious conditions of confinement have behaved similarly; but in the compounds of Koje-do, the "inside law" was more severe than that imposed by the captors.

There were many non-Communists in the compounds. The North Koreans had drafted thousands into their army, and they had used corvée labor as a matter of military necessity. It was United Nations policy to screen the prisoners, to attempt to separate the civilian laborers and unwilling soldiers from the dedicated Communists. And as *the truce talks droned on, it became an established UN principle that prisoners who did not wish to be returned to the North or to China should have the right to refuse repatriation.*

At the end of World War II a similar situation had arisen when the Soviets demanded forced repatriation of all displaced persons from Eastern Europe and the Soviet Union. To their discredit, the western allies had allowed themselves to become party to the infamous Operation Keelhaul, the repatriation of all Russians and East Europeans, regardless of their wishes, or of the fate awaiting them in their homelands. The UN had no wish to repeat Keelhaul in Korea.

But as the truce talks began, the POW camps were alerted. Responding to direct orders from Nam Il and the Communist High Command, the cadres inside the wire went into action.

Conditions in the compounds were by no means pleasant, but the camps were run according to the terms of the 1949 Geneva Convention. This document assumed, reasonably enough, that prisoners of war were entitled to humane treatment because they were no longer active combatants in war. The same Convention gave the force of treaty law to the proposition that POWs had, by reason of having surrendered, placed themselves under obligation to follow the "laws, regulations, and orders in force in the armed forces of the Detaining Power" which was considered to be "justified in taking judicial or disciplinary measures in respect of any offense committed by a prisoner of war against such laws, regulations, or orders."

Neither North Korea nor the People's Republic of China were signatories of the Geneva Convention, nor did they have the slightest intention of adhering to its terms and conditions. The Red Cross, welcome in the camps under UN authority, was never allowed to inspect the prisoner-of-war establishments in North Korea, and at no time did the Communists ever show the slightest disinclination to mistreat UN prisoners in their hands. What now began to take place in the island compounds should have come as no surprise whatever to the UN Command. Yet it appears that it did so.

The first stirrings came in January of 1952, when the screening of prisoners became a point of contention at the truce talks. Admiral Joy, speaking as much for the United States as for the United Nations, had taken the position that the UN Command would never agree to the forced repatriation of any prisoners from Communist territories. When peace came, he declared, those wishing to return to China and North Korea would, of course, be accommodated. But prisoners who did not wish repatriation would be allowed to stay in the South.

Communist negotiators now stated that in order to discuss this tender point constructively, they required to know exactly how many prisoners would be returned and how many would be granted political asylum.

Determined to be reasonable, the UN Command immediately undertook a screening of the by-now 160,000 prisoners in their hands.

What the negotiators apparently did not know—and very probably should have known—was that the moment the screening was decided upon, orders went out from Panmunjom that screening in the camps was to be resisted, actively and violently.

The policy was implemented at once. The prisoners Koje-do, armed with clubs, axes, knives, barbed-wire flails, sharpened bamboo stakes, and shovels honed into halberds, fearlessly attacked a battalion of the U.S. 27th Infantry Regiment which had been sent into the enclosure to maintain order while the ROK screening committee interrogated the prisoners.

The troop commander was well aware (no doubt he had been warned) that any severity by the guard forces would be immediately exaggerated into a "massacre" by Communist propagandists. The camp cadres were restrained by no such considerations. Violence served the Communist purpose, and they were under orders to resist, regardless of consequences. They used their weapons against the American soldiers and the Korean interrogators to such effect that several American soldiers were wounded and one was killed. Only then did the troop commander order his men to fire on the rioters.

Throughout the spring of 1952, the unrest and disorder in the camps grew steadily worse. Any student of the written works of Lenin might have told the powers at the UN Command what was almost certain to follow. For the better part of a century it has been Communist practice to probe, hold, and when resistance slackens, consolidate.

By June, seven of the seventeen compounds on Koje-do remained unscreened. The people in charge of the camps—General Van Fleet

was now Eighth Army commander—seemed baffled by the rising tide
of mutiny. Despite the fact that it should have been obvious that the
prisoners of Koje-do were under outside control, measures to reestablish UN authority were undertaken with the greatest reluctance—when
they were undertaken at all.

Throughout that spring there were mass meetings of prisoners inside the camps, complete with displays of North Korean flags and
banners bearing anti-American slogans. The prisoners indulged in open
defiance at every opportunity.

Sensing at last that something had to be done, General Van
Fleet transferred an additional battalion of U.S. troops to Koje-do. It
was plain that if the screening was to be accomplished, it would require forced entry and very possibly a loss of life on both sides. In
addition to the unit sent to Koje-do, Van Fleet ordered several combat
units into the Pusan area, where they could be ready to move to Koje-
do if more serious rioting took place. The POWs had now actually
caused combat troops to be taken out of the battle line, where all
available forces were needed to face the still-powerful enemy. It was a
tour de force of Communist discipline and ferocity.

General Ridgway writes that "looking back in the light of later
knowledge" it might have been better at the outset to break the resistance in the compounds with firm action. He also says that if UN
intelligence had supplied him with information showing conclusively
that the POWs were under direct command of the Communist authorities, he might have ordered a crackdown. But he "did not know
then . . . how far the Communist command might have gone in its
readiness to sacrifice the lives of its own people in order to achieve a
propaganda victory."

Instead of seeking permission for firm action, however, General
Ridgway petitioned the Joint Chiefs of Staff in Washington for permission to suspend the screening. The truce negotiations, he felt, seemed
to be taking a favorable turn, and he did not wish to interrupt them.

The Joint Chiefs, with what seems almost indecent alacrity, agreed
to a new arrangement in which the prisoners in the rebellious compounds would simply be counted and listed as favoring repatriation.
With peace apparently in reach, an administration anxious to be rid
of an increasingly unpopular war, and an election year looming on

the near horizon, the powers in Washington were ready to go to great
lengths to avoid quarrels at Panmunjom. And the Communists knew
it.

In May, General Ridgway's provost marshal made a tour of inspection of the POW camps. His report was ominous. There had been
incidents of United Nations officers being seized and held hostage for
short periods by the prisoners. In some compounds the prisoners refused
to perform any work, even the work of carrying their own supplies into
the compounds.

General Ridgway sent a sharp message to General Van Fleet,
reminding him of the need to keep proper order in the camps. General
Van Fleet's reply expressed concern that the provost marshal had reported to General Ridgway before informing Van Fleet of conditions
in the compounds. (It is difficult to see how General Van Fleet could
have been unaware of them.)

Then on 7 May, Brigadier General Francis T. Dodd, the UN
camp commander, committed an indiscretion that boggles the mind.
Dodd, without proper safeguards, chose to meet with the Communist
cadre leaders inside the wire. They promptly took him prisoner and
sent word outside that he would be killed unless their demands (as yet
unstated) were met at once. They also informed the camp authorities
that if there were any attempt to free the general, his life would be
forfeit. Dodd, himself, sent out a message asking that no attempt to
free him be made. General Van Fleet, whose reaction to this turn of
events can only be imagined, directed that nothing be done, no force
employed, save only on his, Van Fleet's, direct orders.

At Eighth Army headquarters, which now resembled an over-
turned beehive, it was assumed that a full-scale breakout was imminent, and that the use of force would almost certainly result not only
in the death of General Dodd, but in great loss of life among the
prisoners—and a propaganda bonanza for the Communists.

General Ridgway was at the point of departing Korea to take
over his new post as NATO commander in Europe. General Mark
Clark, his designated successor as UN commander, was already in
Tokyo.

After a series of hastily convened staff meetings, General Ridgway decided to go to Korea to meet the crisis in person. His orders
from the JCS specified 12 May as the date for the change in command

in Korea, and to his credit Ridgway did not wish to leave this unresolved dilemma in the lap of the new commander, Mark Clark.

Ridgway and Clark flew to Korea and a tense meeting with the Eighth Army commander. Van Fleet had already ordered the reinforcing troops from Pusan to Koje-do, and had ordered Brigadier General Charles F. Colson, the chief of staff of the U.S. I Corps, to assume command of the POW camps. Colson arrived at Koje-do on 8 May and informed the Communist cadre inside the camp that General Dodd was no longer camp commander. He warned them that if Dodd were not released before a specified time, UN troops would enter the compounds and set him free by force.

The Communists were far from intimidated. With General Dodd acting as intermediary, they submitted demands of truly staggering insolence. As mere preliminaries they demanded recognition for a "POW association" and for telephone and motor vehicle communications between the several prison compounds.

Meanwhile, Generals Ridgway and Clark were en route to Korea, unaware that Communist demands were being entertained by officers on the scene.

When Ridgway and Clark reached Korea they were met by General Van Fleet, who informed Ridgway that he intended to negotiate with the prisoners for General Dodd's release. Ridgway concluded that such a course would mean delay of at least twenty-four hours before any action could be taken. A delay of that length would carry with it overtones of capitulation and defeat. He found this unacceptable and so informed Van Fleet.

He consulted with Admiral Turner Joy, the chief negotiator at the truce talks. The admiral agreed that any vacillation at this point would have disastrous effects on the negotiations. Any hint of surrender, he said, would only embolden the Communists to demand still further concessions.

Ridgway then ordered Van Fleet, in writing, to establish order in the camps immediately, using whatever force was required, even tanks. And once control was reestablished, it was to be maintained.

Van Fleet promptly ordered a battalion of tanks from the U.S. 3d Division to move 200 miles by road to Pusan and then to transship by LST to Koje-do. General Ridgway was plainly near the end of his patience. He was resolved to put down the disorder with deadly force *if need be. He realized, too, that such a course of action might be the death of General Dodd. But as he later wrote: "I felt that Dodd, like every other professional soldier, had accepted the risk of violent death when he chose his profession."*

Van Fleet, however, postponed carrying out Ridgway's order, citing the late arrival of the tank battalion. And Dodd, in his role as intermediary, had received from the Communist cadre in the camp a further list of demands, together with a list of charges against the camp authorities. They accused the custodial forces of injuring and murdering prisoners.

Colson had ordered his troops to prepare for forcible entry into the camp if General Dodd were not released unconditionally by 1000 hours on the morning of 10 May. Yet with troops and tanks finally ready for action, still another set of Communist demands was sent out. These were, if anything, more inflammatory and blustery than the previous set.

The following is a short extract from that extraordinary document, exactly as it was rendered into English on the spot:

> Immediate ceasing of the barbarous behavior, insults, torture, forcible protest with blood writing, threatening confinement, mass murdering, gun and machinegun shooting, using poison gas, germ weapons, experiment object of A-bomb, by your command.
>
> Immediate stopping of the so-called illegal and unreasonable volunteer repatriation of NKPA and CPVA PWS.
>
> Immediate ceasing the forcible investigation (screening) which thousands of PWs of NKPA and CPVA be armed and falled in slavery.

Despite the absurd language and Marxist hyperbole displayed in the document, what it demanded was no more nor less than the admission that the United Nations Command was guilty of very nearly every crime it had been accused of by the Communist High Command. To have even accepted such demands would have crippled the negotiators at Panmunjom.

Colson consulted with his immediate superior, General Paul F. Yount, and then drafted a reply denying all the Communists' charges

but, unbelievably, agreeing to one of the prisoners' demands. He agreed
to cease all further screening.

Meanwhile, the language of the new demands had reached General Ridgway's headquarters, and he immediately radioed to Van Fleet, telling him to hold Colson's reply, lest great damage be done to the UN's negotiating position at Panmunjom. He also demanded to know why Van Fleet had not carried out his previous order (of 8 May) to use what force was needed to establish control of the camps.

At 2000 hours on 10 May, ten hours after Colson's deadline, Colson and Dodd had worked out a draft reply that proved quite acceptable to the Communists. In it, General Dodd actually pleaded guilty to one of the most specious of the many charges brought by the POWs.

He wrote:

> With reference to your item 1 of that message I do admit that there have been instances of bloodshed where many PWs have been killed or wounded by UN forces. I can assure in the future that PWs can expect humane treatment in this camp according to the principles of International Law. I will do all in my power to eliminate further violence and bloodshed. If such incidents happen in the future, I will be responsible.

At the most charitable, and recognizing that General Dodd was negotiating under duress, it is almost inconceivable that an officer of his rank and experience should have put his name to such a document. But what was happening here was something new in the American experience. A war was being fought with a ruthless and absolutely dedicated enemy. And it was a war only reluctantly supported at home, a war all concerned were eager to put behind them. Furthermore, it was a political war of a sort unfamiliar to Americans, a war with sanctuaries where our fighting men were denied the right to go, a war in which representatives of the Republic sat at a negotiating table with enemies who were still actively in command of substantial forces still engaged in killing Americans. The naïveté of UN negotiators was still on the rise, and the behavior of the convinced Marxists with whom America found itself at war was still incomprehensible.

One suspects that the notion that if one deals fairly but firmly with an opponent, one will receive like treatment lies at the core of American—indeed Western—political thought. In Korea, generally, and at Koje-do specifically, Americans were being instructed in the new morality of the late twentieth century. General Dodd's confusion is, perhaps, understandable.

The Communists continued to hold out for even more damaging admissions until late that night. But when no further concessions were forthcoming, they released General Dodd and airily declared that there was now no need for armed confrontation.

On 12 May General Ridgway turned his command over to General Mark Clark and departed for Europe.

Despite General Ridgway's stated concern, Clark had been handed if not a hot potato, at least an uncomfortably warm one. The United Nations was not yet truly in command of the prisoners of Koje-do, and the Communists had achieved an enormous propaganda coup.

Perhaps General Clark remembered that his military judgment had once been severely criticized for indecisiveness at Salerno. That is conjecture. What is not conjecture is that immediately upon assuming the post of UN commander, he acted decisively to recover control of the compounds of Koje-do. Perhaps, like Crassus in the Roman Republic's Servile War, he felt some distaste at the need to deal with what amounted to a mutiny among prisoners. But he clearly recognized the necessity. He instructed Brigadier General Haydon L. Boatner to take action—and at once.

General Boatner ordered all civilians off the island and reorganized the staff. He set his engineers to building new compounds that would hold no more than 500 men in each. Guards were ordered to be prepared to enter any enclosure where North Korean flags or anti-UN placards were displayed, and to destroy such symbols.

The Communist cadres resolved to resist these attempts to reestablish United Nations control of their compounds. They secretly amassed an arsenal of crude weapons, including a substantial supply of Molotov cocktails made with the gasoline the UN authorities had given them for cooking and heating. They dug trenches and prepared to make a stand.

General Van Fleet ordered the 187th Airborne Combat Team to the island to reinforce Boatner's troops. Other UN formations were moved to Koje-do. Among these was a company of the Royal Canadian Regiment.

Lt. JOHN CLARK
B Company/Royal Canadian Regiment

It was a dirty night, and we were in the process of a changeover in the line, which at the best of times is a rather difficult operation. I was to take my platoon over to our left and relieve the French Canadians, so I had my houseboy—batman, call him what you will—at work packing my gear. I was about halfway between our old position and the new when a runner caught up with me and informed me that the CO had given instructions that I was to report to Tokch'on railhead for further instructions.

I turned over to my platoon sergeant and managed to liberate a vehicle, but it was still about 0200 hours when I arrived at Tokch'on. I was then informed that I was no longer with C Company, the company I had come with to Korea, but that I was now part of Baker Company.

I said, "Very well. Now can you tell me where B Company is going, then?" No one seemed to know the answer to that, but there were plenty of rumors. The hottest of them was that since everyone on hand at Tokch'on seemed to be airborne-qualified, we were going off on some airborne operation.

We got aboard a rickety train and started moving. Even our company commander didn't know where we were going, or what we were going to do when we got there. Neither did the brigade commander. But he did have an envelope that he was instructed to open a couple of hours after leaving Tokch'on.

But when he did, all he could tell us was that we had been ordered to Seaforth Camp, a camp run by the British in Pusan.

We finally arrived in Pusan and were taken in charge immediately by a full colonel, no less, of the Seaforth Highlanders. He confined us to barracks without a by-your-leave. We were still mystified about what our job might be.

Two days we spent in Pusan, while the rumors flew. Then, on the morning of the third day, we were marched down to the docks and put aboard some LSTs. As soon as we were aboard, the LSTs sailed out of Pusan harbor and we *still* didn't know where we were going. But eventually we saw an island, and since we were heading straight for it, we assumed that it was our destination. It was Koje-do.

As we approached the shore, we could see all these people, a great mob of them, waving. They were behind barbed wire. Some of them had signs that said, Welcome, Canadians. Well, that was a bit of a puzzle because as yet we didn't even know what this island was. We knew almost nothing about what was going on, yet the prisoners—they were North Koreans and Chinese, of course—seemed to know all about us.

We got landed and bivouacked, and shortly thereafter came General "Bull" Boatner, the commander of the American 2d Division. He had us gather around, and he gave us a short talk about what had been happening on Koje-do, and what he intended—with our help—to do about setting things right.

We entrenched near Compound 87, the Chinese compound. They were quite docile. There were about 4,000 of them in the enclosure, and they seemed to be well pleased to be out of the war. We only needed four men to do perimeter guard at Compound 87. The Chinese were not about to give anyone trouble.

Meanwhile we were getting some riot training from the American MPs, and some lectures on the Geneva Convention. When that was done, we were moved from Compound 87 over to Compound 66. This was where 6,000 North Korean officers were being held, and it was very different from the Chinese compound. The North Koreans were restless, hostile, and as arrogant as could be, considering they were prisoners of war.

We shared the patrolling of the perimeter of 66 with B Company of the King's Shropshire Light Infantry of the British Army. A Major Bancroft was their commander. Not really a popular officer with the KSLIs—or with us, for that matter. The combined force, the KSLIs and ourselves, were known as Peter Force.

General Boatner had told us we were going to establish order in the POW compounds, and that we were going to teach these Communists a lesson or two. Always within the terms of the Geneva Convention, he said, but we were not to take anything from the prisoners.

He said a number of other things that sounded better there than they would look in print. But no matter. To set things right at the very outset, General Boatner ordered that the North Korean flags and all the signs and placards the North Korean officers had raised had to come down. Boatner went to the wire and informed the Communist honcho that he had one hour to get all the flags and signs down, and if they weren't taken down on the double, why, then we were coming in to do the job for them.

General Boatner moved on down the line, but I could see that the prisoners weren't making any move to obey his orders. So I had our interpreter come with me to the sally port, and I told the NK honcho that time was slipping by, and that Boatner meant what he said. We heard later that these people had just about had everything their way for months. They had even taken an American general hostage.

About fifteen minutes before the deadline, I went to the wire again and told the Communist cadre there that they had better get cracking or we were coming in with bayonets.

What I got in return was a lot of cheeky talk. The honcho argued that the Geneva Convention allowed them to have and fly their national flag—which is absolute nonsense, of course. The Convention says no such thing. We went around a few times about this, and I finally told him that I wasn't interested in arguments, or lectures, or dialectic materialism. What I *was* interested in was seeing them obey General Boatner's order, and without any more delay.

When the deadline was five minutes away and the NK still hadn't obeyed the order, I lined up my troops and had them put on their gas masks and fix bayonets. It finally got through to the cadre inside the wire that the holiday was over, and that we meant what we said. Just as we opened the sally port gates, they bagan to gather up their flags and signs and stack them.

It's a good thing they did it, because it's hard to know what might have happened if we had had to take them on with rifles and bayonets. No one really likes to face, and quite possibly kill, unarmed men.

Lieutenant Clark's men of Peter Force were relatively fortunate. In the other compounds, where the Communist leaders had refused to form their men into small groups for reassignment, General Boatner's troops, including the paratroopers of the 187th Airborne Combat Team, entered the compounds and divided the prisoners by force. Tear gas was used, and the gas grenades set fire to the gasoline stoves and the caches of Molotov cocktails the POWs had accumulated. The American troops methodically cleaned out the resisting compounds. Within two hours, resistance was at an end. A hundred fifty prisoners had been killed or injured in the fighting. One American was killed, and thirteen were wounded. The prisoner barracks had been destroyed by fire, but the POWs were now segregated into smaller groups. And though there were subsequent riots and flurries of defiance, they were shortlived and ineffectual.

Only at Pongam-do, in December of 1952, was there another serious outbreak of POW violence. An attempted mass breakout of hardcore cadres resulted in the killing of 85 and the wounding of 100.

As if to confirm that all of these actions were undertaken at the direct instigation of the Communist High Command, a summary of the escape was presented as a complaint to the negotiators at Panmunjom—and to the world through the North Korean, Chinese, and Soviet propaganda media:

> Our fighting comrades were determined to die a glorious death. They lost nothing but their shameful lives in the fight [Shameful, perhaps, because they had allowed themselves to be captured?], and these were for liberation and glorious victory. . . . The sons of Korea, the fatherland, and honorable fighters of the Great Stalin, exposed nakedly the inhumanitarian, brutal, cannibalistic, slaughtering violence of the American imperialists, causing the peaceable peoples of the world, the fatherland, the party and all democratic nations to shout for revenge.

The gulf between the democratic nations and the Communist adversary was perhaps never better illustrated than in that ideological polemic.

THE BLACK WATCH ON THE HOOK

18-19 November 1952

While negotiations dragged on interminably at Panmunjom, minor actions continued all along the Main Line of Resistance. It is probably gratuitous to call these engagements "minor," since they were fought viciously and casualties on both sides were heavy. But the fact is that the United Nations forces were operating under a political injunction not to undertake any major offensive action, and the Communists, despite the presence in the field of 800,000 ground troops, were unable appreciably to better their position.

Approximately 92,000 UN troops had fallen into Communist hands. Ten thousand were American, 80,000 were Korean, and some 2,500 were members of the various components contributed by other United Nations members: British, Canadian, Turkish, Greek, and French. No Red Cross inspections of Communist prison camps had been permitted, nor were any such inspections ever to be allowed. In 1951 the Communists admitted to holding only 11,500 UN POWs. Two thirds of the Americans held in Communist prison camps were destined never to return.

The military situation clearly favored the United Nations. Command of the air was, to all intents and purposes, complete. The Communist forces dared not move in daylight.

The war had become a test of willingness to pay the cost in blood of a favorable bargaining position at Panmunjom.

In October the talks at the truce table were yet again interrupted by a Communist walkout, and the war became a political football in the United States as the elections approached. The American People, tired of the struggle, elected as president Dwight D. Eisenhower, who had promised to "go to Korea" and bring about an end to the war.

By March of 1953, apparently because of the uncertainty in the Communist world brought about by the death of Joseph Stalin, Premier Kim Il Sung of North Korea would be approving a resumption of the talks at Panmunjom and an acceptance of the (previously ignored) UN proposal to exchange sick and wounded prisoners of war. The talks would once again resume their ponderous progress.

On 3 November 1952, the 1st Battalion of the Black Watch, a storied British regiment, relieved the 1st Battalion of the 7th Marines in the area west of the Sami-ch'on River known as The Hook.

On the night of 26–27 October, the Marines had repelled a heavy attack by Chinese in the first battle of The Hook.

On 1 December, the Black Watch was in turn relieved by a battalion of the Princess Pat's Canadian Light Infantry.

The following are excerpts from the war diary of the Black Watch describing the action of 18–19 November 1952—the second battle of The Hook.

SECRET

Subject:- Second Battle of the HOOK   BW/INT/1
To: - See Distribution   26 Nov 52

1. This report on the second battle of the HOOK, which took place during the night 18/19 Nov 52 is compiled as detailed below.

   Appx "A" Outline of events

   Appx "B" Report on patrol led by SGT KERRY

   Appx "C" Reports made by PTES [Privates] MACDONALD 16   [the sixteenth man of that name presently serving in the Black Watch], MACDONALD 80 [It is a Scottish regiment, after all.] and GRAHAM on their return from SGT KERRY'S patrol.

   Appx "D" Reports made by PTES BEATON and REID on their return from the Ronson [an advanced position] patrol.

Appx "E" Details of events on the HOOK as told by CPL
WILSON and PTE COLEY of "A" Company.

Appx "F" Details of the escape made by PTE STANLEY
of "A" Company.

Appx "G" Report on interrogation of KSC labourer who
was captured during the battle and later escaped.

2. It is recorded here as there seems to be no other place to do
so that to all those who saw the enemy on the HOOK he
gave them the appearance that he was doped. He rushed
about madly in all directions and seemed quite oblivious of
all the shells landing around him. He was then seen suddenly to stop—no doubt when the effect had worn off. These
reports are confirmed by the fact that opium seeds were picked
out of a captured cigarette packet. There was a most repul-
sive odor on the position the next morning from the dead
bodies.

J. G. Moncrieff
Lieut,
Intelligence Officer,
1st Battalion The Black Watch (RHR)

OUTLINE OF EVENTS
(Appx "A")

[Time]

1. 1909 Report hearing burp gun and SA [small-arms] fires
from the area of 2/Lt Doig's patrol which was on the ridge
leading to Warsaw [ridge] having been delayed going out
owing to shellfire.

2. 1924 Report NO contact with either Warsaw or 2/Lt DOIG'S
patrol.

3. 1942 One wounded man returned to "B" Company from
Warsaw patrol. For details of the above action see Appx
"B".

5. 2101 "A" Company being attacked. The attack appeared to
come from three directions, along Warsaw ridge, along the
Ronson ridge and up the valley to the south of the HOOK.
Enemy arrived in fwd trenches of 1 pl [1st Platoon] before

their own barrage had even lifted. *[In other words, the Chinese attackers charged into their own falling artillery shells.]*

6. 2102 Own arty asked to fire close DF No 4092 which covers the approaches to Ronson. *[UN artillery is asked to fire a preregistered concentration between Ronson and the battalion command post.]*

7. 2103 Recall your patrols. All heads down.

8. 2105 [Tanks] ordered to fire on Ronson. They used their searchlights but were unable to see enemy in the smoke and haze.

14. 2127 Offered a ripple of rockets by U.S. Marines. Asked for it to come down on 096104 [map coordinates].

15. 2130 Report at least 4 mor [enemy mortars] firing from WARSAW on both sides of the spur at 105106 and a fire on WARSAW.

16. 2137 Company standing patrol in with one man wounded.

17. 2140 SITREP Heavy fire on the HOOK. Patrol on Ronson overrun.

20. 2145 Bde [brigade] warned 3 PPCLI [3d Battalion, Princess Pat's Canadian Light Infantry] to stand up [alert] one company.

21. 2147 Enemy on the HOOK. This info was obtained by a messenger who got round the fwd trenches to 2/Lt BLACK in his CP and reported back on the 88 [radio] set. Almost immediately after this, arty DF(VT) was fired on the HOOK itself. *[In plainer language, when the Chinese were reported in amongst the Black Watch outposts, a UN artillery concentration was called in.]*

22. 2150 U target. Coming down. Keep in your caves. *[This was a message from the artillery, brief and succinct.]*

23. 2150 Ripple fired, Marine battery. *[The U.S. Marines added their rockets to the incoming barrage on The Hook.]*

24. 2152 Report of enemy attacking 1st platoon of "A" Company and that shelling on the HOOK has restarted. This shelling thought to be both enemy and our own. *[A platoon of "A" Company was fighting hand-to-hand with the Chinese while artillery from both sides rained down on the battle.]*

25. 2201 [Message from the artillery command post] Fire on you stopping now.
26. 2202 HOOK being heavily mortared.
27. 2203 Shelling on "D" Company increasing.
28. 2205 OC [Officer commanding] "A" Company requested VT [artillery fire] to continue on the HOOK itself since he discovered the enemy were still there.
29. 2207 ["A" Company] ordered to stand by to be relieved by [a company] of the 3PPCLI [3d Battalion, Princess Pat's Canadian Light Infantry].
30. 2214 PPCLI getting ready to move.
31. 2217 [From battalion commander] Prepare to lift all fire on the HOOK and put a belt of fire around the perimeter of it in order to stop the next wave of enemy attack.
33. 2224 Report that enemy numbers on the HOOK are considerable.
34. 2225 [Relayed from "A" Company through "C" Company] Fire now lifting off the HOOK. [Platoon commander] going out to have a look. Nothing seen.
35. 2225 The P/M [pipe major] being wounded, the Pipes and Drums were put under command of 2/Lt RATTRAY to reinforce his own platoon. 2/Lt RATTRAY's platoon then moved up the hill in order to take over the high ground and look after the RIGHT flank of the company position since these positions had been vacated by 2 platoon on moving forward to the HOOK.
38. 2237 Shelling decreasing.
39. Request for ambulances.
40. 2244 SA fire from Warsaw.
41. 2247 First platoon thinks the enemy are forming up for another attack.
42. 2247 One Company 3PPCLI on its way to "B" Company now.
46. Following intercept received: "Chinese ordered to move to [Hill] 164."
47. 2259 Tanks on 121 have been firing hard for the last five minutes.
48. 2300 HOOK still being shelled.

51. [From officer commanding "A" Company] Shelling continues. Unable to search area.

54. 2331 A ripple of rockets coming in shortly. One more will come in thirty minutes later.

56. 2335 SITREP There has been considerable damage to the positions. Now consolidating.

57. 2337 Two Chinamen came into 1 pl CP and were shot at point-blank range. Were presumed to be lying there wounded. However, when the situation eased and a light was produced it was found they had gone.

58. 2340 Ripple of rockets shot.

59. 2359 Company of 3PPCLI now moving on foot toward the positions.

60. 0001 Five men returned from Sgt KERRY's patrol on Warsaw.

61. 0010 SITREP Mopping up. A few enemy are still hiding in what is left of the fwd trenches.

[The first flurry of fighting on The Hook and its flanking ridges died down. The Scots in the forward positions, after taking long periods of heavy shelling from their own and enemy guns, and after a number of vicious hand-to-hand encounters with the attacking Chinese, awaited reinforcements by the Canadian Light Infantrymen moving up the slopes of Ronson and Warsaw ridges. By twenty minutes after midnight, the Canadians had completed the relief of the Black Watch's "B" Company. The respite was shortlived.]

67. 0026 [From the officer commanding "A" Company] Attack coming in. Chinese in forward trenches.

68. 0029 [From the battalion commander to the officer commanding "A" Company] You must mop up.

69. 0031 [From "B" Company, en route via Warsaw ridge to the administrative area in the rear] Asks if there is any indication the attack is coming from Warsaw. [It was, in fact, coming from Ronson.]

70. 0032 "A" Company being attacked now.

71. 0032 CO ordered tanks to fire at enemy on Ronson.

72. 0045 [To OC "A" Company from battalion commander]

Counterattack forces to remain in deep trenches by your CP area. 2/Lt SMART's platoon of "B" Company arrived and was put in the trench in front of "A" Company's command post. Soon after this Lt HAW's platoon of "D" Company arrived and was told to hold the high ground formerly occupied by elements of 2 and 3 platoons, and to bring fire to bear on the HOOK when counterattack was launched on green Verey Light signal.

74. 0052 Tanks say it is NOT on to go up on the HOOK. *[Apparently the tanks had been requested to move up the mountainside, but the terrain made such a movement impossible. There was a discussion, and a compromise satisfactory to the Black Watch battalion commander was reached. Agreement, however, did not change the realities of the terrain.]*

76. 0059 Tank is to move up to the HOOK. Intention was to put a tank on the HOOK at the time of the counterattack in order to give the infantrymen some support. OC "A" Company, hearing that a tank was coming up, delayed his counterattack. His plan was then altered to move 4 platoon up with the tank until it reached its firing position on the top of the HOOK, and then swing 4 platoon around the right flank in front of the tank to clear up the HOOK.

78. 0110. Intercept. Enemy calling for reinforcements.

79. 0121 [To "A" Company] Can you see to fight? *[At this point the tank commander reported that his path was blocked by a jeep and a 15-cwt lorry.]*

81. 0125 OC Company "A" told tank commander to drive through the jeep and lorry blocking his way to the HOOK.

83. 0132 Artillery barrage now lifting off the HOOK. [This was "A" Company's signal to begin counterattacking.]

84. 0137 Intercept. Tank hit. Driver hurt. [It happened at the very moment the attack was to go forward. The tank was hit with a round from a bazooka, wounding the driver. At the same moment four machine guns opened up on the tank from the ridge between the "A" Company command post and The Hook.]

85. 0147 Putting down artillery barrage for two minutes to deal

with enemy on the ridge. After that the attack will go forward whether the tank is ready or NOT.

86. 0147 Counterattack went in the moment artillery lifted. Advanced about 50 yards. It was then held up by fresh machine guns opening up. OC "A" Company then ordered 4 platoon to give covering fire to 3 platoon (2/Lt RATTRAY's platoon reinforced with the Pipes and Drums) who had meanwhile been moved to the starting line. 3 platoon then went forward and reached the lateral trench across the HOOK. They were there held up by light machine gun fire and grenades from the enemy established on the highest point of the HOOK.

87. 0223 Green flare seen on top of the HOOK.

90. 0247 SITREP. Elements of 1 platoon holding line of crawl-trench from platoon CP. Other platoons are to pass through. The counterattack force is still holding the lateral trench and trying to mop up.

92. 0253 All clear behind HOOK CP.

93. 0255 Shortly after this 2/Lt BLACK reported he was being fired at from behind.

94. 0302 [From brigade] All Chinese radio sets have closed down. This infers (a) Attack has failed or (b) operators have been killed by counterbombardment.

97. 0310 "C" Company being heavily mortared. [Evidently the Chinese did not agree with brigade's assessment in Item 94.]

98. 0311 Intercept. Chinese calling frantically for reinforcements.

99. 0327 Intercept. [From "A" Company radio net] 1 to 1-A: "Are you happy where you are?" 1-A to 1: "No, never have been." 1 to 1-A: "Don't be a clown."

102. 0345 Group of enemy on RIGHT of the HOOK.

103. 0348 SITREP. One platoon now established on the HOOK. One platoon of "B" Company reforming and distributing ammunition. (They are being fired at from the RIGHT-rear.) Lt. HAW's platoon ordered to move down from the company command post and round the LEFT flank with the task of mopping up and occupying the forward trenches

on the SOUTH side of the HOOK. This platoon, having got so far forward, came under heavy machinegun fire from the hilltop designated BETTY GRABLE.

105. 0345 Machinegun on BETTY GRABLE engaged with Stens and Brownings.

106. 0355 OC 1 platoon reports the remainder of "A" Company, now all on the HOOK, is being attacked from all sides.

107. 0358 Fire mission RESIST [planned earlier before the first assault on The Hook and aimed at isolating the Chinese on the ridges Ronson and Warsaw] shot.

110. 0415 CO called for sitrep from OC "A" Company. OC "A" said he was still battling to get on the HOOK. CO told him reinforcements on way to him had been attacked. Ordered him to hold on in his present position. OC "A" replied: "That's what I hoped you would say."

112. 0425 12 platoon, on the way to the HOOK encountered approximately twenty Chinese on the ridge between 12 and 11 platoons' positions. Sgt. ROBERTSON, with eleven men, ordered to push through to the HOOK. Was fired on from both sides of the ridge.

118. 0503 Intercept from U.S. Marines. A new attack forming up.

119. 0515 2/Lt WALKER, on arrival at Company "A" command post was reinforced with what men were available and sent up to 1 platoon on the ridge to assist clearing the enemy from there.

120. 0522 [From Walker] Making progress. Opposition appears light.

121. 0524 Twenty-nine casualties evacuated so far.

122. 0526 Positions on HOOK receiving artillery fire. Intercept. 1-A to 1: "Our own [fire] is falling short. Can you rectify this?" 1 to 1-A: "It is NOT, repeat NOT, our [fire]."

126. 0550 [From the artillery observer] Firing airburst over WARSAW.

127. 0552 Few enemy still on slopes forward of CP. OC Company "A" ordered 6 platoons of "B" Company to move forward and safeguard the RIGHT flank to prevent further

penetration from WARSAW approach. It was at this time that 2/Lt GRAY and Major ROWAN-HAMILTON were wounded by one of our own grenades thrown at them by the enemy.

128. 0557 CO ordered 11 platoon to go out at first light and deal with enemy on the ridge between them and the HOOK.

129. 0557 Twelve men of 12 platoon arrived at 1 platoon CP. 12 platoon was ordered to go round the LEFT flank of the HOOK and 10 platoon around the RIGHT flank to clear the enemy from both sides of it. Just after 12 platoon moved off from the CP to carry out this task, the officer commanding, 2/Lt WALKER, was wounded.

130. 0558 Request for more men from "A" Company CP. CO asked for a sitrep. Reply was: "Situation very confused. Small parties of the enemy have appeared again all over the place." The CO asked: "Have you any reserve left?" Reply: "No." CO: "Stick it out." CO then informed Brigade that all reserves had now been expended. Brigade informed CO that Company "C" of the 3rd Princess Pat's would relieve our men on the HOOK at first light.

132. 0602 Fire mission BD4092 [planned earlier] fired. Results unknown.

133. 0602 Not much left of 3 Section 11 platoon.

134. 0610 PPCLI counterattack moving on the HOOK [to relieve the Black Watch].

137. Company "A" still holding its ground. Reports small parties of enemy on the HOOK with small piles of grenades ready for use. CO informed Canadians their relieving force would have to do some fighting on arrival.

138. 0630 Artillery firing smoke screen between 093106 and 095103.

139. 0643 Intercept of Company "A" radio net: 1-A to 1: "Some enemy are throwing grenades down on us." 1 to 1-A: "Don't wish to sound facetious, but why not throw some back?"

140. 0653 Mopping up on the HOOK.

141. 0708 One platoon of 3PPLCI on the HOOK, the other platoon is just below it. This unit met NO enemy when they occupied the position.

143. 0801 Evacuation of wounded being carried out.
144. 0820 Command on the HOOK passed to Company "C" of the Princess Pat's Canadian Light Infantry (to be known as "Z" Company).
144. 0933 All wounded off the HOOK. Wounded and two dead removed from WARSAW ridge. Chinese are still on WARSAW, but are being engaged by the Canadians.
145. 0945 Officer commanding the 26th Field Ambulance estimates the battalion has taken more than 70 casualties [in approximately eighteen hours of fighting].
148. 1000 Intercept. Heard on Battalion Command 31 set net— a Canadian voice: "Chinky, Chinky; hullo Chinky here."

[Something of the "fog of war" comes through the lines of Lieutenant Moncrieff's chronology of the Black Watch's eighteen hours atop a Korean mountain. The account is confusing—and so is war. But the account cannot be read without some realization of what it took to spend those hours atop The Hook and its ancillary ridges.

At the very least it should help Americans to remember—if they ever knew—that they did not fight the Korean War alone.

There is more.]

REPORT ON PATROL LED BY SGT KERRY
(Appx "B")

The combined "D" Company ambush patrol commanded by SGT KERRY AND "B" Company recce patrol commanded by 2/Lt DOIG left "A" Company through WARSAW gate in the wire and proceeded along the ridge toward WARSAW. It was at WARSAW that SGT KERRY's patrol was going to set up an ambush and 2/Lt DOIG was going to move from there with his patrol to obtain information about previously reported enemy activity in the valley below. [The combined force] was led by SGT KERRY, behind him were 2/Lt DOIG and his two men, then followed by the remainder of SGT KERRY's patrol. The two patrols totaled 14 men. The patrols had been delayed going out at the scheduled time [of last light] owing to enemy shelling.

They were moving very quietly along the ridge and had reached the bottom of the last rise on this ridge before arriving at the

position of WARSAW itself. It was here that they heard movement ahead of them on this knoll and got down. SGT KERRY
and 2/Lt DOIG decided to wait a little to see what would happen. Neither of them saw any enemy, although the noise was
increasing. Other members of the patrol who were behind later
reported that they did see one or two enemy moving on the top
of this rise. They waited in this position for a few moments with
the two patrols strung out in single file along the path. Suddenly
2/Lt DOIG got up and shouted "CHARGE!" and ran forward
firing his weapon together with SGT KERRY. There were flashes
on the ridge above them. Almost simultaneously, they only having gone a few yards, a grenade landed in front of SGT KERRY
and another between him and 2/Lt DOIG, parting them and
causing them to fall out away from each other.

*[The foibles of subalterns in combat are the stuff of legend in all ar-
mies. Evidently Second Lieutenant Doig's rash action earned him the
disapproval not only of the probably more experienced Sergeant Kerry,
but of the war diarist as well. In any case, at this point Second Lieutenant Doig vanishes from the account of the action. This is the military equivalent of being "sent to Coventry."]*

The remainder of the patrol, being spread out in single file, had
hardly any time to act before being blinded by [the flash of]
these enemy grenades. So they remained where they were and
engaged the enemy with their rifles and LMGs [light machine
guns]. There was a belt of wire separating them from the enemy.
Groans were heard after they returned the enemy's fire. SGT
KERRY, having got up, returned to his patrol and quickly gave
orders to the two Bren gunners, putting one to cover each flank.
He reorganized the patrol in an ambush posture. PTE
O'ROURKE was wounded in this action and taken away back
up the ridge. SGT KERRY then ordered L/Cpl FINDLAY with
a party of men to move back to the next knoll behind them on
the ridge to cover his [Kerry's] withdrawal. After L/Cpl FIND-
LAY had established himself there SGT KERRY withdrew the
remainder of the patrol to this position. SGT KERRY with PTES
GILL and GLASS then went forward again and made a search

and sweep of the area [searching for the enemy] but found nothing. The patrol then moved back along the ridge and took up an ambush position about 150 yards from the WARSAW gate [in the wire]. SGT KERRY found that his wireless was not working. He therefore sent PTE GILL back to "A" Company to report what had happened. PTE O'ROURKE, the wounded man, was then taken back to "A" Company by PTES MCGREGOR and GILL. PTE GILL reached the CP of Number 1 platoon of "A" Company where he had to stay all night. L/Cpl MACKAY and three men, all of "D" Company, came out to reinforce the patrol. SGT KERRY then put L/Cpl MACKAY in front of the patrol and proceeded to go round from man to man making a check on ammo, etc. He was checking the fourth man when a heavy enemy barrage came down on and around [the patrol] which lasted for some time. He thought he heard the sound of a Chinese bugle. Then quite a number of Chinamen came rushing up the ridge but were halted at the wire fence. It appeared that the Chinese were surprised to encounter this belt of wire. A fierce grenade battle then ensued. The Chinese appeared in further waves. The signal for each wave to attack was four blasts on the bugle. It was observed that only about three in ten Chinese grenades thrown went off. The patrol by this time was very low on ammunition, and when it ran out SGT KERRY got up and ordered the patrol to follow him. He led the patrol down a steep reentrant running down from the ridge— the alternative being to withdraw the patrol through the heavy enemy barrage which was falling on "A" Company's position. PTE RAYNHAM of the patrol did return by this route to "A" Company, but he was wounded and evacuated immediately. When [the patrol] reached the bottom of the reentrant, PTE LYNCH was wounded by shellfire. The only others who had followed [Sgt. Kerry] were L/Cpl MACKAY, PTE ROBERTSON 62, and PTE DINGWALL.

[Kerry] then led the patrol downward toward WARSAW, keeping halfway up the ridge in order to avoid both the valley and the path along the top [which was under heavy bombardment].

[Kerry] proceeded along the ridge almost to the finger running off from WARSAW itself at [coordinates] 107106. He heard Chinamen talking on the finger, so he decided to go down and cross the valley at 108105 and then [return] up to the ridge at 109104 to his own platoon's position. The patrol made very slow progress due to one casualty it brought along with it. SGT KERRY sent L/Cpl MACKAY and one man on ahead to make contact with the Company and warn them of the return of the remainder of the patrol. Lt GURDON sent down a stretcher to bring in the wounded man. The patrol returned to the Company position at 0001 hours.

REPORTS MADE BY PTES MACDONALD 16, MACDONALD 80 AND GRAHAM ON THEIR RETURN FROM SGT KERRY'S PATROL
(Appx "C")

PTE MACDONALD 16 was a member of SGT KERRY's patrol. When engaged by the enemy during the arty [artillery] barrage he became separated from the rest of the patrol. He was captured by a single Chinaman who took his rifle. But [MacDonald] engaged him with his fists and got away, *probably having killed him.*

[Emphasis added. The diarist is saying that Private MacDonald killed a Chinese soldier, who had disarmed him, with his bare hands.]

He spent the remainder of the night among the wire in the valley between the WARSAW ridge and 11 platoon's position. He returned to 11 platoon, badly gored by wire, at 0745 hours the next morning.

PTE MACDONALD 80, who was [also] a member of SGT KERRY's patrol, was wounded in the grenade battle on the ridge of the HOOK. He tried to return to "A" Company's position, but found the Chinamen there. Then he crawled back along the ridge to WARSAW. It was here that he was forced to take cover in the scrub due to the continual passage above him of Chinese parties coming forward to collect their wounded. He made the following observations:-

(a) Each party was led by one soldier with a burp gun. Following him was a soldier with a white band on his arm and a box at his side containing field dressings. Presumably this was the medical orderly. There were then about twenty to thirty unarmed gooks. The rear was brought up by another soldier armed with a burp gun.

[It is likely that the "twenty to thirty unarmed gooks" were Korean civilians forced to serve as laborers by the Chinese.]

(b) Men wounded in the legs were carried back by two men, one on each side of the casualty. Men wounded in the chest and upwards were carried by one man in a fireman's lift position.

Many such parties passed PTE MACDONALD 80 during the night. He eventually made his way back to his company's position at first light.

PTE GRAHAM, too, was a member of SGT KERRY's patrol and was separated from them during the enemy barrage. He killed or wounded four Chinamen with a phosphorous grenade before he left the ridge for the valley below. While lying [hidden] in the valley between WARSAW ridge and the spur running down from 11 platoon position, [MacDonald 80] encountered one Chinaman whom he may have killed or wounded with his Bren gun.

He made his way back to his platoon area, arriving there at 0715 hours the following morning, with two grenade wounds in his leg.

REPORT MADE BY PTES BEATON AND REID AFTER RETURNING FROM THE RONSON AMBUSH PATROL
(Appx "D")

The patrol, consisting of 2/Lt YOUNGER and six men, left the company position at last light. At about 2025 hours shelling began. The barrage lasted about ten minutes.

Three Chinamen came along the trench in which the patrol had taken cover. PTE EVANS was out front of the patrol's position with an LMG.

The Chinamen opened fire with burp guns. We discovered that our weapons were stuck and would NOT fire.

[That seven men would have a simultaneous failure of their weapons is improbable. It is more likely that the Chinese achieved total surprise.]

We threw three grenades at the Chinamen and then bailed out. Yells were heard from the Chinamen after the grenades exploded. PTE BEATON went straight back to 2 platoon command post and reported to SGT GAIT [the platoon sergeant] what had happened. PTE REID [who had evidently accompanied Beaton] got stuck in the wire and reported to SGT GAIT later.

More Chinamen came in after those reported above. PTE BLAIR, who was behind PTE BEATON, seemed to have been killed. PTE BEATON tried to get him to make a run with him, but there was NO life in him, nor any response from him. L/Cpl WOOD, PTES BEATON and REID returned from the patrol. It is thought that PTE FORD was wounded.

Note: It has not been possible to obtain an account of this patrol from 2/Lt YOUNGER since he was wounded during it [sic] and has been evacuated out of reach.

[Clearly, the Ronson ambush patrol was an unmitigated disaster. Not only was the ambush patrol ambushed, but it scattered under fire and returned to 2 Platoon's command post as stragglers. The final tally was one man killed and two men wounded.]

DETAILS OF ACTION AS TOLD BY CPL WILSON OF 1 PLATOON "A" COMPANY
(Appx "E")

When the heavy bombardment started we made for our tunnels as ordered by 2/Lt BLACK. The barrage was exceptionally heavy and only PTES STANLEY, MURPHY, MILLAR 11, and DOW 34 reached the tunnels. There were also two RE [Royal

Engineers] personnel and two KSC [Korean Service Corps] por-
ters in the tunnel. L/Cpl WATSON, PTES SWAN and ORAM
of my section did NOT make the tunnel, neither did PTES
DELLOW and COLEY who were manning the Browning [ma-
chine gun] which fired out to RONSON.

I was the last man to get into the tunnel, and standing at the
entrance, I saw the Chinamen come over the [breastworks] in
their own barrage. They fired a burp gun at me but missed. I
took what cover I could and fired back with my Sten. They
managed to get into a part of the tunnel and I heard them lighting matches to try to get some light. I reported over the 88 [ra-
dio] set to 2/Lt BLACK that I had five men of my section in the
tunnel, along with some unknown number of Chinamen.

There was another burst of burp gun fire into the tunnel.
PTE MILLAR threw a grenade, but it bounced against the wall
and landed six feet away from me. It exploded and a piece of it
went straight into my knee. There was another burst from a burp
gun down the tunnel that didn't hit anything. There had been
a lot of shooting and suddenly I realized from the quiet that we
had nothing left to fight with.

I therefore let out a great many groans and very shortly a
Chinaman appeared and realized that I was wounded. Everyone
else in the tunnel was unhurt because they had all been in another compartment when the grenade went off. The Chinaman
peered in, lit a match and burned some leaflets to give himself
some light.

The fighting outside seemed to have stopped. The Chinamen
herded all of us out, where they lined us up and handed out
leaflets. Then they searched us and took everything we had in
our pockets. We were all driven along the trench by a man with
a burp gun. We still had to keep down because the shelling
hadn't completely stopped.

They drove us over the edge of the trench and down the bank.
Wounded, I was being helped by two of our men. Then the
Chinese noncom realized that the shelling was still too bad and
that we would never get through it, so he signalled us to come
back up again. Once we were back in the trench, they left me
lying there and took away PTES MILLAR, DOW, MURPHY,

STANLEY, and the two engineers. They left me where I was, with two Korean laborers. After about five minutes a Chinese commander of some kind came along, lifted me onto his back and carried me along twenty or thirty yards of trench and around a corner into a hutchie [bunker] which happened to be my own. It had about ten Chinamen in it. I stayed there for an hour or more, while the shelling went on and on. I kept looking out to see what was going on. I noticed, to my surprise, that the Chinese had no regard at all for their own safety. They were running around the position, jabbering as though nothing whatever were happening—and all the while the shells kept falling on us. Ours or theirs, I really didn't know, and the Chinese didn't seem to care. Those outside were running around and shouting, and those in the hutchie were looting all my belongings.

The Chinese officer brought in his wireless set and began to set up communications. I tried to indicate to them all that this bunker was NOT a safe place, and that I had no intention of staying in it. They accommodated me by taking me to one of the scrapes dug into the walls of the trench. I found two Korean laborers there. Chinese kept coming in and going out all night long. During the hours of darkness, I took note of three separate attempts by our people to retake the position.

About 0500 hours—I still had my watch and took note of the times—the Chinese started to pull out, taking their dead. They worked like Trojans to get them away. The last man wasn't carried away until about 0700 hours. At the end, one Chinaman came along and shook my hand and said, in broken English, "Good luck."

DETAILS OF ACTION AS TOLD BY PTE COLEY

I was at the Browning position when the barrage started and, thinking it not safe to make for the tunnel opening, I remained where I was. PTE DELLOW, who was with me, opened up with the Browning as the Chinamen started coming up the hill. We then started hearing Chinamen behind us, and a grenade landed and exploded in the pit near us. I started firing the Browning myself. The Chinese then threw two more grenades into our weapon-pit from behind and one of those wounded me.

I didn't know how badly. I lay there half-conscious for the rest of the night. Chinamen came into the pit, looked around, then went away. All the while shells kept falling on the position. Then after a long while the Chinese came back and took away the Browning, the ammo, my rifle and my watch. Different Chinamen came in at odd times all during the night. Each one searched me and then went off. One of them tried to take off my flak-vest, but couldn't manage it because it was the kind that slips on over the head, like a sweater. Then about the time it started getting light they decided to retreat. I heard them take three of our chaps away. I heard one of our people say, "Here now, take your time, boy."

The three taken away were PTES DELLOW, STANLEY and DOW. The Chinese didn't want any wounded prisoners.

DETAILS OF THE ESCAPE MADE BY PTE STANLEY OF "A" COMPANY
(Appx "F")

As has been told previously in Cpl WILSON's story we were lying in the trench after having been captured in one of the tunnels.

The Chinamen first took away PTES MILLAR, MURPHY and the two Sappers with an armed escort. Then they came for me and PTE DOW. There was one Chinaman in front acting as scout, then came PTE DOW and myself and after us about nine Chinamen. They were all loaded down with loot. They had our steel helmets and our weapons and two LMGs, a Sten gun and about eight rifles. They also had two 88 sets [radios]. One of these was taken from PTE MILLAR. The other they brought with them. I saw it strapped to a pack when they first arrived at the position.

On crossing the wire, I got caught up in it and they all were waiting for me to untangle myself. I was second in line. The scout had already crossed the wire. He was kneeling covering one of the approaches with his burp gun. The rest of them were still standing behind the wire.

When I untangled myself I suddenly made a run for it. A big shout went up. They threw grenades at me and fired their burp

221   guns but I got away unscathed and returned to the Company
223   through the 3 platoon position.

224   *The Black Watch's defense of The Hook was a bloody, confused, costly*
225   *business. There were casualties, men were wounded and died. On the*
226   *Communist side, a great many died. No ground was won or lost. The*
227   *Hook was typical of the battles still to be fought before the war's end.*

THE NEVADA
CITIES

October 1952–March 1953

Vegas, Carson, and Reno were the names given to three positions forward of the MLR in an area covering the left flank of the Second U.S. Army northwest of the Imjin River.

Manned by units of the 1st Marine Division, the mountaintop outposts stood like islands in the tumbled terrain of the no-man's-land between the United Nations forces and the lines occupied by the Communist enemy.

To the north and east of the "Nevada Cities," Marines held outposts Berlin and East Berlin. Still farther to the northeast, the Chinese held outposts Detroit, Little Rock, and Frisco.

The actions that took place there were typical of those which were to characterize the last eight months of the war.

Cpl. JAMES D. PREWITT
2/5

Days on the MLR were slow and sometimes boring. The tedium was broken when someone started shooting at the rats in his bunker. Guaranteed to wake things up and bring some brass up to the line. Korea was in the "truce-talk" stage. There were no large movements on the MLR [General Ridgway's order to cease all "offensive" actions was in force], but shooting would break out from time to time for no reason that anyone could see.

Nights on outpost duty were long and, as the year waned, became cold. They were always lonely. Others got two-man posts, but not me. It was always my luck to draw a solo post. I would try to tell time by the rotation of the Big Dipper around the North Star—a leftover from my Boy Scout days. There was always the fear of unexplained noises and movements down the draw where the garbage was thrown. Empty C-ration cans were always tossed down into the gulleys and ravines leading to the outpost. This trash made the footing very unstable and cut down on the chance of a sneak attack from below. But when the cans clattered in the dark, you never knew whether it was the Chinese or just the rats foraging for food.

Rotation was one week on an outpost, then two weeks on the MLR. The outposts stank. Flies, rats, garbage, fecal wastes all contributed to the effluvium. The worst job was covering the Chinese bodies that lay on the side of the hill. Korean laborers were hired to go down and bury the dead, but it took armed Marines to "escort" them. It was part protection, part compulsion. Then a few mortar rounds would fall and the buried bodies would turn up again, smelling worse than before.

Outpost Reno was an L-shaped ridge, with the short base of the L pointed toward a goonie outpost [possibly Little Rock] and our MLR. At the distal end of the base there was a two-man bunker. From this vantage point we could watch the goonie outpost across the valley and observe the trail and trench leading to the outpost proper. The vertex of the L was the highest point on the ridge, and there was located a bunker for the use of the artillery forward observer. To use binoculars there was asking for trouble, because the lenses could reflect the light. One FO was shot through the binoculars by a Chinese sniper.

Between the two small bunkers was a third, larger and more heavily fortified, with two .30-caliber machine guns. The entrance to this bunker was also the entrance to a large, deep tunnel. I hated to go near the thing. When I was a child I helped to dig my brother out of a collapsed play tunnel, and I was left with a real horror of such places.

There was also an observation bunker at the top of the L. All the bunkers were below the ridgeline. There was a trench that crossed the ridge and ran down the hill to the base and came out in a field. This was supposed to keep the goonies in their outpost from knowing when Reno was being supplied or reinforced.

The machine-gun bunker had a step at each end for the gunner and ammo handler. There was a kind of shelf at chest height. On the night of October 30 I went off duty at about 2200, left my M1 on the step, and went back into the bunker. I didn't go into the tunnel; I seldom did.

About an hour later the goonies decided to attack us, and I heard a lot of shooting and yelling and explosions nearby. My only thought was to retrieve my rifle, and I came out of the bunker heading for the gun step. Someone yelled "Grenades!" and at almost the same instant some object hit my steel helmet and bounced onto the gunner's shelf right in front of me.

My immediate reaction was to throw my arms up in front of my eyes. The grenade exploded about six inches from my chest—about at the level of the lower sternum. My helmet was blown off my head and into the bunker. My right forearm and elbow were badly cut up. Two weeks' beard was burned off my face. I had no feeling at all in my right hand and arm. I picked dirt and bits of steel out of my face for weeks afterward.

The Good Lord was really with me. I had been wearing my flak vest, and wonder of wonders, I had even been wearing it properly, zipped up. It saved my life. Some pieces of the grenade did penetrate the vest, but they were stopped by my ribs and didn't go deeper.

My friend Dale Auschenbacher was standing on the step when the grenade went off, and he was wounded in the legs. There was another Marine nearby, an American Indian, who took part of the explosion—I only remember the grenade that wounded me, but there must have been others—at the level of his groin and thighs. His inner legs were a bloody mess. He later lost his testicles.

My first words after the blast were something like "I'm hit. Is anyone else hurt?"

The Indian—whose nickname, for some fool reason, was "Marine"—spoke up. "It's me, Marine," he said. "Help me."

It was dark and I was having trouble seeing, but I recognized his voice and pulled him back into the bunker. No lights, of course. Just by feel I located his wounded legs, felt the blood flowing, took off my belt, and put a tourniquet on him. I don't know if I used my right hand. I must have, but I will never be sure.

The attack petered out, but we stayed in the bunker. From time to time I loosened the tourniquet. I remember trying to talk to Marine, but he wouldn't let me. He kept saying the Chinese were right outside, and to be quiet. His voice sounded strange and my head was still ringing. It turned out later that my eardrums had ruptured when the grenade went off.

I don't really know how long we were in the bunker. But when some others and a Navy corpsman reached us, I told them to take Marine out first because he was hurt badly. The corpsman told me to take it easy, and then he gave both of us a shot of painkiller. My last thought before passing out was, I hope they don't take me into the tunnel.

But they did. I woke up in the tunnel about daybreak. Marine was still in the bunker, alone. More incoming rounds or another attack had prevented his being evacuated. But after another hour or so, more of our people arrived at Reno with some Korean stretcher bearers.

As we came out of the trench and started over the crest of the ridge, some mortar rounds began falling around us. My stretcher bearers dropped me and dived for the trench. I remember a big Marine pulled one of them out and threw me in. The Korean was furious and terrified. He cursed that Marine all the way back to the evacuation point. A helicopter arrived then, and we were moved out to another point behind the lines, where a truck picked us up. The driver did his best to miss the bumps, but considering the condition of the roads, it really wasn't possible. I got to ride in the truck cab, and that, combined with the effect of the painkiller, made the trip to Charlie Med Company at least bearable.

[Corporal Prewitt was evacuated from Charlie Med to the hospital ship USS Repose, *and thence to the naval hospital at Yokosuka, Japan. In December he was flown by Navy R4D to Travis Air Force Base in California, and by 28 December Corporal Prewitt was in the Naval Medical Facility in Oakland, California. From there he was transferred to the Great Lakes Naval Training Facility for recovery*

and rehabilitation. His war was over. In the Nevada Cities, it went on unchecked.

Robert Hall had spent two years as a light machine gunner in Item Company, 3d Battalion, 8th Marines, at Camp Lejeune, North Carolina. In 1950, Hall's second college year, he had decided to leave school and enlist in the Marine Corps. His family had provided three Marines to the Corps during World War II. Enlisting, he says, seemed the proper thing to do.

Throughout 1951 Hall wrote several requests for transfer to WESPAC—the Western Pacific. But it was not until November of 1952, after his promotion to corporal, that he was assigned to the 29th Replacement Draft at Camp Pendleton, California.

He arrived at Inch'on, Korea, on 8 February 1953.]

Cpl. ROBERT HALL
F/2/5

We were told on the ship [the USNS *General Nelson M. Walker*] what our regimental assignments were to be. Trains took us to Munsan-ni, and from there trucks took us to regimental HQ. It was dark when we arrived.

The regimental replacements were assigned for a talk by Colonel Lewis Walt, the 5th Marines' commanding officer. He introduced Major General Edwin Pollack, the CO of the 1st Marine Division. Walt said it was an indication of the importance of the 5th Marines that General Pollack was addressing us, rather than the replacements intended for other regiments.

General Pollack told us how proud he was to command the division and the 5th Marines. He was very complimentary to Colonel Walt. I had read some WW2 history, and I'd heard of General Pollack. He had also been commanding officer of the 2d Marine Division at Lejeune when I was there. I hadn't heard of Colonel Walt, but he impressed me.

The battalion assignments were read out, and about 135 of us were loaded up again to go to 2d Battalion headquarters. It was very late, and had grown very cold when we crossed the Imjin and finally arrived at 2/5 [2d Battalion, 5th Marines].

We spent several days at battalion HQ. The units there were

situated in heavily protected bunkers down in a draw by the main road back to the Imjin. The mess tent was across the road near an open paddy area. The replacement troops were housed in sixteen-man tents with sandbagged sides.

We were issued equipment, heard lectures about the war and why we were fighting, and were briefed on the Chinese units facing us on the other side of the MLR.

We did some practice patrols in the paddies at night, which was when the Chinese tried to shell the battalion headquarters. Once or twice they came fairly close to hitting something, but their artillery wasn't a threat to the battalion area. We found out they were using it for other things. You could always hear the sound of it, a kind of muttering noise beyond the hills. It was like a World War I movie.

But we were closer than it seemed. One day a Marine Corsair, hit while flying over the MLR, came in low over the ridges. It was smoking and losing altitude. You could tell it was in trouble. The troops came running out to watch as a parachute opened and the Corsair crashed beyond the hills to the south. We watched the pilot drift down out of sight and hoped he made it all right. We never knew.

We replacements were used on work details, loading and un-loading trucks and filling sandbags. There never seemed to be enough filled sandbags. We learned a new meaning for the word. In Korea *sandbagging*, used as a verb, meant "goofing off." Like *gold-bricking* in another, older war. Troops would work at filling bags pretty well, but soon boredom would set in—there can't be anything quite as boring as shoveling sand into burlap sacks—and enthusiasm, never really great for the job in hand, would vanish.

We used all the local slang we could pick up. I think soldiers always do that, not wanting to sound green. So we used words like *Luke, goonies,* and *gooks* to describe the Chinese and North Koreans, and we included them in all our letters home so we would sound a little strange and exotic, like veterans.

Living conditions were not bad. The food was not great, but it was plentiful. And the weather was bitterly cold but dry.

After about a week, we were all assigned to companies within the battalion. I drew the 3d Section of the Heavy Machine Gun Platoon of 2/5's Weapons Company. Weapons Company platoons were armed with water-cooled .30-caliber machine guns, 81-mm mortars, and assault and demolitions explosives. A platoon was divided into three sections, and each assigned to one of the three lettered rifle companies in the battalion. 3d Section, mine, was assigned to Fox Company, the third lettered company in the 2d Battalion.

We were sent off to the MLR on 17 February 1953. I was put into the crew of a heavy machine gun in a bunker to the right of the gate in the wire around Observation Post Berlin.

Most of the bunkers were on the forward—north—slope of the hills. The trenches were on the north slope of the ridges rather than on the true skyline. Some were "living bunkers" which housed sometimes five, sometimes twice that many, men. Others were "gun bunkers" for the .30- and .50-caliber machine guns. These bunkers usually had only three or four of the gunners living in them, next to their weapons. The bunkers were heated by kerosene or fuel-oil stoves vented through the roof. The temperature inside was kept high. The walls were dug out of the earth or built up with sandbags. Doors were curtains made of blankets or sheets of heavy canvas to keep the cold out and the light in. Interior lighting was by candle, although some of the bunkers on the reverse slopes had power generators and electricity. Ceilings were beams, usually six inches by six inches, covered over with layers of sandbags, dirt, and trash.

Some of the bunkers were new; others, old and dangerous. These had been constructed with prefabricated materials sent from Japan or from the States; but rain, frost, and the constant impact of explosions had separated the beams and allowed the sandbags to rot. In March an engineer sergeant came through the trenchline inspecting the bunkers. He said that ours would have to be rebuilt. This sort of work was done at night, after the occupants had moved to temporary digs elsewhere. The engineers acted as foremen on these projects, and the infantrymen did the actual work.

The gun bunkers had a firing aperture, whereas the living bunkers had only a door. The gun apertures had chicken wire fastened across the opening to prevent the Chinese throwing things inside. [By "things" Hall means grenades.] But after a few boxes of ammo had been fired through the chicken wire, it wasn't exactly functional and would have to be replaced. This, too, was done at night.

The whole trenchline was a messy, rambling series of ditches five to seven feet deep. One could spot the location of the bunkers by the piles of trash, ration cans, scrap papers, and protruding stove-pipes. The Chinese must have known where every bunker was. They couldn't have missed.

When I first came up to the line, Sergeant Blanchard, my section leader, pointed out the terrain features visible from the bunker. Each machine-gun bunker had a range card posted. It identified the visible targets and noted the adjustments needed to hit them.

I looked through binoculars. Over on a ridge we called Little Rock was the body of a Marine. I was told he had been killed on a Dog Company patrol. On night patrols, when the Chinese suspected there were Marines nearby, they would work the bolt of a weapon back and forth to draw our fire. This Marine had reacted and had been killed. The patrol had withdrawn without his body—a thing Marines very seldom do. The Chinese had ambushed other patrols sent to recover the dead Marine. When I got there, they had been displaying the body, moving it from place to place for several days. When I first saw it, it was propped in a sitting position against a bush. A few days latter, an air strike dropped napalm on it.

There were two others in the bunker to which I was assigned. We were left pretty much on our own to organize work and watch schedules. The most senior man naturally took the best duty. In Korea "most senior" had nothing to do with rank. It had to do with time in-country.

The gunner took the daylight watches. The other two of us split the night watches. For better hearing and visibility, these night watches were stood in a "fighting hole" outside the bunker. A fighting hole was simply a niche in the forward wall of the trench, usually covered with planks and a few sandbags. There was a shelf for grenades and a sound-powered telephone connected to the company CP.

There were also "rabbit holes" dug into the walls of the trench near the bottom. They could be found all along the trenchline so that a casual stroller would not be caught without protection from the stray Chinese mortar rounds that sometimes dropped into the trench.

The length of our night watches depended on how cold it was and our personal schedules. The cold-weather clothing we had been issued was usually adequate, except for on the windiest nights. But even with our Mickey Mouse thermal boots, standing in a fighting hole without moving around could be very uncomfortable. So watches were generally limited to thirty minutes or three quarters of an hour.

Our gunner, a corporal like me, had been in Korea almost a year. He was due to rotate home when the 30th Replacement Draft arrived in-country. He was a "short-timer" and had the day watches. Even so, he rarely left the bunker. And the shorter he became, the less time he would stand outside. One day after several incoming rounds had hit the hill nearby, he wouldn't even leave to go to the head. He used a ration box and heaved it out through the gun aperture.

We would clean the machine gun daily and fire a few bursts to make sure it was ready to go. I read a lot, wrote frequent letters. Most of the companies had chow lines on the reverse slope for one hot meal a day. The F Company didn't. In January, before I arrived, the sandbagged area near the company CP was hit by incoming. Two killed and nine wounded. So F Company men were given two meals of C rations per day. But there was plenty of food. Most bunkers had a large backlog of unused rations. From time to time we could scrounge onions, carrots, or other vegetables from the battalion mess. Great mixtures were cooked with Tabasco or Worcestershire sauce from back home. A couple of times we got fresh bread from battalion, and once a crate of oranges was sent; but by the time the word was passed on the sound-powered and someone detailed to go down to the CP to get a share, most of the oranges were gone. Command post personnel got first pick of everything, so even up on the MLR there was the usual Us-versus-Them feeling among the frontline infantry against the men a few hundred yards to the rear, who had things a fraction better.

One morning a Red Cross man came striding down the trenchline. He was giving away candles—a much-valued commodity. Here was this civilian on the front line. He was dressed in a brown jacket and tan whipcord jodhpurs, looking for all the world as though he were heading out for a canter in the park.

It was strange standing watch at night. It was almost always very cold, with a north wind blowing across the dark paddies and up the slopes into our faces. Quavering snatches of Chinese propaganda broadcasts urging us to surrender were carried on the wind. Sometimes the Chinese played country music. From time to time Marine Ops might call in a "rocket ripple." These would be launched from trailer-mounted 4.5-inch launchers somewhere in the rear area. Up on the MLR the first thing we would hear would be a swishing noise going overhead. Then a tight rectangle of the Chinese hill would be lighted by the impacts. Then silence again.

Halftracks with quad .50s would fire missions, too. They were called Whispering Death because of the sound the tracers made coming over us in a tight bunch on the way to somewhere in Luke's Land. An artificial moonlight was created when the searchlights in the rear illuminated the low-hanging overcast. When conditions were right, the reflected light cast a weird glow on the rice paddies below.

We stood watches with the sound-powered telephone inside our parka hoods, leaving our hands free for our weapons. The line was always open, and the sentries could hear all the message traffic. To alert for sending a message, the microphone was scratched with a fingernail. The codes for activities were "Mercury" for a recon patrol, "Cadillac" for an ambush, "Ford" for a roving patrol. "Chevrolet" was the MLR. When at a listening post in front of the MLR, or in an outpost, we would just tap the phone two or three times to avoid having to speak.

All through the nights there were sporadic shots, grenades going off, artillery firing. Almost every morning at first light a ripple of random shots would greet the new day. Sometimes a machine gun would crank off a burst paced to "shave and a haircut," and down the line someone else would fire off two more for the "six bits." After a very short time all this became routine, unremarkable—a way of life.

In the daytime—here, at least—things tended to be quiet along the MLR. The troops pretty much did their own thing. There was little contact with the staff NCOs and the officers. Nightwatch and patrol people slept well into the day, and no one disturbed them unless it was absolutely necessary.

Someone from each bunker would go every day down to the company CP area with a packboard to collect the rations and kerosene for the stoves. A few enlivened their trip by playing mortar with grenades, heaving them up and out into the forward area. I doubt they ever hit anything, but the explosions were very satisfying.

One of the most pleasurable things was a walk back to battalion for a hot meal and a shower. It didn't happen often, or even regularly, because the schedule had to be worked out with your bunker mates. But when it did happen, it was pure pleasure. The battalion mess people treated the men from the line very well, allowing us to straggle in and feeding us on our schedule rather than theirs. Hot showers were available at what we called the "changie-changie." This was a trio of squad tents joined together with a hot water unit inside. It was steamy and warm inside, in contrast to the cold outside. You'd walk in, remove your helmet and flak jacket and dirty clothes, then have a hot shower and draw clean socks, skivvies, longjohns, and utilities [fatigue uniforms] and go on your way scrubbed and refreshed.

A source of amusement was making "shower rates." You might be given a clean utility jacket with staff sergeant's chevrons inked on the sleeves. Later, the Marine Corps adopted small interchangeable metal collar insignia of rank. After a trip to the changie-changie, you could never be sure what a person's true rank was unless you knew him.

There was one thing about these trips to battalion. Going back and forth meant one had to walk along a section of road called Seventy-six Alley. This was about a mile of valley floor that was under direct Chinese observation from the hills around the Vegas area. The Chinese *usually* wouldn't waste rounds on a pair of infantrymen or a single jeep. But from time to time they would call in some artillery just to prove, I suppose, that Korea was not a place where you could take things for granted.

Sometimes, during the day, the machine gunners would go over to the .50 bunker. This was a position on the right flank of the Fox Company trenchline with a .50-caliber machine gun in place. This gun was used to mark targets for artillery and tank fire. It was the only one on our company front. The position was also used for sniping.

Up the slope behind the .50-caliber was the Arty FO [artillery forward observer] bunker. The FOs had a powerful set of binoculars, called a BC [battery commander's] scope. Using these, the FOs would pick out the areas where the Chinese tended to appear—a curve in their trenchline, stairs, a bunker opening. These targets were all at extreme range, sometimes as much as 4,000 yards away. The big machine gun would be registered on such a target by firing a few single rounds of tracer. Then it would be locked into position and left pointing at that one spot for hours, until the word came from the FO that there were live Chinese in the target area.

The .50 bunker was a kind of casual gathering place for us. Kind of like a coffee shop or even a tavern—but without the booze. You'd meet people from other squads. Two or three were always on hand, just sitting around, shooting the shit, or listening to some Marine play the guitar. Visiting the .50 bunker was what passed for a social occasion.

Most days nothing much would happen with the gun. It just sat there, locked into position, ready but silent. But once in a while the sound powered phone would alert us with a word from the FO behind us who had spotted something with his BC scope. He'd say, "Gook on the stairs" or just "Stand by." Then one of us in the bunker, usually the man closest to the gun, would grab the handles; and when the FO said, "Let'er go," a long burst of ten or more rounds would be fired. The FO would then report the results. Our mini-artillery barrage wasn't going to win the war, but it always made us feel good.

But most of the action—and the danger—came at night, when the patrols, the manning of the listening posts, and the relief and resupply of the outposts took place.

During the spring thaw it rained steadily. Trenches and bunkers flooded, and turned into mudholes that required constant attention. Chiggies [Korean Service Corps laborers] did much of the work needed to clean them out. Chiggies were also used to carry supplies to outpost Berlin. Berlin was on a rounded hill at about the same elevation as the MLR, and connected to it by a 400-yard ridge. There was a trench along the top of the ridge with a listening post about halfway to Berlin. Then there were gates, or protected fighting holes, guarding access to the trench at either end. Unlike the trip to Vegas or Reno, it was possible to go back and forth to Berlin without being observed by the enemy. The KSC convoys—we called them Chiggie trains—were not allowed into the trenches of the OP itself. They had to drop the packboards loaded with ammo, food, and kerosene at the gate. They then returned to the MLR under the watchful eyes of the Chiggie chasers, the Marines overseeing the resupply operation.

The name *Chiggie* came from our inability to pronounce the Japanese and Korean word for "move" or "hurry." The Koreans were willing and cheerful. They liked it when we would get into the mud and dig alongside them, and they loved American cigarettes. *"Lucky numbah one, Sarghie. Kool numbah fuckin ten!"*

Pfc. DONALD K. JOHNSON
F/2/5

A typical day on the MLR began at dark. If it was a patrol night, you learned what kind—combat or recon—what time, where you were going, and what you should carry. It was important to travel as lightly and quietly as possible. If you missed patrol duty, you could count on freezing your butt on listening post, or if you were really unlucky, you might draw the job of probing for mines.

Most patrols were led by the platoon leader, the platoon sergeant, or occasionally by your squad leader. If it was a combat patrol, you were expected to keep on going until you made contact with the enemy. Or you might set up an ambush on some Chinese trail and hope they wandered in. A recon patrol would probe deeply enough into the Chinese positions to check if they were up to something nasty—which they often were. Almost all patrols were accompanied by a Navy medical corpsman. They were often needed.

In some sections of the line you might have outpost responsibility, too. We, however, didn't have any outposts to man, because the Chinese controlled the two hills in front of us [Detroit and Little Rock].

Patrols would set out after dark. The patrol sector would be as wide as your platoon front, maybe 150 yards by 800 yards deep. Not a lot of real estate to cover in an evening, but the pace was very slow, very careful. You always worried about being ambushed, stepping on a mine, or that someone back on the MLR would panic and set off a flare, leaving your patrol standing naked and exposed in the middle of a rice paddy. Then there were artillery short rounds to worry about. Men were sometimes killed by our artillery falling short.

I think what I won't ever forget is the blackness, the absolute dark. When the night was moonless, patrolling was like moving through a coal mine. You imagined Chinese all around you. Sometimes you could smell them.

The Chinese had an outpost we called Detroit about 500 yards from our lines. They would send night patrols of their own out from there. They hoped they wouldn't run into us; we hoped we wouldn't run into them.

At the listening posts you could tell when patrols stumbled into one another in the darkness from the sound. If the first noise was the staccato sort of *bbrrrrpp* of a Chinese submachine gun, you just held your breath, because you knew our guys had walked into it. You'd listen for the *crack* of our carbines or the kind of *bum-bum-bum* our BARs made. When you did hear the sound of our weapons, you kind of relaxed. You knew somebody on our side was alive out there and giving it to the Chinese.

When your patrol checked back in through the listening post, the night's work was done, and it was chow time. We ate in our bunkers and heated our C rations with Sterno. Dinner could be any one of a number of military delights: sausage patties with gravy, corned-beef hash, or beans and franks. C rations have taken a lot of bad press, but they were really quite remarkable. They came in a box, about six by twelve by two inches, and they contained everything needed to keep a Marine fueled and going for twenty-four hours: three tin cans with one of the goodies mentioned above, plus packets of candy, a cookie, crackers, coffee, cocoa, cigarettes, canned fruit, a can opener, even toilet paper. Everything was used, even the oiled cardboard box, into which a man could relieve himself.

As soon as it was light enough to see across the rice paddies, it was bedtime. The day watch took over. We knew the Chinese would never dare start anything in daylight, so we slept like babies.

On the line it was a squad-sized war. The only people you really got to know well were your bunker mates. All the others were almost like strangers. In the bunker we talked about the events of the previous night, about women—about the things troops in wars all through history have talked about, I guess.

We cleaned and recleaned our weapons; then we cleaned them again. We were filthy, but our rifles gleamed. I used to remember a drill instructor in Boot Camp telling us, "If you get killed, no one can pick you up and use you again. But your clean rifle might save a fellow Marine's life."

Cpl. ROBERT HALL
F/2/5

Occasionally tanks would be brought up to the MLR to fire missions. Due to our complete command of the air, the CCF were, of necessity, far more careful about camouflage than we were. We rarely saw a Chinese soldier, or even movement in their outposts. So most targets were chosen from the observations made by patrols or air recon. Then, when a "hit list" had been compiled, a tank platoon would be sent up to prepared revetments on the ridges behind our trenchlines.

Usually the word would be passed that the tanks were coming, but sometimes not. But you could always hear their motors. Four or six tanks would come roaring up the roads behind the hill and tear into their slots. Then they would fire off twenty or so rounds of ear-splitting 90-mm, as an observer or the .50-caliber pointed out targets. Then, after five or ten minutes of rapid firing, they would crank it up and roar away back down the hill just before a shitload of Chinese mortar round began to fall all over the area. We regarded the tanks as a mixed blessing.

In late February Fox Company staged a daylight raid on the Chinese OP we called Detroit. My .30-caliber machine gun was assigned the task of giving supporting fire on Detroit's left flank, then shifting to OP Little Rock to deliver suppressing fire. We burned off thirty boxes of ammo during the early part of the day. The raiders took heavy casualties, and from my bunker I saw them being brought back to the MLR. The word that was passed around said that we had eight KIA, sixty-six WIA, and one man missing. It was not a good day.

[The February raid on outpost Detroit was only one of many attacks against Chinese positions that had been launched by the 2d Battalion, 5th Marines, but it touched off a flurry of raids and counter-raids destined to be costly both to the 2d Battalion and the Chinese enemy.]

Pfc. DONALD K. JOHNSON
F/2/5

On February 23 Fox Company was taken out of the line to practice for a daylight raid on Chinese outpost Detroit, which was about 500 yards forward of our line. We hadn't taken any prisoners recently, and so we were ordered to go get some live Chinese from Detroit.

We zeroed in our rifles and practiced our assault, and on the twenty-fourth, before dawn, we moved across the rice paddy that lay at the base of Detroit. Artillery and rockets just pounded the hill, and planes strafed and dropped bombs.

When the planes left, our squad leader, Sergeant Kelly, said, "Let's go, Marines!" That was the last thing he said. He was hit by rifle fire and went down. I ran up the slope as fast as I could, but I seemed to just run out of gas after a few yards. I got a second wind and kept on going. I could see we were taking a lot of casualties. The fire from the outpost was heavy and accurate. All the shelling and bombing hadn't killed the Chinese on Detroit.

As we approached the wire on the top, the Chinese started throwing potato-masher grenades down at us. Our platoon was supposed to enter the Chinese trenchline from the point and then meet up with the 1st Platoon, which would sweep in from the left.

But only four of us made it to the trenchline: A. P. Goff, who had taken over from Kelly as squad leader; Houseman; Jones; and me. Our platoon leader, Lieutenant Russell, was killed as he stepped into the trench. Goff's left arm was shattered by a burp-gun blast, Houseman was hit in the leg, and I somehow got a piece of tin embedded in my chin.

We cleaned out a lot of Chinese, and we didn't worry about taking prisoners. Goff, who refused even to look at his arm, spotted a lot of Chinese massing on the reverse slope of the hill, so he ordered us out. We were four, who should have been forty.

We fought our way back out, carrying Lieutenant Russell's body with us. On the way down the hill, Jones went into shock, and we lost him for a week or ten days.

Goff was taken to an aid station, and I never did see him again until we met a long time later in Oakland, California. He never did regain the use of his arm, but he was awarded a Silver Star for bravery.

Despite our losses, and even though we didn't bring back a single live Chinese prisoner, the raid on Detroit was considered to have been a great success.

[Fox Company's raid of 24 February on Chinese outpost Detroit was costly. Against the backdrop of the wrangling and bargaining at Panmunjom, it was almost macabre. But worse was to come.]

Pfc. DONALD K. JOHNSON
F/2/5

On March 24, Fox Company was ordered into reserve. I was delighted. I had been up front since arriving in Korea. In reserve you could have a whole case of beer, eat three hot meals a day, and take a shower.

But when we reached the reserve area, and I had only begun to work on my beer, we were informed that we were going back into the line the next day, the twenty-fifth. When we got back, my outfit spent the day filling in for Able Company while they, Able, were out on a combat patrol.

Then we were told we could go back to the reserve area, which we did—only to be told still again (after a couple of hours' sleep) to turn out ready to move.

On March 26 we did. We were introduced to our new platoon leader. I never did remember his name. He was replacing Lieutenant "Truck" Collum, who had replaced Lieutenant Russell. Collum had stepped on a mine a few days before we were pulled back the first time. And the new officer, whose name I never remembered, was twelve hours away from being killed.

He told us that the Army and lost Old Baldy [one of the outposts in the Second Army sector], and that we Marines were going to hit Detroit again in hopes of forcing the Chinese to divert troops from Baldy.

We were loaded into trucks and taken back to the same area we had used to practice for the February 24 raid. I played it smart and brought along an M1 instead of my BAR—the M1 being about ten pounds lighter and much easier to carry.

We spent another morning running up and down a hill practicing the assault again. The attack was scheduled for the next morning, and I was not looking forward to it. I had already been to Detroit, and I had a good idea what we could expect.

It was dark when we reboarded the trucks to return to the reserve area for some rest. In the west there was a whole lot of noise, and flares were lighting up the sky. We couldn't figure out what was going on. It seemed early for a Chinese probe. The trucks didn't move, and we began to get impatient. We watched the new platoon lieutenant and the company commander huddled over a field telephone.

Then we got the word: Reno, Vegas, and Carson had been overrun. There was an unknown number of Marines trapped in a cave on top of Reno. Easy Company was going to attack Vegas and retake it, and we, Fox Company, were going to retake Reno.

We would not, the lieutenant told us, be going back to the reserve area. I was stuck with only an M1, instead of my much more powerful BAR. So much for being clever.

We moved out, and started drawing artillery fire even before we could get out of the trucks in the assembly area. I received one bandolier of ammunition and two grenades. I knew that would never be enough. It wasn't. Fox Company was, for all practical purposes, wiped out.

[*Private Johnson's comment is no exaggeration. Fox Company's mission demanded a run across 2,000 yards of open country under enemy fire before reaching the base of the hill to be attacked. Many men fell before the climb to the outpost began. And as they started up the steep slope, Fox Company came under intense artillery and mortar attack. The company commander, the platoon leader, the platoon sergeant, and some fifty others were either killed or wounded. Private Johnson was hit by an exploding mortar shell and lost his right leg.*

The remnants of Fox Company were joined with survivors of Easy Company's attack on its own objective and used to assault and capture outpost Vegas.

Outpost Reno was not taken that day, or ever. It remained in Chinese hands until the armistice. Private Johnson was evacuated and returned to the United States.

What was in the process of developing was one of the last major Chinese attacks of the war. The Communists had been massing troops for several weeks in the area facing IX Corps's sector of the MLR. They had resolved to seek a major breakthrough east of Old Baldy, and before them lay the Nevada Cities outposts. They came on 25 March just after dark, and they came in regimental strength.]

Pvt. JAMES A. LARKIN
Forward Observer Team/B/1/5
Our team and another, attached to Charlie Company, 1st Battalion, were responsible for artillery support for the reinforced platoon holding outpost Vegas. Each team kept a man in Vegas for five days, after which he was relieved.

Each of the five days I had been on Vegas the incoming had seemed to get heavier and heavier. The Chinks were really laying it in, which made us wonder when the major attack was coming. They wouldn't have bombarded us so intensely if they hadn't been planning to move south.

Just getting around on Vegas was a nightmare. You had to keep low and move fast. The tangle of communications wires in the trenches made this damned hard to do, but we did it to stay alive.

My spot on Vegas was at Able gate, where the trench was deepest. I needed a deep place because the antenna on my 619 radio stuck up ten to twelve feet, making a perfect aiming point for the Chinese on Hills 150, 153, and 190, who could look straight down on Vegas. But Able gate was on the reverse slope of the Vegas hill, which provided some protection, even if not very much.

On the afternoon of the twenty-sixth the Chinese went all out. As intense as the shelling had been for the previous four and a half days, it suddenly got even worse. That afternoon three seriously wounded and one dead Marine had been carried down from the hilltop by Chiggie-Bears. Most of the day everyone remaining had stayed in deep cover, pinned down by the constantly incoming artillery.

About 1740 on the twenty-sixth, Steve Drummond, my relief, arrived, having crawled all the way out from the MLR through the battered trenchline that was getting such a pounding.

Steve and I made with the small talk for a few minutes while I prepared myself for the running crawl back to the MLR. Steve was sure, and I agreed with him, that the Chinese were going to jump on us before dawn, and they were going to come in force. That was what Intelligence thought, and they were usually pretty sharp in guessing what the goonies were going to do.

I helped Steve carry his FO gear to the bunker, where it would be relatively safe from the incoming. He also had to make up a watch schedule with another FO named Doyle, who belonged to another team. I never got to know Doyle. He was new, and seemed a good man. As it happened, he never got off the hill.

I shook hands with Steve and wished him good luck. I wasn't a bit sorry to be getting away from outpost Vegas and back to the relative safety of the MLR. I waited for an imaginary pause in the shelling and got my butt out of there fast. But going through the trenchline in the twilight I was spotted by the Chinese up on the hills, and they tried to bracket me with mortar shots. We had rabbit holes all along the trenchline to take care of situations like this, and the holes worked pretty good.

Buy by the time I reached the bottom of the hill, I was in a stretch where the trench connecting the outpost with the MLR was just about destroyed from the constant shelling. That meant a run of about 1,500 yards across what amounted to open country.

When I hit the bottom, my breath was coming in gasps and I was soaking wet, muddy, and half-frozen. I began to worry about whether or not the Chinese had set up an ambush between me and the MLR. They often tried that, and sometimes it worked. It was too dark to see anything, but I was anxious enough to get moving that I just started to run across the paddies.

As I humped along I could tell that the tempo of the incoming was increasing. It sounded like a continuous roar, and the shells were lighting up the landscape and sending up huge gouts of water and mud.

When I reached the listening post fifty or so yards in front of the line, I didn't even bother to give a password. In fact, I wasn't challenged for one. Everyone was head down in the dirt to stay away from the fragments of artillery shell whistling through the air all around.

Once past the line I headed straight for the 1/5 area to make my report to the battalion FO. And while I had been humping across the open paddies, the Chinese had started attacking in force—attacking all of the Nevada Cities outposts: Reno, Carson, and, of course,

Vegas—the place I had just left. I talked to one of the officers at 1/5 CP and learned that the gooks were in at least regimental strength. Against an understrength platoon on Vegas, is what I thought.

After reporting, I managed to rush through a hot shower and put on a fresh set of utilities. Then I got some hot food and reported back to Baker Company, where the rest of my FO team was attached. I no sooner settled down with them than the word came for me to get my gear together again and report to the company command post.

When I reported to the company CP, the duty officer told me to draw a radio and to join the FO attached to Dog Company as their radio operator. They were getting ready to go back to Vegas.

It is amazing that all the Nevada Cities outposts were not reduced to anthills with all the artillery they had taken, first from the Chinese, and now from our own arty firing "box-me-in" missions.

It must have been about 2100 when we finally got under way. We worked our way across the paddies from the MLR to Reno Block, a hill that supported both Reno and Vegas with covering fire.

Our objective was to secure Reno Block and then jump off from there and secure Vegas. We were together with a reinforced platoon from Dog Company, a platoon from Charlie Company, and another from Echo. The infantrymen were to take Vegas back. (This was the first we had heard about it falling.)

But the Chinese were in regimental strength, and the minute we were in Reno Block they came at us. Four times we pushed them back. In one attack they reached our trenchline, and the fighting was hand-to-hand. They came at us from all sides.

White phosphorus shells from our guns illuminated everything; the whole area was like the Fourth of July. Our artillery was firing, our tanks were firing, machine guns on the MLR were firing. The Chinese were falling like bowling pins everywhere, but there always seemed to be more of them. It was somewhere near midnight, and it was as bright as day from all the pyrotechnics and explosions.

The fighting lasted until about 0500 hours on the twenty-seventh, when the Chinese finally started to withdraw.

But the MLR had lost contact with Vegas by this time. No one knew what the situation was there. We had fought our way to within a couple hundred yards of the position, but we couldn't tell if there were any of our Marines left alive there. Suddenly, we got the order to fall back and regroup.

When we got back to the MLR, we were told there would be a major coordinated attack later in the day. It was after 0500 hours when we reached the MLR, and I was exhausted. I slept most of that day.

The battle for Vegas lasted five full days. I didn't participate in any of the other attacks, after all. I didn't see Vegas again until much later, when I was attached as FO to the Turkish Brigade, which took over from us and held Vegas almost until the end.

["Hero" is a word that has fallen into disrepute in America in the declining years of the twentieth century. But there are those who define the word by their actions. There were many such men with the Marines during the assault on Reno and Carson on the night of 26– 27 March.]

HM3 JOSEPH F. KEENAN
Attached to F/2/5

February 25, 1953

Dear Mother and Dad,

Sorry I haven't written, and am asking you to forgive me for my last letter, it was in anger and I didn't mean the harsh words I said. We arrived in Korea on Friday the 13th, and it is a good thing I am not superstitious.

We went to Confession and Communion the night we left for the front. We were lucky and stayed here at Batt. Aid Station, 2,000 yards behind the Main Line of Resistance, for a week or more. Fox Company pulled a daylight raid on a Goonie hill and it was a slaughter compared to what results were expected. Sixty wounded and six killed. Some may die from wounds later on, but that's what our log read for this morning. Many will awaken with either arms or legs or both missing. And one will never see again. I saw some pretty awful sights today and expect to see many more, I hope not, but there's no getting away from it, this is a real war here and not just a police action. It is terrible over here and it is going to take a lot of doing and much praying to end the spilling of blood here.

Everything that happens here usually happens at night and it is rough on the nerves. Once every two weeks they pull a daylight raid to get "Luke the Gook" worried. The hill had one thousand rounds of bombs and heavy artillery shells and mortars and rockets dropped on it for eight minutes before zero hour, yet when the Marines got close to the top, Goonies were all over the place. Some just stayed in their holes and threw grenade after grenade over the top hardly showing themselves at all.

They asked for a volunteer Corpsman to go up to evac some patients, I said I would go but didn't realize what I said 'til after I was in the halftrack, then I got scared. I went up but when I got there it was too late so I came back to the aid station. I loaded eight or nine cases on the "copter's" bay, they sure are life saving machines.

Well, that's all for now I'll write again as soon as possible.

Your son,

Joe

P.S. Say hello to the kids for me.

[Hospitalman Keenan arrived at the MLR "too late," as he wrote to his parents, to be a participant in Fox Company's first daylight raid on outpost Detroit. But between 24 February and Fox Company's second raid on the "Goonie hills," he had plenty to keep him occupied.]

March 16, 1953

Dear Mother and Dad,

Just a few lines to let you know I am okay and getting along all right.

I had my first casualty the other morning. Got it off an ambushed patrol out in front of the outpost. . . . this kid Jones had tried to disarm a hand grenade and in the process it blew off his thumb down to the second joint and tore his fingernails off and most of the flesh on his hand. He also had some fragments in his left leg. . . .

We went on a combat patrol last night and the Marines were disappointed that we didn't meet any of "Luke the Gook's" boys. . . .

Tomorrow I go back to the outpost for six days and then I'll have only a couple more patrols to go on before getting off this hill on the 25th of the month. . . .

March 21, 1953

Dear Mother and Dad,

Received your letter today and was glad to hear from home. . . .

Well, we have caught a lot of close mortar rounds today. The Goonies have their summer troops up in front of us now and they are hot for combat. . . .

I have to close now on account of I volunteered to help dig outposts on the trenchline tonight where the rain and the shellfire cave them in. . . .

Your son,
Joe

WESTERN UNION

BA175 MA257

M.WA203 LONG GOVT RX PD-WUX WASHINGTON DC

MR AND MRS THOMAS FRANCIS KEENAN

43 MATHER ST DORCHESTER MASS

IT IS WITH DEEP REGRET THAT I OFFICIALLY REPORT THE DEATH OF YOUR SON JOSEPH FRANCIS KEENAN HOSPITAL CORPSMAN THIRD CLASS US NAVY WHICH OCCURRED ON 26 MARCH 1953 AS A RESULT OF ACTION IN THE KOREAN AREA. WHEN FURTHER DETAILS INCLUDING INFORMATION AS TO THE DISPOSITION OF THE REMAINS ARE RECEIVED YOU WILL BE INFORMED. YOUR SON DIED WHILE SERVING HIS COUNTRY AND I EXTEND TO YOU MY SINCEREST SYMPATHY IN YOUR GREAT LOSS.

VICE ADMIRAL J L HOLLOWAY JR CHIEF OF NAVAL PERSONNEL

[Death of the young is always tragic, but in war it is commonplace. The tragedy is compounded by the confusion of combat—the "fog of war." In battles surrounding the Nevada Cities, with outnumbered

Marines fighting hand-to-hand with a determined enemy, men saw much that did not happen, and failed to see what did.]

Pfc. FLOYD W. CATON
F/2/5

March 27, 1953

Dear Mrs. Keenan,

Just a few lines to let you know I was on the raid last night when Joe got hit, he never got hit bad so don't worry about Joe. He got hit in the wrist and also got a little sand in his eyes but not enough to hurt them. He was with our fireteam when it happened. So believe me Mrs. Keenan when I tell you Joe will be alright. When we were out there Joe was doing a wonderful job taking care of the wounded and when the corpsman came over to take care of Joe when he got hit [Joe] said to go help the other guys who need care more than I do.

Mrs. Keenan I haven't known Joe too long but in my books he's tops, he's one of the finest guys I've ever met.

Well there isn't much more I can tell about Joe. But Mrs. Keenan don't worry about Joe he will be just fine in a couple of days. I will close for now.

A very dear friend of Joe's
Floyd W. Caton

Pvt. DAN HOLL
F/2/5

March 27, 1953

Dear Mrs. Keenan,

This is just a short note to let you know about your son Joe. He got hit slightly in the arm by a mortar last night while on a raid with our company. He was with my firing team when we started the attack on the hill [Reno] and during most of the raid. He done the job of a platoon of men before he got hit and quite a while after. He also refused medical aid from anyone until he was sure everyone else was properly cared for. Your son is and will always be one of the most well liked guys in our company. I became good friends with him shortly after he arrived in Fox Co. We seen him leave the hill and I also checked in the aid station to see if he was allright. He got quite a bit of dust in his eyes but it didn't bother his vision after they were cleaned.

Joe's friend,
Dan Holl

Joe is in fine hands and there is no serious wounds.

WESTERN UNION

MR THOMAS F KEENAN

43 MATHER ST DORCHESTER MASS

ANOTHER REPORT RECEIVED FROM THE COMMANDING OFFICER OF THE FIRST DIVISION STATES THAT YOUR SON MADE THE REQUEST THAT PFC CATON AND PVT HOLL WRITE TO YOU IN CASE OF INJURY. PRIOR TO BEING KILLED IN ACTION ON 26 MARCH 1953 YOUR SON HAD BEEN TREATED FOR TEMPORARY BLINDNESS DUE TO SAND IN THE EYES CAUSED BY EXPLODING SHELL. UPON TREATMENT HE WAS RETURNED TO FULL DUTY. THE LETTER[S] TO YOU BY PFC CATON AND PVT HOLL [WERE] WRITTEN AT THIS TIME. AGAIN MY SINCEREST SYMPATHY IS EXTENDED TO YOU.

VICE ADMIRAL J L HOLLOWAY JR CHIEF OF NAVAL PERSONNEL
WASHINGTON DC

Pfc. FLOYD W. CATON
F/2/5

April 17, 1953

Dear Mr. and Mrs. Keenan,

Just a few lines to let you know I received your very kind letter today.

There isn't a lot I can say. The only thing that I know is that I found out about a week after that awful night on that hill that Joe had died and please believe me when I tell you that that hurt me almost as bad as if I had lost my own brother.

Joe was one of the best boys I have ever met and he was also a man every inch of the way.

Dan Holl the other boy that wrote you is in the hospital now. He got wounded on another hill a couple of nights later. So now I haven't got Dan or Joe with me and I sure do miss them.

Mrs. Keenan I want you to know that if I ever get to come up to Boston I will sure look you and Mr. Keenan up and I know I would love to meet you.

Well there isn't anything more for me to write at this time, but I was so happy when I found you and Mrs. Keenan weren't mad at me.

Well I will close for this time hoping to hear from you again.

God bless you and Mrs. Keenan

A friend,

Floyd

If there is ever anything I can do for you let me know.

Pvt. DAN HOLL
F/2/5

April 27, 1953

Dear Mr. and Mrs Keenan,

Thank you very much for answering my letter and for not being angry at me for misinforming you about your son Joe. I asked the Doctor the night he got hit how bad it was and he said Joe had very slight wounds. Before we left the raid Joe asked me to notify you if anything happened to him and of course being as close to him as I was I agreed. I was sent back to three Medical Companies after I got hit and one of them, "A" Med. Joe was supposed to have died at. I checked the records in all the wards and he wasn't known by anyone of them.

I know for a positive fact that Joe left the hill because I was the last man off that hill and I checked for Joe cause I knew he was hit and I wanted to make sure he got off alright.

I come home in July and I promise you one thing that I'll come and visit you as soon as I possibly can. There are things that you might want to ask me if there is please do so no matter how important or unimportant they may seem. I will continue to try to find out just what must have happened to Joe and let you know the outcome.

So long for now, a true friend of Joe's and yours,

Dan Holl

[There is an ineffable sadness about the story of medic Joe Keenan. It appears that during F Company's firefight at the base of outpost Reno he was wounded in the right arm and partially blinded by debris. He was treated briefly at an aid station and then voluntarily returned to the battle. At some dark moment thereafter, in the confusion and anarchy of the fighting, he was struck again by enemy fire and killed. Apparently no one saw him fall.]

Cpl. ROBERT HALL
F/2/5

By the Berlin gate a Marine had a battery-operated radio—one of the big, short-wave kind with a fold-out antenna and time zone maps on the dial. We sat and listened to what was evidently a reporter filing a story with a news service. The speaker said a few words, and then he would spell them out; speak again, then spell. We could look out over Berlin to Vegas and see in the distance the huge hill we'd been on only hours before. I heard the reporter talking about "the body-littered west front hill," then spell "b-o-d-y l-i-t-t-e-r-e-d w-e-s-t. . . ." The group listened quietly with an occasional comment or curse. Later, I went back to my bunker and wrote a long letter home.

PORKCHOP TO CHRISTMAS HILL

March–July 1953

During February the command of the Eighth Army had changed hands yet again. General Van Fleet, after nearly two years as commander, relinquished his post to Lt. Gen. Maxwell D. Taylor.

While the Marines fought and died among the Nevada Cities hills and outposts, the U.S. I Corps met repeated Chinese attacks all along its front line. Apparently in retaliation for UN raids in January and February, the Chinese launched a series of assaults.

On 1 March an enemy battalion attacked Hill 355, held by elements of the U.S. 2d Division. The enemy managed to reach the defensive trenchline before being beaten off. The Chinese hit the hill again on 17 March, again in battalion strength. With two elements attacking from the north and northeast, the Communists breached the mine fields and wire, and penetrated the trenchline on the crest. The center gave ground, but two platoons in reserve were moved up to contain the penetration. The fighting on the crest was hand-to-hand and lasted through the night. At dawn an infantry company reinforced the Americans, and the Chinese withdrew through a heavy barrage of UN artillery.

On the evening of 23 March, as the Marines at the Nevada Cities outposts were being heavily attacked, the Chinese sent another full regiment to attack the 7th Division positions on Hills 266, 255, and 191, twenty miles east of Carson and Vegas.

Hill 266, defended by the 7th Division's Colombian Battalion, was the focus of the Chinese attack. A Chinese battalion, supported by heavy artillery fire, penetrated the defensive positions on the west slope of 266 at about 2100 hours. The Colombians were reinforced with a company, but this was insufficient to contain the Chinese, and the defenders were forced to fall back to positions on the southeastern slope.

At first light on the twenty-fourth, a battalion from the 7th Division counterattacked, penetrated the trenchlines the Chinese had won, and engaged them in a nightmare battle in the tunnels and bunkers. The Chinese refused to give up the position, and the Americans broke off the attack after some five hours of hand-to-hand combat in which both sides were heavily supported by artillery.

Early the following day, 25 March, another American counterattack was launched and repulsed. The Chinese retained control of Hill 266.

Concurrently with the battle for Hill 266, two enemy battalions had assaulted Hills 255 and 191. The fight for 191 was brief and vicious. As the Chinese advanced up the slopes, the Americans decimated their ranks, and the Chinese never reached the trenchline. Their attack broke, and they retreated in confusion.

The enemy had more success at Hill 255. Supported by tanks, artillery, and mortar fire, the Chinese pushed the defenders back nearly 800 yards. But shortly after midnight, two companies from 7th Division reserve counterattacked and drove the Chinese off the crest.

The Chinese gained and held their main objective, Hill 266, but the cost was heavy. Almost 1,000 casualties, 750 of them KIA, were the price the Communists paid for their assaults on the three hills.

Cpl. JOE SCHEUBER
I Company/31st Infantry
Little fighting occurred during January or February of 1953, but with the approach of March there had been rumors and more rumors of an allout attack by the enemy on the Porkchop area. Of course, the Army being the Army, there were always rumors, and no one knew really what to believe. We had spent the last few weeks patrolling and testing out new equipment. One such article was, so help me, *flak shorts* to wear over our fatigues. We dutifully tried them out and

reported back that they rubbed our legs raw and "hindered our mobility." No more was heard of the iron pants.

On March 23, Item Company got word from battalion that a fifty-man patrol was needed to patrol the perimeter of Porkchop. I should have suspected it was more than a routine mission, because we were told that the reg against carrying personal effects would be strictly enforced—something that seldom happened. I left my wallet with Clark Stewart, who had not been chosen for this patrol.

We were loaded into trucks and taken as near to the "finger" of Porkchop as possible without being observed by the enemy. We got out of the trucks with our gear and weapons and were warned to be alert—which meant that the enemy had to be close by. I carried an M1 rifle, three grenades, and as much ammo as I could beg or borrow. If I had known what was coming, I would have loaded up with grenades.

The patrol was set up right there on the finger that came down from Porkchop. There was a senior noncom there, a sergeant, who was directing traffic with a pistol in his hand. (He was older than the rest of us, and was a survivor of the Bataan Death March. What he was doing in Korea, I will never know.) There were some ROK soldiers around, and I was told to get into a foxhole with one of them.

We had no more than taken cover when enemy mortar and artillery started falling all around us. It was dark, and the flashes lit up the night.

I told the ROK we had better fix bayonets. I expected a Chinese attack following the artillery barrage. I could hear Chinese whistles and bugles blowing, but the enemy didn't come. We were all scattered on and across the finger, crouching in our holes, waiting for something to happen. But after a while there was a lull in the shelling, and John Pringle, our BAR man, appeared from the other side of the finger. He was leaning on his assistant, who was carrying their weapon. Pringle had been wounded, they said, in beating off a Chinese attack on the other side of the hill. Not only had Pringle been hit, but the BAR had, too. There was a dent from a bullet on the muzzle-flash suppressor.

Pretty soon, people started emerging from their holes and asking what we should be doing. The sergeant with the handgun had vanished, and no one seemed to be in charge. When the people started asking questions, they looked at me because I was a corporal. I told someone to go up to the ridge of the finger and see if he could figure out what was going on. He came back down and reported that he hadn't seen anything at all.

I tried to work the BAR, but it was jammed. Someone else had a radio, but it didn't work. Off to the right we could see the flashes of incoming artillery landing. There were columns of Chinese moving. Then we saw that there were Chinese behind us as well. We were surrounded. There was nothing to do but gather what men we could and try to reach the top of the hill, where we could at least make a stand.

I gathered perhaps a dozen men by the time we reached the trenchline on the top. But the Chinese had got there before us, and as soon as we appeared, the fighting began.

The fighting was heavy and confused. I turned to look back, hoping that some more of our people might be coming up to reinforce us. As I did, an enemy soldier shot my steel helmet off my head. I hit the ground and lost my rifle. I grabbed a grenade and threw it, never hearing it explode, though it must have. I saw the Korean soldier who had been with me in the foxhole run his bayonet into a Chinese. There was a tremendous amount of noise and confusion, with bullets flying in every direction. It looked to me as though we were being pushed off the hill. A bullet tugged at my field jacket and nicked my arm. I got up and started back down the hill. As I did that, I caught sight of a Chinese soldier shooting at me. I lobbed a grenade at him and killed him.

Then, quite suddenly, I found myself in a foxhole—a shallow one—holding my last grenade with the pin pulled. I tried to think what I would do if the Chinese came upon me. Would I throw the grenade—my last weapon of any sort—or would I blow myself up and hope to take one of them with me? Among the many things that crossed my mind in those moments was the question, What in hell was I, an American, doing here, in Korea, fighting Chinese?

It grew quiet, but I didn't think it wise to raise my head to look out of the foxhole. The grenade made my hand ache. I decided that life could be damned cruel, and that only a strong person could handle it.

I could hear sporadic crackles of rifle fire somewhere out there in the dark. I wondered if I was alone on the hill. Had someone else been killed? Flares would explode from time to time, but even then everything was darkness and shadows.

About this point I remember I told myself that I would rather eat hamburger every day for the rest of my life if having steak meant I had to fight Chinese for it.

As the time passed I began to think that maybe I could risk getting to my feet and trying to get off the hill. I had just made up my mind to do this when shells started landing again all around me. A hot piece of shrapnel hit me in the butt, but instead of complaining about the pain, I congratulated myself for having been lying on my stomach at the time, because given where it hit me, I could easily have been a penis amputee.

The shells kept landing really near me, and I was being pelted with dirt and stones from the explosions. I figured out that I had been hit twice already, though not seriously. It just wasn't my time to go.

As the night went on, I could hear Chinese screaming and yelling as they were hit on their way back off the hill. From the sound of their voices, I could tell they were very near my foxhole. Then, as the sky began to get light, I really began to worry about what was going to happen to me at dawn. I resolved that I would commit suicide and try to take a few of the enemy with me, rather than surrender and become a prisoner.

Just as the dawn broke, I hear a great commotion and movement back down the slope. I didn't know whether the men making the racket were Americans or Chinese, so I held on to my live grenade. But when I finally turned over on my back and looked up, there was a friendly patrol looking down at me. It was led by a former commander of Item Company.

They were looking for wounded and missing—the survivors of our ill-fated patrol. I stood and spoke with the captain. He told me to stay where I was, and to tell him where the rest of our people had gone. I had no answer to that. I pointed out the trenchline where we had fought the Chinese, but there were no men in sight.

Pretty soon my ROK soldier came wandering up. He appeared to have been horribly wounded. His clothes were stiff with blood. But it turned out he had crawled into a hole for safety and a man had fallen on top of him—bleeding to death, I suppose. He stayed under the bleeding man, and in that way saved his own life.

The captain reappeared from his search of the trenchline looking grim. He had found no one.

[After the flash of fighting in March, activity along the MLR subsided into patrolling and small harassing attacks. This low level of activity persisted through April and into May. But as May began, the armistice negotiations at Panmunjom approached a critical stage. There were many indications that the Communists intended to increase the scale and frequency of their attacks. Air observation of enemy troop movements showed that the Chinese and North Koreans were moving their forces out of the northern coastal areas and concentrating them in the south. Artillery and armor were being positioned in attack deployments close to the MLR, and there was a great surge of counter-reconnaissance patrolling by all forward units.]

Pvt. ANGELO PALERMO
A Company/17th Infantry
I arrived in Korea in May, green and twenty-one years old. We landed at Inch'on and were immediately loaded on a train for the MLR. We got to the battalion reserve area behind Porkchop on a holy day. The Catholic chaplain said Mass, and afterward he gave us words of encouragement and told us not to worry, that the war would soon be over. His words gave me courage.

Able Company pulled outpost duty all the time that I was up there on the line. We went to outposts Erie, Arsenal, Hill 200, and of course, Porkchop.

Things were pretty quiet during the month of May. The veterans all said that the Chinese were sure to attack again soon. There had been a number of battles for the outposts in March and April, but things were calm as May came along.

There were a few light skirmishes and some bombardments, and there was a big air strike on Baldy by our jets, but that was about all.

One day—I think it was late in June—Companies Able, Baker, and Charlie were pulled off the line and sent back to practice for an assault. One of the companies, an officer told us, was going to attack Baldy.

It turned out that Charlie got the job of making the assault, with Baker in a blocking position. Able was sent as a reserve to Porkchop.

The operation took several days to organize, and so it was on July 4 that it began. From our position on Porkchop, we members of Able Company could see Charlie going up the slope of Baldy. It was a terrible sight. The casualties were very heavy, and Charlie had to retreat. For some reason this weakened the entire position on our sector of the line, and on the next day the Chinese were on their loudspeakers telling us that we should surrender. If we did not, they said, we were all going to die. They announced that they were going to take Porkchop "if they had to wade through blood," and that they would take no prisoners.

Their intelligence was good. They knew which of our units was where, and just about how strong it was. It gave us a cold feeling in the belly.

On the night of July 6, as it was starting to get dark, the Chinese attacked in force. I was on a .50-caliber machine gun when they started swarming up the hill. I could have sworn that all of China was on that slope. It was like a moving carpet of yelling, howling men—whistles and bugles blowing, their officers screaming like women and driving their men up the hill.

With enough firepower we could have killed a thousand gooks, but we hadn't nearly enough ammunition to turn back this kind of attack.

We fired the .50 until we ran out of ammo, and by that time the Chinese were in our trenchline, so we fought them with rifle butts, bayonets, and even fists and helmets. They were pushing us back, but before we were driven off the hill, Baker Company came up the other side to help us.

We didn't recognize our people, and some of the men fired on them. Later, the story was that Baker was badly hurt by misdirected fire from Americans on the ridge. It was a real tragedy.

The screw-up and the sheer numbers of Chinese drove us off the top of Porkchop, but within an hour we had re-formed—those of us who were left—to counterattack. There was this officer, a second lieutenant named Richard Shea, who regrouped us and led us back up the hill at the Chinese. We had almost secured the hill when the Chinese took their turn at counterattacking, and they drove *us* back off the hill. Lieutenant Shea was killed about this time. I heard later that he won the Medal of Honor.

We had very heavy casualties in the fight that night. Our first sergeant was killed, and several of the other noncoms and officers with him.

About noon on the next day we counterattacked again, and this time we drove the gooks off the hill to stay. This day or the next—it was hard to keep track of time exactly—I was wounded by a grenade.

Fortunately, I wasn't in the aid station when it took a direct hit from a Chinese 76-mm. When that happened, all the medics, the doctor, and all the wounded inside were killed.

We still had Chinese on the side of the hill, and down at the base were our tanks firing quad .50s at them. In addition to this, their artillery and ours were making a shambles of the slopes. The Chinese were being literally chewed up by shellfire, but there always seemed to be more of them. The supply seemed inexhaustible.

After five days the battle began to wear itself out. About that time General Trudeau came up on an inspection and told us that Porkchop had to be held at all costs. I thought generals only talked like that in the movies, but apparently I was mistaken.

I was one of the soldiers chosen to act as the general's body-guards. Our CO, First Lieutenant Roberts, picked me and a few others from the men who were slightly wounded.

At my suggestion the general removed the stars from his collar and covered the star on his helmet. "Call me Private Trudeau," he said.

After he left we were reinforced and resupplied. I guess Private Trudeau had good connections at battalion HQ.

My wound turned out to be more serious than I thought at first. Two weeks after the battle, I was in a hospital in Japan. It was there I heard that the people at Panmunjom had signed the armistice.

Cpl. JOE SCHEUBER
I Company/31st Infantry

Because of the way we were living, I came down with a cold, and the cold ran its course but left me with a severe lingering cough. I decided to go down to the aid station and get some cough syrup. But when I got down there, the medics and the doctors were exhausted from being up for several nights taking care of casualties from the fighting of the last days. I didn't have the gall to bug them about something as trivial as a cough, so I headed back up to Porkchop. It was along the path that I saw at least fifteen dead Americans. They were all laid out in a row, their faces covered, and I could see their boots.

I was still wearing my winter-issue thermo boots; my regular boots had been stolen. Seeing all those summer boots on the dead bodies, it went though my mind to help myself to a pair. I was actually tempted to steal from the dead. But somehow, I couldn't bring myself to do it.

After seeing those dead men, my cough suddenly seemed much less serious. A couple of days later, I went down to supply and drew a pair of used summer boots.

[*From March until early July, attack and counterattack flickered like swamp fire along the entire length of the MLR. The very nearness of a cease-fire gave the action urgency. Each side considered it vital to be in a superior position when the shooting stopped.*

At Panmunjom the negotiations were as bitter and acrimonious as ever. The Western members of the UN Command were growing anxious for peace and agreement. President Syngman Rhee clung desperately to negotiating positions that would leave his nation in a position to defend itself when, as he suspected, his allies would quit Korea in relief. The Communist conferees, schooled by a lifetime of dedication to what they believed were the historical imperatives of world communism, bargained with flinty determination.

In May the Nevada Cities outposts had been turned over to the U.S. 25th Division's Turkish Brigade. On the twenty-eighth of that month, the Chinese launched heavy attacks against these positions.

Moving under heavy artillery support, a Chinese battalion ad-

vanced on Carson and Elko. Simultaneously, another battalion, screened by smoke, attacked the much-bloodied slopes of Vegas, while a third battalion assaulted Berlin and East Berlin.

After three hours of savage combat, the Communists had reached the Turkish positions on Carson and Elko, and the battle was hand-to-hand. The Turks repulsed the Chinese, who withdrew, re-formed, and attacked again. At Elko, the fighting continued until late morning on the twenty-ninth, when the Chinese broke contact. The respite was a short one. Within minutes, more Chinese had been thrown at Elko, and the fight lasted until midnight, at which time the division ordered the outpost abandoned, and the Turks withdrew to the Main Line of Resistance.

At Vegas, a further fight developed. The Chinese attacked with a battalion, and within an hour had reinforced it with another. Charging through their own artillery and mortar barrages, they broke through to the Turkish trenchlines, and once again the fighting was hand-to-hand. A Turkish company was sent from the MLR to reinforce the defenders, and after two hours the enemy broke and retreated. The 25th Divisional artillery raked the withdrawal routes and inflicted terrible casualties on the Chinese. But by daylight they had regrouped, were reinforced, and were once again on the attack.

This attack, too, failed, and the enemy withdrew. Two hours later the Turks counterattacked the enemy on the north slope of Vegas and drove them off. The Turks now had control of the entire outpost and its approaches, but the Communists appeared determined to take Vegas, whatever the cost.

In the afternoon of 29 May another full battalion of Chinese struck the savaged outpost again. The fight continued until 2300 hours, when the Turks were ordered to retreat to the MLR. The Chinese, willing to pay exorbitantly in lives for the outposts, now commanded Vegas.

The Chinese attacks on Berlin and East Berlin were less successful. After a further two-hour firefight, they gave up and retreated. But the Chinese had succeeded in occupying Vegas, Elko, and Carson. The 25th Division reported that it had cost them 2,200 killed and 1,057 wounded. The Turks suffered losses of 104 killed, 324 wounded, and 47 missing.

In June the Communists struck again. This time the attack was aimed at dislodging the ROK II Corps from its positions near Kumsong.

Attacking on both sides of the Pukhan River, two full divisions of Chinese forced the right wing and center of the ROK II Corps back almost 5,000 yards in six days of heavy fighting. It was an offensive comparable to those of the spring of 1951.

While the Chinese were attacking the South Koreans, a lighter enemy force struck at the ROK 20th Division on the left of the U.S. X Corps. This had been intended, apparently, as a holding attack only, but the collapse of the ROK 5th Division on II Corps's right presented a sudden danger to the U.S. X Corps. General I. D. White, II Corps commander, met the threat by narrowing the ROK 20th's front and committing the ROK 7th Division to strengthen the 20th's left flank.

The withdrawal of the ROK 5th east of the Pukhan opened a gap that needed swiftly to be filled. The ROK II Corps commander committed the ROK 3d Division. At the same time General Taylor, deeply concerned by the possibility of a major Communist breakthrough to the south, shifted the boundary between II and X Corps westward to the Pukhan and gave the 5th ROK Division to X Corps.

The Chinese maintained the pressure on the ROK 8th Division. The South Koreans reeled. On 16 June a counterattack by reserve elements of the Division tried but failed to push the Chinese back. A new Main Line of Resistance was established 3,000 yards south of the original. Plainly, this was the UN defeat, and while the territory gained was inconsequential, the psychological effect on the UN negotiators at Panmunjom was significant.

The Communists had concentrated their pressure on the ROK II Corps, but they had mustered sufficient strength to deliver several attacks on other sectors of the line. Two outpost positions in front of the ROK 1st Division—a part of the U.S. I Corps—fell after a prolonged enemy attack. To the east, in IX Corps's sector, regimental-strength attacks against the U.S. 3d and ROK 9th Divisions failed to dislodge the defenders. In the eastern sector of the Eighth Army's front, the North Koreans forced small retreats.

By 18 June it appeared that the Chinese offensive had begun to slow down. At the cost of terrible casualties, the Communists had

made gains and appeared to have exhausted themselves in the process.
The enemy made no further attacks in force until the middle of July,
just before the signing of the armistice agreement.]

2d Lt. EARL R. OWENS
E Company/180th Infantry

I spent a week at Camp Drake in Tokyo in early July, just before
being shipped out to Korea. I had ridden out to Japan in company
with a surgeon on his way back to Korea after a special leave in the
States. Through Bill I met a number of other doctors at Camp Drake.

One of these, Brown, a tall, fair-haired man with a quick and
friendly smile, had been a battalion surgeon in Korea, serving in a
frontline aid station. He had been transferred to Tokyo and was awaiting
an assignment to a military hospital either in Japan or in the States.

A few days after Dr. Brown's arrival, he and I were together one
evening in the BOQ [Bachelor Officers' Quarters] talking and passing
the time of evening.

Several Japanese houseboys came in and huddled at the end of
the bay, talking and whispering.

I noticed that they glanced frequently at Brown. After a hushed
discussion they approached him and began talking and gesturing. The
boys quite evidently wanted him to do something for them, because
they were gesticulating with papers held in their hands. Brown smiled
and signed the papers. The boys smiled and bowed and departed,
chattering excitedly among themselves.

Having been in the Army long enough to know that one signed
papers at one's peril, I went immediately to Brown with a warning. I
told him that he ought not to be signing things for the Japanese on a
military post. They might use his name and medical standing for all
manner of illegal things.

Brown looked at me with a kind of secret amusement and said
only, "Oh, I don't think they had anything illegal in mind, Earl.
You don't have to worry about it." He walked away smiling.

I watched for a day or two to see if anything untoward developed
from Dr. Brown's penchant for signing papers for the houseboys.
Nothing did, but I was still concerned, and so the next day I mentioned the incident to my friend Bill.

He listened to me carefully, and at the end of my tale he laughed out loud. "Earl," he said, "you never played much baseball when you were a kid, did you?"

I said that, no, as a matter of fact, I hadn't, and that I didn't quite see what baseball had to do with a military surgeon being free with his signature.

"Well, Earl, I'll tell you," Bill said. "Those boys probably don't know or care that Brown is a battalion surgeon. But they care a great deal that he is Bobby Brown, seven years with the New York Yankees, the clutch hitter who set a World Series pinch-hitting record in his first full season with the Yankees in 1947, and the man whose hit in the seventh game of the Series probably won the game and the Series for New York." Bill grinned at me and added, "They were asking for his autograph, soldier."

On the night of 13 July, the Chinese attacked the IX Corps in the ROK Capital Division's sector. The South Koreans fell back in confusion, exposing the U.S. II Corps's flank.

The Chinese had coordinated their attack on the South Koreans with an attack, in division strength, on the ROK 6th Division, which was protecting the II Corps's left.

Once again, as he had in the earlier attacks, General Taylor was forced to redeploy his units to the south, establishing a new Main Line of Resistance along the south bank of the Kumsong River, a tributary of the Pukhan. Taylor reinforced IX Corps by moving the U.S. 3d Division from Ch'orwon into the right wing of the IX Corps, and added the strength of the 187th Airborne Combat Team to the U.S. 2d Division. Simultaneously, he ordered the 34th Regimental Combat Team up from Pusan to assume the post of counterattacking force behind 2d Division. With these, and several other reinforcements, II Corps was in sufficient strength to counterattack the Chinese salient with three divisions, seizing the high ground along the Kumsong River and establishing the MLR there.

A Department of the Army history states, "No attempt was made to restore the original line, in as much as the imminence of an armistice made it tactically unnecessary to expend lives for terrain not essential to the security of the Eighth Army's front."

The enemy's July losses were tremendous: 72,000 casualties, more than 25,000 killed. The war was all but over.

But not quite.

2d Lt. EARL R. OWENS
E Company/180th Infantry

In July I was given command of the 2d Platoon of Company E, 2d Battalion, 180th Infantry Regiment. Echo Company was located on a point of land in front of the MLR, just below Christmas Hill and very close to the enemy on the hills surrounding Christmas. We could hear them at night, digging.

Second Platoon was in the central position and on the point, forward of 1st Platoon on the left and 3d Platoon on the right. Each platoon had a headquarters bunker where the platoon leader and the first sergeant bunked. The field telephone was there. The rest of the platoon was spread out around the HQ bunker, in trenches and other bunkers. Casual shelling went on day and night. Mortar rounds dropped around us indiscriminately, in a haphazard pattern—or lack of it. You tried to be careful, but of course there was no way you could tell when a round of incoming was going to hit, or where. We lost a man who had been sunning himself on top of his bunker. A mortar round dropped beside him and killed him instantly.

As platoon leader, I regularly made the rounds of our position to check on the men and let them know I was around. One night I heard a mortar round explode nearby and rushed to check on what had happened. There were a pair of South Korean troopers serving with my platoon. The shell had dropped between them, decapitating one man. The other was dead, as well, but without a mark on him. I had to listen with my ear to his chest to convince myself there was no life in him.

It was close to the armistice. Our job was to stay alive. To watch the enemy and stay alive.

Early before dawn on July 12, Echo Company was relieved. It was pitch black. We moved off the point and were relieved silently by another platoon. The same thing happened all along our front. At the base of the mountain, just after first light, we were given breakfast—hot C rations. All I could tolerate was the canned fruit, and they were all out by the time I got to the server. A smiling black soldier from my platoon apologized for the lack and said he would see to it some fruit was saved for me in the future.

There was no future to speak of for him. Later that day, while the company was resting, he was watching the engineers do some heavy construction—earth and rock moving, I don't know what they were up to. But someone put too much dynamite in the wrong place, or didn't take the proper precautions, because when the charge went off, my would-be benefactor was crushed by a falling rock.

I always thought that of all the deaths I saw, that was one of the most senseless and tragic.

We were given a few days to rest, clean up, eat, and sleep. Then, on July 15, we were told to move on out and return to our old positions below Christmas Hill. There was a catch. The Chinese had overrun our positions, and we were to drive them off. It was a battalion operation, but my view was limited to the things Echo Company had to do. One of these was to rescue any Americans who might still be out there below Christmas Hill, pinned down by the Chinese.

We marched back to the MLR and prepared to move out to the point. I went to each of my people, checking gear and offering words of encouragement. I came across one of our medics crying and crouched down, really terrified of what was coming. I tried to talk to him, but he couldn't even seem to hear me, he was so afraid.

(Yet not more than one hour later, I saw him in the midst of the battle, going from one casualty to another, totally oblivious of the grenades and mortar rounds and machine-gun fire. The only thing that appeared to concern him was taking care of us when we were wounded. He was the medic who bandaged me when I was hit.)

We left the rest area and started out for our company CP. Artillery was already beginning to fall. Some of it ours, some theirs. As we moved up the trail a single soldier was bringing in a Chinese prisoner. The man was short, slightly built, haggard, soaking wet, and miserable. As miserable as most of us felt going up to the line.

After a while we started seeing the dead from the battle in which the company relieving us had been overrun. Dead Americans. I remember one man especially. Pale as alabaster, eyes partially open.

Not older than seventeen. And next to him another, with no head, his dog tags still hanging around the bloody stump of his neck.

At the company CP I was ordered to take my platoon out to the point and attack. First Platoon was on our right, advancing on the other side of a shallow ridge. After we had left the MLR, I decided I would go to the top of the rise and see where 1st Platoon was, and whether they were covering our flank.

When I reached the ridge, they had vanished. The only thing there was a dead Chinese, still and white as chalk, his eyes staring up at the overcast sky and the drizzling rain that had started to fall.

We reached our old positions and attacked the Chinese—who were sheltering in the bunkers we had built—with hand grenades. They threw back their own small grenades, and with them came mortar shells and machine-gun fire.

I saw a South Korean soldier leading a group into the attack. He went down in a mortar burst. We were taking heavy casualties, and so were the Chinese. We had reached the trenchline, and we were fighting with anything that came to hand, even rocks. My platoon sergeant—one of the very best—was everywhere, pushing, shouting, encouraging, leading. I did my part, too, trying to set an example to my men.

First Platoon materialized out of the smoke and mist. I saw their platoon leader, one of the officers I had come from Japan with, go down with shrapnel in his legs and back.

Most of our wounded were hit by fragments and small-caliber bullets. We had many wounded but relatively few killed. The Chinese grenades were not very effective, but they were plentiful. One landed near a man who was ducking another on his other side. He had his chest rather badly torn up by the second explosion.

One of the Chinese threw a grenade straight at me. I ducked away desperately. And while I was doing that, another landed near my right arm. I never saw it. When it exploded, it knocked me head over heels down the hill.

It felt as though someone—Bobby Brown?—had hit my right bicep as hard as he could with a baseball bat. The arm was numb. There was scarcely any pain. I recovered my helmet and carbine. The medic came to me, tore off my sleeve, and put on a pressure bandage. There was a hole about the size of a dime in the underside of my arm. But presently I began to get some feeling back in the arm. I could hold my weapon, so I went back up the hill into the fighting. I even managed to throw some grenades and shoot with my wounded arm. The second time I tried to shoot the carbine, it jammed. It was grimed with mud and grit.

We were pretty well pinned down on the hillside, so I called the company commander on the radio and asked him if I could withdraw my men. We were taking a lot of casualties to no purpose that I could see. But he was reluctant to let us withdraw. I lost my temper and told him my men were dying for no reason, and that I was pulling them back with his approval or without it. He relented and okayed our withdrawal.

So we retreated. Unfortunately, most of the men who had relieved us for a few days before had been killed. None of those pinned down up there had survived for us to rescue. I learned later that the lieutenant who replaced me had been killed in the first Chinese attack.

When we had pulled back a few hundred yards and had some high ground between us and the Chinese holding the outpost, I sat my platoon down for a rest and to wait for further orders. I didn't want to spend the night where we were, so near the point, where the Chinese could counterattack in the night.

But I needn't have worried. Within the hour our battalion was ordered to abandon the point and return to the MLR.

I took myself down to the battalion aid station to have the doctor look at my arm. Things had suddenly grown very quiet. The Chinese were exhausted, and so were we. The battalion surgeon examined my wound and told me that the steel fragment inside might have nicked an artery. If that had happened, it could be serious. He ordered me to climb aboard a truck waiting at the bottom of the hill to take the wounded to the nearest MASH unit.

I was uncertain what to do. The wound wasn't giving me any real pain, and I was in command of a platoon that might soon be going back into action. I felt I owed it to my people to stay with them. Yet at the same time I felt great relief that I had been *ordered* to go to the rear. I argued with myself, trying to decide what the right thing, the honorable thing, was. But after a time I realized that I was going to do what the doctor had ordered me to do, and I started down the hill toward the truck.

I was still feeling very guilty. I walked with my head down and a frown on my face. About halfway down the mountain, I encountered an old Korean gentleman coming up. He moved to one side and gestured politely for me to pass. To me it was a sign that my decision to head for the MASH unit was the right one. I don't know. Does God give out signs like that?

At the base of the mountain I joined a number of other casualties, and the truck dropped us off at the MASH. It was grim there. The wounded were everywhere. The Chinese had hit all along the line, and we had taken heavy casualties. Every bed was filled—and most of the open space, it seemed. I came across our medic, the one who had been so frightened and so brave when it came to the crunch. He had been badly wounded, and he lay on a stretcher, unconscious, hooked up to a plasma bottle. I stayed with him for a while to see if he would wake up. He didn't. I touched him and prayed for him.

Sometime in the very early morning I was awakened, taken into an operating tent, and put to sleep. When I awoke again, my arm had been bandaged and splinted, and I was stark naked under blankets on a cot. Later that day, still clothed only in a blanket, I was carried to a truck, then to a train, and finally to a hospital in Pusan. After the medics looked me over there, they gave me some slippers and a robe, and I was put on an airplane and flown to a hospital in Osaka.

The hospital was jammed with wounded from Korea. The doctors sewed up my arm, which the MASH people had opened for inspection. No severed artery.

I was still in the hospital in Osaka when, on July 27, 1953, Lt. Gen. William K. Harrison, senior United Nations delegate to the armistice negotiations, signed the document they had been quarreling over for so long.

The Korean War was over.

THE
UNCERTAIN
VICTORY

To most Americans, Korea is a forgotten war. To many, it was unreal. Ordinary lives were unruffled by the distant echoes of battle. In
Korea the West was challenged for the first time by the military power
of the Communist world—and neither America's leaders nor her people wanted such a challenge.

The home front made no sacrifices. If neither one's friends nor
one's family were directly involved, the war could have been taking
place on the deserts of Mars.

And not least of all, it was a war fought with a quality that is
unsuited both to war and to the American character: restraint.

But to the men who fought there, the Korean War was the seminal experience of their lives. The task of the authors has been not to
find living memories, but to select from among so many, so vividly
recalled.

Robert Hall, whose experiences as a combat Marine are recorded elsewhere in this volume, remembers the ending of his great
ordeal:

The cease-fire was announced for ten o'clock that night. There
had been artillery fire all evening from both sides—not a barrage, just banging away. We were all up for it. The artillery
gradually tapered off as the hour approached. Flares were shot
up by both sides all along the MLR. Then it became very quiet
as even the morons who wanted to be the one who fired the last

shot of the war quit cranking off. A few showed flashlights. I turned in about midnight. It had grown very still.

At earliest light the troops came up out of the ground to look. At first we stood in the trenches. Then some climbed up to the forward edges, then to the tops of the bunkers, for a better look. It was unheard of—standing in the open in daylight. An incredible feeling. I think the infantrymen all across the peninsula, on both sides of the line, must have been awed by it. Just the simple, natural act of standing erect in the sunshine. Then to look, and eventually to walk through the land ahead of the trenches, a thing that would have meant sure death twenty-four hours before. That's when we began to realize that it was really over.

In Hall's straightforward remembrance we can hear the echo of soldiers' voices through all of history. A Theban hoplite on the newly silent field of Leuctra must have spoken so. And surely a doughboy in the trenches greeted the eleventh hour of the eleventh day of the eleventh month of 1918 with the same relief, the same eagerness to return to the commonplaces of peace.

But this time, there was a difference for Americans, a difference we find difficult, even now, to accept.

The Korean War was the first America ever waged that was not fought for national survival, for territory, for Manifest Destiny, or for hegemony. Korea was the first ideological war. For the first time in the nation's history, Americans were asked to fight and die to contain an idea. In Korea, America was asked to make good on her rhetoric.

It was done, but the price was high. Years later, an American president was to say in his inaugural address that we would pay any price, endure any hardship to ensure the survival of liberty. In Korea, America paid the first installment.

Korea ended in an ambiguous victory. The Communists' war aims were denied them, though it had been a near thing. But the conflict left a legacy of uncertainty.

As the first postnuclear war, Korea was fought under strictures designed to keep the conflict limited. The men in Washington were never certain that the war with China would not erupt with sudden fury into a nuclear confrontation with the Soviets. With hindsight one may question their choices, but the fact that such choices had to be made tells us something about the nature of war in the last half of the twentieth century, and it affected forever the manner in which military decisions must now be made.

In the eighties, after the bitter experience of Vietnam, it has become popular to say that World War II was the last "good" war, and that our wars since then should be a source of shame. This is nonsense. There are no "good" wars; there never have been. But there are wars that must be fought, and Korea was such a war. The only shame is the shame those of us who were not involved should feel for having understood so poorly the sacrifices of the men who fought there. They were men of many nations dragooned into defending an idea of freedom while others went about their ordinary lives untouched.

What does a nation owe to the men who fought its wars? The answer to that, I think, is simple enough. The nation owes respect and remembrance.

Bill Menninger is a Californian who has spent years trying to interest the state's congressional delegation in a Korean War Memorial. His voice is heard elsewhere in this work, but recently he wrote: "I enclose a copy of the letter [on the subject of a Memorial] I sent to the news media. As expected, it was ignored. But we [Korean veterans] are used to this. Congress has stated that a Korean Memorial is out of the question because of the deficit. Yet when I read that Senator [Alan] Cranston's salary when he was state controller was $23,000, and that he is now entitled to a state pension of almost $150,000, plus, when he retires, a Senate pension as well, I wonder at the callousness of these people. Kipling wrote a poem about it a long time ago."

The attitude of the senior senator from California is not unique. Politicians have very short memories. The democratic folk of Athens thanked Miltiades, who saved them from the Persians, by rejecting his demand for a pension and then exiling him.

But there are certain indisputable facts about the Korean War that should always be remembered. South Korea suffered total casualties of 400,167 killed, wounded, and missing. For the United States, the price of defending freedom in Korea came to 54,246 dead, 103,248 wounded, and 5,178 missing. The other United Nations components took casualties of 17,260.

For the first time in modern history, the United States concluded a war with no enemy territory under its control. It is this fact that probably accounts for the appalling number of soldiers, sailors, and airmen listed as missing. You cannot account for your casualties if you are not free to search the territory where they might have fallen. The more recent Vietnam experience is a bitter repetition of this melancholy circumstance.

The war extracted a blood price from the Communist enemy. China suffered total casualties of 967,000 men; North Korea, 624,000. Perhaps a million South Korean civilians were killed and several million made homeless. The United States spent $67,000,000,000 on the war, and property worth perhaps $1,000,000,000 was destroyed in South Korea. The uncertain victory was purchased dearly.

It would be disingenuous to ignore the fact that the war could never have been fought as a United Nations operation had not the Soviets foolishly walked out of the UN before the North Koreans struck. The men in the Kremlin have never again made so costly a miscalculation.

For quite possibly the last time in this century, American arms were fully supported by fellow members of the United Nations. Representatives of the British Commonwealth, France, Greece, Turkey, and a dozen other nations fought bravely on the Korean peninsula.

And for the first, and possibly the only, time in its short history, the United Nations fulfilled the role envisioned for it by its founders: to stop aggression, by force if need be.

Military historians will long debate the strategy and tactics of the war. Was it well done, well planned? Perhaps, perhaps not. That is a question out of the purview of this volume. The intention of the authors has been to give the long-silent men who fought and bled in America's first limited war a chance to speak.

They have done so.

Index